CompTIA®
Security+® Deluxe Study Guide
Fourth Edition

CompTIA®
Security+® Deluxe Study Guide

Exam SY0-501

Fourth Edition

Emmett Dulaney

Chuck Easttom

SYBEX®
A Wiley Brand

Senior Acquisitions Editor: Kenyon Brown
Development Editor: Gary Schwartz
Technical Editors: Buzz Murphy and Warren Wyrostek
Production Editor: Christine O'Connor
Copy Editor: Elizabeth Welch
Editorial Manager: Mary Beth Wakefield
Production Manager: Kathleen Wisor
Associate Publisher: Jim Minatel
Book Designers: Bill Gibson and Judy Fung
Proofreader: Kim Wimpsett
Indexer: John Sleeva
Project Coordinator, Cover: Brent Savage
Cover Designer: Wiley
Cover Image: Getty Images/Jeremy Woodhouse

ISBN: 978-1-119-41685-2
ISBN: 978-1-119-47960-4
ISBN: 978-1-119-47958-1
ISBN: 978-1-119-47957-4

Manufactured in the United States of America

For general information on our other products and services or to obtain technical support, please contact our Customer Care Department within the U.S. at (877) 762-2974, outside the U.S. at (317) 572-3993 or fax (317) 572-4002.

Wiley publishes in a variety of print and electronic formats and by print-on-demand. Some material included with standard print versions of this book may not be included in e-books or in print-on-demand. If this book refers to media such as a CD or DVD that is not included in the version you purchased, you may download this material at http://booksupport.wiley.com. For more information about Wiley products, visit www.wiley.com.

Library of Congress Control Number: 2017955410

For Emmett Buis and Wolfgang Scisney: bookends.
—Emmett

Acknowledgments

This book would not exist were it not for Mike Pastore, the author of the first edition. He took a set of convoluted objectives for a broad exam and wrote the foundation of the study guide that you now hold in your hands. While the exam and their associated objectives improved with each iteration, all subsequent editions of this text are forever indebted to his knowledge, hard work, and brilliance so early on.

Thanks are also due to Gary Schwartz, for being one of the best editors in publishing to work with, and to all of those at Wiley who helped with this title.

About the Authors

Emmett Dulaney   is a professor at a small university in Indiana and the former director of training for Mercury Technical Solutions. He is a columnist for Certification Magazine and the author of more than 30 books on certification, operating systems, and cross-platform integration. Emmett can be reached at eadulaney@comcast.net.

Chuck Easttom   is a researcher, consultant, and trainer in computer science and computer security. He has expertise in software engineering, operating systems, databases, web development, and computer networking. He travels the world teaching and consulting on digital forensics, cyber security, cryptology, and related topics. He has authored 22 books and counting, as well as dozens of research papers. Chuck is additionally an inventor with 10 patented computer science inventions. He also frequently works as an expert witness in computer-related cases. His website is http://chuckeasttom.com/.

Contents at a Glance

Contents

Chapter 8   Cryptography   231

Table of Exercises

CompTIA.

Becoming a CompTIA Certified
IT Professional is Easy
It's also the best way to reach
greater professional opportunities and rewards.

LEARN ➤ **CERTIFY** ➤ **WORK**

Learn more about what the exam covers by reviewing the following:	**Purchase a voucher at a Pearson VUE testing center or at CompTIAstore.com.**	**Congratulations on your CompTIA certification!**
• Exam objectives for key study points. • Sample questions for a general overview of what to expect on the exam and examples of question format. • Visit online forums, like LinkedIn, to see what other IT professionals say about CompTIA exams.	• Register for your exam at a Pearson VUE testing center. • Visit pearsonvue.com/CompTIA to find the closest testing center to you. • Schedule the exam online. You will be required to enter your voucher number or provide payment information at registration. • Take your certification exam.	• Make sure to add your certification to your resume. • Check out the CompTIA Certification Roadmap to plan your next career move.

Why Get CompTIA Certified?

- **Growing Demand** Labor estimates predict some technology fields will experience growth of over 20% by the year 2020.* CompTIA certification qualifies the skills required to join this workforce.

- **Higher Salaries** IT professionals with certifications on their resume command better jobs, earn higher salaries and have more doors open to new multi-industry opportunities.

- **Verified Strengths** 91% of hiring managers indicate CompTIA cer-tifications are valuable in validating IT expertise, making certifica-tion the best way to demonstrate your competency and knowledge to employers.**

- **Universal Skills** CompTIA certifications are vendor neutral—which means that certified professionals can proficiently work with an exten-sive variety of hardware and software found in most organizations.

Learn more: Certification.CompTIA.org/securityplus

*Source: CompTIA 9th Annual Information Security Trends study: 500 U.S. IT and Business Executives Responsible for Security

** Source: CompTIA Employer Perceptions of IT Training and Certification

Introduction

If you're preparing to take the Security+ exam, you'll undoubtedly want to find as much information as you can about computer and physical security. The more information you have at your disposal and the more hands-on experience you gain, the better off you'll be when attempting the exam. This study guide was written with that in mind. The goal was to provide enough information to prepare you for the test, but not so much that you'll be overloaded with information that's outside the scope of the exam.

This book presents the material at an intermediate technical level. Experience with and knowledge of security concepts, operating systems, and application systems will help you get a full understanding of the challenges that you'll face as a security professional.

We've included review questions at the end of each chapter to give you a taste of what it's like to take the exam. If you're already working in the security field, we recommend that you check out these questions first to gauge your level of expertise. You can then use the book mainly to fill in the gaps in your current knowledge. This study guide will help you round out your knowledge base before tackling the exam.

If you can answer 90 percent or more of the review questions correctly for a given chapter, you can feel safe moving on to the next chapter. If you're unable to answer that many correctly, reread the chapter and try the questions again. Your score should improve.

> Don't just study the questions and answers! The questions on the actual exam will be different from the practice questions included in this book. The exam is designed to test your knowledge of a concept or objective, so use this book to learn the objectives behind the questions.

Before You Begin the CompTIA Security+ Certification Exam

Before you begin studying for the exam, it's imperative that you understand a few things about the Security+ certification. Security+ is a certification from CompTIA (an industry association responsible for many entry-level certifications) granted to those who obtain a passing score on a single entry-level exam. In addition to adding Security+ to your résumé as a stand-alone certification, you can use it as an elective in many vendor-certification tracks.

> The CompTIA Advance Security Practitioner (CASP) certification is designed for those with up to 10 years of security experience. It builds on Security+ and authenticates knowledge at a higher level. Between Security+ and CASP, CompTIA created a Cybersecurity Analyst certification (CSA+) as a bridge that remains vendor-neutral and verifies that successful candidates have the knowledge and skills required to configure and use threat detection tools, perform data analysis, and interpret the results to identify vulnerabilities, threats, and risks to an organization, with the end goal of securing and protecting applications and systems within an organization.

When you're studying for any exam, the first step in preparation should always be to find out as much as possible about the test: the more you know up front, the better you can plan your course of study. The current exam, and the one addressed by this book, is the 2017 update. Although all variables are subject to change, as this book is being written, the exam consists of 100 questions. You have 90 minutes to take the exam, and the passing score is based on a scale from 100 to 900. Pearson VUE testing centers administer the exam throughout the United States and several other countries.

The exam is predominantly multiple choice with short, concise questions, usually followed by four possible answers. Don't expect lengthy scenarios and complex solutions. This is an entry-level exam of knowledge-level topics; you're expected to know a great deal about security topics from an overview perspective rather than implementation. In many books, the glossary is filler added to the back of the text; this book's glossary (located on the book's online test bank at www.wiley.com/go/sybextestprep) should be considered necessary reading. You're likely to see a question on the exam about what a Trojan horse is, not how to identify it at the code level. Spend your study time learning the different security solutions and identifying potential security vulnerabilities and where they would be applicable. Don't get bogged down in step-by-step details; those are saved for certification exams beyond the scope of Security+.

You should also know that CompTIA is notorious for including vague questions on all of its exams. You might see a question for which two of the possible four answers are correct—but you can choose only one. Use your knowledge, logic, and intuition to choose the best answer and then move on. Sometimes, the questions are worded in ways that would make English majors cringe—a typo here, an incorrect verb there. Don't let this frustrate you; answer the question, and go to the next. Although we haven't intentionally added typos or other grammatical errors, the questions throughout this book make every attempt to re-create the structure and appearance of the real exam questions.

CompTIA frequently does what is called *item seeding*, which is the practice of including unscored questions on exams. It does so to gather psychometric data, which is then used when developing new versions of the exam. Before you take it, you are told that your exam may include unscored questions. So, if you come across a question that does not appear to map to any of the exam objectives—or for that matter, does not appear to belong in the exam—it is likely a seeded question. You never really know whether or not a question is seeded, however, so always make your best effort to answer every question.

As you study, you need to know that the exam you'll take was created at a certain point in time. You won't see a question about the new virus that hit your systems last week, but you'll see questions about concepts that existed when this exam was created. Updating the exam is a difficult process and results in an increment in the exam number.

Why Become Security+ Certified?

There are a number of reasons for obtaining a Security+ certification. These include the following:

It provides proof of professional achievement.   Specialized certifications are the best way to stand out from the crowd. In this age of technology certifications, you'll find hundreds of thousands of administrators who have successfully completed the Microsoft and Cisco certification tracks. To set yourself apart from the crowd, you need a little bit more. The Security+ exam is part of the CompTIA certification track that includes A+, Network+, and other vendor-neutral certifications such as Linux+, Project+, and more. This exam will help you prepare for more advanced certifications because it provides a solid grounding in security concepts, and it will give you the recognition you deserve.

It increases your marketability.   Almost anyone can bluff their way through an interview. Once you're Security+ certified, you'll have the credentials to prove your competency. Moreover, certifications can't be taken from you when you change jobs—you can take that certification with you to any position you accept.

It provides opportunity for advancement.   Individuals who prove themselves to be competent and dedicated are the ones who will most likely be promoted. Becoming certified is a great way to prove your skill level and show your employer that you're committed to improving your skill set. Look around you at those who are certified: they are probably the people who receive good pay raises and promotions.

It fulfills training requirements.   Many companies have set training requirements for their staff so that they stay up-to-date on the latest technologies. Having a certification program in security provides administrators with another certification path to follow when they have exhausted some of the other industry-standard certifications.

It raises customer confidence.   As companies discover the advantages of CompTIA, they will undoubtedly require qualified staff to achieve these certifications. Many companies outsource their work to consulting firms with experience working with security. Firms that have certified staff have a definite advantage over firms that don't.

How to Become a Security+ Certified Professional

The first place to start to get your certification is to register for the exam at any Pearson VUE testing center. Exam pricing might vary by country or by CompTIA membership. You can contact Pearson at:

Pearson VUE

www.vue.com/comptia

U.S. and Canada: 877-551-PLUS (7587)

When you schedule the exam, you'll receive instructions regarding appointment and cancellation procedures, ID requirements, and information about the testing center location. In addition, you'll receive a registration and payment confirmation letter. Exams can be scheduled up to six weeks out or as late as the next day (or, in some cases, even on the same day).

 Exam prices and codes may vary based on the country in which the exam is administered. For detailed pricing and exam registration procedures, refer to CompTIA's website at http://certification.comptia.org.

After you've successfully passed your Security+ exam, CompTIA will award you a certification. Within four to six weeks of passing the exam, you'll receive your official CompTIA Security+ certificate and ID card. (If you don't receive these within eight weeks of taking the test, contact CompTIA directly using the information found in your registration packet.)

Who Should Read This Book?

If you want to acquire a solid foundation in computer security and your goal is to prepare for the exam by learning how to develop and improve security, this book is for you. You'll find clear explanations of the concepts that you need to grasp and plenty of help to achieve the high level of professional competency that you need in order to succeed in your chosen field.

If you want to become certified as a certification holder, this book is definitely what you need. However, if you just want to attempt to pass the exam without really understanding security, this study guide isn't for you. It's written for people who want to acquire hands-on skills and in-depth knowledge of computer security.

 In addition to reading this book, you might consider downloading and reading the white papers on security that are scattered throughout the Internet.

What Does This Book Cover?

This book covers everything you need to know to pass the Security+ exam.

Chapter 1: Managing Risk

Chapter 2: Designing and Diagnosing Networks

Chapter 3: Understanding Devices and Infrastructure

Chapter 4: Identity and Access Management

Chapter 5: Wireless Network Threats

Tips for Taking the Security+ Exam

Here are some general tips for taking your exam:

- Bring two forms of ID with you. One must be a photo ID, such as a driver's license. The other can be a major credit card or a passport. Both forms must include a signature.

- Arrive early at the exam center so that you can relax and review your study materials, particularly tables and lists of exam-related information. After you are ready to enter the testing room, you will need to leave everything outside; you won't be able to bring any materials into the testing area.

- Read the questions carefully. Don't be tempted to jump to an early conclusion. Make sure that you know exactly what each question is asking.

- Don't leave any unanswered questions. Unanswered questions are scored against you.

- There will be questions with multiple correct responses. When there is more than one correct answer, a message at the bottom of the screen will prompt you to either "Choose two" or "Choose all that apply." Be sure to read the messages displayed to know how many correct answers you must choose.

- When answering multiple-choice questions about which you're unsure, use a process of elimination to get rid of the obviously incorrect answers first. Doing so will improve your odds if you need to make an educated guess.

- On form-based tests (nonadaptive), because the hard questions will take the most time, save them for last. You can move forward and backward through the exam.

- For the latest pricing on the exams and updates to the registration procedures, visit CompTIA's website at http://certification.comptia.org.

What's Included in the Book

We've included several testing features in this book and on the companion website. These tools will help you retain vital exam content as well as prepare you to sit for the actual exam:

Assessment Test   At the end of this introduction is an assessment test that you can use to check your readiness for the exam. Take this test before you start reading the book; it will help you determine the areas in which you might need to brush up. The answers to the assessment test questions appear on a separate page after the last question of the test. Each answer includes an explanation and a note telling you the chapter in which the material appears.

Objective Map and Opening List of Objectives   After this book's introduction, we have included a detailed exam objective map showing you where each of the exam objectives is covered in this book. In addition, each chapter opens with a list of the exam objectives it covers. Use these to see exactly where each of the exam topics is covered.

Exam Essentials   Just before the Summary, each chapter includes a number of exam essentials. These are the key topics that you should take from the chapter in terms of areas to focus on when preparing for the exam.

Review Questions   To test your knowledge as you progress throughout the book, there are review questions at the end of each chapter. As you finish each chapter, answer the review questions and then check your answers. The correct answers and explanations are found in Appendix A. You can go back to reread the section that deals with each question that you got wrong to ensure that you answer correctly the next time you're tested on the material.

> The Sybex Interactive Online Test Bank, flashcards, bonus labs, and glossary can be accessed at http://www.wiley.com/go/sybextestprep.

Interactive Online Learning Environment and Test Bank

The interactive online learning environment that accompanies *CompTIA Security+ Study Guide: Exam SY0-501* provides a test bank with study tools to help you prepare for the certification exams and increase your chances of passing them the first time! The test bank includes the following elements:

Sample Tests   All of the questions in this book, including the assessment test that you'll find at the end of this introduction and the chapter tests, which include the review questions at the end of each chapter, are provided. In addition, there are two practice exams. Use these questions to test your knowledge of the study guide material. The online test bank runs on multiple devices.

Electronic Flashcards   One set of questions is provided in digital flashcard format (a question followed by a single correct answer). You can use the flashcards to reinforce your learning and provide last-minute test prep before the exam.

Glossary   The key terms from this book and their definitions are available as a fully searchable PDF.

Bonus Labs   Also online, you will find additional bonus labs. These include activities such as labs that you can do on a system as well as mental exercises (crossword puzzles, word searches, and so forth) to help you memorize key concepts.

 You can access the online test bank at www.wiley.com/go/sybextestprep.

How to Use This Book and Study Tools

If you want a solid foundation for preparing for the Security+ exam, this is the book for you. We've spent countless hours putting together this book with the sole intention of helping you prepare for the exam.

This book is loaded with valuable information, and you will get the most out of your study time if you understand how we put it together. Here's a list that describes how to approach studying:

1. Take the assessment test immediately following this introduction. It's okay if you don't know any of the answers—that's what this book is for. Carefully read over the explanations for any question that you get wrong, and make a note of the chapters where that material is covered.

2. Study each chapter carefully, making sure that you fully understand the information and the exam objectives listed at the beginning of each one. Again, pay extra-close attention to any chapter that includes material covered in the questions that you missed on the assessment test.

3. Read over the summary and exam essentials. These will highlight the sections from the chapter with which you need to be familiar before sitting for the exam.

4. Answer all of the review questions at the end of each chapter. Specifically note any questions that confuse you, and study those sections of the book again. Don't just skim these questions—make sure that you understand each answer completely.

5. Go over the electronic flashcards. These help you to prepare for the latest Security+ exam, and they're really great study tools.

6. Take the practice exams.

Performance-Based Questions

CompTIA introduced performance-based questions in their certification exams, including Security+, several years ago. These are not the traditional multiple-choice questions with which you're probably familiar. These questions require the candidate to know how to perform a specific task or series of tasks. Although the new Security+ exam was not live by the time this book was published, we have a pretty good idea of how these questions will be laid out. In some cases, the candidate might be asked to fill in the blank with the best answer. Alternatively, you may be asked to match certain items from one list into another. Some of the more involved performance-based questions might present the candidate with a scenario and then ask them to complete a task. You will be taken to a simulated environment where you will have to perform a series of steps, and you will be graded on how well you complete the task.

The Sybex test engine does not have the ability to include performance-based questions. However, we have included numerous hands-on exercises throughout the book that are designed to measure how well you understand the chapter topics. Being able to think logically is a great way to learn.

Exam SY0-501 Exam Objectives

CompTIA goes to great lengths to ensure that its certification programs accurately reflect the IT industry's best practices. They do this by establishing committees for each of its exam programs. Each committee comprises a small group of IT professionals, training providers, and publishers who are responsible for establishing the exam's baseline competency level and who determine the appropriate target-audience level.

Once these factors are determined, CompTIA shares this information with a group of hand-selected subject matter experts (SMEs). These folks are the true brainpower behind the certification program. In the case of this exam, they are IT-seasoned pros from the likes of Microsoft, Oracle, VeriSign, and RSA Security, to name just a few. The SMEs review the committee's findings, refine them, and shape them into the objectives that follow this section. CompTIA calls this process a job-task analysis (JTA).

Finally, CompTIA conducts a survey to ensure that the objectives and weightings truly reflect job requirements. Only then can the SMEs go to work writing the hundreds of questions needed for the exam. Even so, they have to go back to the drawing board for further refinements in many cases before the exam is ready to go live in its final state. Rest assured that the content you're about to learn will serve you long after you take the exam.

Exam objectives are subject to change at any time without prior notice and at CompTIA's sole discretion. Visit the certification page of CompTIA's website at http://certification.comptia.org for the most current listing of exam objectives.

CompTIA also publishes relative weightings for each of the exam's objectives. The following table lists the six Security+ objective domains and the extent to which they are represented on the exam. As you use this study guide, you'll find that we have administered just the right dosage of objective knowledge by tailoring coverage to mirror the percentages that CompTIA uses.

Domain	% of Exam
1.0 Threats, Attacks and Vulnerabilities	21%
2.0 Technologies and Tools	22%
3.0 Architecture and Design	15%
4.0 Identity and Access Management	16%
5.0 Risk Management	14%
6.0 Cryptography and PKI	12%
Total	100%

SY0-501 Certification Exam Objective Map

Objective	Chapter
1.0 Threats, Attacks and Vulnerabilities	
1.1 Given a scenario, analyze indicators of compromise and determine the type of malware	Chapter 9
Viruses; Crypto-malware; Ransomware; Worm; Trojan; Rootkit; Keylogger; Adware; Spyware; Bots; RAT; Logic bomb; Backdoor	
1.2 Compare and contrast types of attacks	
Social Engineering: Phishing; Spear phishing; Whaling; Vishing; Tailgating; Impersonation; Dumpster diving; Shoulder surfing; Hoax; Watering hole attack; Principles (reasons for effectiveness): (Authority; Intimidation; Consensus; Scarcity; Familiarity; Trust; Urgency)	Chapter 10

Objective	Chapter
Application/service attacks: DoS; DDoS; Man-in-the-middle; Buffer overflow; Injection; Cross-site scripting; Cross-site request forgery; Privilege escalation; ARP poisoning; Amplification; DNS poisoning; Domain hijacking; Man-in-the-browser; Zero day; Replay; Pass the hash; Hijacking and related attacks (Click-jacking; Session hijacking; URL hijacking; Typo squatting); Driver manipulation (Shimming; Refactoring); MAC spoofing; IP spoofing	Chapter 9
Wireless attacks: Replay; IV; Evil twin; Rogue AP; Jamming; WPS; Bluejacking; Bluesnarfing; RFID; NFC; Disassociation	Chapter 5
Cryptographic attacks: Birthday; Known plain text/cipher text; Rainbow tables; Dictionary; Brute force (Online vs. offline); Collision; Downgrade; Replay; Weak implementations	Chapter 8
1.3 Explain threat actor types and attributes	Chapter 7
Types of actors: Script kiddies; Hacktivist; Organized crime; Nation states/APT; Insiders; Competitors	
Attributes of actors: Internal/external; Level of sophistication; Resources/funding; Intent/motivation	
Use of open-source intelligence	
1.4 Explain penetration testing concepts	Chapter 12
Active reconnaissance; Passive reconnaissance; Pivot; Initial exploitation; Persistence; Escalation of privilege; Black box; White box; Gray box; Pen testing vs. vulnerability scanning	
1.5 Explain vulnerability scanning concepts	Chapter 12
Passively test security controls; Identify vulnerability; Identify lack of security controls; Identify common misconfigurations; Intrusive vs. non-intrusive; Credentialed vs. non-credentialed; False positive	
1.6 Explain the impact associated with types of vulnerabilities	Chapter 7
Race conditions; Vulnerabilities due to: (End-of-life systems; Embedded systems; Lack of vendor support); Improper input handling; Improper error handling; Misconfiguration/weak configuration; Default configuration; Resource exhaustion; Untrained users; Improperly configured accounts; Vulnerable business processes; Weak cipher suites and implementations; Memory/buffer vulnerability (Memory leak; Integer overflow; Buffer overflow; Pointer dereference; DLL injection); System sprawl/undocumented assets; Architecture/design weaknesses; New threats/zero day; Improper certificate and key management	

Objective	Chapter

2.0 Technologies and Tools

2.1 Install and configure network components, both hardware- and software-based, to support organizational security

Chapter 3

Firewall (ACL; Application-based vs. network-based; Stateful vs. stateless; Implicit deny); VPN Concentrator (Remote access vs. site-to-site; IPSec (Tunnel mode, Transport mode, AH, ESP); Split tunnel vs. full tunnel; TLS; Always-on VPN); NIPS/NIDS (Signature-based; Heuristic/behavioral; Anomaly; Inline vs. passive; In-band vs. out-of-band; Rules; Analytics (False positive, False negative)); Router (ACLs; Antispoofing); Switch (Port security; Layer 2 vs. Layer 3; Loop protection; Flood guard); Proxy (Forward and reverse proxy; Transparent; Application/multipurpose); Load balancer (Scheduling (Affinity, Round-robin); Active-passive; Active-active; Virtual IPs); Access point (SSID; MAC filtering; Signal strength; Band selection/width; Antenna types and placement; Fat vs. thin; Controller-based vs. standalone); SIEM (Aggregation; Correlation; Automated alerting and triggers; Time synchronization; Event deduplication; Logs/WORM); DLP (USB blocking; Cloud-based; Email); NAC (Dissolvable vs permanent; Host health checks; Agent vs. agentless); Mail gateway (Spam filter; DLP; Encryption); Bridge; SSL/TLS accelerators; SSL decryptors; Media gateway; Hardware security module

2.2 Given a scenario, use appropriate software tools to assess the security posture of an organization

Chapter 4

Protocol analyzer; Network scanners (Rogue system detection; Network mapping); Wireless scanners/cracker; Password cracker; Vulnerability scanner; Configuration compliance scanner; Exploitation frameworks; Data sanitation tools; Steganography tools; Honeypot; Backup utilities; Banner grabbing; Passive vs. active; Command line tools (ping; netstat; tracert; nslookup/dig; arp; ipconfig/ip/ifconfig; tcpdump; nmap; netcat)

2.3 Given a scenario, troubleshoot common security issues

Chapter 4

Unencrypted credentials/clear text; Logs and events anomalies; Permission issues; Access violations; Certificate issues; Data exfiltration; Misconfigured devices (Firewall; Content filter; Access points); Weak security configurations; Personnel issues (Policy violation; insider threat; Social engineering; Social media; Personal email); Unauthorized software; Baseline deviation; License compliance violation (availability/integrity); Asset management; Authentication issues

Objective	Chapter
2.4 Given a scenario, analyze and interpret output from security technologies	Chapter 4

HIDS/HIPS; Antivirus; File integrity check; Host-based firewall; Application whitelisting; Removable media control; Advanced malware tools; Patch management tools; UTM; DLP; Data execution prevention; Web application firewall

2.5 Given a scenario, deploy mobile devices securely	Chapter 11

Connection methods (Cellular; WiFi; SATCOM; Bluetooth; NFC; ANT; Infrared; USB); Mobile device management concepts (Application management; Content management; Remote wipe; Geofencing; Geolocation; Screen locks; Push notification services; Passwords and pins; Biometrics; Context-aware authentication; Containerization; Storage segmentation; Full device encryption); Enforcement and monitoring for: (Third-party app stores; Rooting/jailbreaking; Sideloading; Custom firmware; Carrier unlocking; Firmware OTA updates; Camera use; SMS/MMS; External media; USB OTG; Recording microphone; GPS tagging; WiFi direct/ad hoc; Tethering; Payment methods); Deployment models (BYOD; COPE; CYOD; Corporate-owned; VDI)

2.6 Given a scenario, implement secure protocols	Chapter 7

Protocols (DNSSEC; SSH; S/MIME; SRTP; LDAPS; FTPS; SFTP; SNMPv3; SSL/TLS; HTTPS; Secure POP/IMAP); Use cases (Voice and video; Time synchronization; Email and web; File transfer; Directory services; Remote access; Domain name resolution; Routing and switching; Network address allocation; Subscription services)

3.0 Architecture and Design

3.1 Explain use cases and purpose for frameworks, best practices and secure configuration guides	Chapter 2

Industry-standard frameworks and reference architecture (Regulatory; Non-regulatory; National vs. international; Industry-specific frameworks); Benchmarks/secure configuration guides (Platform/vendor-specific guides (Web server; Operating system; Application server; Network infrastructure devices); General purpose guides); Defense-in-depth/layered security (Vendor diversity; Control diversity (Administrative; Technical); User training)

3.2 Given a scenario, implement secure network architecture concepts	Chapter 2

Zones/topologies (DMZ; Extranet; Intranet; Wireless; Guest; Honeynets; NAT; Ad hoc); Segregation/segmentation/isolation (Physical; Logical (VLAN); Virtualization; Air gaps); Tunneling/VPN (Site-to-site; Remote access); Security device/technology placement (Sensors; Collectors; Correlation engines; Filters; Proxies; Firewalls; VPN concentrators; SSL accelerators; Load balancers; DDoS mitigator; Aggregation switches; Taps and port mirror); SDN

Objective	Chapter
3.3 Given a scenario, implement secure systems design	Chapter 2

Hardware/firmware security (FDE/SED; TPM; HSM; UEFI/BIOS; Secure boot and attestation; Supply chain; Hardware root of trust; EMI/EMP); Operating systems (Types (Network; Server; Workstation; Appliance; Kiosk; Mobile OS); Patch management; Disabling unnecessary ports and services; Least functionality; Secure configurations; Trusted operating system; Application whitelisting/blacklisting; Disable default accounts/passwords); Peripherals (Wireless keyboards; Wireless mice; Displays; WiFi-enabled MicroSD cards; Printers/MFDs; External storage devices; Digital cameras)

3.4 Explain the importance of secure staging deployment concepts	Chapter 2

Sandboxing; Environment (Development; Test; Staging; Production); Secure baseline; Integrity measurement

3.5 Explain the security implications of embedded systems	Chapter 7

SCADA/ICS; Smart devices/IoT (Wearable technology; Home automation); HVAC; SoC; RTOS; Printers/MFDs; Camera systems; Special purpose (Medical devices; Vehicles; Aircraft/UAV)

3.6 Summarize secure application development and deployment concepts	Chapter 7

Development life-cycle models (Waterfall vs. Agile); Secure DevOps (Security automation; Continuous integration; Baselining; Immutable systems; Infrastructure as code); Version control and change management; Provisioning and deprovisioning; Secure coding techniques (Proper error handling; Proper input validation; Normalization; Stored procedures; Code signing; Encryption; Obfuscation/camouflage; Code reuse/dead code; Server-side vs. client-side execution and validation; Memory management; Use of third-party libraries and SDKs; Data exposure); Code quality and testing (Static code analyzers; Dynamic analysis (e.g., fuzzing); Stress testing; Sandboxing; Model verification); Compiled vs. runtime code

3.7 Summarize cloud and virtualization concepts	Chapter 6

Hypervisor (Type I; Type II; Application cells/containers); VM sprawl avoidance; VM escape protection; Cloud storage; Cloud deployment models (SaaS; PaaS; IaaS; Private; Public; Hybrid; Community); On-premise vs hosted vs. cloud; VDI/VDE; Cloud access security broker; Security as a Service

3.8 Explain how resiliency and automation strategies reduce risk	Chapter 1

Automation/Scripting (Automated courses of action; Continuous monitoring; Configuration validation); Templates: Master image; Non-persistence (Snapshots; Revert to known state; Rollback to known configuration; Live boot media); Elasticity: Scalability; Distributive allocation; Redundancy; Fault tolerance; High availability; RAID

Objective	Chapter
3.9 Explain the importance of physical security controls	Chapter 10

Lighting; Signs; Fencing/gate/cage; Security guards; Alarms; Safe; Secure cabinets/enclosures; Protected distribution/Protected cabling; Airgap; Mantrap; Faraday cage; Lock types; Biometrics; Barricades/bollards; Tokens/cards; Environmental controls (HVAC; Hot and cold aisles; Fire suppression); Cable locks; Screen filters; Cameras; Motion detection; Logs; Infrared detection; Key management

4.0 Identity and Access Management

| 4.1 Compare and contrast identity and access management concepts | Chapter 4 |

Identification, authentication, authorization and accounting (AAA); Multifactor authentication (Something you are; Something you have; Something you know; Somewhere you are; Something you do); Federation; Single sign-on; Transitive trust

| 4.2 Given a scenario, install and configure identity and access services | Chapter 4 |

LDAP; Kerberos; TACACS+; CHAP; PAP; MSCHAP; RADIUS; SAML; OpenID Connect; OAUTH; Shibboleth; Secure token; NTLM

| 4.3 Given a scenario, implement identity and access management controls | Chapter 4 |

Access control models (MAC; DAC; ABAC; Role-based access control; Rule-based access control); Physical access control (Proximity cards; Smart cards); Biometric factors (Fingerprint scanner; Retinal scanner; Iris scanner; Voice recognition; Facial recognition; False acceptance rate; False rejection rate; Crossover error rate); Tokens (Hardware; Software; HOTP/TOTP); Certificate-based authentication (PIV/CAC/smart card; IEEE 802.1s); File system security; Database security

| 4.4 Given a scenario, differentiate common account management practices | Chapter 11 |

Account types (User account; Shared and generic accounts/credentials; Guest accounts; Service accounts; Privileged accounts); General concepts (Least privilege; Onboarding/offboarding; Permission auditing and review; Usage auditing and review; Time-of-day restrictions; Recertification; Standard naming convention; Account maintenance; Group-based access control; Location-based policies); Account policy enforcement (Credential management; Group policy; Password complexity; Expiration; Recovery; Disablement; Lockout; Password history; Password reuse; Password length)

Objective	Chapter

5.0 Risk Management

5.1 Explain the importance of policies, plans and procedures related to organi-   Chapter 1
zational security

Standard operating procedure; Agreement types (BPA; SLA; ISA; MOU/MOA);
Personnel management (Mandatory vacations; Job rotation; Separation of
duties; Clean desk; Background checks; Exit interviews; Role-based awareness
training (Data owner; System administrator; System owner; User; Privileged
user; Executive user); NDA, Onboarding; Continuing education; Acceptable
use policy/rules of behavior; Adverse actions); General security policies (Social
media networks/applications; Personal email)

5.2 Summarize business impact analysis concepts   Chapter 1

RTO/RPO; MTBF; MTTR; Mission-essential functions; Identification of critical
systems; Single point of failure; Impact (Life; Property; Safety; Finance; Reputation); Privacy impact assessment; Privacy threshold assessment

5.3 Explain risk management processes and concepts   Chapter 1

Threat assessment (Environmental; Manmade; Internal vs. External); Risk
assessment (SLE; ALE; ARO; Asset value; Risk register; Likelihood of occurrence; Supply chain assessment; Impact; Quantitative; Qualitative; Testing
(Penetration testing authorization; Vulnerability testing authorization); Risk
response techniques (Accept, Transfer, Avoid, Mitigate)); Change management

5.4 Given a scenario, follow incident response procedures   Chapter 12

Incident response plan (Documented incident types/category definitions;
Roles and responsibilities; Reporting requirements/escalation; Cyber-incident
response teams; Exercise); Incident response process (Preparation; Identification; Containment; Eradication; Recovery; Lessons learned)

5.5 Summarize basic concepts of forensics   Chapter 12

Order of volatility; Chain of custody; Legal hold; Data acquisition (Capture system image; Network traffic and logs; Capture video; Record time offset; Take
hashes; Screenshots; Witness interviews); Preservation; Recovery; Strategic
intelligence/counterintelligence gathering (Active logging); Track man-hours

Objective	Chapter
6.3 Given a scenario, install and configure wireless security settings	Chapter 8
Cryptographic protocols (WPA; WPA2; CCMP; TKIP); Authentication protocols (EAP; PEAP; EAP-FAST; EAP-TLS; EAP-TTLS; IEEE 802.1x; RADIUS Federation); Methods (PSK vs. Enterprise v. Open; WPS; Captive portals)	
6.4 Given a scenario, implement public key infrastructure	Chapter 8
Components (CA; Intermediate CA; CRL; OCSP; CSR; Certificate; Public key; Private key; Object identifiers (OID)); Concepts (Online vs. offline CA; Stapling; Pinning; Trust model; Key escrow; Certificate chaining); Types of certificates (Wildcard; SAN; Code signing; Self-signed; Machine/computer; Email; User; Root; Domain validation; Extended validation); Certificate formats (DER; PEM; PFX; CER; P12; P7B)	

Exam objectives are subject to change at any time without prior notice and at CompTIA's discretion. Please visit CompTIA's website (www.comptia.org) for the most current listing of exam objectives.

Assessment Test

1. Which type of audit can be used to determine whether accounts have been established properly and verify that privilege creep isn't occurring?

   A. Privilege audit

   B. Usage audit

   C. Escalation audit

   D. Report audit

2. What kind of physical access device restricts access to a small number of individuals at one time?

   A. Checkpoint

   B. Perimeter security

   C. Security zones

   D. Mantrap

3. Which of the following is a set of voluntary standards governing encryption?

   A. PKI

   B. PKCS

   C. ISA

   D. SSL

4. What is the acronym associated with the point of maximum tolerable loss for a system due to a major incident?

   A. ARO

   B. RPO

   C. RTP

   D. WML

5. What type of exercise involves discussing possible security risks in a low-stress environment?

   A. White box

   B. Tabletop

   C. Black hat

   D. DHE

6. You want to install a cryptoprocessor chip that can be used to enhance security with the PKI systems. Which of the following is the one you are looking for?

   A. OCSP

   B. HSM

   C. MTU

   D. PIV

7. Which design concept limits access to systems from outside users while protecting users and systems inside the LAN?

    A. DMZ

    B. VLAN

    C. I&A

    D. Router

8. In the key recovery process, which key must be recoverable?

    A. Rollover key

    B. Secret key

    C. Previous key

    D. Escrow key

9. Which kind of attack is designed to overload a particular protocol or service?

    A. Spoofing

    B. Back door

    C. Man in the middle

    D. Flood

10. Which component of an IDS collects data?

    A. Data source

    B. Sensor

    C. Event

    D. Analyzer

11. Which of the following is included in an SSID broadcast (choose the best answer)?

    A. Network name

    B. MAC address

    C. DHCP configuration information

    D. DNS default values

12. The integrity objective addresses which characteristic of information security?

    A. Verification that information is accurate

    B. Verification that ethics are properly maintained

    C. Establishment of clear access control of data

    D. Verification that data is kept private and secure

13. Which mechanism is used by PKI to allow immediate verification of a certificate's validity?

    A. CRL

    B. MD5

    C. SSHA

    D. OCSP

14. To increase security, TKIP places a wrapper around the WEP encryption with a key that is based on things such as the MAC address of the host device and the serial number of the packet. What is the size of the wrapper?

A. 64-bit

B. 128-bit

C. 256-bit

D. 512-bit

15. A user has just reported that he downloaded a file from a prospective client using IM. The user indicates that the file was called account.doc. The system has been behaving unusually since he downloaded the file. What is the most likely event that occurred?

A. Your user inadvertently downloaded a virus using IM.

B. Your user may have a defective hard drive.

C. Your user is imagining what cannot be and is therefore mistaken.

D. The system is suffering from power surges.

16. Which mechanism or process is used to enable or disable access to a network resource based on an IP address?

A. NDS

B. ACL

C. Hardening

D. Port blocking

17. Virtualization that does not utilize hypervisors can be accomplished through the use of which of the following?

A. Wrappers

B. Containers

C. Portals

D. Sinks

18. What type of program exists primarily to propagate and spread itself to other systems?

A. Virus

B. Trojan horse

C. Logic bomb

D. Worm

19. An individual presents herself at your office claiming to be a service technician. She wants to discuss your current server configuration. This may be an example of what type of attack?

A. Social engineering

B. Access control

C. Perimeter screening

D. Behavioral engineering

20. Which of the following is a type of man-in-the-middle attack in which a Trojan horse manipulates calls between the browser and its security mechanisms yet still displays back the user's intended transaction?

   A. PFS

   B. MITB

   C. P12

   D. SDN

21. Which system would you install to provide active protection and notification of security problems in a network connected to the Internet?

   A. IPS

   B. Network monitoring

   C. Router

   D. VPN

22. The process of verifying the steps taken to maintain the integrity of evidence is called what?

   A. Security investigation

   B. Chain of custody

   C. Three As of investigation

   D. Security policy

23. What encryption process uses one message to hide another?

   A. Steganography

   B. Hashing

   C. MDA

   D. Cryptointelligence

24. Penetration/vulnerability testing that takes a passive approach rather than actually trying to break into the network is known as which one of the following?

   A. Flaccid testing

   B. Noncredentialed testing

   C. Nonintrusive testing

   D. Pedestrian testing

25. Which algorithm is used to create a temporary secure session for the exchange of key information?

   A. KDC

   B. KEA

   C. SSL

   D. RSA

26. You've been hired as a security consultant for a company that's beginning to implement handheld devices, such as smartphones. You're told that the company must use an asymmetric system. Which security standard would you recommend that it implement?

  A. ECC

  B. PKI

  C. SHA

  D. MD

27. Which of the following backup methods will generally provide the fastest backup times?

  A. Full backup

  B. Incremental backup

  C. Differential backup

  D. Archival backup

28. You want to grant access to network resources based on authenticating an individual's retina during a scan. Which security method uses a physical characteristic as a method of determining identity?

  A. Smart card

  B. I&A

  C. Biometrics

  D. CHAP

29. Which access control method is primarily concerned with the role that individuals have in the organization?

  A. MAC

  B. DAC

  C. RBAC

  D. STAC

30. The process of investigating a computer system for clues about an event is called what?

  A. Computer forensics

  B. Virus scanning

  C. Security policy

  D. Evidence gathering

Answers to Assessment Test

1. **A.** privilege audit is used to determine that all groups, users, and other accounts have the appropriate privileges assigned according to the policies of an organization. For more information, see Chapter 11.

2. **D.** A mantrap limits access to one individual at a time. It could be, for example, a small room. Mantraps typically use electronic locks and other methods to control access. For more information, see Chapter 10.

3. **B.** Public Key Cryptography Standards is a set of voluntary standards for public key cryptography. This set of standards is coordinated by RSA. For more information, see Chapter 8.

4. **B.** The Recovery Point Objective (RPO) is the point of maximum tolerable loss for a system due to a major incident. For additional information, see Chapter 1.

5. **B.** A tabletop exercise involves sitting around the table and discussing (with the help of a facilitator) possible security risks in a low-stress format. For more information, see Chapter 12.

6. **B.** A Hardware Security Module (HSM) is a cryptoprocessor chip (or circuit mounted within the computer) that can be used to enhance security, and it is commonly used with PKI systems. For more information, see Chapter 3.

7. **A.** A DMZ (demilitarized zone) is an area in a network that allows restrictive access to untrusted users and isolates the internal network from access by external users and systems. It does so by using routers and firewalls to limit access to sensitive network resources. For more information, see Chapter 2.

8. **C.** A key recovery process must be able to recover a previous key. If the previous key can't be recovered, then all the information for which the key was used will be irrecoverably lost. For more information, see Chapter 8.

9. **D.** A flood attack is designed to overload a protocol or service by repeatedly initiating a request for service. This type of attack usually results in a DoS (denial-of-service) situation occurring because the protocol freezes or since excessive bandwidth is used in the network as a result of the requests. For more information, see Chapter 3.

10. **B.** A sensor collects data from the data source and passes it on to the analyzer. If the analyzer determines that unusual activity has occurred, an alert may be generated. For additional information, see Chapter 2.

11. **A.** An SSID (Service Set Identifier) broadcast includes the network name. For additional information on hardening, see Chapter 3.

12. **A.** To meet the goal of integrity, you must verify that the information being used is accurate and hasn't been tampered with. Integrity is coupled with accountability to ensure that data is accurate and that a final authority exists to verify this, if needed. For more information, see Chapter 8.

13. D. Online Certificate Status Protocol (OCSP) is the mechanism used to verify immediately whether a certificate is valid. The Certificate Revocation List (CRL) is published on a regular basis, but it isn't current once it's published. For additional information, see Chapter 8.

14. B. TKIP places a 128-bit wrapper around the WEP encryption with a key that is based on things such as the MAC address of the host device and the serial number of the packet. For additional information, see Chapter 5.

15. A. IM and other systems allow unsuspecting users to download files that may contain viruses. Due to a weakness in the file extension naming conventions, a file that appears to have one extension may actually have another extension. For example, the file account.doc.vbs would appear in many applications as account.doc, but it's actually a Visual Basic script and could contain malicious code. For additional information, see Chapter 9.

16. B. Access control lists (ACLs) are used to allow or deny an IP address access to a network. ACL mechanisms are implemented in many routers, firewalls, and other network devices. For additional information, see Chapter 3.

17. B. Virtualization that does not utilize hypervisors can be accomplished through the use of containers, also known as "Docker containers." For more information, see Chapter 6.

18. D. A worm is designed to multiply and propagate. Worms may carry viruses that cause system destruction, but that isn't their primary mission. For more information, see Chapter 9.

19. A. Social engineering is using human intelligence methods to gain access or information about your organization. For additional information, see Chapter 10.

20. B. A man-in-the-browser attack (abbreviated as MITB, MitB, MIB, and MiB) is a type of man-in-the-middle attack in which a Trojan horse manipulates calls between the browser and its security mechanisms, sniffing or modifying transactions as they are formed on the browser yet still displaying back the user's intended transaction. For additional information, see Chapter 9.

21. A. An intrusion prevention system (IPS) provides active monitoring and rule-based responses to unusual activities on a network. A firewall, for example, provides passive security by preventing access from unauthorized traffic. If the firewall were compromised, the IPS would notify you based on rules that it's designed to implement. For more information, see Chapter 3.

22. B. The chain of custody ensures that each step taken with evidence is documented and accounted for from the point of collection. Chain of custody is the Who, What, When, Where, and Why of evidence storage. For additional information, see Chapter 12.

23. A. Steganography is the process of hiding one message in another. Steganography may also be referred to as electronic watermarking. For additional information, see Chapter 8.

24. C. Penetration/vulnerability testing that takes a passive approach rather than actually trying to break into the network is known as nonintrusive testing. For additional information, see Chapter 12.

25. B. The Key Exchange Algorithm (KEA) is used to create a temporary session to exchange key information. This session creates a secret key. When the key has been exchanged, the regular session begins. For more information, see Chapter 8.

26. A. Elliptic Curve Cryptography (ECC) would probably be your best choice. ECC is designed to work with smaller processors. The other systems may be options, but they require more computing power than ECC. For additional information, see Chapter 8.

27. B. An incremental backup will generally be the fastest of the backup methods because it backs up only the files that have changed since the last incremental or full backup. See Chapter 12 for more information.

28. C. Biometrics is the authentication process that uses physical characteristics, such as a palm print or retinal pattern, to establish identification. For more information, see Chapter 11.

29. C. Role-based access control (RBAC) is primarily concerned with providing access to systems that a user needs based on the user's role in the organization. For more information, see Chapter 4.

30. A. Computer forensics is the process of investigating a computer system to determine the cause of an incident. Part of this process would be gathering evidence. For additional information, see Chapter 12.

Chapter

1

Managing Risk

THE FOLLOWING COMPTIA SECURITY+ EXAM OBJECTIVES ARE COVERED IN THIS CHAPTER:

✓ **3.8 Explain how resiliency and automation strategies reduce risk.**

- Automation/Scripting: Automated courses of action; Continuous monitoring; Configuration validation
- Templates
- Master image
- Non-persistence: Snapshots; Revert to known state; Rollback to known configuration; Live boot media
- Elasticity
- Scalability
- Distributive allocation
- Redundancy
- Fault tolerance
- High availability
- RAID

✓ **5.1 Explain the importance of policies, plans, and procedures related to organizational security.**

- Standard operating procedure
- Agreement types: BPA; SLA; ISA; MOU/MOA
- Personnel management: Mandatory vacations; Job rotation; Separation of duties; Clean desk; Background checks; Exit interviews; Role-based awareness training (Data owner; System administrator; System owner; User; Privileged user; Executive user); NDA, Onboarding; Continuing education; Acceptable use policy/rules of behavior; Adverse actions
- General security policies: Social media networks/applications; Personal email

✓ **5.2 Summarize business impact analysis concepts.**

- RTO/RPO
- MTBF
- MTTR
- Mission-essential functions
- Identification of critical systems
- Single point of failure
- Impact: Life; Property; Safety; Finance; Reputation
- Privacy impact assessment
- Privacy threshold assessment

✓ **5.3 Explain risk management processes and concepts.**

- Threat assessment: Environmental; Manmade; Internal vs. External
- Risk assessment: SLE; ALE; ARO; Asset value; Risk register; Likelihood of occurrence; Supply chain assessment; Impact; Quantitative; Qualitative; Testing (Penetration testing authorization; Vulnerability testing authorization); Risk response techniques (Accept, Transfer, Avoid, Mitigate)
- Change management

As an administrator, you are responsible. You are responsible for data that gets created, stored, transmitted, viewed, modified, deleted, and just about everything else that can be done with it. Because of this, not only must you enable it to exist, but you must protect it, authenticate it, secure it, and keep it in the form that complies with every applicable law, policy, and regulation. Counter to this are all of the dangers that can befall the data: it can be accidentally deleted, overwritten, stolen, and lost. These potential harms represent *risks*, and you must know the risks involved in working with data. You have to know and accept that data can be corrupted, it can be accessed by those who shouldn't see it, values can be changed, and so on.

If you think that being armed with this knowledge is enough to drive you into taking the steps necessary to keep any harm from happening, however, you are sadly mistaken. One of the actions that administrators can be instructed to take by upper management regarding potential threats is to accept that they exist. If the cost of preventing a particular risk from becoming a reality exceeds the value of the harm that could occur, then a cost-benefit risk calculation dictates that the risk should stand.

Risk calculations weigh a potential *threat* against the *likelihood* or *probability* of it occurring. As frustrating as it may seem, you should accept the fact that some risks, often called *residual risk*, will and must remain. This chapter focuses on risk and the various ways of dealing with it, all of which you will need to understand fully in order to succeed on the Security+ exam.

We will start out by looking at some of the *vernacular*, or terms associated with the field of risk. Then we will move into risk assessment; policies, standards, and guidelines; and change management.

Risk Terminology

Every field of study has a few terms or words that are unique to that particular field in order to help those in the profession to communicate among themselves. The study of risk is no different. A number of terms are associated with risk that will appear at various places in this chapter and throughout the book. The following terms (also found in the online glossary) are those that CompTIA is fond of using and testing. They are provided in order to make it easier for you to know what each is intended to convey.

Security+ Terminology

acceptable use policy/rules of behavior   Agreed-upon principles set forth by a company to govern how the employees of that company may use resources such as computers and Internet access.

annual loss expectancy (ALE)   A calculation used to identify risks and calculate the expected loss each year.

annualized rate of occurrence (ARO)   A calculation of how often a threat will occur. For example, a threat that occurs once every five years has an annualized rate of occurrence of 1/5, or 0.2.

asset value (AV)   The assessed value of an item (server, property, and so on) associated with cash flow.

business impact analysis (BIA)   A study of the possible impact if a disruption to a business's vital resources were to occur.

business partners agreement (BPA)   An agreement between partners in a business that outlines their responsibilities, obligations, and sharing of profits and losses.

exposure factor (EF)   The potential percentage of loss to an asset if a threat is realized.

interconnection security agreement (ISA)   As defined by NIST (in Publication 800-47), it is "an agreement established between the organizations that own and operate connected IT systems to document the technical requirements of the interconnection. The ISA also supports a Memorandum of Understanding or Agreement (MOU/A) between the organizations."

maximum tolerable downtime (MTD)   The maximum period of time that a business process can be down before the survival of the organization is at risk.

mean time between failures (MTBF)   The measurement of the anticipated lifetime of a system or component.

mean time to failure (MTTF)   The measurement of the average of how long it takes a system or component to fail.

mean time to restore (MTTR)   The measurement of how long it takes to repair a system or component once a failure occurs.

memorandum of understanding (MOU)/memorandum of agreement (MOA)   Most commonly known as an MOU rather than MOA, this is a document between two or more parties defining their respective responsibilities in accomplishing a particular goal or mission, such as securing a system.

recovery point objective (RPO)   The point last known good data prior to an outage that is used to recover systems.

recovery time objective (RTO)   The maximum amount of time that a process or service is allowed to be down and the consequences still to be considered acceptable.

Redundant Array of Independent Disks (RAID)   A configuration of multiple hard disks used to provide fault tolerance should a disk fail. Different levels of RAID exist.

risk   The probability that a particular threat will occur, either accidentally or intentionally, leaving a system vulnerable and the impact of this occurring.

risk acceptance   A strategy of dealing with risk in which it is decided the best approach is simply to accept the consequences should the threat happen.

risk analysis   An evaluation of each risk that can be identified. Each risk should be outlined, described, and evaluated on the likelihood of it occurring.

risk assessment   An evaluation of the possibility of a threat or vulnerability existing. An assessment must be performed before any other actions—such as how much to spend on security in terms of dollars and manpower—can be decided.

risk avoidance   A strategy of dealing with risk in which it is decided that the best approach is to avoid the risk.

risk calculation   The process of calculating the risks that exist in terms of costs, number, frequency, and so forth.

risk deterrence   A strategy of dealing with risk in which it is decided that the best approach is to discourage potential attackers from engaging in the behavior that leads to the risk.

risk mitigation   A strategy of dealing with risk in which it is decided that the best approach is to lessen the risk.

risk transference   A strategy of dealing with risk in which it is decided that the best approach is to offload some of the risk through insurance, third-party contracts, and/or shared responsibility.

service-level agreement (SLA)   An agreement that specifies performance requirements for a vendor. This agreement may use mean time before failure (MTBF) and mean time to repair (MTTR) as performance measures in the SLA.

single loss expectancy (SLE)   The cost of a single loss when it occurs. This loss can be a critical failure, or it can be the result of an attack.

single point of failure (SPOF)   A single weakness that is capable of bringing an entire system down

vulnerability   A flaw or weakness in some part of a system's security procedures, design, implementation, or internal controls that could expose it to danger (accidental or intentional) and result in a violation of the security policy.

Threat Assessment

To protect your resources, you need to be able to identify what threats to them exist—the more specific you can be, the better. It is easy to say that you "might lose data," but that is a danger as opposed to a threat. The *threat* is what would cause you to lose this data. In general terms, a *threat* is anything that can harm your resources, and there are three primary categories of threats that need to be identified and examined:

Environmental Threats from the environment include things such as floods, tornados, hurricanes, and so on. If you share a building with another organization, what would happen if a fire alarm went off in their area? Would sprinklers throughout the entire building be activated and your server room flooded?

Manmade There can be overlap between the categories, and the environmental flooding of a server room could be manmade in nature, caused by an individual holding a match to the bathroom smoke detector.

Internal vs. External If the threat is an individual who is employed by your organization, then it is considered an internal threat. If the individual is not currently employed by your organization, then it is considered an external threat.

One graphical tool that is often used to identify threats is a *risk register*, which is essentially a scatterplot of possible problem areas. With the categories of threats now identified, we will factor them into an assessment of risk in the following sections.

Risk Assessment

Risk assessment is also known as *risk analysis* or *risk calculation*. For purposes of uniformity, we will use *risk assessment* as the term of choice for this discussion. *Risk assessment* deals with the threats, vulnerabilities, and impacts of a loss of information-processing capabilities or a loss of information itself. In simple terms, a *vulnerability* is a weakness that could be exploited by a threat. Each risk that can be identified should be outlined, described, and evaluated for the likelihood of it occurring. The key here is to think outside the box. Conventional threats and risks are often too limited when considering risk assessment.

The chief components of a risk assessment process are outlined here:

Risks to Which the Organization Is Exposed This component allows you to develop scenarios that can help you evaluate how to deal with these types of risks if they occur. An operating system, server, or application may have known risks in certain environments. You should create a plan for how your organization will best deal with these risks and the best way for it to respond to them.

Risks That Need Addressing   The risk assessment component also allows an organization to provide a reality check on which risks are real and which are unlikely. This process helps an organization focus on its resources as well as on the risks that are most likely to occur. For example, industrial espionage and theft are likely, but the risk of a hurricane damaging the server room in Indiana is very low. Therefore, more resources should be allocated to prevent espionage or theft as opposed to the latter possibility.

Coordination with BIA   The risk assessment component, in conjunction with the *business impact analysis (BIA)*, provides an organization with an accurate picture of the situation facing it. It allows an organization to make intelligent decisions about how to respond to various scenarios.

 Real World Scenario

Conducting a Risk Assessment

You've been asked to do a quick assessment of the risks your company faces from a security perspective. What steps might you take to develop an overview of your company's problems?

1. Interview the department heads and the data owners to determine what information they believe requires additional security and to identify the existing vulnerabilities from their perspective.

2. Evaluate the network infrastructure to determine known vulnerabilities and how you might counter them.

3. Perform a physical assessment of the facility to evaluate what physical risks must be countered.

Armed with this information, you have a place to start, and you can determine which countermeasures may be appropriate for the company to mitigate risk.

Computing Risk Assessment

When you're doing a risk assessment, one of the most important things to do is to prioritize. Not everything should be weighed evenly, because some events have a greater likelihood of happening. In addition, a company can accept some risks, whereas others would be catastrophic for the company.

One document you should read is the National Institute of Standards and Technology (NIST) Guide for Conducting Risk Assessments, Publication 800-30. Revision 1 of this document can be found here:

`http://nvlpubs.nist.gov/nistpubs/Legacy/SP/`
`nistspecialpublication800-30r1.pdf`

It is worth noting that the revision to the original document refocuses it from being primarily just about risk management to one that strongly emphasizes risk assessment.

Risk Calculations

For purposes of risk assessment, both in the real world and for the exam, you should familiarize yourself with a number of terms to determine the *impact* an event could have:

- *ALE* is the *annual loss expectancy* value. This is a monetary measure of how much loss you could expect in a year.

- *SLE* is another monetary value, and it represents how much you could expect to lose at any one time: the *single loss expectancy*. SLE can be divided into two components:

  - *AV (asset value)*: the value of the item

  - *EF (exposure factor)*: the percentage of it threatened

- *ARO* is the likelihood, often drawn from historical data, of an event occurring within a year: the *annualized rate of occurrence*.

When you compute risk assessment, remember this formula:

$$SLE \times ARO = ALE$$

As an example, if you can reasonably expect that every SLE, which is equal to asset value (AV) times exposure factor (EF), will be the equivalent of $1,000 and that there will be seven such occurrences a year (ARO), then the ALE is $7,000. Conversely, if there is only a 10 percent chance of an event occurring within a year time period (ARO = 0.1), then the ALE drops to $100.

In Exercise 1.1, we'll walk through some risk assessment computations.

EXERCISE 1.1

Risk Assessment Computations

As a security professional, you should know how to compute SLE, ALE, and ARO. Given any two of the numbers, it's possible to calculate the third. Here are three scenarios detailing a hypothetical risk assessment situation followed by the details for figuring out the ALE. They are intended to give you experience working with scenarios similar to those that you may find on the Security+ exam. For this exercise, compute the missing values:

1. You're the administrator of a web server that generates $25,000 per hour in revenue. The probability of the web server failing during the year is estimated to be 25 percent.

A failure would lead to three hours of downtime and cost $5,000 in components to correct. What is the ALE?

The SLE is $80,000 ($25,000 × 3 hours + $5,000), and the ARO is 0.25. Therefore, the ALE is $20,000 ($80,000 × 0.25).

2. You're the administrator for a research firm that works on only one project at a time and collects data through the web to a single server. The value of each research project is approximately $100,000. At any given time, an intruder could commandeer no more than 90 percent of the data. The industry average for ARO is 0.33. What is the ALE?

The SLE equals $90,000 ($100,000 × 0.9), and the ARO is 0.33. Therefore, the ALE is $29,700 ($90,000 × 0.33).

3. You work at the help desk for a small company. One of the most common requests to which you must respond is to help retrieve a file that has been accidentally deleted by a user. On average, this happens once a week. If the user creates the file and then deletes it on the server (about 60 percent of the incidents), then it can be restored in moments from the shadow copy and there is rarely any data lost. If the user creates the file on their workstation and then deletes it (about 40 percent of the incidents), and if it can't be recovered and it takes the user an average of two hours to re-create it at $12 an hour, what is the ALE?

The SLE is $24 ($12 × 2), and the ARO is 20.8 (52 weeks × 0.4). Therefore, the ALE equals $499.20 ($24 × 20.8).

Key to any risk assessment is identifying both assets and threats. You first have to identify what it is that you want to protect and then what possible harm could come to those assets. You then analyze the risks in terms of either cost or severity.

Quantitative vs. Qualitative Risk Assessment

Risk assessment can be either *qualitative* (opinion-based and subjective) or *quantitative* (cost-based and objective), depending on whether you are focusing on dollar amounts or simply downtime. The formulas for single loss expectancy (SLE), annual loss expectancy (ALE), and annualized rate of occurrence (ARO) are all based on doing assessments that lead to dollar amounts and are thus quantitative.

To understand the difference between quantitative and qualitative, it helps to use a simple example. Imagine that you get an emergency call to help a small company that you have never heard from before. It turns out that their one and only server has crashed and that their backups are useless. One of the lost files was the only copy of the company's history. This file detailed the company from the day it began to the present day and had the various iterations of the mission statement as it changed over time. As painful a loss as this file represents to the company's culture, it has nothing to do with filling orders and keeping customers happy, and thus its loss is qualitative in nature.

Another loss was the customer database. This held customer contact information as well as the history of all past orders, charge numbers, and so on. The company cannot function without this file, and it needs to be re-created by pulling all of the hard copy invoices from storage and re-entering them into the system. This loss can be calculated by the amount of business lost and the amount of time it takes to find/re-enter all of the data, and thus it is a quantitative loss.

> Whenever you see the word *quantitative*, think of the goal as determining a dollar amount. Whenever you see the word *qualitative*, think of a best guess or opinion of the loss, including reputation, goodwill, and irreplaceable information; pictures; or data that get you to a subjective loss amount.

Risk Measurements

Make sure that you understand the scope and terms of hardware and *service-level agreement (SLA)*–related terms. Doing so can help avoid frustration and prevent unanticipated disruptions from crippling your organization. The following are key measures with which you should be familiar:

Likelihood   The meaning of the word *likelihood* is usually self-explanatory; however, actual values can be assigned to likelihood. The National Institute of Standards and Technology recommends viewing likelihood as a score representing the possibility of threat initiation. In this way, it can be expressed either in qualitative or quantitative terms. Table 1.1 shows an assessment scale for the likelihood of threat event initiation adapted from Appendix G of NIST Publication 800-30.

TABLE 1.1   Likelihood assessment scale

Qualitative values	Semi-quantitative values	Description
Very High	10	Adversary is almost certain to initiate threat event.
High	8	Adversary is highly likely to initiate threat event.
Moderate	5	Adversary is somewhat likely to initiate threat event.
Low	2	Adversary is unlikely to initiate threat event.
Very Low	0	Adversary is highly unlikely to initiate threat event.

Guide for Conducting Risk Assessments, National Institute of Standards and Technology, Publication 800-30.

A *supply chain assessment* is similarly used to look at the vendors your organization works with strategically and the potential risks they introduce.

Threat Vectors The term *threat vector* is the way in which an attacker poses a threat. This can be a particular tool that they can use against you (a vulnerability scanner, for example) or the path(s) of attack that they follow. Under that broad definition, a threat vector can be anything from a fake email that lures you into clicking a link (phishing) or an unsecured hotspot (rouge access point) and everything in between.

Mean Time Between Failures The *mean time between failures (MTBF)* is the measure of the anticipated incidence of failure for a system or component. This measurement determines the component's anticipated lifetime. If the MTBF of a cooling system is one year, you can anticipate that the system will last for a one-year period; this means that you should be prepared to replace or rebuild the system once a year. If the system lasts longer than the MTBF, it's a bonus for your organization. MTBF is helpful in evaluating a system's reliability and life expectancy.

Mean Time to Failure Similar to MTBF, the *mean time to failure (MTTF)* is the average time to failure for a nonrepairable system. If the system can be repaired, the MTBF is the measurement to focus on, but if it cannot, then MTTF is the number to examine. Sometimes, MTTF is improperly used in place of MTBF, but as an administrator you should know the difference between them and when to use one measurement or the other.

Mean Time to Restore The *mean time to restore (MTTR)* is the measurement of how long it takes to repair a system or component once a failure occurs. (This is often also referenced as *mean time to repair.*) In the case of a computer system, if the MTTR is 24 hours, this tells you that it will typically take 24 hours to repair it when it breaks.

Although MTTR is considered a common measure of maintainability, be careful when evaluating it because it doesn't typically include the time needed to acquire a component and have it shipped to your location. This author (Emmett Dulaney) once worked with a national vendor who thought MTTR meant mean time to respond—that is, a technician would show up on site within the time called for in the contract, but would only then begin to look at the problem and make a list of any needed supplies. Make sure that the contract or service-level agreement spells out exactly what you want.

Recovery Time Objective The *recovery time objective (RTO)* is the maximum amount of time that a process or service is allowed to be down and the consequences still to be considered acceptable. Beyond this time, the break in business continuity is considered to affect the business negatively. The RTO is agreed on during BIA creation.

Recovery Point Objective The *recovery point objective (RPO)* is similar to RTO, but it defines the point at which the system needs to be restored. This could be where the system was two days before it crashed (whip out the old backup tapes) or five minutes before it crashed (requiring complete redundancy). As a general rule, the closer the RPO matches the item of the crash, the more expensive it is to obtain.

Most SLAs that relate to risk management stipulate the definitions of these terms and how they apply to the agreement. You should understand how these terms are used and what they mean to the vendor and to your organization in order to ensure that there is concurrence.

Assessing Privacy

One area of primary importance for administrators today is privacy. Not only are you charged with keeping data accessible, but that accessibility must be limited to certain parties, and those parties seem to change on a regular basis. In healthcare, for example, records may be limited to only a patient and a doctor, but one patient may have a dozen doctors and all of those doctors need to see that data. Other patients will want their spouse to be able to access their records, while still others won't. And so it goes…

Two privacy-related concepts with which you should be familiar are the *privacy impact assessment (PIA)* and *privacy threshold assessment (PTA)*. A PIA is often associated with a business impact analysis, and it identifies the adverse impacts that can be associated with the destruction, corruption, or loss of accountability of data for the organization. The Department of Homeland Security (DHS), for example, uses it to identify and mitigate privacy risks by telling the public what *personally identifiable information (PII)* it collects, why it is collected, and how it is used, accessed, shared, safeguarded, and stored. According to the DHS, a PIA needs to do three things: ensure conformance with applicable legal, regulatory, and policy requirements for privacy; determine risks and effects; and evaluate protections and alternative processes to mitigate potential privacy risks.

A PTA, on the other hand, is more commonly known as an "analysis" rather than an "assessment." This is the compliance tool used in conjunction with the PIA. An example of the form the DHS uses for this purpose can be found at https://www.dhs.gov/compliance.

Two types of testing that can help identify risks are *penetration testing* and *vulnerability testing*. They are particularly useful with identifying threats associated with authorization. Both are discussed in more detail in subsequent chapters.

Acting on Your Risk Assessment

Once you've identified and assessed the risks that exist, for the purpose of the exam, you have four possible responses that you can choose to follow:

Risk Avoidance   *Risk avoidance* involves identifying a risk and making the decision not to engage any longer in the actions associated with that risk. For example, a company may decide that many risks are associated with email attachments, and it may choose to forbid any email attachments from entering the network. As part of risk avoidance, the company takes steps to remove the risk, chooses to engage in some other activity, or puts a stop to their exposure to the risk. Avoidance should be based on an informed decision that the best course of action is to deviate from what could lead to exposure to the risk. One of the biggest problems with risk avoidance is that you are actually steering clear of activities from which you may benefit. The most effective risk avoidance strategy to avoid computer crime, for example, would simply be to avoid using computers at all. Not only is that solution impractical, but it would also prevent companies from adding social value (not to mention monetary value) for their stakeholders.

Risk Transference   *Risk transference*, contrary to what the name may imply, does not mean that you shift the risk completely to another entity. What you do instead is share some of the burden of the risk with someone else, such as an insurance company. A typical policy would pay you a cash amount if all the steps were in place to reduce risk and your system was still harmed.

The current push is to move many services to the cloud, hosted by a third-party provider. If you do so, you are engaging in a form of risk transference by relying on that third-party provider for uptime, performance, and security measures. Another risk transference possibility involves employing external consultants for assistance with solutions in areas where internal IT is weak and requiring the external consultants to guarantee their work.

Risk Mitigation   *Risk mitigation* is accomplished any time you take steps to reduce risk. This category includes installing antivirus software, educating users about possible threats, monitoring network traffic, adding a firewall, and so on. In Microsoft's Security Intelligence Report, Volume 13, the following suggestions for mitigating risk through user awareness training are listed:

- Keep security messages fresh and in circulation.
- Target new employees and current staff members.
- Set goals to ensure that a high percentage of the staff is trained on security best practices.
- Repeat the information to raise awareness.

CompTIA is fond of risk mitigation and confronting it through the use of routine *audits* that address *user rights* and *permission reviews*; *change management*, the structured approach that is followed to secure a company's assets; and *incident management*, the steps followed when events occur (making sure that controls are in place in order to prevent unauthorized access to, and changes of, all IT assets). Policies addressing data loss or theft need to be in place, and technology controls should be enforced.

Data loss prevention (DLP) systems monitor the contents of systems (workstations, servers, and networks) to make sure that key content is not deleted or removed. They also monitor who is using the data (looking for unauthorized access) and transmitting the data. DLP systems share commonality with network intrusion prevention systems. Other approaches include IPSs, firewalls, and similar devices that can help mitigate risk.

Risk Acceptance   *Risk acceptance* is often the choice that you must make when the cost of implementing any of the other responses exceeds the value of the harm that would occur if the risk came to fruition. To truly qualify as acceptance, it cannot be a risk where the administrator or manager is unaware of its existence; it has to be an identified risk for which those involved understand the potential cost or damage and agree to accept it. *Risk acceptance* is nothing more than acknowledging that a risk exists and choosing to do nothing about it. It does not necessarily mean that you will be affected by the risk, but only that you realize that such a possibility exists. Quite often, this is the choice that you make when the cost of implementing any of the other options exceeds the value of any harm that could occur if the risk is realized. Every firm has a different level of *risk tolerance* (sometimes called a *risk appetite*) that they are willing to accept.

Risk strategies need not be thought of as either/or propositions. It is often possible to combine a bit of mitigation with avoidance. You will often try to combine strategies to reduce your exposure as much as possible. You are then left to accept those issues that cannot be addressed otherwise. In the case of the mailbox analogy, the approach of grouping individual boxes together and placing them all in stone combines elements of both mitigation and transference.

Often you can create interesting or memorable examples to help in understanding or memorizing various lists. This works well for the possible risk responses, too.

Imagine that you are a junior administrator for a large IT department, and you believe that one of the older servers should be replaced with a new one. There are no signs of failure now, but you believe it would be prudent to upgrade before anything disastrous happens. The problem, however, is that all spending requires approval from your superior, who is focused on saving the company as much money as possible and, by doing so, hopes to be considered for a promotion. Thus, she does not want anyone coming up with ways to spend money unnecessarily. You know her well enough to realize that if a problem does occur, she will not hesitate to put all the blame on you in order to save her own career. Table 1.2 shows how you would apply each of the possible risk actions to this scenario.

TABLE 1.2   Risk actions for the scenario

Risk action	Application
Risk avoidance	You begin moving services from the older server to other servers and remove the load to avoid the risk of any services being affected by its demise.
Risk transference	You write up the possibility of the server failing along with details of what you think should be done to prevent it, and you submit your findings to your boss while keeping a copy for yourself. If the server does fail, you have proof that you documented this possibility and made the appropriate parties aware of the situation.
Risk mitigation	You write up the possibility of failure and submit it to your boss while also moving crucial services from that server to others.
Risk acceptance	You know the server could fail but hope that it doesn't. You neither write nor submit reports because you don't want to rock the boat and make your boss unhappy with you. With luck, you'll have transferred to another division before the server ever goes down.

Risk transference, mitigation, and avoidance are all proactive solutions that require planning and implementation ahead of time. Risk acceptance, on the other hand, merely adopts a "do nothing" approach. These constitute the four response strategies that CompTIA expects you to know for the risk management portion of the Security+ exam.

Risks Associated with Cloud Computing

The term *cloud computing* has grown in popularity recently, but few agree on what it truly means. For the purpose of the Security+ exam, *cloud computing* means hosting services and data on the Internet instead of hosting it locally. Some examples of this include running office suite applications such as Office 365 or Google Docs from the web instead of having similar applications installed on each workstation; storing data on server space, such as Google Drive, SkyDrive, or Amazon Web Services; and using cloud-based sites such as Salesforce.com.

From an exam standpoint, there are three different ways of implementing cloud computing:

Platform as a Service   The *Platform as a Service (PaaS)* model is also known as *cloud platform services*. In this model, vendors allow apps to be created and run on their infrastructure. Two well-known models of this implementation are Amazon Web Services and Google Code.

Software as a Service   The *Software as a Service (SaaS)* model is the one often thought of when users generically think of cloud computing. In this model, applications are remotely run over the web. The big advantages are that no local hardware is required (other than that needed to obtain web access) and no software applications need to be installed on the machine accessing the site. The best-known model of this type is Salesforce.com. Costs are usually computed on a subscription basis.

Infrastructure as a Service   The *Infrastructure as a Service (IaaS)* model utilizes virtualization, and clients pay a cloud service provider for resources used. Because of this, the IaaS model closely resembles the traditional utility model used by electric, gas, and water providers. GoGrid is a well-known example of this implementation.

A number of organizations have examined risk-related issues associated with cloud computing. These issues include the following:

Regulatory Compliance   Depending on the type and size of your organization, there are any number of regulatory agencies' rules with which you must comply. If your organization is publicly traded, for example, you must adhere to Sarbanes-Oxley's demanding and exacting rules, which can be difficult to do when the data is not located on your servers. Make sure that whoever hosts your data takes privacy and security as seriously as you do.

User Privileges   Enforcing user privileges can be fairly taxing. If the user does not have least privileges (addressed later in this chapter), then their escalated privileges could allow them to access data to which they would not otherwise have access and cause harm to it— intentional or not. Be cognizant of the fact that you won't have the same control over user accounts in the cloud as you do locally, and when someone locks their account by enter-ing the wrong password too many times in a row, you or they could be at the mercy of the hours that the technical staff is available at the provider.

Data Integration/Segregation   Just as web-hosting companies usually put more than one company's website on a server in order to be profitable, data-hosting companies can put more than one company's data on a server. To keep this from being problematic, you should use encryption to protect your data. Be aware of the fact that your data is only as safe as the data with which it is integrated. For example, assume that your client database is hosted on a server that another company is also using to test an application that they are creating. If their application obtains root-level access at some point (such as to change pass-words) and crashes at that point, then the user running the application could be left with root permissions and conceivably be able to access data on the server for which they are not authorized, such as your client database. Data segregation is crucial; keep your data on secure servers.

Data integration is equally important. Make sure that your data is not comingled beyond your expectations. It is not uncommon in an extranet to pull information from a number of databases in order to create a report. Those databases can be owned by anyone connected to the extranet, and it is important to make certain that the permissions on your databases are set properly to keep other members from accessing more information than you intended to share.

 Among the groups focused on cloud security issues, one worth noting is the Cloud Security Alliance (https://cloudsecurityalliance.org). They have published a number of whitepapers on security-related issues that can be found on their site and should be considered highly recommended reading for security administrators.

Risks Associated with Virtualization

If cloud computing has grown in popularity, *virtualization* has become the technology du jour. Virtualization consists of allowing one set of hardware to host multiple virtual machines. It is in use at most large corporations, and it is also becoming more common at smaller businesses.

Some of the possible security risks associated with virtualization include the following:

Breaking Out of the Virtual Machine   If a disgruntled employee could break out of the virtualization layer and were able to access the other virtual machines, they could access data that they should never be able to access.

Intermingling Network and Security Controls   The tools used to administer the virtual machine may not have the same granularity as those used to manage the network. This could lead to privilege escalation and a compromise of security.

Most virtualization-specific threats focus on the hypervisor. *Hypervisor* is the virtual machine monitor—that is, the software that allows the virtual machines to exist. If the hypervisor can be successfully attacked, the attacker can gain root-level access to all virtual systems. Although this is a legitimate issue, and one that has been demonstrated as possible in most systems (including VMware, Xen, and Microsoft Virtual Machine), it is one that has been patched each time it has arisen. The solution to most virtualization threats is always to apply the most recent patches and keep the system(s) up to date. Be sure to look for and implement suggestions that the vendor of your virtualization system may have published in a hardening guide.

Developing Policies, Standards, and Guidelines

The process of implementing and maintaining a secure network must first be addressed from a policies, standards, and guidelines perspective. This sets the tone, provides authority, and gives your efforts the teeth they need to be effective. Policies and guidelines set a standard of expectation in an organization. The process of developing these policies will help everyone in an organization become involved and invested in making security efforts successful. You can think of policies as providing high-level guidance on large issues. Standards tell people what is expected, and guidelines provide specific advice on how to accomplish a given task or activity.

 There is a difference between "top-down policies" (those that use the support of upper management) and "bottom-up policies" (often generated by the IT department with little intradepartmental support).

The following sections discuss the policies, standards, and guidelines that you'll need to establish in order for your security efforts to be successful.

Implementing Policies

Policies provide the people in an organization with guidance about their expected behavior. Well-written policies are clear and concise, and they outline the consequences when they aren't followed. A good policy contains several key areas besides the policy itself.

Scope Statement   A good policy has a *scope statement* that outlines what the policy intends to accomplish and which documents, laws, and practices the policy addresses. The scope statement provides background to help readers understand what the policy is about and how it applies to them.

The scope statement is always brief—usually not more than a single sentence in length.

Policy Overview Statement A *policy overview statement* provides the goal of the policy, why it's important, and how to comply with it. Ideally, a single paragraph is all you need to provide readers with a sense of the policy.

Policy Statement Once the policy's readers understand its importance, they should be informed about the substance of the policy. A *policy statement* should be as clear and unambiguous as possible. The policy may be presented in paragraph form, as bulleted lists, or as checklists.

The presentation will depend on the policy's target audience as well as its nature. If the policy is intended to help people determine how to lock up the building at the end of the business day, for example, it might be helpful to provide a specific checklist of the steps that need to be taken to accomplish this task.

Accountability Statement This policy should address who (usually expressed as a position, not the actual name of an individual) is responsible for ensuring that the policy is enforced. The *accountability statement* provides additional information to the reader about who to contact if a problem is discovered. It should also indicate the consequences of not complying with the policy.

The accountability statement should be written in such a way as to leave no room for misinterpretation on the part of users.

Exception Statement Sometimes, even the best policy doesn't foresee every eventuality. The *exception statement* provides specific guidance about the procedure or process that must be followed in order to deviate from the policy. This may include an escalation contact in the event that the person who is dealing with the situation needs to know whom to contact next.

The policy development process is often time-consuming. The advantage of this process, though, is that the decisions can be made in advance and can be sent to all involved parties so that the policy doesn't have to be restated over and over again. In fact, formally developing policies saves time and provides structure: Instead of using valuable time trying to figure out what to do, employees will know exactly what to do.

Incorporating Standards

A *standard* deals with specific issues or aspects of a business. Standards are derived from policies. A standard should provide enough detail that an audit can be performed to determine whether the standard is being met. Standards, like policies, have certain structural aspects in common.

The following five points are the key aspects of standards documents:

Scope and Purpose   The *standards document* should explain or describe the intention. If a standard is developed for a technical implementation, the scope might include software, updates, add-ins, and any other relevant information that helps the implementer carry out the task.

Roles and Responsibilities   This section of the standards document outlines who is responsible for implementing, monitoring, and maintaining the standard. In a system configuration, this section would outline what the customer is supposed to accomplish and what the installer is supposed to accomplish. This doesn't mean that one or the other can't exceed those roles; it means that, in the event of confusion, it's clear who is responsible for accomplishing which tasks.

Reference Documents   This section of the standards document explains how the standard relates to the organization's different policies, thereby connecting the standard to the underlying policies that have been put in place. In the event of confusion or uncertainty, it also allows people to go back to the source and figure out what the standard means. You'll encounter many situations throughout your career where you're given a standard that doesn't make sense. Frequently, by referring to the policies, you can figure out why the standard was written as it was. Doing so may help you carry out the standard or inform the people responsible for the standard of a change or problem.

Performance Criteria   This part of the standards document outlines how to accomplish the task. It should include relevant baseline and technology standards. Baselines provide a minimum or starting point for the standard. Technology standards provide information about the platforms and technologies. Baseline standards spell out high-level requirements for the standard or technology.

 An important aspect of performance criteria is benchmarking. You need to define what will be measured and the metrics that will be used to do so.

If you're responsible for installing a server in a remote location, for example, the standards spell out what type of computer will be used, what operating system will be installed, and any other relevant specifications.

Maintenance and Administrative Requirements   These standards outline what is required to manage and administer the systems or networks. For instance, in the case of a physical security requirement, the frequency with which locks or combinations are changed would be addressed.

As you can see, the standards documents provide a mechanism for both new and existing standards to be evaluated for compliance. The process of evaluation is called an *audit*. Increasingly, organizations are being required to conduct regular audits of their standards and policies.

Following Guidelines

Guidelines are slightly different from either policies or standards. *Guidelines* help an organization implement or maintain standards by providing information on how to accomplish the policies and maintain the standards.

Guidelines can be less formal than policies or standards because their nature is to help users comply with policies and standards. An example might be an explanation of how to install a service pack and what steps should be taken before doing so.

Guidelines aren't hard-and-fast rules. They may, however, provide a step-by-step process to accomplish a task. Guidelines, like standards and policies, should contain background information to help a user perform the task.

The following four items represent the minimum contents of a good guidelines document:

Scope and Purpose The *scope and purpose* section provides an overview and statement of the guideline's intent. It is not uncommon to see the heading "Purpose and Scope" or "Scope and Purpose" at the beginning of a document followed by verbiage to the effect: "This document contains the guidelines and procedures for the assignment and use of *xyz* and establishes the minimum requirements for governing the acceptable use of…"

Where scope and purpose are two separate headings, the information beneath the "Purpose" section states why it exists (for example, "This policy establishes guidelines and minimum requirements governing…"), and the "Scope" section tells to whom it applies (for instance, "This policy applies to any employee who…").

Roles and Responsibilities This section of the guidelines identifies which individuals or departments are responsible for accomplishing specific tasks. This may include implementation, support, and administration of a system or service. In a large organization, it's likely that the individuals involved in the process will have different levels of training and expertise. From a security perspective, it could be disastrous if an unqualified technician installed a system without guidelines.

Guideline Statements The *guideline statements* provide the step-by-step instructions or procedures on how to accomplish a task in a specific manner. Again, these are guidelines or recommendations—they may not be hard-and-fast rules and can even include shortcuts and suggestions.

Operational Considerations A procedure's *operational considerations* specify and identify what duties are required and at what intervals. This list might include daily, weekly, and monthly tasks. Guidelines for systems backup, for example, might provide specific guidance as to which files and directories must be backed up and how frequently.

Guidelines help an organization in three ways:

- If a process or set of steps isn't performed routinely, experienced support and security staff will forget how to do them; guidelines will help refresh their memory.

- When you're trying to train someone to do something new, written guidelines can reduce the new person's learning curve.

- When a crisis or high-stress situation occurs, guidelines can keep you from coming unglued.

Business Policies to Implement

Business policies also affect the security of an organization. They address organizational and departmental business issues as opposed to corporate-wide personnel issues. When developing your business policy, you must consider these primary areas of concern. Policies can be divided into two general categories: those for vendors and those for personnel.

Implementing Policies for Vendors

The overriding policy for operations is the *standard operating procedure (SOP)*. This serves as the baseline for business and, if properly written, covers what is expected on a regular basis. More importantly, from a crisis management standpoint, it outlines what to do when things aren't running as well as they should, such as which vendor to call when the communications server crashes, who to notify when their keypads won't allow access to the server room, and so on.

Service-level agreements (SLAs) were discussed previously, and equally important are *business partner agreements (BPAs)*. These outline responsibilities and obligations (as well as the sharing of profits and losses) between business partners. These documents can be important when you need authorization before or after a disaster to get the help and equipment needed to have everything functioning as it should be.

For the most part synonymous, *memorandum of understanding (MOU)* and *memorandum of agreement (MOA)* define the terms and conditions for securely sharing data and information resources. It is important that it identify the purpose for the interconnection's existence. It should also identify who the relevant authorities are within each organization and define their responsibilities. Since nothing lasts forever, conditions of terminating the agreement should be included in it as well as expected cost apportionment.

An *interconnection security agreement (ISA)* documents the technical and security requirements for establishing, operating, and maintaining the interconnection. It works in conjunction with the MOU/A between organizations by spelling out the requirements for connecting the IT systems and describing the security controls to be used to protect the systems and data, and it includes any necessary topological drawings of the interconnection.

Although the two can overlap, the general guideline is that the ISA specifies the technical and security requirements of the interconnection, whereas the MOU/A defines the responsibilities of each organization. As such, the MOU/A should not have technical details, such as how the interconnection is going to be established or maintained within it. Those details are contained within the ISA.

Given the sensitive nature of the information contained within the ISA and MOU/A, it is imperative that their physical copies be stored in a safe and secure location to keep them from prying eyes. It is also important that electronic copies be protected from those same prying eyes.

Implementing Policies for Personnel

For exam purposes, there are more policies related to personnel—employees and contractors—with which you should be familiar than for vendors. The following sections look at them and guidelines associated with them.

Mandatory Vacations   A *mandatory vacation policy* requires employees to take time away from work to refresh, and it is primarily used in jobs related to the financial sector. As contradictory as it may seem, an employee who doesn't take their vacation time can be detrimental to their own health as well as the organization's health. If the company becomes too dependent on one person, they can end up in a real bind if something should happen to that person. Not only does mandatory vacation give the employee a chance to refresh, but it also gives the company a chance to make sure that others can fill in any gaps in skills, and it satisfies the need to have replication or duplication at all levels. Mandatory vacations also provide an opportunity to discover fraud.

Job Rotation   A *job rotation policy* defines intervals at which employees must rotate through positions. Similar in purpose to mandatory vacations, it helps to ensure that the company does not become too dependent on one person (who then has the ability to do enormous harm). Rotate jobs on a frequent enough basis so that you are not putting yourself—and your data—at the mercy of any one administrator. Just as you want redundancy in hardware, you want redundancy in abilities.

When one person fills in for another, such as for mandatory vacations, it provides an opportunity to see what the person is doing and potentially uncover any fraud.

Separation of Duties Policies   *Separation of duties policies* are designed to reduce the risk of fraud and to prevent other losses in an organization. A good policy will require more than one person to accomplish key processes. This may mean that the person who processes an order from a customer isn't the same person who generates the invoice or deals with the billing.

Separation of duties helps prevent various problems, such as an individual embezzling money from a company. To embezzle funds successfully, an individual would need to recruit others to commit an act of *collusion*—that is, an agreement between two or more parties established for the purpose of committing deception or fraud. Collusion, when part of a crime, is also a criminal act in and of itself.

In addition, separation-of-duties policies can help prevent accidents from occurring in an organization. Let's say that you're managing a software development project. You want someone to perform a quality assurance test on a new piece of code before it's put into production. Establishing a clear separation of duties prevents development code from entering production status until quality testing is accomplished.

Many banks and financial institutions require multiple steps and approvals to transfer money. This helps reduce errors and minimizes the likelihood of fraud.

Very small assaults are often called "salami attacks." In banking, various forms of salami attacks can occur, such as shaving a few cents from many accounts, rounding to whole numbers and compiling the remainder into one account, and so on.

Clean Desk   As secure as data within a computer system may be, equally insecure are printed copies of the data resting in a pile on someone's desk. A clean desk policy increases the physical security of data by requiring employees to limit what is on their desk to what they are working on at the present time, safely securing (locking in a drawer, for example) anything not presently needed.

Background Checks   Given the need to protect data, one of the best ways to do so is to make sure those who are given access to it can be trusted. All potential employees should be thoroughly screened with an extensive background check before being hired and given access to the computer systems.

Nondisclosure Agreement   A nondisclosure agreement (NDA) is a legal contract intended to cover confidentiality. An NDA can be crafted and accepted to cover almost any scale. It can, for example, be limited to only what is discussed in a single meeting with a vendor or cover everything you learned during the course of your employment.

Onboarding   The process used to train a new employee and bring them up to speed with the organization, its clients, its products, and so forth is known as onboarding. From the organization's prospective, this process can represent a substantial investment in the new employee and thus the organization typically wants to make sure they made a smart hiring decision and are going to keep the employee for a while. From the new employee's stand-point, they are usually much more valuable after the onboarding has concluded.

Continuing Education   Lifelong learning is a necessity in the workplace of today. Not only does additional learning add to the skills an employee has and make them more valuable to the employer, but often it is required to maintain certifications. Most CompTIA certifications today (including Security+), for example, require a minimum number of continuing education units (CEUs) in order for the certified administrator to keep that certification over time.

Exit Interviews   One of the best ways to find problems is to listen—not talk—to those with whom you work. The last real opportunity for that communication occurs when an individual leaves the organization and they are given an exit interview. Never bypass this learning opportunity, and be sure to listen carefully to what is being said and ask questions that can help you determine if any changes should be made.

Role-Based Awareness Training   Not all employees are equal, and that is especially truly when it comes to data access. Depending on your organization, you may use groups with lots of different names and assign users to those groups. You should, however, at a minimum have the following: Data Owner, System Administrator, System Owner, User, Privileged User, and Executive User.

When deciding what group each user should be a member of, the *least privilege policy* should be used, particularly when assigning permissions. Give users only the permissions that they need to do their work and no more. For example, a temporary employee should never have the right to install software, a receptionist does not need the right to make backups, and so on. Every operating system includes the ability to limit users based on groups and individual permissions, and your company should adhere to the policy of always applying only those permissions users need and blocking those that they do not.

 Any time you see the phrase "least privilege," always equate it with giving only the minimum permissions needed to do the work that must be done.

Acceptable Use Policies *Acceptable use policies (AUPs)* describe how the employees in an organization can use company systems and resources, both software and hardware. This policy should also outline the consequences for misuse. In addition, the policy (also known as a *use policy*) should address the installation of personal software on company computers and the use of personal hardware such as USB devices. When portable devices are plugged directly into a machine, they bypass the network security measures (such as firewalls) and allow data to be copied in what is known as *pod slurping*. This can also be done if employees start using free cloud drives instead, and that scenario should be addressed in the AUP.

 Even secure workstations that do not contain traditional media devices (CD, DVD, and so forth) usually contain USB ports. Unless those ports are disabled, a user can easily connect a flash drive and copy files to and from it. Not only should you make every effort to limit USB ports, but you should also have the use of such devices spelled out in the acceptable use policy to circumvent the "I didn't know" defense.

 Real World Scenario

The Trouble with Not Having a Policy

A few years ago, an employee in a large company was using corporate computer systems to run a small accounting firm that he had started. He was using the computers on his own time. When this situation was discovered, he was immediately fired for the misuse of corporate resources. He sued the company for wrongful discharge and won the case. The company was forced to hire him back and pay his back wages, and he was even awarded damages. The primary reason the company lost the case was that its acceptable use policy didn't state that he couldn't use company computers for personal work—only that he couldn't use them for personal work during work hours. The company was unable to prove that he did the personal work during work hours.

Every acceptable use policy today should include a section on smartphone usage (and even presence) within the workplace. Although a smartphone is a convenience for employees (they can now more easily receive and make personal calls at work), it can be a headache for the security administrator. Most smartphones can store files in the same way as any USB device, and they can be used to copy files to and from a workstation. Additionally, the camera feature on most phones makes it possible for a user to take pictures of things such as company documents, servers, and physical security implementation, among many other things that the company may not want to share. For this reason, most secure facilities have stringent restrictions on the presence of smartphones within the facility.

Make sure your acceptable use policies provide your company with adequate coverage regarding all acceptable uses of corporate resources.

Adverse Actions   It is a sad but true condition in the workplace that administrative (usually adverse) actions must be taken against employees. This could be due to an employee being forced to take an administrative leave, being terminated, or any number of other situations. An adverse action policy should be in place detailing exactly what must be done—suspending the user's account, revoking privileges, and so forth.

The more detailed the policy, the less opportunity there is for something important to fall through the cracks and put all of your valuable data at risk. You may truly work with the best co-workers on the planet, but it is surprising how vindictive they can become if they feel they've been wronged. You will be much happier if you can stick to preventive measures and head off problems before they ever have the opportunity to manifest themselves.

General Security Policies   *Security policies* define what controls are required to implement and maintain the security of systems, users, and networks. This policy should be used as a guide in system implementations and evaluations, addressing what one might consider common sense.

Issues that should be defined in these policies include the difference between company and personal email and how to deal appropriately with social media—reminding users that they are seen as an extension of the company and that they must always put the interests of the company first. Both social media and personal use of email are items that can cause companies to lose big in the marketplace and the courtroom. Users need to understand that with a company email account and/or use of company resources, they are serving as representatives of the company and any offensive comments they make could reflect poorly on the company.

Network/Application Policies

As you just learned, anything owned by the company is thought to represent the company in both the marketplace and the courtroom. This is true of employees using company email accounts for personal email, the use of company computers for social media, and for all other applications and networks that the employees access while at work or in the line of work.

Understanding Control Types and False Positives/Negatives

Risk assessment and analysis involves calculating potential risks and making decisions based on the variables associated with those risks (likelihood, ALE, impact, and so forth). Once you've identified risks that you want to address with actions other than avoidance, you put controls in place to address those risks.

Control Types

The National Institute of Standards and Technology places controls into various types. The control types fall into three categories: Management, Operational, and Technical, as defined in Special Publication 800-12. Table 1.3 lists the control types and the controls with which they are associated.

TABLE 1.3 Control types and controls

Control type	Controls
Management	Risk Assessment
Management	Planning
Management	System and Services Acquisition
Management	Certification, Accreditation, and Security Assessment
Operational	Personnel Security
Operational	Physical and Environmental Protection
Operational	Contingency Planning
Operational	Configuration Management
Operational	Maintenance
Operational	System and Information Integrity
Operational	Media Protection
Operational	Incident Response
Operational	Awareness and Training
Technical	Identification and Authentication

Control type	Controls
Technical	Access Control
Technical	Audit and Accountability
Technical	System and Communication Protection

Another series of security controls worth examining is NIST 800-53, used by government and industry and viewed as more of a global standard. As of this writing, the current publication is revision 4.

 Although we discussed risk assessment in this chapter, we address most of the other controls in subsequent chapters.

After you have implemented security controls based on risk, you must perform routine audits. These audits should include reviews of user rights and permissions as well as specific events. Pay particular attention to false positives and negatives.

False positives are events that aren't really incidents. Event flagging is often based on established rules of acceptance (deviations from which are known as *anomalies*) and things such as attack signatures. If the rules aren't set up properly, normal traffic may set off an analyzer and generate an event. You don't want to declare an emergency unless you're sure that you have one. The opposite of a false positive is a *false negative*. With a false negative, you are not alerted to a situation when you should be alerted. In this case, you miss something crucial and it slips right by.

Error Types

A number of error types exist beyond what you need to know for the exam. Type I errors are those with false positives—that is, you think that evil is present when it is not. You have to be careful with them because if you erroneously raise a red flag and it turns out nothing is wrong, it becomes more difficult to get anyone to listen to you the next time you think you've uncovered something wrong because you've lost credibility.

Type II errors are those with false negatives, where you fail to notice a problem even though it is there—that is, you were looking directly at the evil and didn't recognize it. These errors are generally considered less harmful than Type I errors, though they allow the wrongdoer to get away with the act and maybe even keep doing it.

Type III errors are those in which you come to the right conclusion for all of the wrong reasons. You may conclude that someone broke into your systems because users are having trouble logging in. Someone did indeed break into the system, but you should have noticed it because all of the valuable data is gone.

Risk Management Best Practices

One of the leading ways to address *business continuity* is to do a BIA and implement *best practices*. Best practices are based on what is known in the industry and those methods that have consistently shown superior results over those achieved by other means.

> You need only a passing knowledge of business continuity issues for the Security+ exam. If you plan on taking the Project+ exam, also from CompTIA, you will need a more thorough knowledge of these topics.

Undertaking Business Impact Analysis

Business impact analysis (BIA) is the process of evaluating all of the critical systems (important to core business functions) in an organization to define impact and recovery plans. BIA isn't concerned with external threats or vulnerabilities; the analysis focuses on the impact a loss would have on the organization.

Here are the key components of a BIA:

Identifying Critical Functions   To identify critical functions, a company must ask itself, "What functions are necessary to continue operations until full service can be restored?" This identification process will help you establish which systems must be returned to operation in order for the business to continue. In performing this identification, you may find that a small or overlooked application in a department may be critical for operations. Many organizations have overlooked seemingly insignificant process steps or systems that have prevented business continuity planning (BCP) from being effective. Every department should be evaluated to ensure that no critical processes are overlooked.

Prioritizing Critical Business Functions   When business is continued after an event, operations must be prioritized as *mission-essential* or nonessential functions. If the organization makes resources available to the recovery process, these resources may be limited. Furthermore, in a widespread outage, full operation may not be possible for some time. What would happen, for example, if your data communications services went down? You can usually establish temporary services, but you probably won't be able to restore full network capability. There should be no internal disagreement about the *identification of critical systems*, and you should be clear about which applications or systems have priority based on the resources available. For example, your company may find itself choosing to restore email before it restores its website.

Calculating a Timeframe for Critical Systems Loss   How long can the organization survive without a critical function? Some functions in an organization don't require immediate action whereas others do. Which functions must be reestablished and in what timeframe? If your business is entirely dependent on its web presence and is e-commerce oriented, how long can the website stay inoperable? Your organization may need to evaluate and attempt to identify the maximum time that a particular function can be unavailable. When you look at the *impact*, be sure to factor in the following variables:

Life   Is anyone in immediate jeopardy because of the failure?

Property   Will anything be lost as a result of the malfunction?

Safety   Is anyone in harm's way due to the crash?

Finance   How much will be lost due to the stoppage?

Reputation   How harmful is the breakdown to the trust of the organization?

This component dictates the contingencies that must be established to minimize losses due to exceeding the allowable period.

Estimating the Tangible and Intangible Impact on the Organization   Your organization will suffer losses in an outage. These losses will be tangible in nature, such as lost production and lost sales. Intangible losses will also be a factor. For example, will customers lose faith in your service? Knowing the true cost of these impacts in advance will greatly increase the organization's effectiveness in responding to such outages.

A thorough BIA will accomplish several organizational goals:

- The true impact and damage that an outage can cause will be visible.

- Understanding the true loss potential may help you in your fight for a budget.

- Most important, perhaps, the process will document which business processes are being used, the impact they have on the organization, and how to restore them quickly.

The BIA will gain power in the organization as the true costs of an outage become known. People buy insurance not because they intend to have an accident but just in case they have one. A BIA can help identify what insurance is needed for the organization to feel safe.

Identifying Critical Systems and Components

Sometimes your systems are dependent on things that you would not normally consider. Basic utilities such as electricity, water, and natural gas are key aspects of business continuity. In the vast majority of cases, electricity and water are restored—at least on an emergency basis—fairly rapidly. The damage created by blizzards, tornadoes, and other natural disasters is managed and repaired by utility companies and government agencies. Other disasters, such as a major earthquake or hurricane, can overwhelm these agencies, and services may be interrupted for quite a while. When these types of events occur, critical infrastructure may be unavailable for days, weeks, or even months.

Real World Scenario

The Importance of Utilities

When the earthquake of 1989 occurred in San Francisco, California, portions of the city were without electricity, natural gas, and water for several months. Entire buildings were left unoccupied because the infrastructure was badly damaged. This damage prevented many businesses whose information systems departments were located in those buildings from returning to operation for several weeks. Most of the larger organizations were able to shift the processing loads to other companies or divisions.

When you evaluate your business's sustainability, realize that disasters do indeed happen. If possible, build infrastructure that doesn't have a *single point of failure (SPOF)* or connection. After the September 11, 2001, terrorist attack on the World Trade Center (WTC), several ISPs and other companies became nonfunctional because the WTC housed centralized communications systems and computer departments. If you're the administrator for a small company, it is not uncommon for the SPOF to be a router/gateway. The best way to remove an SPOF from your environment is to add redundancy.

Consider the impact of weather on your *contingency plans*. What if you needed to relocate your facility to another region of the country due to a tornado hitting your server room? How would you get personnel there? What personnel would be relocated? How would they be housed and fed during the time of the crisis? You should consider these possibilities in advance. Although the possibility of a crippling disaster is relatively small, you still need to evaluate the risk.

 Real World Scenario

Formulating Business Continuity Plans

As a security administrator, you need to think through a way to maintain business continuity should a crisis occur. Imagine that your company is involved in each of the following three scenarios:

Scenario 1

Your company is in the business of monitoring criminal offenders who are under electronic house arrest nationwide. Every offender wears an ankle bracelet that wirelessly communicates with a device in his or her home. The home device communicates to your site in real time over phone lines by calling a toll-free number to report if the offender is in or out of the home, and you alert local authorities immediately if someone isn't in compliance. The number of offenders, and the number of home devices that call your center, is in the tens of thousands. How could business be maintained if the trunk line for the toll-free phone carrier were disrupted in the middle of the night? How could you verify offender compliance if the problem took hours to correct?

Scenario 2

You're the administrator for a small educational company that delivers certification exams locally. The exams are downloaded the night before and delivered throughout the day as students—who have registered over the Internet—arrive. You show up at 8 a.m. on Friday, knowing that there are more than 20 exams to be administered that were downloaded Thursday night. What you find, however, is that someone has broken into the testing room and trashed all of the workstations and monitors. Some of those coming to take the exams are driving from far away. How will you approach the situation?

Scenario 3

You're the database administrator for a large grocery chain. When you leave on Wednesday, there are no problems. When you arrive on Thursday—the day a new sale starts—you learn that the DSL lines are down. They went down before the local stores could download the new sale prices. All scanned goods will ring up at the price they were last week (either sale or regular) and not at current prices. The provider says it's working on the DSL problem but can't estimate how long the repairs will take. How do you approach the problem?

Just like in the real world, there are no right or wrong answers for these scenarios. However, they all represent situations that have happened and for which administrators planned ahead of time.

There are several ways to plan for such scenarios, including implementing redundant technology, fault-tolerant systems, and RAID. A truly redundant system won't use just one of these methods, but rather it will support some aspect of all of them. The following sections address these topics in more detail.

As an administrator, you should always be aware of problems that can occur and have an idea of how you'll approach them. It's impossible to prepare for every emergency, but you can plan for those that could conceivably happen.

Automation/Scripting

The days of relying on someone in the server room to see a problem and push a button to head it off are coming to a close. Thanks to sophisticated monitors and sensors, it is possible to use *automation/scripting* in a wide variety of scenarios to preplan *automated courses of action*. Scenarios in which the automated courses of action can be taken range from *configuration validation* of new equipment added on the network to *continuous monitoring* of server operations.

Frameworks and Templates

Templates can be helpful in the risk assessment process by providing a means to summarize and document results of threat source identification, characterization, vulnerabilities, and impacts. Typical templates include scales for evaluating the threats and deciding the best responses to them.

Master Image

Most newer operating systems allow you to create a model user system as a disk image on a server; the disk image is downloaded and installed when a failure occurs. This method makes it easier for administrators to restore a system than it would be to do it manually.

Nonpersistence

Persistent images are those that stay the same, while nonpersistent are those that are temporary. They can exist only in RAM or be changes that are overwritten on a reboot by a persistent/frozen image.

In a nutshell, a system image (referenced earlier) is a *snapshot* of what exists. Capturing an image of the operating system in its exploited state can be helpful in revisiting the issue after the fact to learn more about it. As an analogy, think of germ samples that are stored in labs after major outbreaks so that scientists can revisit them later and study them further.

Most newer operating systems take snapshots of the configuration at various times and these can be manually created as well (which is highly recommended before updates or major system changes). When something goes awry, you can *revert to known state*—that is, go back to the configuration as it was before the last major change. This ability to *roll back to a known configuration* is helpful on workstations as well as servers.

When all else fails, you can often use *live boot media* to boot a system and begin troubleshooting it. You can usually create bootable flash drives and/or DVDs based on the operating system you are using and the abilities it offers. Bear in mind that for the live boot media to work, the system on which you are working must be configured to boot from that media.

Elasticity

Elasticity is a major feature of cloud computing, meaning the ability to scale up resources as needed. A number of other benefits go along with it: the time to service is a possibility, as is the mean time to implement being quicker inside rather than outside the virtual model, or resource pooling. Other features that make elasticity so valuable include using multitenant models, and the fact that it is scalable not only up but also down, and applications are both available and portable.

Scalability

Speaking of scaling both up and down, *scalability* is always a desired attribute of any system. A virtual datacenter, for example, appears the same as a physical datacenter from an administration standpoint, and it features elasticity, scalability, and so forth. A big benefit of the virtual center is that it can employ a pay-as-you-go model.

Distributive Allocation

Commonly known as load balancing, *distributive allocation* allows for distributing the load (file requests, data routing, and so on) so that no device is overly burdened. This can help with redundancy, availability, and fault tolerance.

High Availability

High availability (HA) refers to the measures, such as redundancy, failover, and mirroring, used to keep services and systems operational during an outage. In short, the goal is to provide all services to all users, where they need them and when they need them. With high availability, the goal is to have key services available 99.999 percent of the time (also known as *five nines availability*).

Planning for Resiliency

Resiliency is the capacity to recover quickly from difficulties. Few things are as difficult in the world of IT as a crash or failure—be it at the server level or the server room level. This chapter is focused on how to compute and manage risk and increase your resiliency when it is economically feasible to do so. For the most part, risk resilience is a buzzword that can be equated with risk management.

Redundancy

Redundancy refers to systems that either are duplicated or *fail over* to other systems in the event of a malfunction. *Failover* refers to the process of reconstructing a system or switching over to other systems when a failure is detected. In the case of a server, the server switches to a redundant server when a fault is detected. This strategy allows service to continue uninterrupted until the primary server can be restored. In the case of a network, this means processing switches to another network path in the event of a network failure in the primary path.

Failover systems can be expensive to implement. In a large corporate network or e-commerce environment, a failover might entail switching all processing to a remote location until your primary facility is operational. The primary site and the remote site would synchronize data to ensure that information is as up to date as possible.

Many operating systems, such as Linux, Windows Server 2012, and Novell Open Enterprise Server, are capable of *clustering* to provide failover capabilities. *Clustering* involves multiple systems connected together cooperatively (which provides *load balancing*) and networked in such a way that if any of the systems fail, the other systems take up the slack and continue to operate. The overall capability of the server cluster may decrease, but the network or service will remain operational.

To appreciate the beauty of clustering, contemplate the fact that this is the technology on which Google is built. Not only does clustering allow you to have redundancy, but it also offers you the ability to scale as demand increases.

Most ISPs and network providers have extensive internal failover capability to provide high availability to clients. Business clients and employees who are unable to access information or services tend to lose confidence. The trade-off for reliability and trustworthiness, of course, is cost: failover systems can become prohibitively expensive. You'll need to study your needs carefully to determine whether your system requires this capability. For example, if your environment requires a high level of availability, your servers should be clustered. This will allow the other servers in the network to take up the load if one of the servers in the cluster fails.

Fault Tolerance

Fault tolerance is the ability of a system to sustain operations in the event of a component failure. Fault-tolerant systems can continue operation even though a critical component, such as a disk drive, has failed. This capability involves over-engineering systems by adding redundant components and subsystems.

Fault tolerance is discussed in more detail in Chapter 7, "Data and Privacy Security Practices," but it appears here as it relates to risk.

Fault tolerance can be built into a server by adding a second power supply, a second CPU, and other key components. Several manufacturers (such as HP, Unisys, and IBM) offer fault-tolerant servers. These servers typically have multiple processors that automatically fail over if a malfunction occurs.

In addition to fault-tolerant servers, you can have fault-tolerant implementations such as Tandem, Stratus, and HP. In these settings, multiple computers are used to provide 100 percent availability of a single server.

There are two key components of fault tolerance that you should never overlook: spare parts and electrical power. Spare parts should always be readily available to repair any system-critical component if it should fail. The redundancy strategy "N+1" means that you have the number of components you need, plus one to plug into any system should it be needed. For example, a small company with five stand-alone servers that are all the same model should have a power supply in a box nearby to install in any one of the servers should there be a failure. (The redundancy strategy 1+1 [or 2N] has one spare part for every component in use.)

Since computer systems cannot operate in the absence of electrical power, it is imperative that fault tolerance be built into your electrical infrastructure as well. At a bare minimum, an *uninterruptible power supply (UPS)*—with surge protection—should accompany every server and workstation. That UPS should be rated for the load it is expected to carry in the event of a power failure (factoring in the computer, monitor, and any other device connected to it) and be checked periodically as part of your preventive maintenance routine to make sure that the battery is operational. You will need to replace the battery every few years to keep the UPS operational.

A UPS will allow you to continue to function in the absence of power for only a short duration. For fault tolerance in situations of longer duration, you will need a *backup generator.* Backup generators run off of gasoline, propane, natural gas, or diesel and generate the electricity needed to provide steady power. Although some backup generators can come on instantly in the event of a power outage, most take a short time to warm up before they can provide consistent power. Therefore, you will find that you still need to implement UPSs within your organization.

Redundant Array of Independent Disks

Redundant Array of Independent Disks (RAID) is a technology that uses multiple disks to provide fault tolerance. There are several designations for RAID levels.

RAID stands for not only *Redundant Array of Independent Disks* but also *Redundant Array of Inexpensive Disks*. Although the latter term has lost its popularity, you might still encounter it in some books.

The most commonly implemented RAID levels are as follows:

RAID Level 0   RAID 0 is *disk striping*. It uses multiple drives and maps them together as a single physical drive. This is done primarily for performance, not for fault tolerance. If any drive in a RAID 0 array fails, the entire logical drive becomes unusable.

RAID Level 1   RAID 1 is *disk mirroring*. Disk mirroring provides 100 percent redundancy because everything is stored on two disks. If one disk fails, another disk continues to operate. The failed disk can be replaced, and the RAID 1 array can be regenerated. This system offers the advantage of 100 percent data redundancy at the expense of doubling the storage requirements. Each drive keeps an exact copy of all information, which reduces the effective storage capability to 50 percent of the overall rated storage. Some implementations of disk mirroring are called *disk duplexing* (*duplexing* is a less commonly used term). The difference between mirroring and duplexing is one more controller card. With mirroring, one controller card writes sequentially to each disk. With duplexing, the same data is written to both disks simultaneously. Disk duplexing has much faster write performance than disk mirroring. Many hardware implementations of RAID 1 are actually duplexing, but they are still generally referred to as mirrors.

The data is intact in a RAID 1 array if either one of the two drives fails. After the failed drive is replaced with a new drive, you remirror the data from the good drive to the new drive to re-create the array.

RAID Level 3   RAID 3 is *disk striping with a parity disk*. RAID 3 arrays implement fault tolerance by using striping (RAID 0) in conjunction with a separate disk that stores parity information. *Parity information* is a value based on the value of the data stored in each disk location. This system ensures that the data can be recovered in the event of a failure. The process of generating parity information uses the arithmetic value of the data binary. This process allows any single disk in the array to fail while the system continues to operate. The failed disk is removed, a new disk is installed, and the new drive is then regenerated using the parity information. RAID 3 is common in older systems, and it's supported by most Unix systems.

RAID Level 5   RAID 5 is *disk striping with parity*, and it is one of the most common forms of RAID in use today. It operates similarly to disk striping, as in RAID 0. The parity information is spread across all of the disks in the array instead of being limited to a single disk, as in RAID 3. Most implementations require a minimum of three disks and support a maximum of 32.

These four types of RAID drives, or arrays, are illustrated in Figure 1.1.

FIGURE 1.1 The four primary RAID technologies used in systems

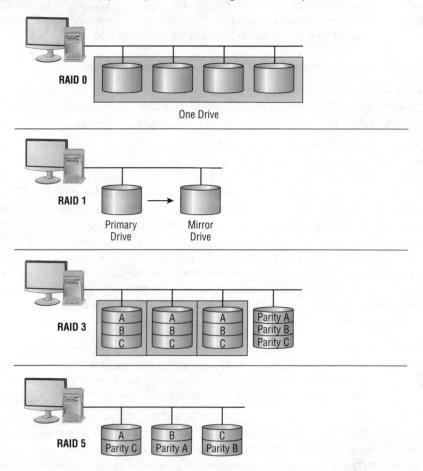

A RAID 5 array can survive the failure of any one drive and still be able to function. It can't, however, survive the failure of multiple drives.

You aren't required to know the current RAID capabilities for the Security+ exam. They are presented here primarily for your edification. They are commonly used in highly reliable systems.

RAID levels 0, 1, 3, and 5 are the ones most commonly implemented in servers today. RAID 5 has largely replaced RAID 3 in newer systems. When two levels are combined for a more potent solution, the numbers simply move into double digits representing the two RAID levels combined. For example, combining RAID 1 with RAID 0 is now called RAID 10 (or RAID 0+1 in older documentation). Combining RAID 1 with RAID 5 is now known as RAID 15, and so on.

RAID levels are implemented either in software on the host computer or in the disk controller hardware. A RAID hardware-device implementation will generally run faster than a software-oriented RAID implementation because the software implementation uses the system CPU and system resources. Hardware RAID devices generally have their own processors, and they appear to the operating system as a single device.

You must do a fair amount of planning before you implement RAID. Within the realm of planning, you must be able to compute the number of disks needed for the desired implementation.

 Real World Scenario

How Many Disks Does RAID Need?

As a security administrator, you must determine how many RAID disks you'll need. Compute how many disks will be needed for each of the following scenarios or the amount of storage capacity that results. *(Answers appear after each scenario.)*

Scenario 1

Your company has standardized on 5 TB disks. A new server will go online next month to hold the data files for a new division. The server will be disk-duplexed and needs to be able to store 8 TB of data. How many drives should you order?

Disk duplexing is the same as disk mirroring except that there is also a second controller. Fifty percent of the overall storage capacity must be used for RAID, so you must purchase four 5 TB drives. This will give you excess data capacity of 2 TB.

Scenario 2

Your primary server is currently running four 3 GB disks in a RAID 5 array. Storage space is at a premium, and a purchase order has just been approved for four 5 TB disks. If you still use a RAID 5 array, what is the maximum data storage space this server will be able to host?

The solution that will generate the most data storage capacity is to install all eight drives (the four current ones and the four new ones) into the server. The array must use the same size storage on each drive; thus, all eight drives will appear as if they are 3 TB drives. Under this scenario, 21 TB can be used for data storage, and 3 TB will be used for parity.

Scenario 3

Access speed is of the utmost importance on a web server. You want to purchase some fast 3 TB hard drives and install them in a RAID 0 array. How many drives will you need to purchase to host 900 GB of data?

RAID 0 doesn't perform any fault tolerance and doesn't require any extra disk space. You can obtain 9 TB of data by using three disks.

Change Management

One of the biggest risks an organization faces involves change: either implementing or failing to implement. The discipline of *change management* is focused on how to document and control for change. A subset of project management, change management is focused on controlled implementation and identification of changes. Those changes can be to the actual physical resources themselves (new servers, moving to the cloud, etc.), to individuals (new teams, reorganization, etc.), or even to the organization (merger, acquisition, and so on). The key in every instance is to document everything and focus on the extent and scope of what is affected by every change.

Summary

Risk assessment is the process of evaluating and cataloging the threats, vulnerabilities, and weaknesses that exist in the systems being used. Risk assessment should ensure that all bases are covered.

Security models begin with an understanding of the business issues that an organization is facing. The following business matters must be evaluated:

- Policies
- Standards
- Guidelines

A good policy design includes scope statements, overview statements, accountability expectations, and exceptions. Each of these aspects of a well-crafted policy helps in setting expectations for everyone in a company. For a policy to be effective, it needs the unequivocal support of senior management and decision makers in an organization.

Exam Essentials

Name the three categories of control types.   The three types of controls that can be administered are technical, management, and operational.

Know how to calculate risk.   Risk can be calculated either qualitatively (subjective) or quantitatively (objective). Quantitative calculations assign dollar amounts, and the basic formula is SLE × ARO = ALE, where SLE is the single loss expectancy, ARO is the annualized rate of occurrence, and ALE is the annual loss expectancy.

Be familiar with the four different approaches to risk.   The four risk response strategies are avoidance (don't engage in that activity), transference (think insurance), mitigation (take steps to reduce the risk), and acceptance (be willing to live with the risk).

Know the importance of policies, standards, and guidelines.   The process of implementing and maintaining a secure network must first be addressed from a policies, standards, and guidelines perspective. Policies and guidelines set a standard of expectation in an organization. Standards tell people what is expected, and guidelines provide specific advice on how to accomplish a given task or activity.

Understand important elements of key levels of RAID.   RAID level 0 does not include any fault tolerance. RAID level 1 can be implemented as mirroring or duplexing; the difference is that the latter includes multiple controllers. RAID level 5 is known as disk striping with parity.

Review Questions

You can find the answers in the Appendix.

1. You're the chief security contact for MTS. One of your primary tasks is to document everything related to security and to create a manual that can be used to manage the company in your absence. Which documents should be referenced in your manual as the ones that identify the methods used to accomplish a given task?

   A. Policies

   B. Standards

   C. Guidelines

   D. BIA

2. Consider the following scenario. The asset value of your company's primary servers is $2 million, and they are housed in a single office building in Anderson, Indiana. Field offices are scattered throughout the United States, but the workstations located at the field offices serve as thin clients and access data from the Anderson servers. Tornados in this part of the country are not uncommon, and it is estimated that one will level the building every 60 years. Which of the following is the SLE for this scenario?

   A. $2 million

   B. $1 million

   C. $500,000

   D. $33,333.33

   E. $16,666.67

3. Refer to the scenario in question 2. Which of the following amounts is the ALE for this scenario?

   A. $2 million

   B. $1 million

   C. $500,000

   D. $33,333.33

   E. $16,666.67

4. Refer to the scenario in question 2. Which of the following is the ARO for this scenario?

   A. 0.0167

   B. 1

   C. 5

   D. 16.7

   E. 60

5. Which of the following strategies involves identifying a risk and making the decision to discontinue engaging in the action?

   A. Risk acceptance

   B. Risk avoidance

   C. Risk mitigation

   D. Risk transference

6. Which of the following policy statements may include an escalation contact in the event that the person dealing with a situation needs to know who to contact?

   A. Scope

   B. Exception

   C. Overview

   D. Accountability

7. Which of the following policies are designed to reduce the risk of fraud and prevent other losses in an organization?

   A. Separation of duties

   B. Acceptable use

   C. Least privilege

   D. Physical access control

8. What is the term used for events that were mistakenly flagged although they weren't truly events about which to be concerned?

   A. Fool's gold

   B. Non-incidents

   C. Error flags

   D. False positives

9. Which of the following is the structured approach that is followed to secure a company's assets?

   A. Audit management

   B. Incident management

   C. Change management

   D. Skill management

10. Which of the following strategies involves sharing some of the risk burden with someone else, such as an insurance company?

   A. Risk acceptance

   B. Risk avoidance

   C. Risk deterrence

   D. Risk mitigation

   E. Risk transference

11. The risk assessment component, in conjunction with the _____, provides the organization with an accurate picture of the situation facing it.

    A. RAC

    B. ALE

    C. BIA

    D. RMG

12. Which of the following policy statements should address who is responsible for ensuring that the policy is enforced?

    A. Scope

    B. Exception

    C. Overview

    D. Accountability

13. Which of the following strategies is accomplished any time you take steps to reduce risk?

    A. Risk acceptance

    B. Risk avoidance

    C. Risk transference

    D. Risk mitigation

14. If you calculate the SLE to be $4,000 and that there will be 10 occurrences a year (ARO), then the ALE is:

    A. $400

    B. $4,000

    C. $40,000

    D. $400,000

15. Which of the following policies describes how the employees in an organization can use company systems and resources, both software and hardware?

    A. Separation of duties

    B. Acceptable use

    C. Least privilege

    D. Physical access control

16. Separation of duties helps to prevent an individual from embezzling money from a company. To embezzle funds successfully, an individual would need to recruit others to commit an act of _____ (an agreement between two or more parties established for the purpose of committing deception or fraud).

    A. Misappropriation

    B. Misuse

    C. Collusion

    D. Fraud

17. Which of the following agreements contains the technical information regarding the technical and security requirements of the interconnection between two or more organizations?

A. BPA

B. MOA

C. ISA

D. MOU

18. If you calculate SLE to be $25,000 and that there will be one occurrence every four years (ARO), then what is the ALE?

A. $6,250

B. $12,500

C. $25,000

D. $100,000

19. Which of the following policies should be used when assigning permissions, giving users only the permissions they need to do their work and no more?

A. Separation of duties

B. Acceptable use

C. Least privilege

D. Physical access control

20. Which of the following strategies necessitates an identified risk that those involved understand the potential cost/damage and agree to live with it?

A. Risk acceptance

B. Risk avoidance

C. Risk transference

D. Risk mitigation

Chapter

2

Monitoring and Diagnosing Networks

THE FOLLOWING COMPTIA SECURITY+ EXAM OBJECTIVES ARE COVERED IN THIS CHAPTER:

✓ **3.1 Explain use cases and purpose for frameworks, best practices and secure configuration guides.**

- Industry-standard frameworks and reference architectures: Regulatory; Non-regulatory; National vs. international; Industry-specific frameworks

- Benchmarks/secure configuration guides: Platform/vendor-specific guides—Web server; Operating system; Application server; Network infrastructure devices

- General purpose guides

- Defense-in-depth/layered security: Vendor diversity; Control diversity; User training

✓ **3.2 Given a scenario, implement secure network architecture concepts.**

- Zones/topologies: DMZ; Extranet; Intranet; Wireless; Guest; Honeynets; NAT; Ad hoc

- Segregation/segmentation/isolation: Physical; Logical (VLAN); Virtualization; Air gaps

- Tunneling/VPN: Site-to-site; Remote access

- Security device/technology placement: Sensors; Collectors; Correlation engines; Filters; Proxies; Firewalls; VPN concentrators; SSL accelerators; Load balancers; DDoS mitigator; Aggregation switches; Taps and port mirror

- SDN

✓ **3.3 Given a scenario, implement secure systems design.**

■ Hardware/firmware security: FDE/SED; TPM; HSM; UEFI/
BIOS; Secure boot and attestation; Supply chain; Hardware
root of trust; EMI/EMP

■ Operating systems: Types—Network; Server; Workstation;
Appliance; Kiosk; Mobile OS—Patch management; Disabling
unnecessary ports and services; Least functionality; Secure
configurations; Trusted operating system; Application
whitelisting/blacklisting; Disable default accounts/passwords

■ Peripherals: Wireless keyboards; Wireless mice; Displays;
Wi-Fi-enabled MicroSD cards; Printers/MFDs; External
storage devices; Digital Cameras

✓ **3.4 Explain the importance of secure staging
deployment concepts.**

■ Sandboxing

■ Environment: Development; Test; Staging; Production

■ Secure baseline

■ Integrity measurement

The ability to monitor systems and networks is vital to security. If you cannot effectively monitor systems and networks, you'll find it impossible to detect security breaches and therefore address them.

Monitoring and Diagnosing Networks Terminology

The Security+ exam depends heavily on your knowledge of both terms and acronyms. The following terms (also found in the online glossary) are those CompTIA is fond of using and testing on in this category. They are provided in order to make it easier for you to know what each is intended to convey.

Security+ Terminology

demilitarized zone (DMZ)   A network segment between two firewalls. One is outward facing, connected to the outside world, the other inward facing, connected to the internal network. Public-facing servers, such as web servers, are often placed in a DMZ.

honeynet   A network that functions in the same manner as a honeypot.

honeypot   A fake system designed to divert attackers from your real systems. It is often replete with logging and tracking to gather evidence.

information security management system (ISMS)   A broad term that applies to a wide range of systems used to manage information security.

intrusion detection system (IDS)   A system that monitors the network for possible intrusions and logs that activity.

intrusion prevention system (IPS)   A system that monitors the network for possible intrusions and logs that activity and then blocks the traffic that is suspected of being an attack.

personally identifiable information (PII)   Any information that could identify a particular individual.

software-defined network (SDN)   The entire network, including all security devices, is virtualized.

stateful packet inspection (SPI)   A firewall that not only examines each packet but also remembers the recent previous packets.

Frameworks, Best Practices, and Configuration Guides

There are many standards and best practices that you can reference for guidance in securing and monitoring your network. The Security+ exam will ask you questions about widely used standards. Unfortunately, CompTIA does not publish exactly which standards it will query you about. For that reason, in this chapter, we review some of the most widely used standards and frameworks. The more common the standard, the more likely it is to appear on the exam.

Industry-Standard Frameworks and Reference Architectures

Although cybersecurity can be a complicated topic, there is excellent news: plenty of standards, frameworks, and guidelines are available to assist you in planning and implementing your organization's cybersecurity. These include national and international standards, industry-specific standards, product-specific guidelines, and vendor-specific guidelines. All of these will be useful in helping you determine the best practices for your network's security.

It must be noted, however, that it is beyond the scope of a single chapter, or even an entire book, to cover every regulation or standard. In this chapter, we will explore some of the most widely known standards, frameworks, and regulations. You should also consult the regulations relevant to your locality and industry.

ISO Standards

The International Organization for Standardization (ISO), as the name suggests, is the de facto source for international standards. They have published a wide range of standards, many related to cybersecurity. One in particular stands out as being worthy of closer examination: ISO/IEC 27001:2013. This standard was published in October 2014, and its full title is "ISO/IEC 27001:2013 – Information technology – Security techniques – Information security management systems – Requirements."

This standard is divided into several parts. There is an outline for good practices for managing cybersecurity. The goal is to provide guidelines for those organizations that wish to obtain ISO certification.

According to the ISO (https://www.iso.org/standard/54534.html):

> ISO/IEC 27001:2013 specifies the requirements for establishing, implementing, maintaining and continually improving an information security management system within the context of the organization. It also includes requirements for the assessment and treatment of information security risks tailored to the needs of the organization. The requirements set out in ISO/IEC 27001:2013 are generic and are intended to be applicable to all organizations, regardless of type, size or nature.

One interesting aspect of this framework is that it encourages you to look at those issues specific to your organization. This includes your organization's capabilities as well as its corporate culture. These factors can significantly influence what security measures are even feasible for your organization.

This framework also asks that you identify all the relevant parties that have an interest in your organization's security management. This includes executives and department heads, but it could also include vendors, partners, and, in some cases, customers. After identifying the relevant parties, next identify their requirements as well as their expectations.

As you can see from this brief description, this framework is more of a generalized approach to security management. This framework will not provide you with specific to-do lists. However, a generalized approach of how you manage security is the correct place to begin.

ISO 27002 is another ISO standard widely used in cybersecurity. This standard recommends best practices for initiating, implementing, and maintaining *information security management systems (ISMSs)*. The standard itself starts with five introductory chapters that provide guidance such as terminology and scope of the standard. It is the main chapters that are an issue, starting with Chapter 5. They provide recommended best practices on many areas of ISMSs. A list of the chapters is given here:

5. Information Security Policies
6. Organization of Information Security
7. Human Resource Security
8. Asset Management
9. Access Control
10. Cryptography
11. Physical and Environmental Security
12. Operation Security: Procedures and Responsibilities
13. Communication Security
14. System Acquisition, Development and Maintenance
15. Supplier Relationships
16. Information Security Incident Management
17. Information Security Aspects of Business Continuity Management

Each of these topics is addressed in chapters in this book. For example, Chapter 4 of this book will address identity and access management; Chapter 8, cryptography; and Chapter 12, disaster recovery and incident response. Each of the 13 main chapters of ISO 27002 are important topics that any security professional should be familiar with.

ISO 27017 is guidance for cloud security. It does apply the guidance of ISO 27002 to the cloud but then adds seven new controls.

CLD.6.3.1   This is an agreement on shared or divided security responsibilities between the customer and cloud provider.

CLD.8.1.5   This control addresses how assets are returned or removed from the cloud when the contract is terminated.

CLD.9.5.1   This control states that the cloud provider must separate the customers' virtual environment from other customers or outside parties.

CLD.9.5.2   This control states that the customer and the cloud provider both must ensure the virtual machines are hardened.

CLD.12.1.5   It is solely the customer's responsibility to define and manage administrative operations.

CLD.12.4.5   The cloud provider's capabilities must enable the customer to monitor their own cloud environment.

CLD.13.1.4   The virtual network environment must be configured so that it least meets the security policies of the physical environment.

As cloud computing continues to grow, cloud security is increasingly important. It is also likely that the Security+ exam will put some emphasis on cloud security. With that in mind, ISO 27018 is closely related to ISO 27017. ISO 27018 defines privacy requirements in a cloud environment—particularly how the customer and cloud provider must protect *personally identifiable information (PII)*.

North American Electric Reliability Corporation (NERC)

A variety of standards exist that are specific to particular industries. In recent years, the security of infrastructure, such as electrical power grids, has been a focal point for security. The *North American Electric Reliability Corporation (NERC)* publishes standards for electrical power companies. NERC CIP (Critical Infrastructure Protection) 007-6 in particular addresses patching of all systems. This standard requires that all registered entities check for new patches at least once every 35 days. This may seem like too long an interval to some readers, but power systems are not like desktop computers. Patches are not usually issued every day, or even every few days.

The fact that patches are less common in power systems also explains another feature of NERC CIP 007-6. This standard provides registered entities 35 days after identifying that a patch is available to evaluate the patch and then complete mitigation steps. In this particular industry, this process is necessary. As most readers are probably aware, sometimes a patch can actually cause a problem. So, implementing a patch on a power system is a delicate process. It must be confirmed that the patch will not cause any disruption to power.

Although you may not be involved in the electrical industry, this standard is an excellent example of how different industries have different security requirements. You cannot simply take generic security procedures and apply them to all organizations, all industries, or all situations.

It should be noted that NERC also created the NERC Cybersecurity Standards (CSS) in 2003. These have been updated and modernized into NERC 1300. The newest version of NERC 1300 is called CIP-002-3 through CIP-009-3 (CIP stands for Critical Infrastructure Protection).

National Institute of Standards and Technology (NIST)

Where ISO is the most common source for international standards, the National Institute of Standards and Technology (NIST) is the source for many of the national standards in the United States. NIST publishes a number of standards, many of which are related to cybersecurity. These are general guidelines applicable regardless of the specific industry or even the specific devices. The NIST Cybersecurity Framework (NIST CSF) is a group of related standards that are designed to provide guidance on cybersecurity. Each standard is published as an NIST SP (Special Publication) with a numeric designation. Some of these special publications are discussed in this section.

NIST Special Publication 800-12 provides a broad overview of computer security. It primarily deals with areas of security controls. It was written with federal agencies in mind, but it can be useful to any security professional. The full title of the document is "NIST Special Publication 800-12, An Introduction to Computer Security." One of the more important features of this document is that it emphasizes the need to address computer security throughout the system development life cycle, not just after the system is developed.

Special Publication 800-14 describes common security principles that should be addressed within security policies. The purpose of this document is to describe 8 principles and 14 practices that can be used to develop security policies. A significant part of this document is dedicated to auditing user activity on a network. Specific requirements include tracking user actions and, in the event of any investigation, the ability to reconstruct exactly what a user has done. Auditing, monitoring, and intrusion detection are heavily emphasized in this standard.

The eight principles of Special Publication 800-14 are as follows:

1. Computer security supports the mission of the organization.
2. Computer security is an integral element of sound management.
3. Computer security should be cost-effective.
4. System owners have security responsibilities outside their own organizations.
5. Computer security responsibilities and accountability should be made explicit.
6. Computer security requires a comprehensive and integrated approach.
7. Computer security should be periodically reassessed.
8. Computer is security is constrained by societal factors.

The 14 practice areas of Special Publication 800-14 are as follows:

1. Policy
2. Program Management
3. Risk Management
4. Life Cycle Planning
5. Personnel/User Issues
6. Preparing for Contingencies and Disasters

7. Computer Security Incident Handling

8. Awareness and Training

9. Security Considerations in Computer Support and Operations

10. Physical and Environmental Security

11. Identification and Authentication

12. Logical Access Control

13. Audit Trails

14. Cryptography

Many of these areas will be addressed as you progress throughout this book.

NIST SP 800-53 is an important cybersecurity standard. As of 2017, the current revision for NIST SP 800-53 is revision 4. This document organizes security measures into families of controls, such as risk assessment, access control, incident response, and others. The document also defines three levels of minimum security controls.

Special Publication 800-82, Revision 2, Guide to Industrial Control System (ICS) Security, is specific to industrial control systems. Industrial systems include SCADA (Supervisor Control and Data Acquisition) and PLCs (primary logic controllers). This document begins by examining the threats to these systems in detail. The standard then discusses how to develop a comprehensive security plan for such systems. The plan outlined in this document includes firewall issues, network segregation (discussed later in this chapter), network protocols, and security controls for mitigating threats to industrial systems.

NIST 800-30 is the U.S. standard for how to conduct risk assessments. The standard is divided into three chapters. The first is just introductory information such as the target audience and purpose of the standard. Chapter 2 discusses the risk management process and concepts. Chapter 3 provides a process for conducting a risk assessment.

NIST 800-35, titled "Guide to Information Technology Security Services," is an overview of information security. In this standard, six phases of the IT security life cycle are defined:

Phase 1: Initiation   At this point the organization is looking into implementing some IT security service, device, or process.

Phase 2: Assessment   This phase involves determining and describing the organization's current security posture. It is recommended that this phase use quantifiable metrics.

Phase 3: Solution   This is where various solutions are evaluated and one or more is selected.

Phase 4: Implementation   In this phase, the IT security service, device, or process is implemented.

Phase 5: Operations   Phase 5 is the ongoing operation and maintenance of the security service, device, or process that was implemented in Phase 4.

Phase 6: Closeout   At some point, whatever was implemented in Phase 4 will be concluded. Often this is when a system is replaced by a newer and better system.

This NIST standard is rather broad in scope, but it's useful in helping any organization select and implement information security services.

ISA/IEC-62443

ISA/IEC-62443 is a series of standards that define procedures for implementing electronically secure industrial automation and control systems (IACSs). The guidance in this document is divided into four general categories: General, Policies and Procedures, System, and Component. This is another standard that is specific to a particular industry.

Payment Card Industry Data Security Standard (PCI-DSS)

The Payment Card Industry Data Security Standard is the one used by Visa, Mastercard, American Express, and Discover. Though there are in fact a great many parts to the standard, we will only briefly summarize the general standard itself and then focus on the details of the penetration testing portion of it.

The first version of PCI-DSS was released in December 2004. The standard has routinely been updated. As of April 2016, the current version was 3.2.

The main focus of the PCI-DSS is the security controls and objectives that companies that process credit cards should implement. Security auditing and penetration testing are done to ensure that such controls are implemented and the objectives met. This is one reason why you will need a basic understanding of PCI-DSS in order to truly understand a PCI-DSS penetration test.

PCI-DSS defines some rather broad objectives of security that must be met in order for a network to be security compliant. You can see the control objectives in Figure 2.1.

FIGURE 2.1   PCI-DSS control objectives

Build and Maintain a Secure Network

Protect Cardholder Data

Maintain a Vulnerability Management Program

Regularly Monitor and Test Networks

Maintain a Vulnerability Management Program

Although this overview is somewhat broad, the PCI-DSS standards do get more specific. In fact, companies that process credit cards must be aware of all the specific requirements of PCI-DSS. Periodic audits to ensure compliance are part of the PCI process.

Open Web Application Security Project (OWASP)

If your concern is web application security, then the Open Web Application Security Project is the logical place to begin your search for standards, frameworks, and guidelines. On the OWASP website, www.owasp.org, you can find a range of resources for web application security. Among other resources is the OWASP list of security controls for web developers (https://www.owasp.org/):

1. Verify for security early and often
2. Parameterize queries
3. Encode data
4. Validate all inputs
5. Implement identity and authentication controls
6. Implement appropriate access controls
7. Protect data
8. Implement logging and intrusion detection
9. Leverage security frameworks and libraries
10. Error and exception handling

Perhaps OWASP is most well-known for their top 10 vulnerability list. Every few years they publish the top 10 vulnerabilities found in web applications during the previous year. This is a great place for anyone concerned about web application security to begin. At a minimum, you should address these well-known vulnerabilities.

Benchmarks/Secure Configuration Guides

Regardless of the other security controls that you implement, secure configuration is fundamental to overall cybersecurity. Without properly configured servers, workstations, routers, and other devices, other security measures will be far less effective. Fortunately, a number of guidelines have been published for securing individual systems. These are often vendor specific.

Web Server

Web servers are an obvious security concern. By their very nature, they are exposed to the entire world and thus are susceptible to a variety of attacks. At the same time, they cannot be locked down as securely as other servers. This is due to the fact that you must allow unknown visitors to connect to your website. That is, in fact, the very reason why you publish a website.

Microsoft publishes some security guidelines for their IIS (Internet Information Services) web and FTP server (`https://technet.microsoft.com/en-us/library/cc731278` `(v=ws.10).aspx`). Some of the items in this list include the ability to deny access to IP addresses, to configure authentication and authorization, and to configure digital certificates properly. Microsoft also provides an IIS lockdown tool that has an easy-to-use wizard that will walk you through the process of securing your IIS server (`https://support.microsoft` `.com/en-us/help/325864/how-to-install-and-use-the-iis-lockdown-wizard`).

The Apache foundation offers a number of tips on how to secure an Apache web server (`https://httpd.apache.org/docs/2.4/misc/security_tips.html`). Their website has an entire section on how to configure Apache to resist common web attacks such as denial-of-service (DoS) attacks. The website is very thorough. Among the recommendations are methods to protect server-side files, securely configure Common Gateway Interface (CGI), and properly configure permissions.

IIS and Apache account for the overwhelming majority of websites around the world. But regardless of the specific web server you are using, the goal is to configure it as securely as possible. This will usually involve consulting the vendor that distributes the web server you are using and following those recommendations.

Operating System

Obviously, the operating system running on your computer(s) must be securely configured. This is a fundamental aspect of cybersecurity. Fortunately, all operating system vendors provide security frameworks for use with their operating systems.

Microsoft has a Windows Security page (`https://technet.microsoft.com/en-us/` `library/cc772066.aspx`), which has subsections for Windows security–related applications (AppLocker, Authorization Manager, and so on), as well as how to use various security-related features such as BitLocker drive encryption and Kerberos.

Microsoft TechNet also publishes a checklist (`https://technet.microsoft.com/en-us/` `library/bb735870.aspx`) for security best practices. This checklist includes security configuration issues, system updating, physical security, secure communications, and best practices for securing the client computers.

A number of sites publish best practices lists for Macintosh computers. Tech Republic publishes one such list (`http://www.techrepublic.com/blog/apple-in-the-enterprise/` `protect-your-macs-security-best-practices/`). Their list is geared to the common Macintosh user. It addresses issues such as running antivirus software, safe web browsing habits, and user authentication.

Intego publishes a list of 15 tips for protecting your privacy on a Macintosh computer (`https://www.intego.com/mac-security-blog/15-mac-hardening-security-tips-to-` `protect-your-privacy/`). This list includes recommendations such as using a nonadministrative account for normal activities, disabling automatic login, running a firewall, using full-disk encryption, and running antivirus software.

The University of Virginia has a list of security best practices for Unix/Linux (`http://` `its.virginia.edu/unixsys/sec/`). Suggestions include turning off unused services, using a firewall, and keeping the system updated. Red Hat publishes a far more comprehensive guide to Linux security (https://access.redhat.com/documentation/en-US/Red_Hat_ Enterprise_Linux/6/pdf/Security_Guide/Red_Hat_Enterprise_Linux-6-Security_ Guide-en-US.pdf). Their 232-page book, freely available on the Internet as a PDF file, is a comprehensive guide to Linux security.

You have probably noticed that many of these operating system guidelines offer similar suggestions. This is because some security recommendations are ubiquitous—they are not unique to a specific trusted operating system. Keeping your system patched, using antivirus software, using a firewall, and performing day-to-day activities with a nonadministrative account—these are all good ideas regardless of the trusted operating system you are using.

You can derive a single checklist from these various guidelines and benchmarks for operating systems that is an appropriate baseline for any trusted operating system. The following is a list of those essential items that should be implemented to ensure that any operating system is secure:

1. Make certain that the operating system is patched. Without updating the operating system itself, other security measures will be less effective.

2. Turn off any unneeded services, accounts, or other methods of accessing the system.

3. Turn on sufficient logging to allow you to audit the system and to understand what has occurred on the operating system.

4. If the operating system has an inherent firewall, turn it on and see that it is properly configured.

5. Run an appropriate antimalware software package.

These are just general steps that should be taken as the starting point for operating system security, not the end point. The process of making a system as secure as it can be, without the addition of third-party software, devices, or other security controls, is often termed *operating system hardening*.

Network Infrastructure Devices

As important as the security of your operating system, web server, and other services is, the infrastructure that makes up your networks backbone is equally important. This means that the switches, routers, and similar network devices must be secured. Cisco has a lengthy article regarding security compliance, "Achieving NSA Security Compliance," available at http://www.cisco.com/c/en/us/about/security-center/intelligence/05-11-nsa-security-compliance.html. Striving for compliance with the U.S. National Security Administration guidelines is a laudable goal. This particular guideline is thorough. The article discusses network topology, risk assessment, deployment, and even using hashing algorithms to verify routing path decisions.

There is some overlap between securing operating systems and securing your network infrastructure. For example, in both scenarios patching is important as is proper configuration. However, with network infrastructure, topological layout is just as important.

Secure Network Architecture Concepts

In addition to specific technologies that can be used to create a more secure network, architectural concepts can assist in making a network more secure. Essentially how you design the network can enhance security.

Zones

One of the most elementary aspects of network security is to segment your network into zones. Each zone has a different level of security. Furthermore, should a given zone be breached, only that zone is affected—the entire network is not necessarily vulnerable.

At the simplest level, a network can be separated into zones based on security needs for different segments of the network. This requires you to classify the individual computers, systems, and data based on the sensitivity of the data and the criticality of the systems. The following list provides an example:

Secure Zone   These are the most sensitive systems, with mission-critical data.

General Work Zone   These are standard workstations and servers, with typical business data and functionality.

Low Security Zone   These are computers, network segments, and systems that have no highly sensitive information, and the breach of these systems would have minimal impact.

The preceding is just an example. The concept is to divide your network into different zones, each with different levels of security. In this section, we will examine a number of different types of zones and how these affect your network's security.

Demilitarized Zones

A *demilitarized zone (DMZ)* is an area where you can place a public server for access by people whom you might not trust otherwise. By isolating a server in a DMZ, you can hide or remove access to other areas of your network. You can still access the server using your network, but others aren't able to access further network resources. This can be accomplished using firewalls to isolate your network.

When establishing a DMZ, you assume that the person accessing the resource isn't necessarily someone you would trust with other information. Figure 2.2 shows a server placed in a DMZ. Notice that the rest of the network isn't visible to external users. This arrangement lowers the threat of intrusion in the internal network.

FIGURE 2.2 A typical DMZ

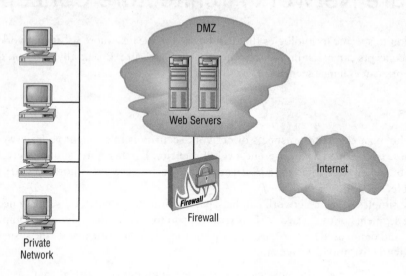

Private
Network

Any time that you want to separate public information from private
information, a DMZ is an acceptable option.

The easiest way to create a DMZ is to use a firewall that can transmit in three
directions:

- To the internal network
- To the external world (Internet)
- To the public information that you're sharing (the DMZ)

From there, you can decide what traffic goes where; for example, HTTP traffic would be
sent to the DMZ and email would go to the internal network.

A host that exists outside the DMZ and is open to the public is often called
a *bastion host*. Routers and firewalls, because of where they must exist,
often constitute bastion hosts.

Extranet and Intranet

Many organizations utilize websites that are only accessible within the organization's network.
These are referred to as *intranets*. These websites can be used to publish internal information
for use within the company. Often items such as human resources information, company policies, and online training can be published via an intranet. Due to the fact that these sites are
completely contained within the organizational network, it is uncommon to implement any
additional security measures. An intranet is only accessible to internal employees, and it is
already protected by the company's firewalls, antimalware, and other security measures.

The situation becomes complicated when the organization wishes to expose some part of their network to a partner organization. A classic example would be a retail chain that uses an intranet so that retail stores can order supplies. Then the company decides to provide a few of their largest suppliers with direct access to that intranet ordering service. This is now an extranet.

Extranets present more security issues than do intranets. You are now allowing an outside entity access to a part of your internal network. The first issue is to ensure that outside party is complying with your security policies and standards. The next issue is to segment that extranet so that it cannot be a bridge to access the rest of your network. Extranets are a good example of network security being accomplished by network segmentation.

Wireless

In today's technology dependent society, it is hard to imagine any company, school, or other organization not providing wireless access. However, wireless is inherently less secure than a physically wired network. This means that segmentation becomes an even greater issue.

The first issue is the wireless protection protocol being implemented. There are three choices: WEP, WPA, and WPA2. The details of these will be explored later in this book. For now, you should know that they are listed in the order of increasing security. This means that, if at all possible, you should simply use WPA2. The problem arises when you have some older computers that cannot support WPA2. This is one area where segmentation can be very helpful. The computers that cannot support WPA2 should be placed on a separate wireless network that is not connected to the primary wireless network.

In addition to the issue of dealing with older technology, there is the more fundamental issue of simply segmenting the wireless network in the same manner that you would segment the wired network. This means having zones that are based on the sensitivity and critically of the data.

It is also a good idea to have an entire separate network (usually wireless, but it could be a wired network) for guests to use. This network will only provide basic Internet access and perhaps access to a single printer. But it should not be connected to the rest of the network. This means that you can be far less concerned about a guest accessing data and resources that he or she should not be able to access.

Some networks simply use ad hoc wireless that involves no predetermined infrastructure and each node participates in routing. This is usually found only in small wireless networks, and it is not recommended from a security perspective. An ad hoc Wi-Fi is the antithesis of segmenting your network into zones.

Segmentation and Defense in Depth

In addition to the specific guidelines previously discussed in this chapter, there are some conceptual issues involved in maintaining a secure network. These are generalized approaches to security that should be considered in addition to specific frameworks and security models.

One of the first issues is that of *defense in depth*. This is a fundamental precept of security. It simply means that it should never be the case that your security is either all or primarily focused on your network's borders. Security should be extended throughout the network. Put another way, it should not be the case that an intruder who breaches your border security measures now has free and unfettered access to your network's resources.

One method for accomplishing defense in depth is to ensure that each device (server, workstation, router, switch, and so forth) is securely configured. The previously discussed security standards will assist you in ensuring that this is accomplished. Another important technique to aid in achieving defense in depth is via network segmentation.

Network segmentation involves dividing your network into zones based on security needs. For example, you might have a zone for sales, a separate zone for technical support, and another zone for research. Each of these zones would have different technical needs. You can separate them by routers/switches or by using *virtual local area networks (VLANs)*. These will be discussed in more detail later in this book, but essentially a VLAN is created when you configure a set of ports on a switch to behave like a separate network. You have essentially segmented your network by creating a logical subnetwork segment.

Whether you use physical devices (switches and routers), VLANs, or a combination of the two to segment your network, segmentation accomplishes two goals. The first is the ability to treat security differently in each of the zones based on the security needs of that zone. The second is the ability to have barriers, such as firewalls, between the zones. This means that if an intruder (or rogue insider) gains access to one zone, this breach would not allow unfettered access to the other zones. A basic example is shown in Figure 2.3.

FIGURE 2.3   Network segmentation

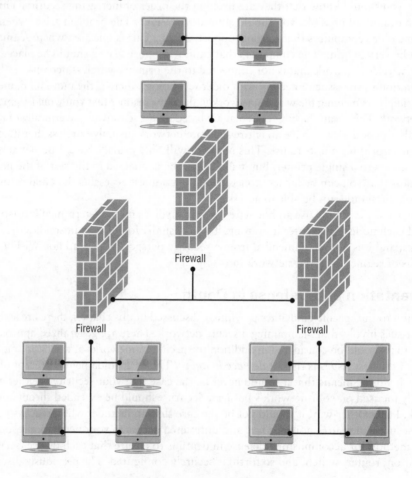

In Figure 2.3, you can see three separate network segments. Each has a firewall protecting it from the other segments. As you can see, network segmentation is a fundamental part of defense in depth. It ensures that each of your network segments has its own security measures.

Another, more extreme example of segmentation is the *air-gap*. This occurs when one or more systems are literally not connected to a network. Obviously, this can reduce the usefulness of many systems, and it is not the right solution for every situation. In some cases, however, a system can be sensitive enough that it needs not to be connected to a network. Having an air-gapped backup server is often a good idea. This is one certain way of preventing malware infections on that system.

Virtualization is another way to segment a network. In later chapters, we will explore virtualization in much more detail. For our current topic, the issue to keep in mind is that it is much easier to segment virtual systems than it is to segment physical systems. As one simple example, consider a virtual machine on your workstation. You can easily configure it so that the virtual machine is completely isolated from the workstation—it does not share a clipboard, common folders, or drives and literally operates as an isolated system. This is just one example of using virtualization to segment your network.

Control Diversity

Another issue is the diversity of vendors and controls. What this means is that you do not address any particular security concern with a single control or a single vendor. Let's assume that you are concerned about malware getting into your network, and one of the controls you are considering is antimalware software. That is an appropriate and logical first step. But that is all it is, the first step, and it should not be your only antimalware security control.

Although most security experts would agree that antimalware is a fundamental aspect of addressing concerns over malware, it is not the only security control. Blocking of suspicious websites, security policies that address attachments and downloads, limited user privileges—all of these also help alleviate the threat of malware. This is what is meant by *control diversity*. You should not rely on a single control to address any security threat.

Vendor Diversity

In addition to diversity of controls, you should strive for diversity of vendors. Returning to the scenario where malware is a concern, you would be correct not only to use antimalware software on each of your computers but also to have antimalware software running on the network and at the firewall. However, this is a situation where diversifying vendors is the best solution. It is not the goal of this book to endorse any particular vendor, but regardless of the vendor you are considering, keep in mind that vendor uses the same malware detection algorithms in all its products. So, if you select vendor A and use their products for workstation, network, and firewall antimalware, then anything missed by one (for example, the firewall) will be missed by all three.

A better solution would be to use vendor A for the firewall antimalware, vendor B for the network, and vendor C for individual computers. The probability of all three products, created by different vendors and using different detection algorithms, missing a specific malware is far lower than any one of them alone missing it.

When implementing controls to mitigate any security issue, controls can be classified into one of three categories: administrative, technical, and physical. In this chapter, we are concerned only with the administrative and technical components. In later chapters, we will discuss physical security.

Administrative controls are all the policies, procedures, and processes that are in place to support security. For example, to mitigate the threat of malware, having policies against downloading unknown attachments and prohibiting the use of unknown external media (such as USB drives) are examples of administrative controls.

Technical controls involve software and hardware. Firewalls, VLANs, antimalware, *intrusion detection systems (IDSs)*, and *intrusion prevention systems (IPSs)* are technical controls. Throughout this book, we will explore these technical controls in depth. It is important, however, to realize that technical controls, by themselves, are usually not going to be adequate. You must couple technical controls to administrative controls in order to mitigate security threats effectively.

Whether we are discussing technical or administrative controls, however, neither is particularly effective without user training. User training is a critical topic in cybersecurity. First and foremost, users (including technical users) must be properly trained in the use of technical controls. The best firewall in the world is far less effective if the technical staff are not appropriately trained (and getting your technical staff Security+ certified is a good first step!).

End users also need to be trained in how to deal with the threats they face, such as phishing emails and attachments. The best security in the world can be undermined by end users who fail to follow security policies. But they cannot really be expected to follow those policies without adequate training.

Honeypots and Honeynets

The concept of a *honeypot* is a separate system that appears to be an attractive target but is in reality a trap for attackers (internal or external). For example, you might set up a server that appears to be a financial database. However, all of the records are fake. This accomplishes two important goals. The first is that the attacker believes that he or she has found what they are looking for and will be occupied with this system, leaving your other systems alone (at least for a short period of time). The second item that a honeypot provides is that since it is not a real system, no legitimate users ever access it. Therefore, you are free to turn on an absurd amount of monitoring and logging for that system. So, when an attacker does access it, you are gathering an impressive amount of evidence to aid in your investigation.

A *honeynet* is the next logical extension of a honeypot. In this case, there is a fake network segment that appears to be a very enticing target. Some organizations set up fake wireless access points for just this purpose.

You can manually set up a honeypot or honeynet, but a variety of products are available that can do this for you. The following is a list of honeynet products. This should not be taken as an endorsement of any specific product but rather as a starting point for you to investigate the honeynet solution that is right for your organization.

Honeyd (www.honeyd.org/)

Symantec Decoy systems (www.symantec.com/region/au_nz/press/au_030701c.html)

Google Hack Honeypot (http://ghh.sourceforge.net/)

Tunneling/VPN

A *virtual private network (VPN)* is a private network connection that occurs through a public network. A private network provides security over an otherwise unsecure environment. VPNs can be used to connect LANs together across the Internet or other public networks. With a VPN, the remote end appears to be connected to the network as if it were connected locally. A VPN requires either special hardware to be installed or a VPN software package running on servers and workstations.

VPNs typically use a tunneling protocol, such as Layer 2 Tunneling Protocol, IPSec, or Point-to-Point Tunneling Protocol (PPTP). Figure 2.4 shows a remote network connected to a LAN using the Internet and a VPN. This connection appears to be a local connection, and all message traffic and protocols are available across the VPN.

FIGURE 2.4   Two LANs connected using a VPN across the Internet

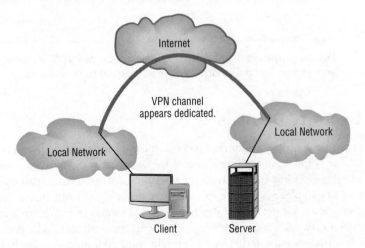

VPNs are becoming the connection of choice when establishing an extranet or intranet between two or more remote offices. The major security concern when using a VPN is encryption. PPTP offers some encryption capabilities, although they're weak. IPSec offers higher security, and it's becoming the encryption system used in many secure VPN environments.

Even though a VPN is created through the Internet or other public network, the connection logically appears to be part of the local network. This is why a VPN connection that is used to establish a connection between two private networks across the Internet is considered a private connection or an extranet.

As mentioned earlier, VPNs are used to make connections between private networks across a public network, such as the Internet. These connections aren't guaranteed to be secure unless a tunneling protocol (such as PPTP) and an encryption system (such as IPSec) are used. A wide range of options, including proprietary technologies, is available for VPN support. Many of the large ISPs and data communications providers offer dedicated hardware with VPN capabilities. Many servers also provide software VPN capabilities for use between two networks.

VPN systems can be dedicated to a certain protocol, or they can pass whatever protocols they see on one end of the network to the other end. A pure VPN connection appears as a dedicated wired connection between the two network ends.

A *VPN concentrator* is a hardware device used to create remote access VPNs. The concentrator creates encrypted tunnel sessions between hosts, and many use two-factor authentication for additional security. Cisco models often incorporate Scalable Encryption Processing (SEP) modules to allow for hardware-based encryption and/or redundancy.

For the purposes of the exam, whenever you see VPN, associate it with encryption and that it only allows authorized remote users.

Placing Security Devices

One issue that has been hinted at but that has not yet been discussed in detail is where to place various security devices. We have discussed segmenting your network, and even network zones, but this does not fully answer the question of where to place all devices.

The easiest device to place is the firewall. You are probably already aware that you need a firewall at your network's perimeter. Beyond that, you should in fact place a firewall at every junction of a network zone. Each segment of your network should be protected by a firewall. This is actually easier to do than you might think. All modern switches and routers have firewall capabilities. Even the most primitive, commercial products for home use have at least basic filtering capabilities. These capabilities just need to be turned on and properly configured.

Along with the firewall, we must discuss correlation engines. These are applications that look at firewall logs, often from diverse firewalls, and attempt to correlate the entries to understand possible attacks. The placement of the correlation engine need not be proximate to the firewall, as long as the correlation engine can access and examine the firewall logs.

Other devices are clearly best suited for the network perimeter. For example, VPN concentrators are used at the networks gateway to connect VPN sites between the outside world and the inside world. Proxies are also most appropriate on the network perimeter. This is because they stand as intermediaries between internal and external traffic.

Another device that obviously belongs on the perimeter would be a distributed DoS (DDoS) mitigator. These are devices that attempt to detect DDoS attacks and to stop them, or at least mitigate the impact. Clearly, such attacks must be stopped before they affect the entire the network.

Some devices are best placed based on the rest of your network configuration. For example, load balancers are used to balance the load for mirrored servers in a server cluster. If we are discussing a cluster of web servers in a DMZ, then the load balancer needs to be in the DMZ as well. However, if we are referring to a cluster of database servers in an interior network segment, then that load balancer must be placed with that cluster.

Port mirroring will also be placed wherever your network demands it. This is often done throughout network switches so that traffic from a given network segment is also copied to another segment. This can be done to ensure that all network traffic is copied to an IDS or IPS.

Network aggregation switches are another device for which there is no definitive placement advice. Such switches aggregate multiple streams of bandwidth into one. This is done wherever there is a need for aggregation on your network. One example would be to use an aggregation switch in conjunction with any network cluster in order to maximize bandwidth to and from the cluster.

Still other devices have to be placed throughout the network. For intrusion detection systems, there must be collectors or sensors in every network segment. Without them, the IDS/IPS will be blind to activity in that segment.

Firewalls

Firewalls are one of the first lines of defense in a network. There are different types of firewalls, and they can be either stand-alone systems or included in other devices such as routers or servers. You can find firewall solutions that are marketed as hardware only and others that are sold as software only. Many firewalls, however, consist of add-in software that is available for servers or workstations.

 Although solutions are sold as "hardware only," the hardware still runs some sort of software. It may be hardened and in ROM to prevent tampering, and it may be customized—but software is present nonetheless.

The basic purpose of a firewall is to isolate one network from another. Firewalls are available as appliances, meaning that they're installed as the primary device separating two networks. *Appliances* are freestanding devices that operate in a largely self-contained manner, requiring less maintenance and support than a server-based product.

The firewall shown in Figure 2.5 effectively limits access from outside networks, while allowing inside network users to access outside resources. The firewall in this illustration is also performing proxy functions, discussed later. A firewall at the gateway will often include network address translation (NAT). This is the process of taking the private IP address of the internal computer, and translating it to a public IP address so that it can be routed across the Internet.

FIGURE 2.5   A proxy firewall blocking network access from external networks

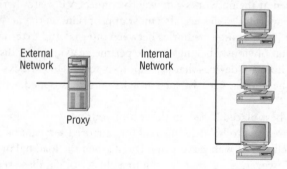

Firewalls function as one or more of the following:

- Packet filter
- Proxy firewall
- Stateful packet inspection firewall

Packet Filter Firewalls

A firewall operating as a *packet filter* passes or blocks traffic to specific addresses based on the type of application. The packet filter doesn't analyze the data of a packet; it decides whether to pass it based on the packet's addressing information. For instance, a packet filter may allow web traffic on port 80 and block Telnet traffic on port 23. This type of filtering is included in many routers. If a received packet request asks for a port that isn't authorized, the filter may reject the request or simply ignore it. Many packet filters can also specify which IP addresses can request which ports and allow or deny them based on the security settings of the firewall.

Packet filters are growing in sophistication and capability. A packet filter firewall can allow any traffic that you specify as acceptable. For example, if you want web users to access your site, you configure the packet filter firewall to allow data on port 80 to enter. If every network were exactly the same, firewalls would come with default port settings hard-coded, but networks vary, so the firewalls don't include such settings.

Proxy Firewalls

A *proxy firewall* can be thought of as an intermediary between your network and any other network. Proxy firewalls are used to process requests from an outside network; the proxy firewall examines the data and makes rule-based decisions about whether the request should be forwarded or refused. The proxy intercepts all the packets and reprocesses them for use internally. This process includes hiding IP addresses.

The proxy firewall provides better security than packet filtering because of the increased intelligence that a proxy firewall offers. Requests from internal network users are routed through the proxy. The proxy, in turn, repackages the request and sends it along, thereby isolating the user from the external network. The proxy can also offer caching, should the same request be made again, and it can increase the efficiency of data delivery.

A proxy firewall typically uses two network interface cards (NICs). This type of firewall is referred to as a *dual-homed firewall*. One of the cards is connected to the outside network, and the other is connected to the internal network. The proxy software manages the connection between the two NICs. This setup segregates the two networks from each other and offers increased security.

Stateful Packet Inspection Firewalls

The last section on firewalls focuses on the concept of stateful inspection. To understand the terminology, you should know that what came before was referred to as *stateless*. *Stateless firewalls* make decisions based on the data that comes in the packet, for example, and not based on any complex decisions.

Stateful inspection is also referred to as *stateful packet inspection (SPI) filtering*. In an SPI firewall, the entire conversation between client and server is examined. Essentially it does what a packet filtering firewall does, but it also remembers what the recent previous packets from the same client contained.

SDN

Software-defined networking (SDN) is a relatively recent trend that can be useful both in placing security devices and in segmenting the network. Essentially in an SDN, the entire network is virtualized. This allows a relatively easy segmentation of the network. It also allows the administrator to place virtualized security devices in any place that he or she wishes.

IDS vs. IPS

Although intrusion detection systems (IDSs) have been popular for a long time, *intrusion prevention systems (IPSs)* have become prevalent in the past few years.

What is now called an IPS was formerly known as an active IDS.

This type of system is an IDS that reacts to the intrusion that has been detected, most often by blocking communication from the offending IP address. The problem with this approach is the issue of false positives. No system is perfect—at some point you will have a situation where network activity is anomalous and the IDS indicates an intrusion, but in reality, it is not an intrusion. For example, if the IDS is set up to react to traffic outside normal bounds, excessive traffic from a given system could indicate an attack. However, it could also indicate an unusually high workload.

Secure Systems Design

Another aspect of security is designing the systems on the network. This is closely related to the previously discussed secure network architecture.

Hardware and Firmware Security

When designing a network, one of the first issues that you must address are secure systems. And one critical aspect of secure systems is the issue of encrypted data. There are many options today for encrypting a hard drive. Later in this book we will discuss encryption, including various algorithms, in more detail. At this point, we are simply interested in the applications of cryptography.

Full disk encryption (FDE) is encrypting the entire disk, rather than a specific file or folder. This is recommended for full security of the system. Windows, beginning with Windows 7, offers BitLocker on the professional and higher versions of its operating system. There are also open source encryption solutions such as VeraCrypt (https://veracrypt .codeplex.com/) that allow you to encrypt your entire drive.

A self-encrypting drive (SED) has a controller chip built into it that automatically encrypts the drive and decrypts it, provided the proper password is entered. The encryption key used in SEDs is called the *media encryption key (MEK)*. Locking and unlocking a drive requires another key, called the *key encryption key (KEK)*, supplied by the user. The KEK is used to decrypt the MEK, which in turn is what encrypts and decrypts the drive.

Trusted platform modules (TPMs) are dedicated processors that use cryptographic keys to perform a variety of tasks. For example, they can be used to authenticate devices. TPMs can also be used to facilitate FDE. Usually a TPM will be on the motherboard of the computer.

Hardware security modules (HSMs) are devices that handle digital keys. They can be used to facilitate encryption as well as authentication via digital signatures. Most HSMs support tamper-resistant mechanisms.

In addition to securing drives, the system BIOS or UEFI must be secured. BIOS (basic input/output system) was the older method for handling bootup information for a computer. UEFI (Unified Extensible Firmware Interface) is the more modern technique. While UEFI has a number of newer and better features compared to BIOS, they both have the same basic purpose: to store information that the computer needs when booting up. For this reason, you should always ensure that access to either BIOS or UEFI is password protected.

Secure boot is a process whereby the BIOS or UEFI makes a cryptographic hash of the operating system boot loader and any boot drivers and compares that against a stored hash. This is done to prevent rootkits and boot sector viruses. The stored hash is often protected or encrypted by a TPM. Another option is to store the hash in some secure server remote from the computer being protected. This leads to *remote attestation*.

Another aspect of secure system design is the *root of trust (RoT)*. A root of trust is a security process that has to begin with some unchangeable hardware identity often stored in a TPM. From this confirmed identity, each layer of the system, starting with BIOS/UEFI, on to the operating system and beyond, is validated upon startup to ensure that no tampering has occurred.

Systems must also be protected against electromagnetic interference and electromagnetic pulses (EMI/EMP). In most environments, this will be a rather small concern. However, computers are susceptible to electronic interference. At the simplest level, this means being aware of devices and processes that might produce EMI/EMP and keeping them away from systems. In other, more secure environments, this may involve taking steps to prevent EMI/EMP from penetrating a room with computers. A common way to do this is via a Faraday cage. A Faraday cage is named after the famous physicist Michael Faraday. They are essentially metal meshes that prevent electromagnetic signals from penetrating. The U.S. government, particularly the Department of Defense, uses secure compartmented information facilities (SCIFs), wherein the room or building itself is a Faraday cage.

Finally, when procuring systems from an outside party, you need to check the supply chain to ensure that it is not compromised. This may be something as simple as using a reputable vendor who signs an agreement to abide by minimal security requirements, or something much more elaborate, depending on your security needs.

Operating Systems

Operating systems come in many types. There are network operating systems, computer operating systems (client or server), appliance operating systems, kiosks, and mobile device operating systems. However, they all share some common needs that must be addressed. In the following sections, we will explore these issues.

Network operating systems define how the network will function. The network operating system is determined by the operating system used on the domain controller. For example, if the domain controller is running Unix, then the network is a Unix network, even if it contains many Windows or Macintosh computers.

Client and server operating systems are very similar. For example, Windows 10 and Windows Server 2016 have a great many similarities, including the basic interface. In general, however, server operating systems usually offer up additional network services and are usually more secure than client operating systems.

Appliance operating systems and kiosk operating systems are both limited to a specific purpose. An appliance operating system might be on a smart device, such as a smart home's thermostat. A kiosk is usually a public computer used for a limited purpose. In both cases, the operating system needs only to support a limited range of functions. This usually makes security easier, since there are fewer issues to address.

Mobile operating systems are now similar to server and client operating systems. The Apple iOS is similar to the Macintosh operating system. Android phones are running a version of Linux. And of course, Windows phones are running Windows 10 (or older phones running Windows 8). With the greater range of functionality supported by mobile devices, there is an increase in the number of security issues to mitigate.

Patch Management

Previously in this chapter, in our discussions of standards, we mentioned updating an operating system. This usually means making sure that it is patched. However, in live systems, particularly critical servers, patch management can be a bit more complicated.

Home users are usually advised to have automatic updates turned on. However, this is not recommended for large organizations—at least not for sensitive systems. It is always possible that a patch will cause some issue for a custom application that runs on your system, or that the patch itself is somehow flawed. For this reason, we recommend the following process:

1. Read the description of the patch in question. Is this simply an update to functionality, or is it a vital security patch? Depending on the nature of the patch, you will decide when to schedule deployment.

2. Deploy the patch on a test system that is identical to the systems to which you intend to roll it out. This should let you quickly detect any serious or obvious issues.

3. If the patch passes the initial test, then roll it out to a small number of live systems. Wait some appropriate period of time and then continue the rollout in stages. What is an appropriate wait time will depend on the nature of the patch. Critical security patches should be deployed with as much haste as you can while still testing the patch. Capability upgrades can be slowly rolled out over a period of time.

Obeying this carefully planned and phased patch rollout plan is one of the cornerstones of patch management. However, it is only part of patch management. Another critical aspect is to have a backout plan. If at any point it appears that the patch is causing a problem, you must have a plan to back the patch out and return to pre-patch operations.

Documentation is also an important aspect of patch management. You need to document all patch deployment decisions, the rationale for such decisions, and any issues encountered. Good documentation will help smooth out future patch management issues.

Secure Configurations

Another issue we touched on when discussing standards was secure configuration. Whether discussing a critical server, a guest workstation, or a network switch, some issues are common to all of these.

The first is *least functionality*. This is similar to the concept of least privileges. The system itself should be configured and capable of doing only what it is intended to do and no more.

The next issue is to lock down the system as much as possible. This involves disabling all default passwords and any default accounts you don't use. It is amazing how often I encounter, in real-world system audits, even gateway routers with default usernames and passwords. And, in case you not aware, a simple Google search is all it takes to find the default username and password for any system.

If there are default accounts that you don't use, shut them down. We suspect that most readers never log in to their home computer as "guest." If not, then why do you have a guest account still active? Simply shutting down anything that you don't need will go quite a long way to improving security.

Along with disabling default accounts is the disabling of default services. If you are not using a service, why do you have it turned on? In the next few figures, we will walk you through how to turn off services in Windows 10. You should be aware that with different versions of Windows, Microsoft sometimes moves items around in the Control Panel, so you may need to look around a little to find the services section. You start with the Control Panel, shown in Figure 2.6.

FIGURE 2.6   Windows 10 Control Panel

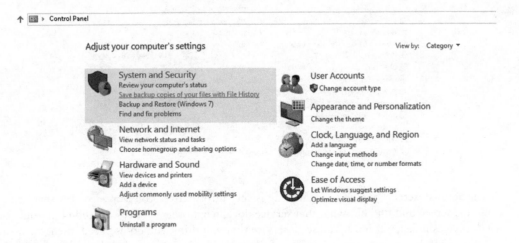

Now, select System and Security. You'll see the screen shown in Figure 2.7.

FIGURE 2.7   Windows 10 System and Security

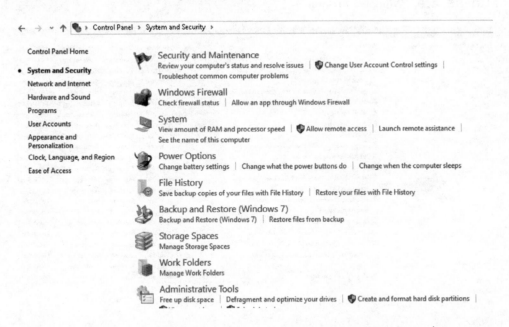

Next select Administrative Tools. You'll see the screen in Figure 2.8. From there launch Services.

FIGURE 2.8 Windows 10 Administrative Tools screen

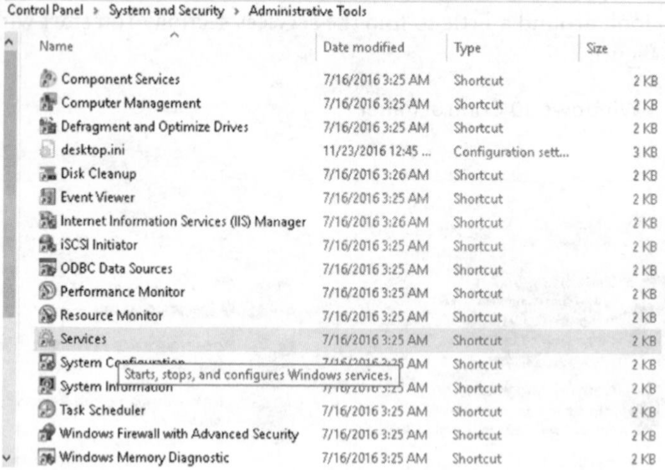

Name	Date modified	Type	Size
Control Panel › System and Security › Administrative Tools			
Component Services	7/16/2016 3:25 AM	Shortcut	2 KB
Computer Management	7/16/2016 3:25 AM	Shortcut	2 KB
Defragment and Optimize Drives	7/16/2016 3:25 AM	Shortcut	2 KB
desktop.ini	11/23/2016 12:45 ...	Configuration sett...	3 KB
Disk Cleanup	7/16/2016 3:26 AM	Shortcut	2 KB
Event Viewer	7/16/2016 3:25 AM	Shortcut	2 KB
Internet Information Services (IIS) Manager	7/16/2016 3:26 AM	Shortcut	2 KB
iSCSI Initiator	7/16/2016 3:25 AM	Shortcut	2 KB
ODBC Data Sources	7/16/2016 3:25 AM	Shortcut	2 KB
Performance Monitor	7/16/2016 3:25 AM	Shortcut	2 KB
Resource Monitor	7/16/2016 3:25 AM	Shortcut	2 KB
Services	7/16/2016 3:25 AM	Shortcut	2 KB
System Configuration	7/16/2016 3:25 AM	Shortcut	2 KB
System Information	Starts, stops, and configures Windows services.	Shortcut	2 KB
Task Scheduler	7/16/2016 3:25 AM	Shortcut	2 KB
Windows Firewall with Advanced Security	7/16/2016 3:25 AM	Shortcut	2 KB
Windows Memory Diagnostic	7/16/2016 3:25 AM	Shortcut	2 KB

The Services screen, shown in Figure 2.9, is very informative. You can select any service from this screen and find out what that service does, what other services depend on it, and what services it depends on. If you see a service that you think you do not need, then you can shut it off. But before you do, first carefully examine the services that depend on it and make sure that you won't be inadvertently shutting down something that you do need. The cardinal rule in services is: if you don't know what it is, leave it alone!

FIGURE 2.9 Windows 10 Services

Name	Description	Status	Startup Type	Log On As
Services (Local)				
Select an item to view its description.				
Sync Host_2a266847	This service ...	Running	Automatic (D...	Local Syst
CDPUserSvc_2a266847	<Failed to R...	Running	Automatic	Local Syst
Intuit Update Service v4	Helps Intuit ...	Running	Automatic (D...	Local Syst
Intel(R) PROSet/Wireless Zero Configuration Service	Manages th...	Running	Automatic	Local Syst
Windows Driver Foundation - User-mode Driver Framework	Creates and...	Running	Manual (Trig...	Local Syst
Windows Update	Enables the ...	Running	Manual (Trig...	Local Syst
Windows Search	Provides co...	Running	Automatic (D...	Local Syst
Security Center	The WSCSV...	Running	Automatic (D...	Local Serv
Windows Push Notifications System Service	This service ...	Running	Automatic	Local Syst
WLAN AutoConfig	The WLANS...	Running	Automatic	Local Syst
Windows Management Instrumentation	Provides a c...	Running	Automatic	Local Syst
WinHTTP Web Proxy Auto-Discovery Service	WinHTTP i...	Running	Manual	Local Serv
Windows Defender Service	Helps prote...	Running	Automatic	Local Syst
Windows Defender Network Inspection Service	Helps guard...	Running	Manual	Local Serv
Diagnostic System Host	The Diagno...	Running	Manual	Local Syst
Diagnostic Service Host	The Diagno...	Running	Manual	Local Serv
Windows Connect Now - Config Registrar	WCNCSVC ...	Running	Manual	Local Serv
Windows Connection Manager	Makes auto...	Running	Automatic (T...	Local Serv
Windows Process Activation Service	The Windo...	Running	Manual	Local Syst
World Wide Web Publishing Service	Provides W...	Running	Automatic	Local Syst
VMware NAT Service	Network ad...	Running	Automatic	Local Syst

For servers, workstations, and mobile devices, the process of securing the system will involve turning off anything that you don't need, whether that is a user account, a service, or anything at all that is not needed for the system. However, you may also wish to consider application whitelisting or blacklisting. *Application blacklisting* is the process of listing banned applications. For example, you may wish to ban password crackers or software that scrubs evidence. The problem is that blacklisting can never be all-inclusive. You simply cannot list every single "bad" app that is available. So, whitelisting is an alternative. In *application whitelisting*, you make a list of allowed apps, and only those applications may be installed.

Peripherals

Peripherals also present security issues. There are so many peripherals available today, including wireless keyboards and mice, displays, Wi-Fi enabled cards, printers, scanners, external drives, digital cameras, and more coming all the time. As you might suspect, these devices have security issues that must be addressed.

For more complex devices, such as printers, the security measures are not so different from the recommendations for computers. For example, any default passwords should be changed. Also, any unused or unneeded services should be turned off. Many printers allow remote access via protocols such as Telnet and SSH. If you are not using those, then turn them off.

Many virus scanners can scan just about any device with nonvolatile storage. That means you should periodically scan your external drives and digital cameras for malware. If a device is Wi-Fi enabled but you don't require that capability, consider disabling it.

Secure Staging Deployment Concepts

When you're deploying anything, a new application, a patch, a new operating system, or a new device, the manner in which you deploy it can have a significant impact on the security of your network. The first and most common way to address this is to have separate environments.

For applications, the first stage is the *development environment*. This is where the application is developed. This is used for both desktop applications and web applications. With proper testing, security flaws can be found while the application is in the development environment.

For applications, operating systems, and devices, there should be a *test environment*. Think of this as a mini-network. The more closely the test environment mimics the real environment, the more likely you are to find and address security issues in testing.

Next is *staging*. Normally, any new addition to a network is deployed in stages, not simply put out to the entire network. This is particularly important with applications or even patches for existing applications and operating systems. Roll the new software out to sections of the network, with a period of time between each new stage. This provides an opportunity to find issues before they are propagated to the entire network. The production environment should always be rolled out in stages.

When there is any doubt about a new item on the network, put the new item into a sandbox. A *sandbox* is a term for a test environment that is completely isolated from the rest of the network. When the new item is an application or patch, an isolated virtual machine can provide a good sandbox. The concept is to test the new item completely while it is isolated from the network and cannot affect it. This way, if some significant issue is discovered in testing, it won't impact the production network.

Establishing a *secure baseline* is an important concept in secure networking. Essentially, this is a process whereby you find a baseline for any system, application, or service that is considered secure. Certainly, absolute security is not possible—the goal is "secure enough," based on your organization's security needs and risk appetite. By establishing a secure baseline, any change can be compared to that baseline to see if the change is secure enough.

Once a baseline is defined, then the next step is to monitor that system (be it a single service, a computer, or application) to ensure that it has not deviated from that baseline. This process is defined as *integrity measurement*. For example, NIST SP 800-155 defines standards for testing the integrity of a system BIOS to ensure that it has not changed.

Part of integrity testing involves a chain of trust. If system A trusts system B, which in turn trusts system C, then the integrity testing should be in reverse order. Start with the root of that chain of trust, system C. Once you have checked the integrity of system C, you can then proceed down the chain, checking the integrity of each system.

Summary

In this chapter, we discussed how to design and implement a network in such a way as to enhance security. We focused on issues such as network security standards, segmentation, and defense in depth.

We also examined firewalls and VPNs, as well as where and how to implement devices. We introduced you to fundamental security devices such as honeypots and intrusion detection systems.

Exam Essentials

Be able to describe the standards.   For the test, you will be asked questions about standards. There are many standards around the world, but expect the emphasis to be on NIST and ISO standards. It is beyond the scope of any chapter, or even an entire book, to describe in detail all of the NIST and ISO standards. In this chapter, we focused on standards that are most commonly used in cybersecurity and that you are most likely to see on the test.

Be able to explain the purpose of a honeypot/honeynet.   A honeypot is a system that is used to gather information or designed to be broken. Honeypot systems are used to gather evidence in an investigation and to study attack strategies.

Be able to explain operating system hardening.   OS hardening is making the OS as secure as you can before adding in antivirus, firewalls, and so forth. It includes patching the system, shutting down unneeded services, and removing unneeded software.

Be able to explain and apply network design and configuration   Make certain that you understand network segmentation, zones, and defense in depth. You should also understand the technologies (such as VPNs) and network devices (firewalls, IDSs/IPSs, and so forth) that have been discussed in this chapter.

Review Questions

You can find the answers in the Appendix.

1. A periodic update that corrects problems in one version of a product is called a(n) _____.

   A. Hotfix

   B. Overhaul

   C. Service pack

   D. Security update

2. Which device monitors network traffic in a passive manner?

   A. Sniffer

   B. IDS

   C. Firewall

   D. Web browser

3. What is a system that is intended or designed to be broken into by an attacker?

   A. Honeypot

   B. Honeybucket

   C. Decoy

   D. Spoofing system

   E. Deleted if the employee has been terminated

4. In intrusion detection system vernacular, which account is responsible for setting the security policy for an organization?

   A. Supervisor

   B. Administrator

   C. Root

   D. Director

5. You are a junior security administrator for a large bank. You have been asked to make the database servers as secure as they can be. The process of making certain that an entity (operating system, application, and so on) is as secure as it can be is known as which of the following?

   A. Stabilizing

   B. Reinforcing

   C. Hardening

   D. Toughening

6. John is working on designing a network for the insurance company where he is employed. He wants to put the web server in an area that has somewhat less security so that outside users might access it. But he does not want that to compromise the security of the rest of the network. What would be John's best approach?

   A. Place the web server in a honeynet.

   B. Place the web server on the guest network segment.

   C. Place the web server in a DMZ.

   D. Place the web server outside his network.

7. Tom has been instructed to find a security standard, applicable to the United States, that will help him develop appropriate security policies. He has found a standard that describes 8 principles and 14 practices that can be used to develop security policies. What standard is Tom most likely reviewing?

   A. ISO/IEC 27001:2013

   B. NIST 800-12

   C. NIST 800-14

   D. ISA/IEC-62443 4

8. Juanita is implementing a security mechanism that will fully encrypt the hard drive of laptops in her organization. The encryption and decryption will be automatic. What best describes what Juanita is implementing?

   A. AES

   B. TPM

   C. FDE

   D. SED

9. Ahmed has been working to mitigate the threat of malware in his network. He has selected a specific vendor (Vendor ABC) for his antivirus software. He is using ABC products everywhere he needs antivirus software. Is this the correct decision? Why or why not?

   A. Yes, consistency is more secure.

   B. Yes, this will make the process more affordable.

   C. No, this violates control diversity.

   D. No, this violates vendor diversity.

10. You are concerned about your backup files becoming infected with malware. Which of the following technologies would be best to protect your backup?

   A. Air-gap

   B. SPI firewall

   C. DMZ

   D. VLAN

Chapter

3

Understanding Devices and Infrastructure

THE FOLLOWING COMPTIA SECURITY+ EXAM OBJECTIVES ARE COVERED IN THIS CHAPTER:

✓ **2.1 Install and configure network components, both hardware- and software-based to support organizational security.**

- Firewall: ACL; Application-based vs. network-based; Stateful vs. stateless; Implicit deny

- VPN Concentrator: Remote access vs. site-to-site; IPSec (Tunnel mode, Transport mode, AH, ESP); Split tunnel vs. full tunnel; TLS; Always-on VPN

- NIPS/NIDS: Signature-based; Heuristic/behavioral; Anomaly; Inline vs. passive; In-band vs. out-of-band; Rules; Analytics (False positive, False negative)

- Router: ACLs; Antispoofing

- Switch: Port security; Layer 2 vs. Layer 3; Loop protection; Flood guard

- Proxy: Forward and reverse proxy; Transparent; Application/multipurpose

- Load balancer: Scheduling (Affinity, Round-robin); Active-passive; Active-active; Virtual IPs

- Access point: SSID; MAC filtering; Signal strength; Band selection/width; Antenna types and placement; Fat vs. thin; Controller-based vs. standalone

- SIEM: Aggregation; Correlation; Automated alerting and triggers; Time synchronization; Event deduplication; Logs/WORM

- DLP: USB blocking; Cloud-based
- NAC: Dissolvable vs. permanent; Host health checks; Agent vs. agentless
- Mail gateway: Spam filter; DLP; Encryption
- Bridge
- SSL/TLS accelerators
- SSL decryptors
- Media gateway
- Hardware security module

This chapter introduces the hardware used within the network. Your network is composed of a variety of *media* and *devices* that both facilitate communications and provide security. Many of these devices provide external connectivity from your network to other systems and networks, whereas others specialize in providing one form of security or another. To provide reasonable security to the entire network, you must know how these devices work and how they provide, or fail to provide, security.

This chapter deals with issues of infrastructure and the common components needed. Some of those components are hardware based (such as a switch) whereas others are software based (such as an NIDS); most (such as a firewall) are a combination of both. Understanding why each of these components exist and why you would use them is key to studying for the Security+ exam, not to mention necessary in order to secure your network.

Infrastructure Terminology

It can sometimes be confusing as to just what each piece of equipment does since so many of them are referenced by their acronyms. Given the bit of redundancy built into the objectives and the fact that you often use multiple pieces of equipment for similar functions, the following terms (also found in the online glossary) are those CompTIA is fond of using and testing on in this category. We provide them in order to make it easier for you to know what each is intended to convey.

Security+ Terminology

access control list (ACL)   A table or data file that specifies whether a user or group has access to a specific resource on a computer or network.

access point (AP)   The point at which access to a network is accomplished. This term is often used in relation to a wireless access point.

active response   A response generated in real time.

alarm   A notification that an unusual condition exists and should be investigated.

alert   An indication that an unusual condition could exist and should be investigated.

all-in-one appliance   An appliance that performs multiple functions.

analyzer   The component or process that analyzes the data collected by the sensor.

anomalies   Variations from normal operations.

anomaly-detection IDS (AD-IDS)   An anomaly-detection intrusion detection system works by looking for deviations from a pattern of normal network traffic.

appliance   A freestanding device that operates in a largely self-contained manner.

application-level proxy   A device or software that recognizes application-specific commands and offers granular control over them.

Authentication Header (AH)   An IPSec header used to provide connectionless integrity and data origin authentication for IP datagrams and to provide protection against replays.

clustering   A method of balancing loads and providing fault tolerance.

compensating controls   Gap controls that fill in the coverage between other types of vulnerability mitigation techniques (where there are holes in coverage, we compensate for them).

data loss prevention (DLP)   Any systems that identify, monitor, and protect data to prevent it from unauthorized use, modification, destruction, egress, or exfiltration from a location.

Encapsulating Security Payload (ESP)   An IPSec header used to provide a mix of security services in IPv4 and IPv6. ESP can be used alone or in combination with the IP Authentication Header (AH).

encapsulation   The process of enclosing data in a packet.

false negative   An event that should be flagged but isn't.

false positive   A flagged event that isn't really an event and has been falsely triggered.

firewall   A combination of hardware and software filters placed between trusted and untrusted networks intended to protect a network from attack by hackers who could gain access through public networks, including the Internet.

host-based IDS (HIDS)   An intrusion detection system that is host based. An alternative is an intrusion detection system that is network based.

HSM (hardware security module)   A software or appliance stand-alone used to enhance security and commonly used with PKI systems.

implicit deny   A condition that states that unless otherwise given, the permission will be denied.

Internet Protocol Security (IPSec)   A set of protocols that enable encryption, authentication, and integrity over IP. IPSec is commonly used with virtual private networks (VPNs) and operates at Layer 3.

intrusion detection system (IDS)   Tools that identify attacks using defined rules or logic and are considered passive. An IDS can be network based or host based.

intrusion prevention system (IPS)   Tools that respond to attacks using defined rules or logic and are considered active. An IPS can be network based or host based.

key management   The management of all aspects of cryptographic keys in a cryptosystem, including key generation, exchange, storage, use, destruction and replacement.

load balancing   Dividing a load for greater efficiency of management among multiple devices.

network access control (NAC)   The set of standards defined by the network for clients attempting to access it. Usually, NAC requires that clients be virus free and adhere to specified policies before allowing them on the network.

network intrusion prevention system (NIPS)   An intrusion prevention system that is network based.

network-based IDS (NIDS)   An approach to an intrusion detection system (IDS); it attaches the system to a point in the network where it can monitor and report on all network traffic.

passive response   A nonactive response, such as logging. Passive response is the most common type of response to many intrusions. In general, passive responses are the easiest to develop and implement.

proxy   A type of system that prevents direct communication between a client and a host by acting as an intermediary.

proxy firewall   A proxy server that also acts as a firewall, blocking network access from external networks.

proxy server   A type of server that makes a single Internet connection and services requests on behalf of many users.

Secure Sockets Layer (SSL)   A protocol that secures messages by operating between the Application layer (HTTP) and the Transport layer.

SIEM   Security information and event management (SIEM) software combines security information management (SIM) and security event management (SEM) functions to provide real-time analysis of security alerts.

signature-based system   A system that acts based on the digital signature it sees and offers no repudiation to increase the integrity of a message.

SSID broadcast   An access point's broadcasting of the network name.

stateful inspection   Inspections that occur at all levels of the network and provide additional security using a state table that tracks every communications channel.

switch   A network device that can replace a router or hub in a local network and get data from a source to a destination. Switching allows for higher speeds.

Designing with Security in Mind

When you design the *security topology* of your network, you are concerned with the access methods, security, and technologies used. These issues have to be factored into the physical elements that comprise the network. Everything you add, or want to add, comes with constraints. Those constraints can run the gamut from number of nodes they support to cost.

Large multinational as well as small and medium-sized corporations are building networks of enormous complexity and sophistication. These networks work by using miles of both wired and wireless technologies. Whether the network is totally wire- and fiber-based, or totally wireless, the method of transmitting data from one place to another opens up vulnerabilities and opportunities for exploitation. Vulnerabilities appear whenever an opportunity exists to intercept information from the media.

The devices briefly described here are the components that you'll typically encounter in a network.

Many network devices contain firmware with which you interact during configuration. For security purposes, you must authenticate in order to make configuration changes and do so initially by using the default account(s). Make sure that the default password is changed after installation on any network device; otherwise, you are leaving that device open for anyone recognizing the hardware to access it using the known factory password.

Firewalls

Firewalls are one of the first lines of defense in a network. There are different types of firewalls, and they can be either stand-alone systems or included in other devices such as routers or servers. You can find firewall solutions that are marketed as hardware only and others that are software only. Many firewalls, however, consist of add-in software that is available for servers or workstations.

Although solutions are sold as "hardware only," the hardware still runs some sort of software. It may be hardened and in ROM to prevent tampering, and it may be customized—but software is present nonetheless.

The basic purpose of a firewall is to isolate one network from another. Firewalls are available as appliances, meaning that they're installed as the primary device separating two networks. *Appliances* are freestanding devices that operate in a largely self-contained manner, requiring less maintenance and support than a server-based product.

Firewalls can work at many levels and, as such, be *application-based* or *network-based*. Most are configured as network based and work with *access control lists (ACLs)* to determine what is allowed in (in terms of traffic, data, applications, or whatever other term for criteria you want to use) and what is left out. All should operate on the principle of *implicit deny*, meaning that any service not specifically allowed is implicitly denied.

The firewall shown in Figure 3.1 effectively limits access from outside networks while allowing inside network users to access outside resources. The firewall in this illustration is also performing proxy functions, which will be discussed later.

FIGURE 3.1   A proxy firewall blocking network access from external networks

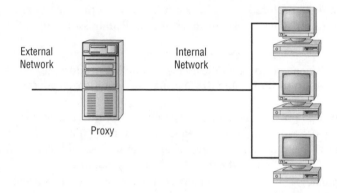

Firewalls function as one or more of the following:

- Packet filter

- Proxy firewall

- Stateful packet inspection firewall (as opposed to stateless)

 Although firewalls are often associated with outside traffic, you can place a firewall anywhere. For example, if you want to isolate one portion of your internal network from others, you can place a firewall between them.

Packet Filter Firewalls

A firewall operating as a *packet filter*, or *static firewall*, passes or blocks traffic to specific addresses based on the type of application. The packet filter doesn't analyze the data of a packet; based on given rules, it decides whether to pass it based on the packet's addressing information. For instance, a packet filter may allow web traffic on port 80 and block Telnet traffic on port 23. This type of filtering is included in many routers. If a received packet request asks for a port that isn't authorized, the filter may reject the request or simply ignore it. Many packet filters can also specify which IP addresses can request which ports and allow or deny them based on the security settings of the firewall.

Packet filters are growing in sophistication and capability. A packet filter firewall can allow any traffic that you specify as acceptable. For example, if you want web users to access your site, you configure the packet filter firewall to allow data on port 80 to enter. If every network were exactly the same, firewalls would come with default port settings hard-coded, but networks vary, so the firewalls don't include such settings.

Proxy Firewalls

A *proxy firewall* can be thought of as an intermediary between your network and any other network. Proxy firewalls are used to process requests from an outside network; the proxy firewall examines the data and makes rule-based decisions about whether the request should be forwarded or refused. The proxy intercepts all of the packets and reprocesses them for use internally. This process includes hiding IP addresses.

 When you consider the concept of hiding IP addresses, think of Network Address Translation (NAT) as part of your internal addressing scheme.

The proxy firewall provides better security than packet filtering because of the increased intelligence that a proxy firewall offers. Requests from internal network users are routed through the proxy. The proxy, in turn, repackages the request and sends it along, thereby isolating the user from the external network. The proxy can also offer caching, should the same request be made again, and it can increase the efficiency of data delivery.

A proxy firewall typically uses two network interface cards (NICs). This type of firewall is referred to as a *dual-homed firewall*. One of the cards is connected to the outside network, and the other is connected to the internal network. The proxy software manages the connection between the two NICs. This setup segregates the two networks from each other and offers increased security.

 Whenever you have a system that is configured with more than one IP address, it can be said to be *multihomed*.

The proxy function can occur at either the application level or the circuit level.

Application-level proxy functions read the individual commands of the protocols that are being served. This type of server is advanced and must know the rules and capabilities of the protocol used. An implementation of this type of proxy must know the difference between GET and PUT operations, for example, and have rules specifying how to execute them.

A *circuit-level proxy* creates a circuit between the client and the server and doesn't deal with the contents of the packets that are being processed.

A unique application-level proxy server must exist for each protocol supported. Many proxy servers also provide full auditing, accounting, and other usage information that wouldn't normally be kept by a circuit-level proxy server.

Stateful vs. Stateless Firewalls

The last section on firewalls focuses on the concept of stateful inspection. To understand the terminology, you should know that what came before was referred to as *stateless*. *Stateless firewalls* make decisions based on the data that comes in—the packet, for example—and not based on any complex decisions.

Stateful inspection is also referred to as *stateful packet inspection (SPI) filtering*. Most of the devices used in networks don't keep track of how information is routed or used. After a packet is passed, the packet and path are forgotten. In stateful inspection (or stateful packet filtering), records are kept using a state table that tracks every communications channel; it remembers where the packet came from and where the next one should come from.

The real difference between SPI and simple packet filtering is that SPI tracks the entire conversation while packet filtering looks only at the current packet.

Stateful inspections occur at all levels of the network and provide additional security, especially in connectionless protocols, such as User Datagram Protocol and Internet Control Message Protocol. This adds complexity to the process. Denial-of-service attacks present a challenge because flooding techniques are used to overload the state table and effectively cause the firewall to shut down or reboot.

For the exam, remember that pure packet filtering has no real intelligence. It allows data to pass through a port if that port is configured and otherwise discards it—it doesn't examine the packets. Stateful packet filtering, however, has intelligence in that it keeps track of every communications channel.

UTM Security Appliances

In the broadest sense of the term, any freestanding device that operates in a largely self-contained manner is considered to be an *appliance*. An *all-in-one appliance*, also known as *unified threat management (UTM)* and *next generation firewall (NGFW)*, is one that provides a good foundation for security. A variety are available; those that you should be familiar with for the exam fall under the categories of providing URL filtering, content inspection, or malware inspection. They are discussed further in the sections that follow. When you combine a firewall with other abilities (intrusion prevention, antivirus, content filtering, and so forth), what used to be called an all-in-one appliance is now known as a *UTM*. The advantages of combining everything into one include a reduced learning curve (you only have one product to learn), a single vendor to deal with, and (typically) reduced complexity. The disadvantages of combining everything into one include a potential single point of failure and dependence on the one vendor.

URL Filters

URL filtering involves blocking websites (or sections of websites) based solely on the URL, restricting access to specified websites and certain web-based applications. This is in contrast to content filters, which block data based on its content rather than from where the data originates. Microsoft, for example, first implemented the Phishing filter, which acted as a URL filter for their browser, and then replaced it with the SmartScreen filter, which runs in the background and sends the address of the website being visited to the SmartScreen filter server, where it is compared against a list that is maintained of phishing and malware sites. If a match is found, a blocking web page appears (in red), and it encourages you to not continue. You can continue to the site (not recommended) or abort the operation.

Content Inspection

Instead of relying on a website to be identified previously as questionable, as URL filtering does, *content inspection* works by looking at the data that is coming in. Microsoft included content filtering in some versions of their browsers (Internet Explorer and Microsoft Edge), which could be configured using Content Advisor.

Internet content filters, though not included with every operating system by default, are plentiful and can be readily found for any operating system with a simple web search. We highly recommend that you place content filters on all servers (NAT, proxy, and so on) facilitating client access as well as on the workstations themselves. This provides two levels of security that can keep errant pages out.

Malware Inspection

It is important to stop malware before it ever gets ahold of a system. Although tools that identify malware when they find it on a system are useful, real-time tools that stop it from ever making it to the system are much better. One of the available tools for Windows is Windows Defender (which replaced its predecessor, Microsoft Security Essentials).

Also note that another free tool from Microsoft is the Malicious Software Removal Tool (MSRT), which helps remove any infection found but is not intended to be a full antimalware suite. An updated version of this tool is released on the second Tuesday of each month, and once installed, it is included, by default, in Microsoft Update and Windows Update.

Web Application Firewall vs. Network Firewall

A *web application firewall (WAF)* is a real-time appliance that applies a set of rules to block traffic to and from web servers and to try to prevent attacks. The rules of blocking can be customized, and WAFs are gaining popularity along with the movement to put everything on the cloud. Among the main threats that a WAF is trying to protect against are cross-site scripting (XSS), injection attacks (such as those using SQL), and forged HTTP requests.

Operating at the highest level of the OSI model, WAFs can not only detect known problems but react to suspected problems as well—making them similar to, though superior than, intrusion protection systems. A traditional network firewall differs from a WAF in terms of the focus of the latter on web-based servers and services and the degree of rule-based logic applied.

Application-Aware Devices

An *application-aware device* is one that has the ability to respond to network traffic based on what is there. Often, such devices combine SNMP and quality of service to be able to prioritize traffic based on the importance and value of the content. This functionality can be added to such devices as a firewall, IPSs, IDSs, and proxies.

VPNs and VPN Concentrators

A *virtual private network (VPN)* is a private network connection that occurs through a public network. A private network provides security over an otherwise unsecure environment. VPNs can be used to connect LANs together across the Internet or other public networks (*site-to-site*) or be used on a much smaller scale to offer security to remote users (known as *remote access* or *host-to-site*).

With a VPN, the remote end appears to be connected to the network as if it were connected locally. A VPN requires either special hardware to be installed or a VPN software package running on servers and workstations.

VPNs typically use a tunneling protocol, such as Layer 2 Tunneling Protocol, IPSec, or Point-to-Point Tunneling Protocol (PPTP). Figure 3.2 shows a remote network connected to a LAN using the Internet and a VPN. This connection appears to be a local connection, and all message traffic and protocols are available across the VPN.

FIGURE 3.2   Two LANs connected using a VPN across the Internet

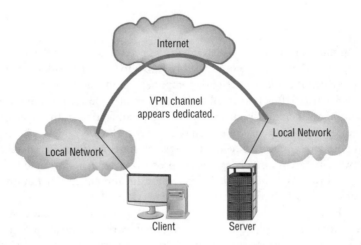

VPNs are becoming the connection of choice when establishing an extranet or intranet between two or more remote offices. The major security concern when using a VPN is encryption. PPTP offers some encryption capabilities, although they're weak. IPSec offers higher security, and it's becoming the encryption system used in many secure VPN environments.

Even though a VPN is created through the Internet or other public network, the connection logically appears to be part of the local network. This is why a VPN connection that is used to establish a connection between two private networks across the Internet is considered a private connection, or an extranet.

As mentioned earlier, VPNs are used to make connections between private networks across a public network, such as the Internet. These connections aren't guaranteed to be secure unless a tunneling protocol (such as PPTP) and an encryption system (such as IPSec) are used. A wide range of options, including proprietary technologies, is available for VPN support. Many of the large ISPs and data communications providers offer dedicated hardware with VPN capabilities. Many servers also provide software VPN capabilities for use between two networks.

VPN systems can be dedicated to a certain protocol, or they can pass whatever protocols they see on one end of the network to the other end. A pure VPN connection appears as a dedicated wired connection between the two network ends.

A *VPN concentrator* is a hardware device used to create remote access VPNs. The concentrator creates encrypted tunnel sessions between hosts, and many use two-factor authentication for additional security. Cisco models often incorporate Scalable Encryption Processing (SEP) modules to allow for hardware-based encryption and/or redundancy.

For purposes of the exam, whenever you see VPN, associate it with encryption and that it is intended to increase security and only allows authorized users.

IPSec

There is a fair amount of overlap between what you need to know for the new version of the Security+ exam and what you would need to know for the Network+ exam. This is particularly true when it comes to network components and technologies—key of which is IPSec. The IP Security (IPsec) protocol is designed to provide secure communications between systems. This includes system-to-system communication in the same network, as well as communication to systems on external networks. IPsec is an IP layer security protocol that can both encrypt and authenticate network transmissions. In a nutshell, IPsec is composed of two separate (mutually exclusive) protocols: *Authentication Header (AH)* and *Encapsulating Security Payload (ESP)*. AH provides the authentication and integrity checking for data packets, and ESP provides encryption services.

Using both AH or ESP, data traveling between systems can be secured, ensuring that transmissions cannot be viewed, accessed, or modified by those who should not have access to them. It might seem that protection on an internal network is less necessary than on an external network; however, much of the data you send across networks has little or no protection, allowing unwanted eyes to see it.

IPsec provides three key security services: data verification (verifying that the data received is from the intended source), protection from data tampering (ensuring that the data has not been tampered with or changed between the sending and receiving devices), and private transactions (ensuring that the data sent between the sending and receiving devices is unreadable by any other devices).

IPsec operates at the network layer of the Open Systems Interconnection (OSI) reference model and provides security for protocols that operate at the higher layers. Thus, by using IPsec, you can secure practically all TCP/IP-related communications.

IPSec can work in either *Tunneling mode* or *Transport mode*. In Tunneling mode, the data or payload and message headers are encrypted. Transport mode encrypts only the payload.

Split and Full Tunneling

The scope of a VPN *tunnel* can vary based on what you route and encrypt through it. The two most common scopes are a *full tunnel* and a *split tunnel*. With a full tunnel configuration, all requests are routed and encrypted through the VPN, whereas with a split tunnel, only some (usually all incoming requests) are routed and encrypted over the VPN.

It is not uncommon for an organization to have both types of connections available. A college campus, for example, might use a split tunnel to encrypt all web mail and not encrypt traffic for Amazon, Facebook, and so on. That same campus would use a full tunnel to require traffic from a remote site to reach the Internet.

In all situations, a full tunnel is the most secure but a split tunnel is implemented when there are constraints (such as bandwidth).

TLS

TLS (Transport Layer Security) is not only an enhancement to SSL (which was first created for use with the Netscape web browser), but also a replacement for it. Because of this, TLS is popular with VPNs (as well as VoIP applications) and "SSL" is often the term used to signify confidentiality whether it is actually SSL in use or TLS. For example, an SSL VPN, also marketed as WebVPN and OpenVPN, can be used to connect locations that would run into trouble with firewalls and NAT when used with IPSec. It is known as an SSL VPN whether the encryption is done with SSL or TLS.

Always-on VPN

A traditional VPN can be thought of as a rather passive entity: sitting and waiting for someone to use it. In the case of a remote user, they must choose it, use extra passwords to connect to it, and so on. To keep up with the times, this type of implementation is being replaced, due to technologies such as the SSL VPN, with *always-on VPNs*. As the name implies, an always-on VPN is one on which the user is already authenticated and able to use as needed. They are popular with mobile devices where persistent connections are common and thus are sometimes alternatively referred to as *mobile VPNs*.

Intrusion Detection Systems

An *intrusion detection system (IDS)* is software that runs either on individual workstations or on network devices to monitor and track network activity. By using an IDS, a network administrator can configure the system to respond just like a burglar alarm. IDSs can be configured to evaluate system logs, look at suspicious network activity, and disconnect sessions that appear to violate security settings.

Many vendors have oversold the simplicity of these tools. They're quite involved and require a great deal of planning and maintenance to work effectively. Many manufacturers are selling IDSs with firewalls, and this area shows great promise. Firewalls by themselves will prevent many common attacks, but they don't usually have the intelligence or the reporting capabilities to monitor the entire network. In conjunction with a firewall, an IDS allows both a reactive posture with the firewall and a preventive posture with the IDS.

Figure 3.3 shows an IDS working in conjunction with a firewall to increase security.

FIGURE 3.3   An IDS and a firewall working together to secure a network

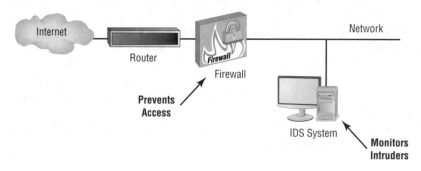

The issue is the description of what the IDS does in the event of a penetration. IDS only detects and reports on compromises and penetrations; an IPS acts on compromises and penetrations.

Understanding Intrusion Detection Systems

In the original *Walking Tall* movies, the sheriff puts small strips of clear tape on the hood of his car. Before getting in the vehicle, he would check the difficult-to-detect tape to see if it was torn. If it was, it tipped him off that someone had been messing beneath the hood and that saved his life. Do you have clear tape on your network?

IDSs are becoming integral parts of network monitoring. *Intrusion detection (ID)* is the process of monitoring events in a system or network to determine if an intrusion is occurring. An *intrusion* is defined as any activity or action that attempts to undermine or compromise the confidentiality, integrity, or availability of resources. Firewalls, as you may recall, were designed to prevent access to resources by an attacker. An IDS reports and monitors intrusion attempts.

Know the Resources Available in Linux

Security information is readily found at a number of Linux-related sites. The first to check is always the distribution vendor's site. Its pages usually provide an overview of Linux-related security issues with links to other relevant pages. You should also keep abreast of issues and problems posted at www.cert.org and www.linuxsecurity.com.

You can also find information on any Linux command through a number of utilities in Linux:

- The man tool offers pages on each utility. For example, to find information about the setfacl tool, you can type **man setfacl**. It is a manual of commands and information.

- Most utilities have the built-in option of --help to offer information. From the command line, you can type **setfacl --help** to see a quick list of available options.

- The info utility shows the man pages as well.

- The whatis utility can show if there is more than one set of documentation on the system for the utility.

- The whereis utility lists all the information it can find about locations associated with a file.

- The apropos utility uses the whatis database to find values and returns the short summary information.

It should be understood that every network, regardless of size, should use a firewall. On a home-based network, a personal software firewall can be implemented to provide protection against attacks.

Several key terms are necessary to explain the technology behind intrusion detection:

Activity   An *activity* is an element of a data source that is of interest to the operator. This could include a specific occurrence of a type of activity that is suspicious. An example might be a TCP connection request that occurs repeatedly from the same IP address.

Administrator   The *administrator* is the person responsible for setting the security policy for an organization and is responsible for making decisions about the deployment and configuration of the IDS. The administrator should make decisions regarding alarm levels, historical logging, and session-monitoring capabilities. They're also responsible for determining the appropriate responses to attacks and ensuring that those responses are carried out.

Most organizations have an escalation chart. The administrator is rarely at the top of the chart but is always expected to be the one doing the most to keep incidents under control.

Alert   An *alert* is a message from the analyzer indicating that an event of interest has occurred. The alert contains information about the activity as well as specifics of the occurrence. An alert may be generated when an excessive amount of *Internet Control Message Protocol (ICMP)* traffic is occurring or when repeated logon attempts are failing. A certain level of traffic is normal for a network. Alerts occur when activities of a certain type exceed a preset threshold. For instance, you might want to generate an alert every time someone from inside your network pings the outside using the Ping program.

Analyzer   The *analyzer* is the component or process that analyzes the data collected by the sensor. It looks for suspicious activity among all the data collected. Analyzers work by monitoring events and determining whether unusual activities are occurring, or they can use a rule-based process that is established when the IDS is configured.

Data Source   The *data source* is the raw information that the IDS or IPS uses to detect suspicious activity. The data source may include audit files, system logs, or the network traffic as it occurs.

Event   An *event* is an occurrence—or continuous occurrence—in a data source that indicates that a suspicious activity has occurred (once it's been analyzed and shown to be security related, then it becomes known as an *incident*). It may generate an alert. Events are logged for future reference. They also typically trigger a notification that something unusual may be happening in the network. An IDS might begin logging events if the volume of inbound email connections suddenly spiked; this event might be an indication that someone was probing your network. The event might trigger an alert if a deviation from normal network traffic patterns occurred or if an activity threshold was crossed.

Manager   The *manager* is the component or process the operator uses to manage the IDS or IPS. The IDS/IPS console is a manager. Configuration changes in the IDS/IPS are made by communicating with the IDS manager.

Notification   *Notification* is the process or method by which the IDS/IPS manager makes the operator aware of an alert. This might include a graphic display highlighting the traffic or an email sent to the network's administrative staff.

Operator   The *operator* is the person primarily responsible for the IDS/IPS. The operator can be a user, administrator, and so on, as long as they're the primary person responsible.

Sensor   A *sensor* is the IDS component that collects data from the data source and passes it to the analyzer for analysis. A sensor can be a device driver on a system, or it can be an actual black box that is connected to the network and reports to the IDS/IPS. The important thing to remember is that the sensor is a primary data collection point for the IDS/IPS.

The IDS/IPS, as you can see, has many different components and processes that work together to provide a real-time picture of your network traffic. Figure 3.4 shows the various components and processes working together to provide an IDS. Remember that data can come from many different sources and must be analyzed to determine what's occurring. An IDS isn't intended as a true traffic-blocking device, though some IDSs can also perform this function; it's intended to be a traffic-auditing device.

IDSs use four primary approaches:

Behavior-Based Detection   A *behavior-based system* looks for variations in behavior such as unusually high traffic, policy violations, and so on. By looking for deviations in behavior, it is able to recognize potential threats and to respond quickly to them.

Signature-Based Detection   A *signature-based system*, also commonly known as *misuse-detection IDS (MD-IDS)*, is primarily focused on evaluating attacks based on attack signatures and audit trails. Attack signatures describe a generally established method of attacking a system. For example, a TCP flood attack begins with a large number of incomplete TCP sessions. If the MD-IDS knows what a TCP flood attack looks like, it can make an appropriate report or response to thwart the attack.

FIGURE 3.4   The components of an IDS working together to provide network monitoring

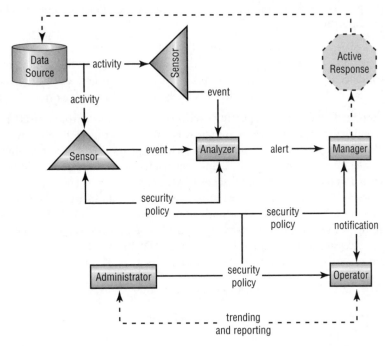

Figure 3.5 illustrates a signature-based detection system in action. Notice that this system uses an extensive database to determine the signature of the traffic. This process resembles an antivirus software process.

FIGURE 3.5   A signature-based detection system in action

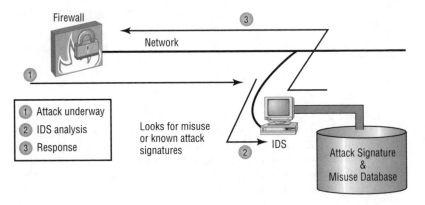

Anomaly Detection   An *anomaly-detection (AD)* system looks for anomalies, meaning it looks for things outside of the ordinary. Typically, a training program learns what the normal operation is and then spots deviations from it. An AD-based system can establish

the baseline either by being manually assigned values or through automated processes that look at traffic patterns. One method is *behavior based*, which looks for unusual behavior and then acts accordingly.

Heuristic   A *heuristic system* uses algorithms to analyze the traffic passing through the network. As a general rule, heuristic systems require more tweaking and fine-tuning than the other types of detection systems to prevent false positives in your network. If the system is working with incomplete information, this it is likely to trigger far more often than it should.

IDSs are primarily focused on reporting events or network traffic that deviate from historical work activity or network traffic patterns. For this reporting to be effective, administrators should develop a baseline or history of typical network traffic. This baseline activity provides a stable, long-term perspective on network activity. An example might be a report generated when a higher-than-normal level of ICMP responses is received in a specified time period. Such activity may indicate the beginning of an ICMP flood attack. The system may also report when a user who doesn't normally access the network using a VPN suddenly requests administrative access to the system. Figure 3.6 demonstrates an AD-IDS tracking and reporting excessive traffic in a network. The AD-IDS process frequently uses artificial intelligence or expert system technologies to learn about normal traffic for a network.

FIGURE 3.6   AD-IDS using expert system technology to evaluate risks

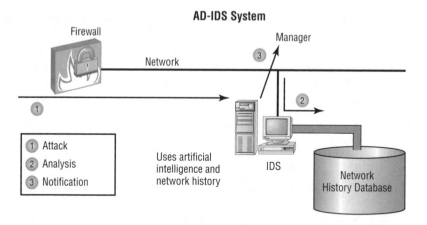

Whenever an attack takes place, there is almost always something created that identifies it—an entry in the login report, an error in a log, and so on. These items (frequently called *indicators of compromise*) represent intrusion signatures, and you can learn from them and instruct an IDS to watch for and prevent repeat performances.

MD-IDS and AD-IDS are merging in most commercial systems. They provide the best opportunity to detect and thwart attacks and unauthorized access. Unlike a firewall, the IDS exists to detect and report unusual occurrences in a network, not to block them.

The next sections discuss network-based and host-based implementations of IDS and the capabilities they provide.

IDS vs. IPS

Although IDSs have been popular for a long time, *intrusion prevention systems (IPSs)* have become prevalent in the past few years. Since the IPS is active and working in real time, it is said to be an *inline* device as opposed to a *passive* one (an evolutionary change from an IDS).

If the monitoring of devices is done remotely, this is known as *out-of-band* management; otherwise, it is known as *in-band* management. For the exam, associate in-band management with local management (the most common method) and out-of-band management with remote monitoring.

 NOTE   What is now called an IPS was formerly known as an active IDS.

This type of system is an IDS that reacts to the intrusion that has been detected, most often by blocking communication from the offending IP address. The problem with this approach is the issue of false positives. No system is perfect—at some point you will have a situation where network activity is anomalous and the IDS indicates an intrusion, but in reality, it is not an intrusion at all. For example, if the IDS is set up to react to traffic outside normal bounds, excessive traffic from a given system could indicate an attack. However, it could also indicate an unusually high workload.

Working with a Network-Based IDS

A *network-based IDS (NIDS)* approach to IDS attaches the system to a point in the network where it can monitor and report on all network traffic. This can be in front of or behind the firewall, as shown in Figure 3.7.

FIGURE 3.7   NIDS placement in a network determines what data will be analyzed.

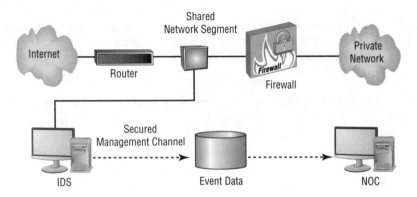

> The best solution for creating a secure network is to place an IDS in front of and behind the firewall. This dual-security approach provides as much defense as possible.

Placing the NIDS in front of the firewall enables the monitoring of all traffic going into the network and can give you data on the attacks that your firewall is blocking. This approach allows a huge amount of data to be processed, and it lets you see all the traffic coming into the network. Putting the NIDS behind the firewall only allows you to see the traffic that penetrates the firewall. Although this approach reduces the amount of data processed, it doesn't let you see all of the attacks that might be developing.

The NIDS can be attached to a switch or a hub, or it can be attached to a tap. Many hubs and switches provide a monitoring port for troubleshooting and diagnostic purposes. This port may function in a manner similar to a tap. The advantage of the tap approach is that the IDS is the only device that will be using the tap. Figure 3.8 illustrates a connection to the network using a hub or tap.

FIGURE 3.8 A hub being used to attach the NIDS to the network

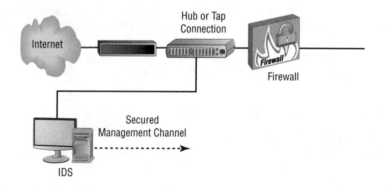

> *Port spanning*, also known as *port mirroring*, copies the traffic from all ports to a single port and disallows bidirectional traffic on that port. Cisco's Switched Port Analyzer (SPAN) is one example of a port-spanning implementation.

In either case, the IDS monitors and evaluates all the traffic to which it has access.

Two basic types of responses can be formulated at the network level: passive and active. They're briefly explained in the following sections.

Real World Scenario

Working with Network Audit Files

You're the network administrator of a relatively busy network. Your company has gone through a couple of cutbacks, and your staffing is limited. You want to make sure that your network stays as secure as you can make it. What can you do to ease your workload?

You have three possibilities. There are two that you should consider to protect your network: Either install an IDS or reduce the logging levels of your network audit files. An alternative is to install an audit log-collection system with filtering.

You might be able to reduce the amount of logged traffic in your audit files by changing the settings that determine what you audit. However, changing audit rules would prevent you from seeing what's happening on your network because most events wouldn't be logged.

Installing an IDS would allow you to establish rules that would provide a higher level of automation than you could achieve by reviewing audit files. Your best solution might be to convince your company to invest in an IDS. An IDS could send you an email or alert you when an event is detected.

Implementing a Passive Response

A *passive response* is the simplest type of response to an intrusion. In general, passive responses are the easiest to develop and implement. The following list includes some passive response strategies:

Logging *Logging* involves recording that an event has occurred and under what circumstances. Logging functions should provide sufficient information about the nature of the attack to help administrators determine what has happened and to assist in evaluating the threat. This information can then be used to devise methods to counter the threat.

Notification *Notification* communicates event-related information to the appropriate personnel when an event has occurred. This includes relaying any relevant data about the event to help evaluate the situation. If the IDS is manned full time, messages can be displayed on the manager's console to indicate that the situation is occurring.

Shunning *Shunning*, or ignoring an attack, is a common response even though it is a violation of every security policy. This might be the case if your IDS notices an Internet Information Services (IIS) attack occurring on a system that's running another web-hosting service, such as Apache. The attack won't work because Apache doesn't respond in the same way as IIS, so why pay attention to it? In a busy network, many different types of attacks can occur simultaneously. If you aren't worried about an attack succeeding, why waste energy or time investigating it or notifying someone about it? The IDS can make a note of it in a log and move on to other more pressing business.

The difference between a passive response and an active response is much like the difference between a security guard and a security camera. All a security camera can do is record what occurs; it cannot react to any incident. A security guard can take action. This is the same with IDSs. A passive IDS simply records what occurs; an active IDS—or IPS—takes action.

Implementing an Active Response

An *active response* involves taking an action based on an attack or threat. The goal of an active response is to take the quickest action possible to reduce an event's potential impact. This type of response requires plans for how to deal with an event, clear/understandable policies, and intelligence in the IPS in order to be successful. An active response will include one of the reactions briefly described here:

Terminating Processes or Sessions If a flood attack is detected, the IPS can cause the subsystem, such as TCP, to force resets to all of the sessions that are under way. Doing so frees up resources and allows TCP to continue to operate normally. Of course, all valid TCP sessions are closed and will need to be reestablished—but at least this will be possible, and it may have little effect on end users. The IPS evaluates the events and determines the best way to handle them. Figure 3.9 illustrates TCP being directed to issue RST commands from the IPS to reset all open connections to TCP. This type of mechanism can also terminate user sessions or stop and restart any process that appears to be operating abnormally.

FIGURE 3.9 An IPS instructing TCP to reset all connections

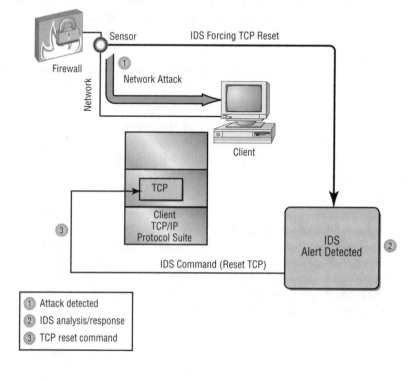

Network Configuration Changes If a certain IP address is found to be causing repeated attacks on the network, the IPS can instruct a border router or firewall to reject any requests or traffic from that address. This configuration change can remain in effect permanently or for a specified period. Figure 3.10 illustrates the IPS instructing the firewall to close port 80 for 60 seconds to terminate an IIS attack.

FIGURE 3.10 An IPS instructing the firewall to close port 80 for 60 seconds to thwart an IIS attack

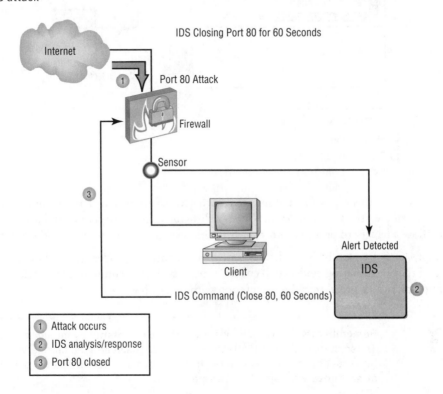

If the IPS determines that a particular socket or port is being attacked, it can instruct the firewall to block that port for a specified amount of time. Doing so effectively eliminates the attack, but it may also inadvertently cause a self-imposed DoS situation to occur by eliminating legitimate traffic. This is especially true for port 80 (HTTP or web) traffic.

Deception A *deception active response* fools the attacker into thinking that the attack is succeeding while the system monitors the activity and potentially redirects the attacker to a system that is designed to be broken. This allows the operator or administrator to gather data about how the attack is unfolding and the techniques being used in the attack. This process is referred to as *sending them to the honeypot*. Figure 3.11 illustrates a honeypot (a decoy system intended to lure in an attacker) where a deception has been successful.

FIGURE 3.11   A network honeypot deceives an attacker and gathers intelligence.

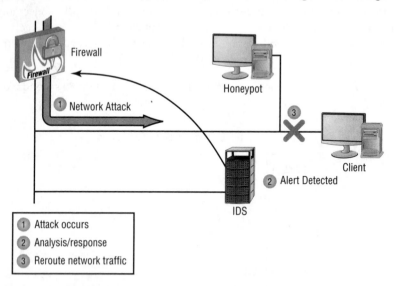

The advantage of this type of response is that all activities are watched and recorded for analysis when the attack is completed. This is a difficult scenario to set up, and it's dangerous to allow a hacker to proceed into your network, even if you're monitoring the events.

This approach is frequently used when an active investigation is under way by law enforcement and they're gathering evidence to ensure a successful prosecution of the attacker. Deception allows you to gather documentation without risking live data.

Remember that active responses are the least commonly implemented. Those that are the most effective are the costliest and the hardest to put into practice, not to mention the trouble you can get into following a "we-attack-those-who-attack-us" strategy.

More common than attacking the attacker is an active response that is non-retaliatory in nature: having the IPS drop the connection.

Working with a Host-Based IDS

A *host-based IDS (HIDS)* is designed to run as software on a host computer system. These systems typically run as a service or as a background process. An HIDS examines the machine logs, system events, and applications interactions; it normally doesn't monitor incoming network traffic to the host. An HIDS is popular on servers that use encrypted channels or channels to other servers.

Figure 3.12 illustrates an HIDS installed on a server. Notice that the HIDS interacts with the logon audit and kernel audit files. The kernel audit files are used for process and application interfaces.

FIGURE 3.12   A host-based IDS interacting with the operating system

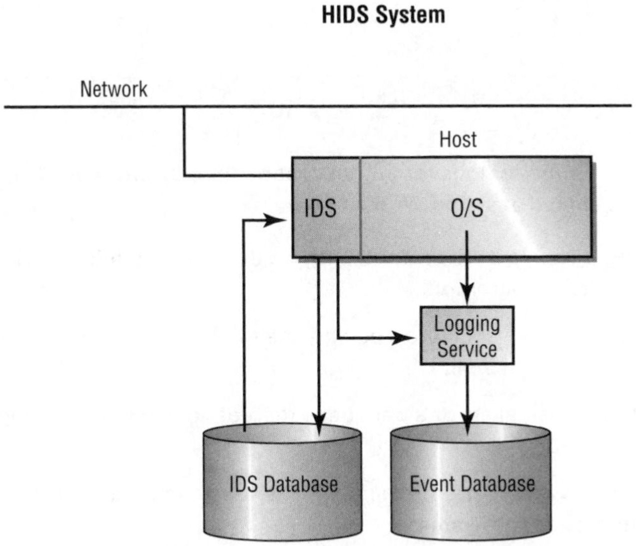

HIDS System

Two major problems with an HIDS aren't easily overcome. The first problem involves a compromise of the system. If the system is compromised, the log files to which the IDS reports may become corrupt or inaccurate. This may make fault determination difficult, or it may make the system unreliable. The second major problem with an HIDS is that it must be deployed on each system that needs it. This can create a headache for administrative and support staff.

One of the major benefits of an HIDS is the potential to keep checksums on files. These checksums can be used to inform system administrators that files have been altered by an attack. Recovery is simplified because it's easier to determine where tampering has occurred. The other advantage is that an HIDS can read memory when an NIDS cannot.

Working with NIPSs

As opposed to NIDSs, *network intrusion prevention systems (NIPSs)* focus on *prevention*. These systems focus on signature matches and then take a course of action. For example, if it appears as though an attack might be under way, packets can be dropped, ignored, and so forth. To do this, the NIPS must be able to *detect* the attack occurring, and thus it can be argued that NIPS is a subset of NIDS.

The line continues to blur between technologies. For example, NIST now refers to these systems as intrusion detection and prevention systems (IDPSs). Though it is important to stay current with the terminology in the real world, know that the exam often wants you to be familiar with older terminology for the questions that you will face on it.

Log Files in Linux

You should check a number of logs for entries that might indicate an intrusion. The primary ones that you should examine are listed here:

/var/log/faillog   Open a shell prompt, and use the `faillog` utility to view a list of users' failed authentication attempts.

/var/log/lastlog   Open a shell prompt, and use the `lastlog` utility to view a list of all users and when they last logged in.

/var/log/messages   Use grep, or a derivative thereof, to find login-related entries in this file.

/var/log/wtmp   Open a shell prompt, and use the `last` command to view a list of users who have authenticated to the system.

Router

The primary instrument used for connectivity between two or more networks is the *router*. Routers work by providing a path between the networks. A router has two connections that are used to join the networks. Each connection has its own address (or more) and appears as a valid address in its respective network. Figure 3.13 illustrates a router connected between two LANs.

FIGURE 3.13   Router connecting two LANs

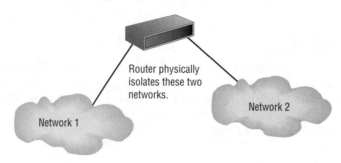

Router physically isolates these two networks.

Network 1

Network 2

Routers are intelligent devices, and they store information about the networks to which they're connected. Most routers can be configured to operate as packet-filtering firewalls and use *access control lists (ACLs)*. Many of the newer routers also provide advanced firewall functions. Many attacks use source IP address spoofing to conceal the true source of an attack. Software programs utilizing an ACL in order to deter attacks that rely on source IP address spoofing are known as *antispoofing* protections. Antispoofing protections work by performing switch port, MAC address, and/or source address verification.

Routers, in conjunction with a channel service unit/data service unit (CSU/DSU), are also used to translate from LAN framing to WAN framing (for example, a router that connects a 100BaseT network to a T1 network). This is needed because the network protocols are different in LANs and WANs. Such routers are referred to as *border routers*. They serve as the outside connection of a LAN to a WAN, and they operate at the border of your network. Like the border patrols of many countries, border routers decide who can come in and under what conditions.

Dividing internal networks into two or more subnetworks is a common use for routers. Routers can also be connected internally to other routers, effectively creating *zones* that operate autonomously. Figure 3.14 illustrates a corporate network that uses a combination of a border router for connection to an ISP and internal routers to create autonomous networks for communications. This type of connection keeps local network traffic off the backbone of the corporate network, and it provides additional security to internal users.

FIGURE 3.14   A corporate network implementing routers for segmentation and security

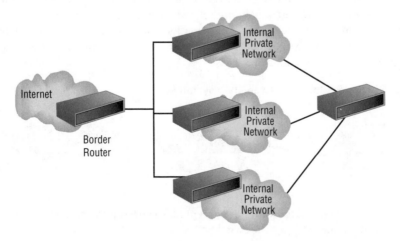

Because broadcasts don't traverse routers, network segmentation decreases traffic.

Routers establish communication by maintaining tables about destinations and local connections. A router contains information about the systems connected to it and where to send requests if the destination isn't known. These tables grow as connections are made through the router.

Routers usually communicate routing and other information using one of three standard protocols: Routing Information Protocol (RIP), Border Gateway Protocol (BGP), or Open Shortest Path First (OSPF). Routing can occur interior to the network or exterior.

Routers are your first line of defense, and they must be configured to pass only traffic that is authorized by network administrators. In effect, a router can function as a firewall if it's configured properly. The best approach is layered; a router shouldn't take the place of a firewall but simply augment it.

The routes themselves can be configured as static or dynamic. If they are static, they are edited manually and stay that way until changed. If they are dynamic, they learn of other routers around them and use information about those routers to build their routing tables.

Switch

A *switch* is a multiport device that improves network efficiency. A switch typically contains a small amount of information about systems in a network—a table of MAC addresses (Media Access Control, or unique physical addresses for each controller) as opposed to IP addresses. Using switches improves network efficiency over hubs or routers because of the virtual circuit capability. Switches also improve network security because the virtual circuits are more difficult to examine with network monitors. You can think of a switch as a device that has some of the best capabilities of routers and hubs combined.

The switch maintains limited routing information about nodes in the internal network, and it allows connections to systems like a hub or router. Figure 3.15 shows a switch in action between two workstations in a LAN.

FIGURE 3.15   Switching between two systems

The connection isn't usually secure or encrypted; the need for that, however, is diminished since the data doesn't leave the switched area.

For the exam, know that switches are used internally because the switching they do is based on MAC addresses that are not routable. Routers, on the other hand, route based on IP address.

A switch can work at either Layer 2 (the data link layer) or Layer 3 (the network layer) of the OSI model. A multilayer switch is one that can operate at both Layer 2 and Layer 3 of the OSI model, which means that the multilayer device can operate as both a switch and a router. Also called a Layer 3 switch, the multilayer switch is a high-performance device that actually supports the same routing protocols as routers. It is a regular switch directing traffic within the LAN. In addition, it can forward packets between subnets.

Loops can occur when more than one bridge or switch is implemented on the network. In this scenario, the devices can confuse each other by leading one another to believe that a host is located on a certain segment when it is not. To combat the *loop* problem, technologies such as the Spanning Tree Protocol (STP) enable bridge/switch interfaces to be assigned a value that is then used to control the learning process and prevent loops. Since switches can be subject to DoS attacks, *flood guards* are used to look for and prevent malicious traffic from bringing the switch to a halt.

Switch ports can represent quite a weakness and *port security* is crucial. Be sure to secure switches, disable unused ports, and be on the lookout or aware of the following: DHCP snooping, ARP inspection, MAC address filtering, and VLAN assignments (as related to network segmentation). Securing switches, disabling unused ports, and using commonsense solutions can go far in improving network security.

Proxy

A *proxy* is any device that acts on behalf of other(s). This can be to access the web, a database, or almost anything else serving a single *application* of *multiple purposes*. In the interest of security, all internal user interaction with the Internet should be controlled through a *proxy server*. The proxy server should automatically block known malicious sites. The proxy server should cache often-accessed sites to improve performance.

Most proxies act as a *forward proxy* and are used to retrieve data on behalf of the clients they serve. If the proxy server is accessible by any user on the Internet, then it is said to be an "open" proxy server. A variation is the *reverse proxy*, also known as a "surrogate." This is an internal-facing server used as a front-end to control (and protect) access to a server on a private network. The reverse scenario is used for tasks like load-balancing, authentication, decryption, and caching. Responses from the proxy server are returned as if they came directly from the original server, so the client has no knowledge of the original servers.

With most proxies being located between the client and the Internet, they are referred to as being a *transparent proxy* (also known as an intercepting proxy, inline proxy, or forced proxy). RFC 2616 defines transparency as "a proxy that does not modify the request or response beyond what is required for proxy authentication and identification." In other words, clients need not be aware of the existence of the proxy. The opposite of this would be a "nontransparent proxy"—that is, one that "modifies the request or response in order to provide some added service to the user agent, such as group annotation services, media type transformation, protocol reduction, or anonymity filtering."

Load Balancer

Load balancing refers to shifting a load from one device to another. Most often the device in question is a server, but the term could be used for a hard drive, a CPU, or almost any device that you want to avoid overloading. Using a server as the device in question, balancing the load between multiple servers instead of relying on only one reduces the response time, maximizes throughput and allows better allocation of resources.

A *load balancer* can be implemented as a software or hardware solution, and it is usually associated with a device—a router, a firewall, Network Address Translation (NAT) appliance, and so on. In its most common implementation, a load balancer splits the traffic intended for a website into individual requests that are then rotated to redundant servers as they become available. (If a server that should be available is busy or down, it is taken out of the rotation.)

Scheduling is a key issue with load balancing: determining how to split up the work and distribute it across servers. Two methods of approaching this are round-robin and affinity. *Round-robin* load balancing is incredibly simple: the first client request is sent to the first group of servers, the second is sent to the second, and so on. When the end of the list is reached, the load balancer loops back and goes down the list again. Conversely, with *affinity* balancing, like services are sent to like servers.

Active-active configuration means that more than one load balancing server is working at all times to handle the load/requests as they come in. An alternative to this is *active-passive* in which case there is one primary server and the secondary one is in listening mode—able to activate and start splitting the load when needed if the first server becomes overwhelmed.

Lastly, you can use *virtual IP (VIP)* to achieve load balancing across multiple interfaces for both inbound and outbound workloads. An advantage of this workload balancing method is that it provides more flexibility than the DNS-based load balancing methods. The disadvantage of this method is that it is really a connection-based solution as opposed to a load-based solution (the load on each interface is not considered and the assumption is that the traffic load is similar for all connections). A VIP has an IP address, which must be publicly available to be usable (such as TCP port 80 for web traffic).

Access Point

While an *access point (AP)* can technically be used for either a wired or wireless connection, in reality the term is almost exclusively associated with a wireless-enabling device today. An AP works at Layer 2 (the data link layer) of the OSI model, and it can operate as a bridge connecting a standard wired network to wireless devices or as a router passing data transmissions from one access point to another. Wireless access points (APs) consist of a transmitter and receiver (transceiver) device used to create a wireless LAN (WLAN). APs typically are a separate network device with a built-in antenna, transmitter, and adapter. APs use the wireless infrastructure network mode to provide a connection point between WLANs and a wired Ethernet LAN. APs also typically have several ports, giving you a way to expand the network to support additional clients.

Depending on the size of the network, one or more APs might be required to provide coverage. Additional APs are used to allow access to more wireless clients and to expand the range of the wireless network. Each AP is limited by a transmission range—that is, the distance a client can be from an AP and still obtain a usable signal. The actual distance depends on the wireless standard used and the obstructions and environmental conditions between the client and the AP.

APs come in all different shapes and sizes. Many are cheaper and designed strictly for home or small-office use. Such APs have low-powered antennas and limited expansion ports. Higher-end APs used for commercial purposes have high-powered antennas, enabling them to extend how far the wireless signal can travel. Saying that an AP is used to extend a wired LAN to wireless clients doesn't give you the complete picture. A wireless AP today can provide different services in addition to just an access point. Today, the APs might provide many ports that can be used to easily increase the network's size. Systems can be added to and removed from the network with no effect on other systems on the network. Also, many APs provide firewall capabilities and Dynamic Host Configuration Protocol (DHCP) service. When they are hooked up, they give client systems a private IP address and then prevent Internet traffic from accessing those systems. So, in effect, the AP is a switch, DHCP server, router, and firewall.

To connect to a wireless AP, you need a service set identifier (*SSID*) name. 802.11 wireless networks use the SSID to identify all systems belonging to the same network, and client stations must be configured with the SSID to be authenticated to the AP. The AP might broadcast the SSID, allowing all wireless clients in the area to see the AP's SSID, but for security reasons, APs can be configured not to broadcast the SSID or to cloak it. This means that an administrator needs to give client systems the SSID instead of allowing it to be discovered automatically.

Wireless devices ship with default SSIDs, security settings, channels, passwords, and usernames. To protect yourself, it is strongly recommended that you change these default settings. Today, many Internet sites list the default settings used by manufacturers with their wireless devices. This information is used by people who want to gain unauthorized access to your wireless devices.

Authentication should be required for access to any network resource. *MAC filtering*, in which each host is identified by its MAC address and allowed (or denied) access based on that, can increase security dramatically. You should also consider the *signal strength* of the AP and make sure that you are not reaching beyond your network and allowing someone to connect who should not. If you are running into interference or other difficulties, consider the *band selection*: many access points allow you to choose which of the Wi-Fi bands you want to use and opt for the one that works best in your environment.

Real World Scenario

Estimating Signal Strength

One of the most troublesome aspects of working with wireless networks is trying to compute the strength of the signal between the wireless AP and the client(s). It is a common joke that a hacker can stand outside a building and tap into your network but a user within the building can't get a strong enough signal to stay on the network.

Think of a wireless signal in terms of any other radio signal—cinderblock walls, metal cabinets, and other barriers will significantly reduce its strength. However, the signal can pass through glass windows and thin walls with no difficulty.

When you're laying out a network, it's highly recommended that you install a strength meter on a workstation—many are free to download—and use it to evaluate the intensity of the signal you're receiving (perform what is known as a site survey). If the signal is weak, you can add additional APs and repeaters to the network, just as you would on a wired network.

Antenna placement can be crucial in allowing clients to reach the access point. There isn't a universal solution to this issue, and it depends on the environment in which the access point is placed. As a general rule, the greater the distance the signal must travel, the more it will attenuate, but you can lose a signal quickly over a short distance as well if the building materials reflect or absorb the signal. You should try to avoid placing access points near metal (which includes appliances) or near the ground. Placing them in the center of the area to be served and high enough to get around most obstacles is recommended. On the chance that the signal is actually traveling too far, some access points include *power level controls*, which allow you to reduce the amount of output provided.

Just as important as antenna placement is the type of antenna used. The default antenna on many (but not all) APs can be replaced to increase or decrease transmission range. The proper antenna can work around obstacles, minimize the effects of interference, increase signal strength, and focus the transmission (which can increase signal speed).

The antenna can be completely internal on an AP, or it can consist of one, two, or three external poles.

An *omnidirectional* antenna is designed to provide a 360-degree pattern and an even signal in all directions, so you usually want to locate the AP in the middle of the area to be covered. A *directional* antenna, on the other hand, forces the signal in one direction, and since it is focusing the signal, it can cover a greater distance with a stronger signal.

All antennas are rated in terms of *gain value*, which is expressed in dBi numbers. A wireless antenna advertised with a 20 dBi would be 20 times stronger than the base of 0 dBi. As a general rule, every 3 dB added to an antenna effectively doubles the power output.

Access points can be said to be *fat* or *thin* and *controller-based* or *stand-alone*. Fat APs, sometimes still referred to as autonomous APs, need to be manually configured with network and security settings. Then they are essentially left alone to serve clients until they can no longer function. Thin APs are an evolutionary change to fat ones and allow for configuration remotely using a controller (typically rack mounted). Since thin clients do not need to be manually configured, they can be easily reconfigured—and monitored—on the fly. Stand-alone access points are also known as thick access points (as opposed to thin) and do not require a controller whereas controller-based access points use that controller for centralized management, updates, policy settings, and a variety of other functions.

 As a general rule, stand-alone access points are often used in small deployments, and controller-based/thin access points are used in large deployments.

SIEM

Combining security information management (SIM) with security event management (SEM) creates one of the newest acronyms in the field: *security information and event management (SIEM)*. SIEM products provide real-time analysis of security alerts that are flagged by network appliances and software applications (*aggregation*). A number of vendors sell all-in-one SIEM as managed services (as opposed to software-only or appliance-based solutions).

Not only do SIEM solutions aggregate and *correlate* the events that come in, but they can perform *time synchronization* as well and *event deduplication*: removing multiple reports on the same instance and then act based on *automated alert and trigger* criteria. Long-term storage of log files is built into many implementations as well as write-once-read-many (*WORM*) protection: information, once written, cannot be modified, thus assuring that the data cannot be tampered with once it is written to the device.

DLP

Data loss prevention (DLP) systems monitor the contents of systems (workstations, servers, and networks) to make sure that key content is not deleted or removed. One way to do this is to *block USB* and other interfaces. DLP systems also monitor who is using the data (looking for unauthorized access) and transmitting the data. DLP systems share commonality with network intrusion prevention systems. This monitoring can be *cloud based* and limited to specific applications (such as email).

One of the best-known DLP systems is MyDLP, an open source solution that runs on most Windows platforms. You can find MyDLP at www.mydlp.org. A large number of commercial programs are available for purchase. RSA is another popular DLP product, and there are others available from McAfee, Palisade Systems, and Global Velocity.

Tripwire is a great system for data protection. Tripwire monitors specific files to see if they have changed. If they have, the Tripwire system can either restore them or simply alert an administrator. Both a commercial and an open source version of Tripwire are available.

Network Access Control (NAC)

Operational security issues include *network access control (NAC)*; authentication, and security topologies after the network installation is complete. Issues include the daily operations of the network, connections to other networks, backup plans, and recovery plans. In short, operational security encompasses everything that isn't related to design or physical security in your network. Instead of focusing on the physical components where the data is stored, such as the server, the focus is now on the topology and connections.

Some vendors use the acronym NAC to signify network *admission* control rather than the more commonly accepted network *access* control.

The best way to think of NAC is as a set of standards defined by the network for clients attempting to access it so that only known devices meeting specified requirements can connect. Usually, NAC requires that clients be virus free and be assigned to trusted users before allowing them on the network.

The device that is attempting to connect to the network must have something (usually an *agent*) running on it to verify the device, whether or not it is running up-to-date virus software, and perform any other *host health check* that the administrator wants to run. If that agent is always on that device, then it is said to be *permanent*, and this is usually the case when connecting with most company-issued devices. If that agent is installed only for that session, then it is said to be *dissolvable*, and this is often the case with browser-based sessions and users connecting from guest machines such as when traveling.

Equate dissolvable NAC software with disappearing from the device after reporting to the NAC.

Agents do not work with every device and every operating system (think of networked printers, for example), and for that reason there are *agentless* solutions. These devices must be known, defined, and trusted and are identified during network scans done by the NAC and allowed on the network.

Mail Gateway

A mail gateway can be used not only to route mail, but to perform other functions as well, such as *encryption* or, to a more limited scope, *DLP*. More commonly, *spam filters* can be added to catch unwanted email and filter it out before it gets delivered internally. The filtering is done based on established rules, such as blocking email coming from certain IP addresses, email that contains particular words in the subject line, and the like. Although spam filters are usually used to scan incoming messages, they can be used to scan outgoing messages as well and thus act as a quick identifier of internal PCs that may have contracted a virus.

It is estimated that over 90 percent of incoming email is spam. Apache SpamAssassin is one of the best-known open source spam filters. You can find more information about it here: http://spamassassin.apache.org/.

A number of vendors make all-in-one security devices that combine spam filters with firewalls, load balancers, and several other services.

Bridge

Bridges are used to divide larger networks into smaller sections by sitting between two physical network segments and managing the flow of data between the two. Bridges have mostly fallen out of favor in recent years and have been replaced by switches, which offer similar functionality and more. Also, switches are sometimes referred to as "multiport bridges" because of how they operate.

By looking at the MAC address of the devices connected to each segment, bridges can elect to forward the data (if they believe that the destination address is on another interface) or block it from crossing (if they can verify that it is on the interface from which it came). Bridges can also be used to connect two physical LANs into a larger logical LAN.

SSL/TLS Accelerators

From an earlier discussion, you may recall that SSL (Secure Sockets Layer) is the acronym commonly used, whether the technology in use is really SSL or its replacement TLS (Transport Layer Security). This is especially true with *SSL accelerators*, a term used for both SSL and TLS accelerators. Since encrypting data is very processor intensive, accelerators can be used to offload the public-key encryption to a hardware accelerator, which is a separate plug-in card (usually into a PCI slot).

SSL Decryptors

Another layer of security can be added to the network with an *SSL decryptor*. These gateways decrypt encrypted traffic (SSL or TLS), inspect it, and then re-encrypt it before sending it on to its destination. It is a processor-intensive process, but the advantage it offers is in the inspection step—making sure that you are not forwarding problems that did not get caught simply because the data was encrypted.

Media Gateway

One of the newest buzzwords is *web security gateway*, which can be thought of as a proxy server (performing proxy and caching functions) with web protection software built in. Depending on the vendor, the "web protection" can range from a standard virus scanner on incoming packets to monitoring outgoing user traffic for red flags as well.

Potential red flags that the gateway can detect and/or prohibit include inappropriate content, trying to establish a peer-to-peer connection with a file-sharing site, instant messaging, and unauthorized tunneling. You can configure most web security gateways to block known HTTP/HTML exploits, strip ActiveX tags, strip Java applets, and block/strip cookies.

Hardware Security Module

In addition to software-based encryption, hardware-based encryption can be applied. Within the advanced configuration settings on some BIOS configuration menus, for example, you can choose to enable or disable TPM. A *trusted platform module (TPM)* can be used to assist with hash key generation. TPM is the name assigned to a chip that can store cryptographic keys, passwords, or certificates. TPM can be used to protect smartphones and devices other than PCs as well. It can also be used to generate values used with whole disk encryption such as BitLocker, which will be discussed in more detail in Chapter 8, "Cryptography." BitLocker can be used with or without TPM. It is much more secure when coupled with TPM (preferable, in fact) but does not require it.

The TPM chip may be installed on the motherboard. When it is, in many cases it is set to off in the BIOS by default. In Exercise 3.1, you'll look for a TPM chip in Windows. Support for TPM is included with most versions of Windows, though that support is limited in some editions.

EXERCISE 3.1

Verifying the Presence of a TPM Chip in Windows

The following steps will allow you to verify whether a TPM chip is installed on your computer:

1. In Windows, open Control Panel and choose Security.

2. Under Security, choose BitLocker Drive Encryption.

3. A dialog box will appear. The contents of the box do not matter. What does matter is a link in the lower-left corner that reads TPM Administration. If the link is there, TPM is installed and active. If you don't see the link but are certain that your computer contains such a chip, you may need to boot into your BIOS Setup menu and enable TPM before trying this again.

More information on TPM can be found at the Trusted Computing Group's website: https://www.trustedcomputinggroup.org/.

In addition to TPM, *HSM (hardware security module)* is a cryptoprocessor that can be used to enhance security. HSM is commonly used with PKI systems to augment security with certification authorities (CAs). As opposed to being mounted on the motherboard like TPMs, HSMs are traditionally packaged as PCI adapters.

> There is an open source product called TrueCrypt (www.Truecrypt.org) that is free; that is available for Windows, Linux, or Macintosh; and that uses 256-bit AES encryption. TrueCrypt is an excellent choice for encrypting hard drives and partitions.

Summary

This chapter focused on the key elements of network infrastructure and some of the hardware components involved in networking. Your infrastructure is the backbone of your network and the key to all of its security capabilities.

Your total network infrastructure includes the hardware and software necessary to run your network. Proper configuration of these infrastructure components is the key to providing services in the way that your network needs them. If your network security devices are improperly configured, you may be worse off than if you didn't have them at all. It's a dangerous situation when you think that you're secure, but in reality, you are not.

Exam Essentials

Be able to describe the various components and the purpose of an infrastructure.   Your network's infrastructure is the backbone of your systems and network operations. The infrastructure includes all of the hardware, software, physical security, and operational security methods in place. Key components of your infrastructure include devices such as routers, firewalls, switches, and the other devices used in the network.

Know the difference between false positives and false negatives.   A false negative is any event that should be flagged but isn't. This is dangerous because it can lure you into a false sense of security. Conversely, a false positive is a flagged event that has been falsely triggered. The danger in it is that you spend a lot of time focused on the wrong things and trying to solve problems where there aren't any.

Know the difference between affinity-based load balancing and round-robin load balancing.   Both are methods of scheduling commonly used with load balancing. With affinity scheduling, like services are sent to like servers. With round-robin, the first client request is sent to the first group of servers; the second is sent to the second; and so on.

Review Questions

You can find the answers in the Appendix.

1. Which of the following devices is the most capable of providing infrastructure security?
   A. Hub
   B. Switch
   C. Router
   D. Modem

2. Upper management has decreed that a firewall must be put in place immediately, before your site suffers an attack similar to one that struck a sister company. Responding to this order, your boss instructs you to implement a packet filter by the end of the week. A packet filter performs which function?
   A. Prevents unauthorized packets from entering the network
   B. Allows all packets to leave the network
   C. Allows all packets to enter the network
   D. Eliminates collisions in the network

3. Which device stores information about destinations in a network (choose the best answer)?
   A. Hub
   B. Modem
   C. Firewall
   D. Router

4. As more and more clients have been added to your network, the efficiency of the network has decreased significantly. You're preparing a budget for next year, and you specifically want to address this problem. Which of the following devices acts primarily as a tool to improve network efficiency?
   A. Hub
   B. Switch
   C. Router
   D. PBX

5. You've been notified that you'll soon be transferred to another site. Before you leave, you're to audit the network and document everything in use and the reason why it's in use. The next administrator will use this documentation to keep the network running. Which of the following protocols isn't a tunneling protocol but is probably used at your site by tunneling protocols for network security?
   A. IPSec
   B. PPTP
   C. L2TP
   D. L2F

6. Which of the following can be implemented as a software or hardware solution and is usually associated with a device—a router, a firewall, NAT, and so on—used to shift a load from one device to another?

   A. Proxy

   B. Hub

   C. Load balancer

   D. Switch

7. Which of the following are multiport devices that improve network efficiency?

   A. Switches

   B. Modems

   C. Gateways

   D. Concentrators

8. Which IDS system uses algorithms to analyze the traffic passing through the network?

   A. Arithmetical

   B. Algebraic

   C. Statistical

   D. Heuristic

9. Which of the following can be used to offload the public-key encryption to a separate hardware plug-in card?

   A. SSL accelerator

   B. Load balancer

   C. Proxy firewall

   D. SIEM

10. Which of the following protections implies that information, once written, cannot be modified?

    A. DLP

    B. ROM

    C. WORM

    D. NAC

11. In which two modes can IPSec work?

    A. Tunneling and Storing

    B. Transport and Storing

    C. Tunneling and Transport

    D. At-Rest and At-Ease

12. With which tunnel configuration are only some (usually all incoming) requests routed and encrypted over the VPN?

    A. Split

    B. Full

    C. Partial

    D. Hybrid

13. With which type of load balance scheduling is the first client request sent to the first group of servers, the second is sent to the second, and so on?

    A. Affinity

    B. Round-robin

    C. Sequential

    D. Progressive

14. Which type of load balancing configuration means that more than one load balancing server is working at all times to handle the load/requests as they come in?

    A. Active-active

    B. Cooperative-sharing

    C. Equal-partner

    D. Proactive-colleague

15. Which of the following work by decrypting encrypted traffic (SSL or TLS), inspecting it, and then re-encrypting it before sending it on to its destination?

    A. SSL filters

    B. SSL gateways

    C. SSL accelerators

    D. SSL decryptors

16. Which of the following is a chip that can store cryptographic keys, passwords, or certificates?

    A. HMP

    B. TPM

    C. MTP

    D. PMH

17. Which AP-based technology can increase security dramatically by allowing or denying access based on a client's physical address?

    A. MAC filtering

    B. UTM (unified threat management)

    C. Round-robin

    D. WORM

18. Which network devices are used to divide larger networks into smaller sections by sitting between two physical network segments and managing the flow of data between the two?

    A. Accelerators

    B. Proxies

    C. Bridges

    D. Balancers

19. Which problem can occur when more than one bridge or switch is implemented on the network, and the devices confuse each other by leading one another to believe that a host is located on a certain segment when it is not?

    A. Backdoors

    B. Dead zones

    C. Collisions

    D. Loops

20. To combat the problem described in Question 19, which of the following technologies enable bridge/switch interfaces to be assigned a value that is then used to control the learning process and prevent problems?

    A. ESSID

    B. SSID

    C. BRD

    D. STP

Chapter

4

Identity and Access Management

THE FOLLOWING COMPTIA SECURITY+ EXAM OBJECTIVES ARE COVERED IN THIS CHAPTER:

✓ **2.2 Given a scenario, use appropriate software tools to assess the security posture of an organization.**

- Protocol analyzer
- Network scanners: Rogue system detection; Network mapping
- Wireless scanners/cracker
- Password cracker
- Vulnerability scanner
- Configuration compliance scanner
- Exploitation frameworks
- Data sanitization tools
- Steganography tools
- Honeypot
- Backup utilities
- Banner grabbing
- Passive vs. active
- Command line tools: ping; netstat; tracert; nslookup/dig; arp; ipconfig/ip/ifconfig; tcpdump; nmap; netcat

✓ **2.3 Given a scenario, troubleshoot common security issues.**

- Unencrypted credentials/clear text
- Logs and events anomalies
- Permission issues
- Access violations

- Certificate issues

- Data exfiltration

- Misconfigured devices: Firewall; Content filter; Access points

- Weak security configurations

- Personnel issues: Policy violation; Insider threat; Social engineering; Social media; Personal email

- Unauthorized software

- Baseline deviation

- License compliance violation (availability/integrity)

- Asset management

- Authentication issues

✓ **2.4 Given a scenario, analyze and interpret output from security technologies.**

- HIDS/HIPS

- Antivirus

- File integrity check

- Host-based firewall

- Application whitelisting

- Removable media control

- Advanced malware tools

- Patch management tools

- UTM

- DLP

- Data execution prevention

- Web application firewall

✓ **4.1 Compare and contrast identity and access management concepts.**

- Identification, authentication, authorization and accounting (AAA)

- Multifactor authentication: Something you are; Something you have; Something you know; Somewhere you are; Something you do

- Federation
- Single sign-on
- Transitive trust

✓ **4.2 Given a scenario, install and configure identity and access services.**

- LDAP
- Kerberos
- TACACS+
- CHAP
- PAP
- MSCHAP
- RADIUS
- SAML
- OpenID Connect
- OAUTH
- Shibboleth
- Secure token
- NTLM

✓ **4.3 Given a scenario, implement identity and access management controls.**

- Access control models: MAC; DAC; ABAC; Role-based access control; Rule-based access control
- Physical access control: Proximity cards; Smart cards
- Biometric factors: Fingerprint scanner; Retinal scanner; Iris scanner; Voice recognition; Facial recognition; False acceptance rate; False rejection rate; Crossover error rate
- Tokens: Hardware; Software; HOTP/TOTP
- Certificate-based authentication: PIV/CAC/smart card; IEEE 802.1x
- File system security
- Database security

This chapter covers a critical topic in security: controlling who can access your system, what resources they can access, and how to ensure that individuals are who they claim to be. At the most basic level, you can consider authentication and access control to be the two foundations of security. If you don't do a good job on these tasks, it is unlikely that the rest of your security strategy will be effective.

This chapter starts by looking at the basics of access control and then explores remote access and authentication services. It concludes by examining access control implementation and best practices.

Security+ Terminology

Challenge Handshake Authentication Protocol (CHAP)   An authentication protocol that periodically reauthenticates.

crossover error rate (CER)   The point at which the FRR and FAR are equal. Sometimes called the *equal error rate (ERR)*.

data execution prevention (DEP)   Any technique that prevents a program from running without the user's approval.

data loss prevention (DLP)   Software or techniques designed to detect attempts to exfiltrate data.

false acceptance rate (FAR)   The rate at which a biometric solution allows in individuals it should have rejected.

false rejection rate (FRR)   The rate at which a biometric solution rejects individuals it should have allowed.

federation   A collection of computer networks that agree on standards of operation, such as security standards.

HIDS   A host-based intrusion detection system. An HIPS is a host-based intrusion prevention system.

Kerberos   An authentication protocol developed at MIT that uses tickets for authentication.

least privileges   The principle that any user or service will be given only enough access privileges to do its job and no more.

NIDS A network-based intrusion detection system. An NIPS is an intrusion prevention system. Unlike an HIDS/HIPS, an NIDS/NIPS scans an entire network segment.

network scanner A tool that enumerates your network and provides a map of the network.

OAUTH Open Authorization standard. It is a common method for authorizing websites or applications to access information.

Using Tools to Assess Your Network

A variety of tools are available that you can use to assess a network's security. Such tools are a valuable part of any security professional's work.

Protocol Analyzer

Protocol analyzers, also called *packet sniffers*, are some of the most common tools used by network administrators. Essentially, these tools look at the current traffic on a network and allow you to view that traffic and capture a copy of the traffic for later analysis. In this section, we will take a brief look at two of the most common tools.

Monitoring the traffic on your network is an essential step in security. Odd traffic could indicate a denial-of-service attack, someone exfiltrating data, or any number of security concerns. Protocol analyzers and packet sniffers are fundamental tools in network security, incident response, and network forensics.

tcpdump

tcpdump is a common packet sniffer for Linux. It works from the shell, and it is relatively easy to use. To start it, you just tell it what interface to listen to, like this:

```
tcpdump -i eth0
```

This causes tcpdump to capture the network traffic for the network card, eth0. You can also alter tcpdump's behavior with a variety of command flags such as the following:

```
tcpdump -c 100 -i eth0
```

This tells tcpdump to capture only the first 100 packets on interface eth0 and then stop.

```
tcpdump -D
```

This command will display all the interfaces on your computer so you can select which one to use. You can see all three of these options in Figure 4.1.

FIGURE 4.1 tcpdump

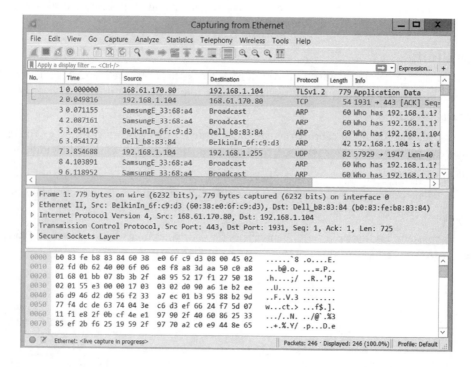

Wireshark

Wireshark is one of the most widely known network packet sniffers. Often a penetration tester can learn a great deal from simply sniffing the network traffic on a target network. Wireshark provides a convenient graphical user interface (GUI) for examining network traffic. It is a free download, which you can get at https://www.wireshark.org/. This tool can be downloaded for Windows or Macintosh. It has a GUI as opposed to being command line based. You can see the main Wireshark interface in Figure 4.2.

FIGURE 4.2 Wireshark

When using Wireshark, you can highlight any packet and then see the details of that packet, including the various network headers such as Ethernet, TCP, and IP. You can also right-click a specific packet and then choose to view the entire conversation associated with that packet. This can be seen in Figure 4.3.

FIGURE 4.3   Wireshark follow conversation

Wireshark is a very versatile tool. It is worth taking the time to learn completely all the features of this tool. Fortunately, you'll find a number of resources on the Wireshark page at `https://www.wireshark.org/#learnWS` to help you learn.

Network Scanners

Network scanning is different from packet sniffing. With *network scanning*, you are literally trying to find out what is on your network. This may seem like an odd task. Shouldn't you already know what is on your network? Ideally you should. However, networks change over time, and not all changes are documented. A network scanner or network mapper can enumerate everything on your network, giving you an up-to-the-minute view of what is on your network.

It is also a perfect way to detect rogue systems. It is entirely possible that someone has added a computer, wireless access point, or even multiple servers that you didn't know about. In some cases, this is just an undocumented addition to your network. In other cases, however, it is added for the specific purpose of circumventing security.

Solar Winds

SolarWinds is a commercial network scanner, and the developer offers a free 14-day trial version. You can see the network topology scan in Figure 4.4.

You select an IP range, subnet, or list of IP addresses to scan and then start the scan. SolarWinds will produce a map of your network. You can then right-click any device on the network to get more details (Figure 4.5).

FIGURE 4.4   SolarWinds network topology scan

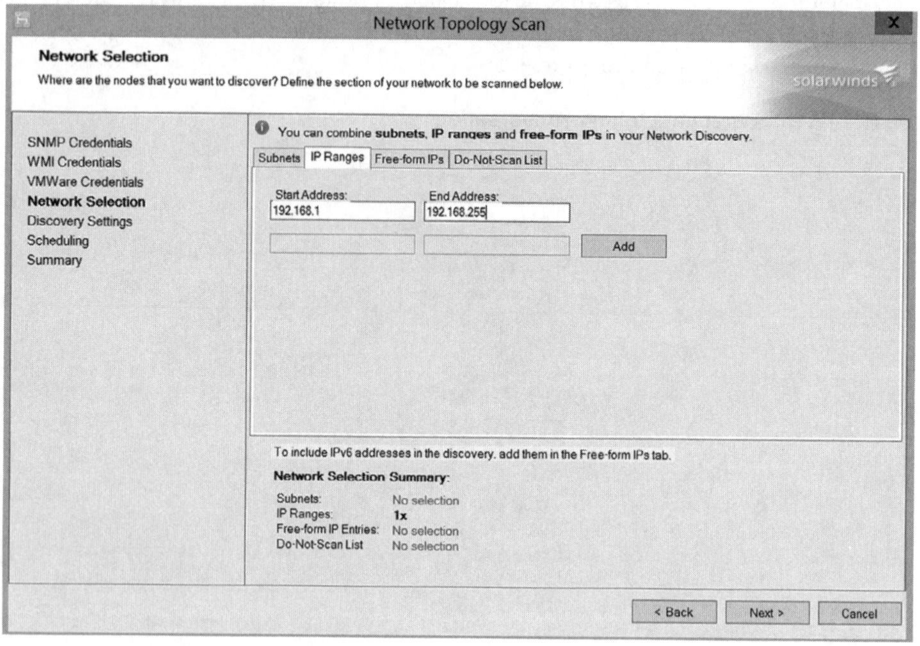

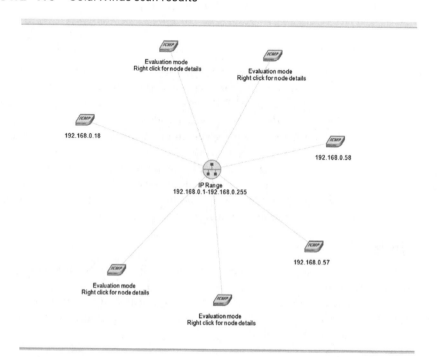

FIGURE 4.5   SolarWinds scan results

This tool is a fully featured, easy-to-use network scanner.

LanHelper

This tool is an inexpensive network mapper and scanner that you can download from www.hainsoft.com/download.htm. It installs rather quickly, and then you simply tell it to scan by clicking Network on the drop-down menu and then selecting one of the following:

- Scan Lan

- Scan IP

- Scan Workgroups

When the scan is done, you will see a list of all devices on the network, and you can click any one of them to get more details, as shown in Figure 4.6.

FIGURE 4.6   LanHelper

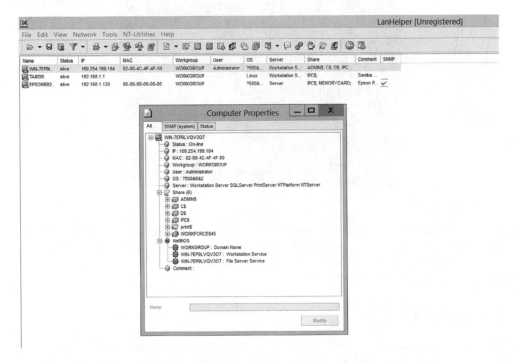

Wireless Scanners and Crackers

Wireless networks are ubiquitous today. For this reason, scanning the wireless network, and even testing its security by attempting to crack it, is an important activity for any network administrator. The network scanners mentioned in the previous section can be used for wireless networks, but there are also tools specifically designed for Wi-Fi that you can use.

In addition to scanning, many of these Wi-Fi tools will attempt to crack your Wi-Fi. They will essentially attempt either to derive the password or to circumvent the security. It is important that network security professionals scan their network with tools like this to find issues before an attacker does.

Aircrack

Aircrack is one of the most popular tools for scanning and cracking Wi-Fi. It is a free download, and you can get it at www.aircrack-ng.org/. There are actually a few tools in this download. One, called wzcook.exe, will try to extract wireless data, including the password, from the local machine on which it is installed. But that is not the part we are interested in here. The main tool is aircrack-ng. It is a command-line tool, and you can see it in Figure 4.7.

FIGURE 4.7 Aircrack

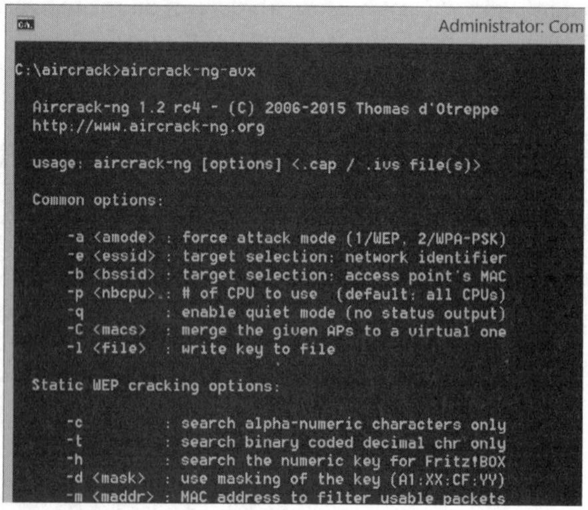

It takes a bit of time to get comfortable with all the command-line flags. However, this is a very important tool and well worth the time spent. The reason why it is so important is that it is popular with attackers. If you scan your wireless network with the same tool that attackers are likely to use and you find problems and correct those, then your network is less vulnerable to wireless attacks.

Password Cracker

It is a reasonable assumption that an attacker will attempt to crack passwords on your network. With this fact in mind, it is also reasonable that you should attempt to use password crackers on your network. If you are able to crack one or more passwords, you are then aware of this security vulnerability and can take appropriate steps to remedy the issue. In this section, we will take a look at three widely used password crackers.

pwdump

pwdump is a common tool used by attackers, so it is a good thing for security professionals to use as well. The first step for many password cracking tools is to get a copy of the local password hashes from the Windows SAM file. The SAM file, or Security Accounts

Manager, is where Windows stores hashes of passwords. The program pwdump will extract the password hashes from the SAM file. pwdump is a free download from www.openwall .com/passwords/windows-pwdump. Figure 4.8 is an image of the output of pwdump7. The actual hashes are redacted, since this was run on a live machine.

FIGURE 4.8   pwdump

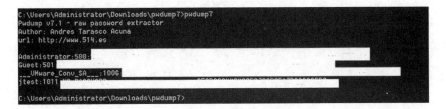

Oftentimes, you will want to dump the hashes to an external file so that you can import them into a rainbow table tool. Rainbow tables are explained in detail in Chapter 8, "Cryptography," but for now just know that they are tables of pre-computed hashes used to guess passwords. That is done quite easily by simply piping the output of pwdump to a test file. For example:

```
pwdump > passwordhashes.txt
```

Once you have the password hashes, you can use any rainbow table tool to check to see if the passwords can be recovered. This is one method for validating the strength of your organization's passwords.

Ophcrack

Ophcrack is one of the most widely used password cracking tools. Ophcrack is important because it can be installed on a bootable CD. If used in that manner, you boot the system to the CD, thus circumventing Windows security, and proceed to try to crack the passwords. Ophcrack offers a small rainbow table free of charge; you must purchase the larger rainbow tables. You can download Ophcrack from http://ophcrack.sourceforge.net/. It also does not require a separate process to dump the Windows SAM file. Instead, it will grab the data from the SAM file for you. The output from Ophcrack is shown in Figure 4.9. The actual hashes and passwords are redacted.

Regardless of which specific password cracking tool you use, such tools can be very important in verifying the security of your passwords. Essentially, you attempt to crack the passwords, and if you are successful, that indicates your passwords are not strong enough.

Vulnerability Scanners

It is important that you scan your network for vulnerabilities. The goal is to find and correct vulnerabilities before an attacker finds them. Some of these tools scan for general vulnerabilities, others specifically scan for web page vulnerabilities, and still others scan to see if your systems are configured properly. A few of the most widely used scanners will be discussed in this section.

FIGURE 4.9   Ophcrack

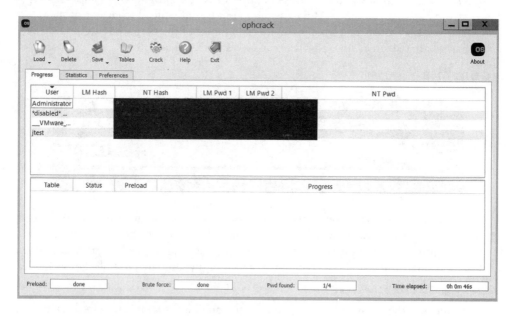

Vulnerability scanners can be classified as active or passive. *Active scanners* will interact directly with the target network. Tools such as Nessus, MBSA, and OWASP ZAP, which will be discussed in more detail in this section, are active scanners. *Passive scanning* involves methods to search your network that do not directly interact with the network. This usually means websites that provide information. A few are listed here, with brief descriptions.

Netcraft.com   This provides information about websites including what operating system they are running.

Shodan.io   This site is a vulnerability search engine. You can search your own network's domain name for vulnerabilities.

isc.sans.edu   This is the SANS Institute cyber storm center, and it will provide information on current cyber threats.

Nessus

Nessus is the most widely used vulnerability scanner. You can find Nessus at https://
www.tenable.com/products/. It is a commercial tool that has tens of thousands of documented vulnerabilities in its library. You can scan Linux machines, Windows machines, routers, and just about everything on your network. The library of vulnerabilities is updated on a continuous basis, so you will always be able to check for the latest vulnerabilities. Nessus produces a report for each scan. You can see an example of such a report in Figure 4.10.

FIGURE 4.10   Nessus report

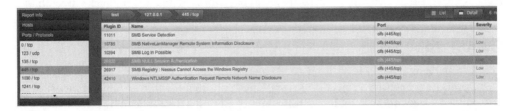

The report is in HTML format, and you can drill down on any specific issue and read a detailed description of the issue as well as recommended remediation steps.

MBSA

Microsoft Baseline Security Analyzer is not the most robust vulnerability scanner. However, it is a free download, and in addition to finding vulnerabilities, it is useful in finding configuration issues with Windows machines. You can download MBSA from `https://www.microsoft.com/en-us/download/details.aspx?id=7558`. In addition to being free, it is very easy to use. You can see the output from MBSA in Figure 4.11.

FIGURE 4.11   MBSA output

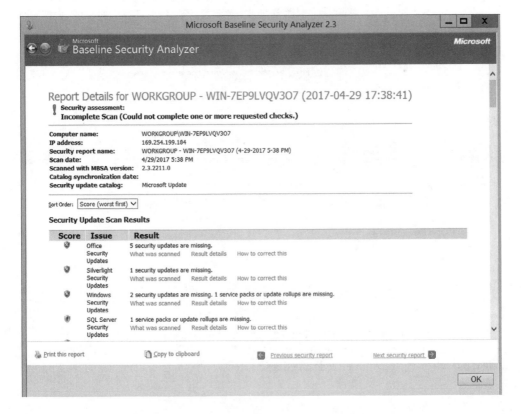

As you can see, MBSA finds common Windows vulnerabilities and also lets you know if patches are required or issues exist with system passwords. Thus, it combines vulnerability scanning with configuration scanning.

OWASP Zap

Recall from Chapter 2, "Monitoring and Diagnosing Networks," we discussed the Open Web Application Security Project (OWASP). They publish a list of top vulnerabilities. They also publish a free tool to scan for website vulnerabilities. This tool can be downloaded from https://www.owasp.org/index.php/OWASP_Zed_Attack_Proxy_Project. It is also easy to use. Just enter the URL of the website you wish to check and click the button. You can see the output from OWASP in Figure 4.12.

FIGURE 4.12   OWASP ZAP output

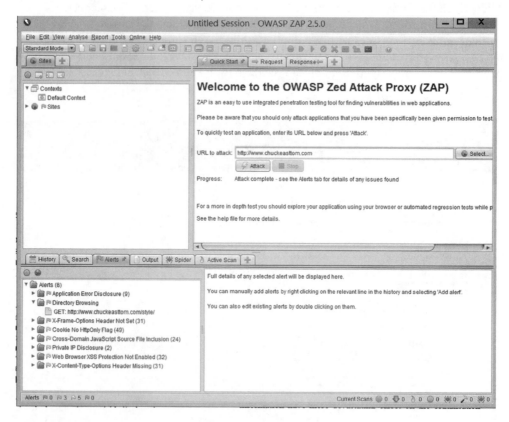

As you can see, the tool provides detailed information on everything it finds. Each item can be double-clicked for more detail. OWASP ZAP will tell you the details of the vulnerability, as well as the recommended remediation steps.

Exploitation Frameworks

In some cases, network administrators will take an additional step of actually attempting exploits on their network. This is often done as part of a penetration test. In such cases, it is often helpful to use an exploitation framework. Perhaps the most widely known such framework is Metasploit. This program can be downloaded from https://www.metasploit.com/. There are free and commercial versions. The free version comes with the Kali Linux distribution.

Entire books have been written on Metasploit, and it is beyond the scope of this chapter to teach you the ins and outs of Metasploit. However, if you are interested in using a framework to test your network, it is highly recommended that you take the time to learn Metasploit.

Command-Line Tools

You can use a number of command line tools to ascertain information about your network. Some of these are basic networking utilities, whereas others are specific to network security. CompTIA often places an emphasis on these tools. It is important that you actually use each of these and be familiar with them for the Security+ exam. Also, as you will see in the following sections, each of these commands has several flags that you can use. The Security+ exam will expect you to know these flags as well as the basic commands. Many of these tools are also essential networking tools, and the Security+ exam will assume that this section is primarily a review, not new material.

ping

ping is a fundamental networking utility. It is part of both Windows and Linux. The ping utility is used to find out if a particular website is reachable. Occasionally *Packet InterNet Gopher* is suggested as an acronym for ping, but the original author of ping says that it is based on the sound of a sonar return. ping operates by sending Internet Control Message Protocol (ICMP) echo request packets to the target host and waits for an ICMP response, sometimes casually called a *pong*. You can see ping in use in Figure 4.13.

FIGURE 4.13 ping

The most common flags for ping are described in Table 4.1.

TABLE 4.1   Common ping flags

-t	Continues pinging until stopped—for example, `ping -t www.google.com`.
-a	Resolves the address to a hostname, if you are pinging an IP address.
-i	Specifies the Time To Live value for packages.
-w	Waits a specified number of milliseconds for a response before sending the next ping.
-l	Sets the size of the packets. For example, `ping -l 20000 www.google.com` will send 20,000 byte packets to `google.com`.

netstat

The netstat command is also part of both Windows and Linux. It displays current network connections. The basic command is shown in Figure 4.14.

FIGURE 4.14   netstat

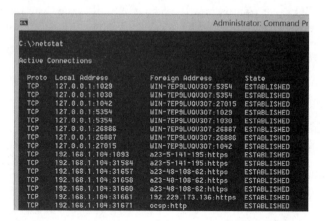

Some of the more commonly used netstat flags are described in Table 4.2.

TABLE 4.2   Common netstat flags

-A	Shows the address of any protocol
-a	Shows the state of sockets
-c	Shows statistics for the network buffer cache

-n	Shows active TCP connections
-o	Shows the active TCP connection and the process ID that started them
-p	Shows protocols
-s	Shows statistics per protocol

tracert

This command is `tracert` in Windows and `traceroute` in Linux. It will tell you the entire path to a given address. It is often said that `ping` tells you if a given address is reachable and `tracert` or `traceroute` tells you how to get there. A basic `tracert` is shown in Figure 4.15.

FIGURE 4.15 tracert

The common flags for this command are described in Table 4.3.

TABLE 4.3 Common tracert flags

-h	Maximum hops. By default it is 30, but you can change it.
-w	Time out.
-6	Force using IPv6.
-4	Force using IPv4.

nslookup/dig

The nslookup command is a bit different than the other commands. It will start by verifying that the machine can connect to the DNS server. Then, however, it also opens a command prompt wherein you can enter DNS-related commands. You can see the basic nslookup in Figure 4.16.

FIGURE 4.16 nslookup

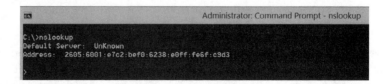

From the prompt, you can attempt a zone transfer:

run: nslookup.exe

type: ls -d domain_name <enter>

A *zone transfer* is when you attempt to get the DNS server to send you all of its zone information. A properly configured DNS server will refuse. It is a good idea to attempt this to verify whether or not your DNS server is secure.

arp

The arp (Address Resolution Protocol) command maps IP addresses to MAC addresses. Unlike the other commands, this one will only work with at least one flag, so let's list the more common flags first in Table 4.4 and then demonstrate arp.

TABLE 4.4 Common arp flags

-d	Removes a listing from the arp cache. You won't use this very often.
-a	Displays all of the current arp entries for all interfaces. This is the most common flag.
-g	Displays all of the current arp entries for all interfaces. Same as -a.
-N	Lists arp cache for a specified interface.

You can see arp in use in Figure 4.17.

ipconfig/ip/ifconfig

ipconfig in Windows (ifconfig in Linux) is one of the more basic network commands. It will provide you with information about your network interfaces. You can see the basic command in use in Figure 4.18.

FIGURE 4.17   arp

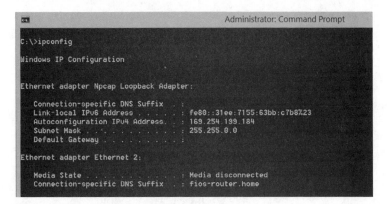

FIGURE 4.18   ipconfig

The common ipconfig flags are shown in Table 4.5.

TABLE 4.5   Common ipconfig flags

/all	Show all information for all network interfaces.
/release	Release any dynamically assigned IP addresses.
/renew	Renew the dynamically assigned IP address.

nmap

nmap is a free download for Windows or Linux. It is not part of the operating system. It is often used to port scan machines. This can reveal what services are running as well as information about the target machine's operating system. You can scan a range of IP addresses as well as a single IP.

nmap also lets you set a number of flags (either with the command-line version of nmap or the Windows version) that customize your scan. The allowed nmap flags are listed in Table 4.6.

TABLE 4.6 Allowed nmap flags

-O	Detects operating system
-sP	Is a ping scan
-sT	TCP connect scan
-sS	SYN scan
-sF	FIN scan
-sX	Xmas tree scan
-sN	NULL scan
-sU	UDP scan
-sO	Protocol scan
-sA	ACK scan
-sW	Windows scan
-sR	RPC scan
-sL	List/DNS scan
-sI	Idle scan
-Po	Don't ping
-PT	TCP ping
-PS	SYN ping
-PI	ICMP ping
-PB	TCP and ICMP ping

-PM	ICMP netmask
-oN	Normal output
-oX	XML output
-oG	Greppable output
-oA	All output
-T	Timing
-T0	Paranoid
-T 1	Sneaking
-T 2	Polite
-T 3	Normal
-T 4	Aggressive
-T 5	Insane

Here are some basic scans:

Basic nmap scan
nmap 192.168.1.1

Scan a range of IP addresses
nmap 192.168.1.1-20

Scan to detect operating system, use TCP scan, and use sneaky speed
nmap -O -PT -T1 192.168.1.1

netcat

The netcat utility also does not come with the operating system, but it is a free download for Windows or Linux. This utility allows you to read and write to network connections using either TCP or UDP. Here are some examples:

Open a connection to a mail server on port 25
nc mymail.server.net 25

listen on port 12345
nc -l -p 12345

You can see a basic netcat command in use in Figure 4.19.

FIGURE 4.19   netcat

Some of the most common `netcat` flags used are listed in Table 4.7.

TABLE 4.7   Common *netcat* flags

-l	Listen mode (default is client mode)
-L	Listen harder (supported only on Windows version of `netcat`). This option makes `netcat` a persistent listener that starts listening again after a client disconnects.
-u	UDP mode (default is TCP).
-p	Local port (in listen mode, this is the port listened on; in client mode, this is the source port for all packets sent).
-e	Program to execute after connection occurs, connecting STDIN and STDOUT to the program.

Additional Tools

There are many other tools with which any network security professional must be familiar. Each of these tools provide assistance with various aspects of security. Some commonly used networking tools are described in this section.

General Networking Tools

Data sanitization tools are used to ensure that data is entirely wiped from a given device before it is repurposed. The prevalence of deleted file recovery tools makes data sanitization very critical.

Backup utilities are also critical for network security. Making regular backups of your servers and workstations is a fundamental part of network security. Specific approaches on to how to back up your data will be discussed in Chapter 12, "Disaster Recovery and Incident Response." However you approach your backup strategy, it is critical that you have utilities that effectively and securely automate the process.

Banner grabbing is a technique that attackers use to gather information about a website before launching an attack. A *banner* is a text file on a web server that describes the operating system and the web server software. If an attacker can grab the banner, then he or she will have information about the web server to plan the attack. Network administrators sometimes use banner grabbing tools or techniques to check their web server to see what sort of information the attacker might have access to.

Honeypot

Honeypots were briefly introduced in Chapter 2, "Monitoring and Diagnosing Networks." Just to review, a *honeypot* is a fake system designed to attract an attacker so that he or she focuses on the fake system rather than on your actual system. Honeypots are also generally set up to perform a great deal of monitoring and tracing in order to gather evidence of an attack. A number of honeypot tools are available, and a few are discussed briefly here:

Nova Network Security   Nova sells a product that is both an intrusion detection system and a honeypot: www.novanetworksecurity.com/.

Honeynet Project   The Honeynet project is an open source honeypot and honeynet project: www.honeynet.org/.

Web Application Security Project   The Web Application Security project has a collaborative project that supports a distributed honeypot: http://projects.webappsec.org/w/page/29606603/Distributed%20Web%20Honeypots.

Steganography Tools

The process of *steganography* will be explored in detail in Chapter 8, "Cryptography." For now, you need to understand that it is a process whereby you can hide data in files. In fact, entire files can be hidden in other files.

A number of tools are available on the Internet, some for free, which allow an attacker to hide data steganographically without even needing to understand how steganography works. These tools are sometimes used by insiders to exfiltrate confidential information. A few such tools are listed here:

Invisible Secrets   This a low-cost commercial product that can hide data in either an image or sound file. You can find out more at www.invisiblesecrets.com.

Deep Sound   This is a free download that allows you to hide data in sound files: http://jpinsoft.net/deepsound.

Open Stego   This is an open source steganography tool that can be found at www.openstego.com. It is somewhat limited, but it will provide basic steganography.

Troubleshooting Common Security Issues

The Security+ exam will assume that you can troubleshoot common security issues. In this section, we will discuss those common issues and how to address them.

Access Issues

Access issues are a broad category of security anomalies that are very common. Whenever there is any situation where someone is able to access data they should not be able to access, then that is an access violation. These violations are divided into two broad categories.

The first involves *permission issues*. One of the cornerstones of security is the concept of *least permissions*. Each user or service is provided only with sufficient permissions to do their job. Any permission beyond that is a permission issue that could lead to an access violation.

One way such permission issues occur is when a user is moved from one role on the network to another. It is important that their old permissions be replaced with the new permissions, rather than the new permissions being added to the old ones. If the network administrator is not careful, the user will ultimately have significantly more permissions than their job requires. The fundamental way to address permissions issues is to compare each user's permissions to the requirements of their job.

Access violations occur when someone accesses, or attempts to access, data that they should not be accessing. For example, if a user accesses files to which they have not been given permission, that is an access violation. Violations can occur from inside employees accessing data beyond what they have been authorized to access, or by outside attackers who have not been authorized to access any data but are doing so anyway.

There is a second definition of access violation, not related to permissions. This definition involves memory management. When an application running on a computer is able to access the memory of another application, this is also an access violation. This is sometimes even more narrowly defined as software trying to access protected memory. When the hardware of a system notifies the operating system that some software has attempted to access a restricted area of memory, this is called a *segmentation fault*, or access violation.

Often, access violations (defined as someone accessing data that they should not be accessing) are best discovered by examining the logs of a given system. For example, a database log should show what users accessed what data and when. By scanning the database log for anomalies, you can detect access violations.

Access violations are closely related to authentication problems. Whenever someone is able to circumvent the normal authentication process, this may lead to an access violation. Here are some common issues that you should check for on your network:

Good Passwords   Passwords should be at least 10 characters long, implement complexity requirements, and be changed from time to time.

Password Storage   Passwords should be stored as a hash using a salt algorithm. Hashes and salt will be discussed in detail in Chapter 8.

Least Privileges   Ensure that once a user is authenticated, he or she is only given just enough privileges to do their job.

Protocols   There are modern authentication protocols, such as Kerberos, which are discussed later in this chapter. You should ensure that you are using these protocols.

Strong Authentication   Later in this chapter, we will be discussing different types of authentication. Make sure that you are using two-factor authentication whenever possible.

When you fail to implement any one of these guidelines, the entire security of your network is compromised.

Configuration Issues

Whenever any device or software is not configured correctly, this presents a significant security concern. Misconfiguration can be failing to enable some security mechanism, using a weak security configuration, or simply incorrectly configuring the system's settings. This applies to workstations, servers, routers, switches, and all other devices on your network. However, the problem is even more disconcerting for certain devices.

Your firewall(s) provide the frontline of protection for your network. Unfortunately, modern firewalls have become increasingly complex. This can lead to a misconfigured firewall. If the firewall is misconfigured, it can lead to a possible point of access for an attacker. Common firewall configuration issues include not properly configuring the rules of the firewall—this includes inbound and outbound rules. Another firewall configuration issue is allowing traffic to exit the network that should not be allowed.

For any system, some common configuration issues include the following:

Default Passwords   All systems come with a default login. This login must be changed immediately.

Failure to Patch   Network items such as firewalls, access points, switches, and routers all have operating systems that must be patched, just as you patch your computers.

Regardless of the system, it should be configured to meet a security baseline. The *security baseline* is essentially an overall approach to security that provides a basic level of protection across the major portions of your network. Configuration issues can lead to deviations from that security baseline.

Issues with configuring content filters also pose a security risk. In addition to the issues just listed, a content filter must be carefully configured so that it blocks the content that you wish to block without accidentally blocking legitimate traffic. Usually it takes a bit of time and effort to get the configuration exactly correct.

Misconfigured access points are a serious security concern. Any access point, particularly a wireless access point, requires careful security configuration. Along with issues such as default passwords and patching, additional security concerns include these:

Limit Admin Access   Wireless access points have an administrative panel. This should only be accessible via a physical connection, not via wireless.

Filtering   Most access points offer some level of filtering. It should be turned on and configured.

Logging   Access points typically offer logging that must be turned on and configured.

Digital Certificate Issues

Although not a device, digital certificates also must be configured and implemented properly. Digital certificates will be discussed in detail in Chapter 8, but let's address a few issues here.

The first step involves issuing certificates in a secure manner. This means ensuring that the proper key size is selected and making certain that the private key is stored securely.

The next common issue involves the use of self-signed certificates. These should be used sparingly since they are not authenticated by a trusted third party. It is better to have an organizational certificate authority issue certificates.

Certificate revocation is another important issue to address. This is particularly important when your organization has its own certificate authority. When you have your own certificate authority, then you are responsible for ensuring that the revoked certificates are not used on your network. This can be as simple as ensuring that the certificate revocation list is updated and published frequently.

Personnel Issues

It is often said in cybersecurity that the greatest threat is the insider. Unfortunately, this is true. Whether it comes from intentional malfeasance from a disgruntled employee or simply a mistake due to lack of knowledge or carelessness, the fact is that insiders can cause a tremendous amount of damage. Sadly, many of the security concerns related to insiders cannot be alleviated with the application of technology.

The most obvious issue with insiders is the failure to follow policies. Policy violations undermine your entire network's security. Policy violations often occur through simple ignorance. The policies have not been adequately communicated to the staff or are not clear. However, intentional violations are also a significant insider threat about which you must be aware.

Insiders are also vulnerable to social engineering. *Social engineering* is essentially using interpersonal skills to attempt to elicit information. Someone could call employees in your organization pretending to be from technical support and attempt to get passwords from users. Other applications of social engineering are less obvious. For example, the attacker might call claiming to be conducting an IT survey for a major company, while all the time attempting to gather information about your network.

Social media is also a problem in many ways. First, it can be a means of distracting employees and reducing productivity. More important, however, it may be a conduit for information exfiltration. Employees might disclose information about confidential projects or other sensitive information. This often occurs in the context of the employee either boasting about some new innovation in your company or complaining about the extra work the new project causes. Either way, the end result is that information about your company is released to the outside world.

The use of personal email at work is another security concern. When an employee checks their personal email from a company workstation, any malware that might be sent to that email address will now infect the company network. Moreover, the employee's personal email may not have the rigorous security precautions that you have on your company network.

Other Issues

One serious risk to all organizations is the installation of unauthorized software. Any organization has a process for vetting and controlling the software that is installed on its network. If unauthorized software is installed, this can be the beginning of many problems.

The most obvious issue is that the unauthorized software could have significant security flaws. Since the software was not tested or vetted, its security won't be known. It is even possible that the unauthorized software is actually a Trojan horse, bringing malware into the organization.

Unauthorized software is closely related to license compliance violations. Copyrights are serious legal issues, and your company should strive to comply with copyright laws. Installing unlicensed software is a violation of copyright law. Whether the software is authorized by your IT department or is unauthorized, you must vigilant in ensuring that unlicensed copies of applications are not installed on your network.

Unlicensed software is itself a subset of the topic of asset management. The larger the organization, the more challenging it can be to have clear management of all of your company IT assets. Whether it is laptops, servers, or software, you have to maintain an accurate inventory of everything your company owns and where it is currently located.

SMS/MMS messages can also be a security risk, albeit a minor one. Many companies choose to limit text messages based on when they can be sent, from where, and what content. Particularly, sending pictures can be a security issue in secure areas.

Security Technologies

You can implement a variety of security technologies to make your network more secure. Most network administrators implement a combination of multiple technologies. However, the challenge becomes how to interpret the output from these technologies. In this section, we will review this issue for various technologies.

Intrusion Detection Systems

A *host-based intrusion detection system (HIDS)* or *host-based intrusion prevention system (HIPS)* is a vital part of your security. Such devices detect activity that indicates a likely intrusion. There are a variety of such systems, some commercial and some open source. Obviously, you will need to consult the documentation of your specific device in order to interpret the output completely from your HIDS/HIPS, but some general guidelines apply to all such devices.

The first thing to keep in mind is that no HIDS/HIPS is 100 percent effective. All such systems will have some false positives (legitimate traffic labeled as an attack) and false negatives (attacks labeled as legitimate traffic). The key is to interpret what your HIDS/HIPS is telling you properly in order to determine if you need to alter the configuration to get more accurate readings.

This leads to the first issue with interpreting HIDS/HIPS output—that is, matching traffic identified as an attack with the actual traffic on your network. As stated earlier, there will be some false positives. Thus, you should expect that some of the traffic that has been identified as an attack will actually match activity on that host, which you can confirm is legitimate traffic. As you note the number of false positives, you can alter the configuration of your HIDS/HIPS to lower the frequency of false positives.

For an HIPS, this will be even easier, since it blocks suspected attacks. Those will be clearly identified in the logs of your HIPS, regardless of which HIPS you are using.

As stated earlier, actually interpreting the logs and output from your HIDS/HIPS will require you to refer to the documentation of that specific product. But let's look at one specific IDS/IPS: the SNORT IDS/IPS. This is an open source HIDS/HIPS, and its logs provide a good example. Here is a sample log:

```
[116:56:1] (snort_decoder): T/TCP Detected
```

This may look very cryptic to you, and it may not provide you with any information that you can use. The first number (116) is the *generator ID*, and it indicates what Snort component generated this alert. The second number (56) is sometimes called a *Signature ID*, or a *Snort ID*. It will identify the rule that triggered this alert. The third number (1) is the *revision ID*, which identifies the revision number of the attack signature that matched this alert. The text tells you what was detected. In this case, it was normal TCP traffic.

NIST SP 800-94 Guide to Intrusion Detection and Prevention Systems (IDPS) provides guidance as to IDS systems, both host based (HIDS) and network based (NIDS). You can view this document here: http://nvlpubs.nist.gov/nistpubs/Legacy/SP/nistspecialpublication800-94 .pdf. The standard describes various types of IDS/IPS, how they function, and typical components. This can be a valuable resource when choosing your own IDS.

Antimalware

There are a variety of antimalware applications, including standard antivirus as well as advanced antimalware applications. Just like HIDS/HIPS, these will sometimes have false positives and false negatives. Fortunately, most of these applications provide much more user-friendly output than HIDS/HIPS, and it is far easier to interpret the output. Figure 4.20 shows the output from Malwarebytes, a popular antivirus tool.

FIGURE 4.20   Malwarebytes

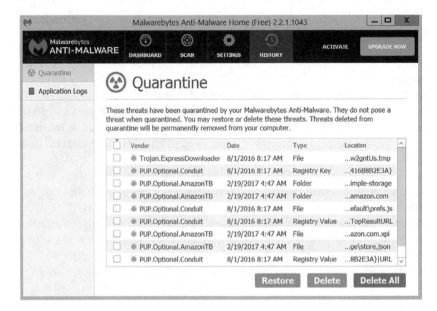

This output is very clear. It identifies the item that was suspect, the date and time it was detected, the type (file, folder, registry key, and so forth), and the exact location. Most antivirus and even more advanced antimalware products provide equally readable output. Then, as the user, you can determine if you wish to restore or delete the item.

More advanced antimalware tools have more robust scanning algorithms, scan for more anomalies, and offer more options in how to deal with such issues. They also often offer add-in features such as HIDS/HIPS, firewall, and similar security services, but they still tend to have the type of easy-to-use interface that you see in Figure 4.20.

Firewalls and Related Devices

Whether you are using a host-based firewall or a web-application firewall (WAF), you will still need to know how to interpret the logs of these systems. As with HIDS/HIPS, you will ultimately have to refer to the documentation for your specific firewall in order to interpret the results properly.

For an example of a firewall log, let's examine the Windows Firewall log.

In most versions of Windows, this will be found at `%windir%\system32\logfiles\` `firewall\`. This log will be empty if you have not turned on logging. You can have the firewall turned on but not be logging. To turn on logging, open the Windows Firewall console (`wf.msc`) and choose Actions ➤ Properties. You will then see a screen much like the one shown in Figure 4.21.

FIGURE 4.21   Windows Firewall

Simply click the Logging button to turn on logging. Here is an example of what log entries might look like:

```
2017-04-09 10:10:45 ALLOW TCP 192.168.0.104 192.168.0.100 52174 23
2017-04-09 10:10:54 DROP TCP 192.168.0.104 192.168.0.100 52175 21
```

Both entries start with a date in year-month-day format followed by the time. Then a description of what occurred follows. In both example entries, TCP traffic was occurring from IP 192.168.0.104 to IP 192.168.0.100. The first entry was allowed, but the second was blocked. The last item is the port that traffic was using. Thus, in this log, traffic was allowed on port 23 (Telnet) but blocked on port 21 (FTP).

Each vendor's logs will have a different format, so you will need to review the documentation that came with your firewall. We've provided a basic understanding of how firewall logs work. It is important to realize that firewall logs can contain a wealth of information about attempted breaches of your network.

Other Systems

In addition to the three most common security technologies (HIDS/HIPS, antivirus, and firewalls), other security technologies have output you may wish to review.

File integrity checking systems are very common. Tripwire is a well-known product that has both an open source and a commercial version. All file integrity products are configured to check to see if certain files have been changed and to record such activity. Many products, like Tripwire, will return the file to its previous state. However, if you don't check the logs, you may not be aware that such a change was even attempted. Even if your file integrity product does correct such issues, it is important to know that they occurred.

Application whitelisting is a common technique used by security professionals. An *application whitelist* is a list of applications that are allowed on a given computer or network. If an application is not on the list, then it is not allowed. A variety of products can be used to enforce these application whitelisting policies. Such products will also log attempts to install unauthorized applications. It is important to check these logs, as you will want to know if, for example, some user on your network attempted to install a password cracker.

Many network administrators also control what removable media can be used, such as USB drives and optical disks. A number of tools exist for enforcing these policies. Again, however, you must review the tool's logs to see if someone has been attempting to violate these policies. If a user on your network repeatedly attempts to install a USB drive that is not allowed, this could indicate a desire to exfiltrate data.

As you are probably aware, patch management is a challenge in a network environment. Unlike with home use, you cannot simply set up automatic updates on all systems. Instead, you must install patches on a test machine and verify that the patch or update works appropriately before rolling it out. Several products are available that can automate this process for you. It is important to check the logs of any patch management software to review issues with failed patches, patches that had to be rolled back, or any scenario in which the patch application was not successful.

A *unified threat management (UTM)* system, sometimes called a *USM (unified security management)* system, includes combinations of all the other devices we discussed earlier in this chapter, including firewall, IDS, and antivirus, as well as other items, such as load balancing and VPN. The procedure for reviewing logs will depend on the specific device you select. However, one major advantage is that you will have a single place to review logs rather than having to check multiple devices and systems logs.

Data loss prevention (DLP) software attempts to detect exfiltration of data. It does this by monitoring outgoing network traffic to look for key files going out. It can also monitor data storage of sensitive documents to log when data is accessed. As with the other technologies that we have examined, you will need to consult your manufacturer's documentation to know how to interpret the logs for your system.

Data execution prevention (DEP) has become increasingly popular. Microsoft introduced this with Windows Vista. When an application tries to launch, the user must approve the execution before it can proceed. Other vendors produce more complex DEP systems. These systems log any time an application tried to execute, even if it was blocked. This could be a valuable resource for learning about malware. Even if the malware is blocked, you would want to know that there was an attempt to execute.

Identity and Access Management Concepts

Understanding the difference between identification and authentication is critical to answering access control questions correctly on the Security+ exam. *Identification* means finding out who someone is. *Authentication* is a mechanism of verifying that identification. Put another way, identification is claiming an identity; authentication is proving it.

Identification vs. Authentication

In the physical world, the best analogy would be that any person can claim to be anyone (identification). To prove it (authentication), however, that person needs to provide some evidence, such as a driver's license, passport, or other nonrefutable proof.

Authentication systems or methods are based on one or more of these five factors:

- Something you know, such as a password or PIN. This is often referred to as Type I.

- Something you have, such as a smartcard, token, or identification device. This is often referred to as Type II.

- Something you are, such as your fingerprints or retinal pattern (often called *biometrics*). This is often referred to as Type III.

- Something you do, such as an action you must take to complete authentication. This does not have a type (I, II, III).

- Somewhere you are (this is based on geolocation). This does not have a type (I, II, III).

Because of the use of mobile computing, "somewhere you are" authentication is not often used, since users are likely to log in from diverse locations. In fact, many sources do not include "somewhere you are" as an authentication factor.

Systems authenticate each other using similar methods. Frequently, systems pass private information between each other to establish identity. Once authentication has occurred, two systems can communicate in the manner specified in the design. Several common methods are used for authentication, and they fall within the categories of either single factor or multifactor. Each offers something in terms of security and should be considered when you're evaluating authentication schemes or methods.

Another method that is becoming popular is *out-of-band authentication*. This is a process whereby the system you are authenticating gets information from public records and asks you questions to help authenticate you. For example, the system might retrieve your credit report and then query you about specific entries in it.

Authentication (Single Factor) and Authorization

The most basic form of authentication is known as *single-factor authentication (SFA)*, because only one type of authentication is checked. SFA is most often implemented as the traditional username/password combination. A username and password are unique identifiers for a logon process. Here's a synopsis for how SFA works: When users sit down in front of a computer system, the first thing a security system requires is that they establish who they are. Identification is typically confirmed through a logon process. Most operating systems use a user ID (username) and password to accomplish this. These values can be sent across the connection as plain text or they can be encrypted.

The logon process identifies that you are who you say you are to the operating system and possibly the network. Figure 4.22 illustrates the logon and password process. Note that the operating system compares this information to the stored information from the security processor, and it either accepts or denies the logon attempt. The operating system might establish privileges or permissions based on stored data about that particular user ID.

Whenever two or more parties authenticate each other, it is known as *mutual authentication*. A client may authenticate to a server, and a server may authenticate to a client when there is a need to establish a secure session between the two and employ encryption. Mutual authentication ensures that the client is not unwittingly connecting and providing its credentials to a rogue server, which can then turn around and steal the data from the real server.

Ordinarily, mutual authentication will be implemented when the data to be sent during the session is of a critical nature, such as financial or medical records.

FIGURE 4.22   A logon process occurring on a workstation

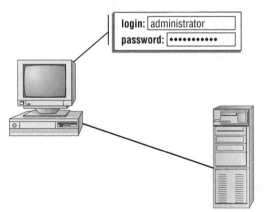

login: administrator
password: ••••••••••

Logon or Security Server

Multifactor Authentication

When two or more access methods are included as part of the authentication process, you're implementing a *multifactor authentication* system. A system that uses smartcards and passwords is referred to as a *two-factor authentication* system. This example requires both a smartcard and a logon password process.

A multifactor system can consist of a two-factor system, three-factor system, or any number of factors. As long as more than one factor is involved in the authentication process, it is considered a multifactor system.

For obvious reasons, the two or more factors employed should not be from the same category. Although you do increase difficulty in gaining system access by requiring the user to enter two sets of username/password combinations, it is much preferred to pair a single username/password combination with a biometric identifier or other security check.

When taking the Security+ exam, keep in mind the number of authentication factors in each type. For example, using a smartcard and a password is two-factor authentication. However, using a password and a PIN is one-factor authentication because both involve "something you know."

Biometrics

A very secure way to authenticate users is via the use of *biometrics*. Biometric authentication is Type III, something you are. These can be fingerprint scanners, full hand scanners, eye scanners (including retinal or iris scanners), facial recognition, or voice recognition.

Eye scanners tend to be very accurate. Full hand scanners are more accurate than simply a single fingerprint scanner. However, all of these methods will have both a *false acceptance rate (FAR)* and a *false rejection rate (FRR)*. Your first thought might be that you want the FRR to be higher than the FAR. However, it is recommended that both rates be equal. This is because the same algorithms are being used to reject or accept. Fluctuations between FRR and FAR indicate a possible issue with the algorithm itself.

The point at which the FRR and FAR are equal is called the *crossover error rate (CER)* or sometimes the *equal error rate (ERR)*. With any biometric system, you want to reach the CER/ERR and then make that rate as low as possible.

Federations

A *federation* is a collection of computer networks that agree on standards of operation, such as security standards. Normally, these are networks that are related in some way. In some cases, it could be an industry association that establishes such standards.

Another example of a federation would be an instant messaging (IM) federation. In this scenario, multiple IM providers form common communication standards, thus allowing users on different platforms with different clients to communicate freely.

In other situations, a group of partners might elect to establish common security and communication standards, thus forming a federation. This would facilitate communication between employees in each of the various partners.

A *federated identity* is a means of linking a user's identity with their privileges in a manner that can be used across business boundaries (for example, Microsoft Passport or Google checkout). This allows a user to have a single identity that they can use across different business units and perhaps even entirely different businesses.

A federated identity sounds similar to a single sign-on, but do not confuse the two. Single sign-on is about having one password for all resources on a given network. Federated identities relate to being able to access resources on diverse networks.

Potential Authentication and Access Problems

There are two problem areas that you should know about for the Security+ exam as they apply to authentication/access issues: transitive access and client-side attacks. Let's address both of these.

Transitive Access

The word *transitive* means involving transition—keep this in mind as you learn how transitive access problems occur. With *transitive access*, one party (A) trusts another party (B). If the second party (B) trusts another party (C), then a relationship can exist where the first party (A) also may trust the third party (C). This is sometimes described as *transitive trust*.

In early operating systems, this process was often exploited. In current operating systems, such as Windows Server 2016, the problems with transitive access are solved by creating *transitive trusts*, which are a type of relationship that can exist between domains (the opposite is *nontransitive trusts*). When the trust relationship is transitive, the relationship between party (A) and party (B) flows through as described earlier (for instance, A now trusts C). In all versions of Active Directory, the default is that all domains in a forest trust each other with two-way, transitive trust relationships.

Although this process makes administration much easier when you add a new child domain (no administrative intervention is required to establish the trusts), it leaves open the possibility of a hacker acquiring more trust than they should have by virtue of joining the domain. We'll explore how to validate the trust relationship in Windows Server 2012, which is a step toward addressing this problem.

LDAP

Lightweight Directory Access Protocol (LDAP) is a standardized directory access protocol that allows queries to be made of directories (specifically, pared-down X.500-based directories). If a directory service supports LDAP, you can query that directory with an LDAP client, but it's LDAP itself that is growing in popularity and is being used extensively in online white and yellow pages.

LDAP is the main access protocol used by Active Directory. It operates, by default, at port 389. The LDAP syntax uses commas between names.

Because a breach of LDAP can be quite serious, some organizations use secure LDAP. With *secure LDAP (LDAPS)*, all LDAP communications are encrypted with SSL/TLS, and port 636 is used.

> Throughout this book, you will see various port numbers mentioned. These port numbers are often the subject of questions on the Security+ exam (as well as other security-related certifications), so it is a good idea for you to get to know them.

PAP, SPAP, and CHAP

These three authentication protocols represent the evolution of authentication. The oldest, PAP (Password Authentication Protocol), will likely seem rather primitive and unsecure to you. However, that is because it is quite old and not used any longer.

PAP

Password Authentication Protocol is an old and insecure method of authentication. Essentially the username and password are sent in clear text. PAP was used before packet sniffers became widely available. It is now insecure and should not be used.

SPAP

Shiva Password Authentication Protocol simply encrypts the username and password. This prevents a packet sniffer from getting the username and password, but it does nothing to limit replay attacks or session hijacking.

CHAP

Challenge Handshake Authentication Protocol is a modern authentication protocol in use today. With this protocol, when users send their username and password to the server (encrypted, of course), the server first authenticates the user. Then once authentication is complete, the server directs the client computer to generate some random number (often a cryptographic hash) and send that to the server (encrypted as well, of course). Then the server will periodically challenge the client to reproduce that number/hash. If the client session has been compromised, then the client will be unable to produce that number/hash, and the server will terminate the session. Microsoft has a proprietary version of this called MS-CHAP.

Kerberos

Kerberos is an authentication protocol named after the mythical three-headed dog that stood at the gates of Hades. Originally designed by MIT, Kerberos is very popular as an authentication method. It allows for a single sign-on to a distributed network.

Kerberos authentication uses a *key distribution center (KDC)* to orchestrate the process. The KDC authenticates the *principal* (which can be a user, program, or system) and provides it with a ticket. After this ticket is issued, it can be used to authenticate against other principals. This process occurs automatically when another principal performs a request or service.

Kerberos is a common standard in network environments. Its only significant weakness is that the KDC can be a single point of failure. If the KDC goes down, the authentication process will stop. Figure 4.23 illustrates the Kerberos authentication process and the ticket being presented to systems that are authorized by the KDC. It should be noted that this figure is a simplified explanation of Kerberos. There are more details, but those are not covered in the Security+ exam.

FIGURE 4.23   Kerberos authentication process

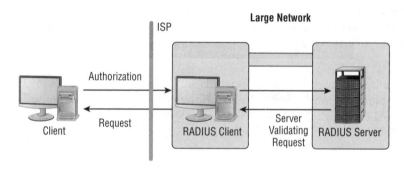

When using Kerberos, the user authenticates to the KDC and is given a *ticket granting ticket (TGT)*. This ticket is encrypted and has a time limit of up to 10 hours. The ticket lists the privileges of that user (much like a token). Each time the user wishes to access some resource on the network, the user's computer presents the KDC with the TGT; the TGT then sends that user's computer a *service ticket*, granting the user access to that service. Service tickets are usually only good for up to 5 minutes. The user's computer then sends the service ticket to the server the user is trying to access. As a final authentication check, that server then communicates with the TGT to confirm and validate the service ticket.

Working with RADIUS

Remote Authentication Dial-In User Service (RADIUS) is a mechanism that allows authentication of remote and other network connections. Originally intended for use on dial-up connections, it has moved well beyond that and offers many state-of-the-art features. The RADIUS protocol is an IETF standard, and it has been implemented by most of the major operating system manufacturers. A RADIUS server can be managed centrally, and the servers that allow access to a network can verify with a RADIUS server whether an incoming caller is authorized. In a large network with many connections, this allows a single server to perform all authentications.

 The term *caller* may seem outdated, but Windows Server 2012 (as well as 2008 and 2003) all refer to the ability to access a system remotely as *dial-in privileges*. Although few people are actually "dialing," or calling in, the terms have stuck.

Figure 4.24 shows an example of a RADIUS server communicating with an ISP to allow access to a remote user. Notice that the remote ISP server is functioning as a client to the RADIUS server. This allows centralized administration of access rights.

FIGURE 4.24   The RADIUS client manages the local connection and authenticates against a central server

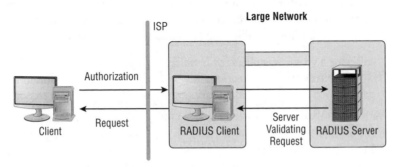

You should use RADIUS when you want to improve network security by implementing a single service to authenticate users who connect remotely to the network. Doing so gives you a single source for the authentication to take place. Additionally, you can implement auditing and accounting on the RADIUS server.

The major difficulty with a single-server RADIUS environment is that the entire network may refuse connections if the server malfunctions. Many RADIUS systems allow multiple servers to be used to increase reliability. All of these servers are critical components of the infrastructure, and they must be protected from attack.

TACACS, TACACS+, XTACACS

Terminal Access Controller Access Control System (TACACS) is a client-server-oriented environment, and it operates in a manner similar to RADIUS. Extended TACACS (XTACACS) replaced the original version and combined authentication and authorization with logging to enable auditing.

The most current method, or level, of TACACS is TACACS+. It replaces the previous two incarnations. TACACS+ allows credentials to be accepted from multiple methods, including Kerberos. The TACACS client-server process occurs in the same manner as the RADIUS process.

Cisco has widely implemented TACACS+ for connections. TACACS+ has become widely accepted as an alternative to RADIUS.

 Remember, RADIUS and TACACS (or any of its variations such as TACACS+ or XTACACS) can be used to authenticate connections.

OATH

Open Standard for Authorization (OATH) is a common method for authorizing websites or applications to access information. It allows users to share information with third-party applications.

It is designed to work with HTTP and allows access tokens to be issued to third-party clients with the approval of the resource owner. Thus a resource owner, such as a social media website user, can authorize a third party to access his or her data.

One-Time Passwords

As the name suggests, these can be used one time and never again. A common application is the time-based one-time password (or TOTP) such that a password is issued but is only good for a finite period of time. After it is used once or the time expires, it is no longer a valid password. Bank websites often use this if you need to reset your password. A TOTP is sent to your phone, and you have a limited time to log in and change your password.

Another variation is the keyed-hash message authentication code (HMAC)-based one-time password (HOTP). These are often used in physical tokens, which we will discuss later in this chapter. Hashes, message authentication code (MAC), and HMAC will be discussed in detail in Chapter 8.

SAML

Security Assertion Markup Language (SAML) is a markup language, much like HTML. It uses tags, but rather than defining web page elements (as HTML does), it defines security authorization.

SAML is used to exchange authentication and authorization information between identity providers and service providers. It is often used in web browser single sign-on implementations.

Shibboleth is a single sign-on system used widely on the Internet. The name derives from a bible story where the word *shibboleth* was used as a password. The Shibboleth system uses SAML.

Open ID

OpenID is an authentication service often done by a third party, and it can be used to sign into any website that accepts OpenID.

Install and Configure Identity and Access Services

There are several approaches to access control, each with its own strengths and weaknesses. In this section, we will review access control methodologies.

Mandatory Access Control

Mandatory access control (MAC) is a relatively inflexible method for how information access is permitted. In a MAC environment, all access capabilities are predefined. Users can't share information unless their rights to share it are established by administrators. Consequently, administrators must make any changes that need to be made to such rights. This process enforces a rigid model of security. However, it is also considered the most secure security model.

For a MAC model to work effectively, administrators and network designers must think relationships through carefully in advance of implementation. The advantage of this model is that security access is well established and well defined, making security breaches easier to investigate and correct. A well-designed MAC model can make the job of information control easier and can essentially lock down a network. The major disadvantages of this model are its lack of flexibility and the fact that it requires change over time. The inability of administrative staff to address these changes can sometimes make the model hard to maintain.

This model is used in environments where confidentiality is a driving force. It often employs government and military classifications (labels), such as Top Secret and others.

Discretionary Access Control

In a *discretionary access control (DAC)* model, network users have some flexibility regarding how information is accessed. This model allows users to share information dynamically with other users. The method allows for a more flexible environment, but it increases the risk of unauthorized disclosure of information. Administrators have a more difficult time ensuring that information access is controlled and that only appropriate access is issued.

A classic example of DAC is the permission structure that exists for "other" files in the Unix/Linux environment. All permissions in this operating system fall within three groups of users: owner, group, and other. The permissions associated with the owner and the group to which the owner belongs are based on their roles, but all of those who are not the owner, or a member of the owner's group, fall within the category of other.

The permissions for this group are set separately from the other two and, with very few special exceptions, are a combination of read, write, and execute. Within this environment, you can create a database and give yourself (owner) permission to read and write, give other admins (group) only read permission, and not give any permission to those not in admin (other).

You could just as easily create a script file that cleans up log files and frees space on a workstation. To do this, you would give yourself (owner) all rights, give other admins (group) the ability to read and execute, and give basic users (other) the right only to execute.

Role-Based Access Control

Role-based access control (RBAC) models approach the problem of access control based on established roles in an organization. RBAC models implement access by job function or by responsibility. Each employee has one or more roles that allow access to specific information. If a person moves from one role to another, the access for the previous role will no longer be available. RBAC models provide more flexibility than the MAC model and less flexibility than the DAC model. They do, however, have the advantage of being strictly based on job function as opposed to individual needs.

Instead of thinking "Denise needs to be able to edit files," RBAC uses the logic "Editors need to be able to edit files" and "Denise is a member of the Editors group." This model is always good for use in an environment in which there is high employee turnover.

This is also sometimes called *group-based control* or *group-based permissions*. Essentially, Windows operating systems work in this fashion. Your permissions on a Windows-based domain are determined by the group(s) into which you are placed. These groups are, in effect, roles.

Rule-Based Access Control

Rule-based access control (RBAC) uses the settings in preconfigured security policies to make all decisions. These rules can be to

- Deny all but those who specifically appear in a list (an allow list)
- Deny only those who specifically appear in the list (a true deny list)

Entries in the list may be usernames, IP addresses, hostnames, or even domains. Rule-based models are often being used in conjunction with role-based models to add greater flexibility.

The easiest way to implement rule-based access control is with access control lists (ACLs), discussed later in this chapter. ACLs create the rules by which the access control model functions.

ABAC

Attribute-based access control (ABAC) is a relatively new method for access control. It is defined in NIST 800-162, Attribute Based Control Definition and Considerations. According to that standard:

> A logical access control methodology where authorization to perform a set of operations is determined by evaluating attributes associated with the subject, object, requested operations, and, in some cases, environment conditions against policy, rules, or relationships that describe the allowable operations for a given set of attributes.

Essentially, the access control mechanism looks at subjects that are attempting to access a given object but considers all of the various attributes associated with the subject and object in making the access control decision. A *subject* is an active entity (generally an individual, process, or device). An *object* is some resource that the subject is attempting to access. *Attributes* are characteristics that define specific aspects of the subject, object, environment conditions, and/or requested actions that are predefined and preassigned by an authority.

If, for example, a traveling sales representative is attempting to access customer records on a company network, an ABAC system would not only look at the sales rep's access rights, but also at the entire scenario. Is the rep logging in from a machine or a location that he or she has not used before? Is the rep logging in at an unusual time? What is the rep attempting to do? The sales rep might be given access to read files, but not to edit or delete files. In essence, ABAC is a more robust access control methodology that examines the entire scenario in making access control decision.

Smartcards

Smartcards are generally used for access control and security purposes. The card itself usually contains a small amount of memory that can be used to store permissions and access information.

Smartcards are difficult to counterfeit, but they're easy to steal. Once a thief has a smartcard, they have access to all that the card allows. To prevent this, many organizations don't put any identifying marks on their smartcards, making it harder for someone to use them. A password or PIN is required to activate most smartcards, and encryption is employed to protect the contents. With many smartcards, if you enter the wrong PIN multiple times (usually three), the card will shut down to enhance security further.

Many European countries are beginning to use smartcards instead of magnetic-strip credit cards because they offer additional security and can contain more information. The United States has made moves in this direction, but it has not fully implemented chip and pin.

Smartcards are now sometimes implemented as proximity cards. These cards have an RFID (radio frequency identifier) chip that will transmit authentication information when the card is in range of an authentication device.

There are two main types of smartcards: common access cards and personal identification verification cards. We will discuss these smartcards in the following sections.

Common Access Card

The first type of smartcard is the *common access card (CAC)*. These cards are issued by the Department of Defense (DoD) as a general identification/authentication card for military personnel, contractors, and non-DoD employees. A picture appears on the front of the card with an integrated chip beneath and a barcode. A magnetic strip and another barcode appears on the back of the card.

A CAC is used for accessing DoD computers, signing email, and implementing PKI (public key infrastructure). In 2008, the most recent year for which data is available, over 17 million cards had been issued. You can find current information on the CAC here: www.cac.mil.

Personal Identification Verification Card

What the CAC is for military employees, the *personal identity verification (PIV)* (referenced by CompTIA as personal identification verification card) is to federal employees and contractors. Per Homeland Security Presidential Directive number 12 (HSPD-12), the PIV will eventually be required of all U.S. government employees and contractors. The PIV will be required to gain access (physical and logical) to government resources.

Tokens

A *token* is some physical device that is used to gain access. It could be a wireless keycard, a key fob, or any physical device. These are sometimes called *security tokens*. Tokens often contain a digital certificate, and the certificate is used to authenticate the user. There are software implementations of tokens, but the original meaning of the term was a hardware device.

Software-based security tokens are part of a two-factor authentication device. Software tokens are stored on the device and used to authenticate the user. They can be as simple as a password that is in an encrypted file, or perhaps a digital certificate.

There are many ways that a token could operate. It might have a stored password, simply called a *static password token*. Another method is to rotate through passwords based on some algorithm. The token and the authentication server used synchronized clocks to determine which password should be used at what time. There are also one-time passwords that are generated based on some algorithm. The last type of token is a challenge response token. The authentication server encrypts a challenge (typically a random number, or at least data with some random parts) with a public key; the device proves it possesses a copy of the matching private key by providing the decrypted challenge.

File and Database Security

Maintaining security of your network will necessitate maintaining security of your most sensitive data. That is usually going to be on a file or database server. When an attacker breaches your network or an insider seeks data to exfiltrate, the most likely target will be either file or database servers.

Much of the security discussed in this chapter already is applicable to file and database servers. For example, both types of servers should have their own firewall, and the logs of that firewall should be reviewed periodically. Both types of servers should have an HIDS, and the log for that HIDS should be reviewed periodically. And, of course, any server (any computer at all) should have antivirus.

The authentication and access control methods discussed in this chapter are also applicable to file and database servers. It is critical that you limit access to these servers to a need-to-know basis. It is also important that any user with access can only access as much as they need to perform their job tasks—that is, the principle of least privileges.

Summary

This chapter introduced you to a number of tools that you can use to gather data about your network. For the Security+ exam, you should be able to define the tool types, such as vulnerability scanners and password crackers. For your job duties as a security administrator, you should be able to utilize several of these tools. The command-line tools also comprise common test questions on the Security+ exam.

Next the chapter examined troubleshooting configuration issues. This is a very broad topic, and no single chapter could fully address it. The main point to understand is that if your security devices and services are not properly configured, that misconfiguration is itself a security vulnerability.

This chapter introduced a number of security technologies and explained how to view their output. That includes IDS, firewall, antivirus, and other related technologies. You should be familiar with how to view outputs from these systems.

The chapter also addressed access control and identity management. The key difference between authentication and identification is that authentication means that someone has accurate information, whereas identification means that accurate information is proven to be in possession of the correct individual.

The most basic form of authentication is known as single-factor authentication (SFA), because only one set of values is checked. To increase security, it is necessary to use multifactor authentication, which involves two or more values that are checked.

This chapter examined the various types of authentication services in use, including RADIUS and different variations of TACACS. It also looked at tunneling protocols, smartcards, and other means of access control.

ACLs are being implemented in network devices and systems to enable the control of access to systems and users. ACLs allow individual systems, users, or IP addresses to be ignored.

Exam Essentials

Be able to describe the various tools.   Understand vulnerability scanners, port scanners, password crackers, and related tools. Know conceptually how they function. Be very familiar with command-line tools such as `ipconfig`, `ping`, and `arp`.

Understand configuration issues.   Proper configuration of all security and network devices is essential and will be on the exam. You should also have a general idea of how to read and interpret output from security devices.

Be able to describe the roles of access control.   The four primary roles are MAC, DAC, and RBAC (both types of RBAC). Mandatory access control (MAC) establishes rigid access control methods in the organization. Discretionary access control (DAC) allows for flexibility in access control. Role-based access control (RBAC) is based on the role the individual or department has in the organization. In a fourth type, rule-based access control (RBAC), settings in preconfigured security policies, are used to make all decisions.

Explain the relative advantages of the technologies available to you for authentication.   You have many tools available to you to help establish authentication processes. Some of these tools start with a password and user ID. Others involve physical devices or the physical characteristics of the person who is requesting authentication.

Understand least privilege.   Least privilege states that when assigning permissions, you should give users only the permissions they need to do their work and no more. The biggest benefit to following this policy is the reduction of risk.

Review Questions

You can find the answers in the Appendix.

1. John is a network administrator for ACME company. He is trying to explain least privileges to a new technician. Which of the following is the basic premise of least privilege?

  A. Always assign responsibilities to the administrator who has the minimum permissions required.

  B. When assigning permissions, give users only the permissions they need to do their work and no more.

  C. Regularly review user permissions and take away one that they currently have to see if they will complain or even notice that it is missing.

  D. Do not give management more permissions than users.

2. The present method of requiring access to be strictly defined on every object is proving too cumbersome for your environment. The edict has come down from upper management that access requirements should be slightly reduced. Which access model allows users some flexibility for information-sharing purposes?

  A. DAC

  B. MAC

  C. RBAC

  D. MLAC

3. Ahmed has been directed to ensure that LDAP on his network is secure. LDAP is an example of which of the following?

  A. Directory access protocol

  B. IDS

  C. Tiered model application development environment

  D. File server

4. Upper management has suddenly become concerned about security. As the senior network administrator, you are asked to suggest changes that should be implemented. Which of the following access methods should you recommend if the technique to be used is one that is primarily based on preestablished access and can't be changed by users?

  A. MAC

  B. DAC

  C. RBAC

  D. Kerberos

5. Your office administrator is being trained to perform server backups. Which access control method would be ideal for this situation?

  A. MAC

  B. DAC

  C. RBAC

  D. Security tokens

6. You've been assigned to mentor a junior administrator and bring her up to speed quickly. The topic you're currently explaining is authentication. Which method uses a KDC to accomplish authentication for users, programs, or systems?

    A. CHAP

    B. Kerberos

    C. Biometrics

    D. Smartcards

7. After a careful risk analysis, the value of your company's data has been increased. Accordingly, you're expected to implement authentication solutions that reflect the increased value of the data. Which of the following authentication methods uses more than one authentication process for a logon?

    A. Multifactor

    B. Biometrics

    C. Smartcard

    D. Kerberos

8. Your company provides medical data to doctors from a worldwide database. Because of the sensitive nature of the data, it's imperative that authentication be established on each session and be valid only for that session. Which of the following authentication methods provides credentials that are valid only during a single session?

    A. Tokens

    B. Certificate

    C. Smartcard

    D. Kerberos

9. Which of the following is the term used whenever two or more parties authenticate each other?

    A. SSO

    B. Multifactor authentication

    C. Mutual authentication

    D. Tunneling

10. You have added a new child domain to your network. As a result of this, the child has adopted all of the trust relationships with other domains in the forest that existed for its parent domain. What is responsible for this?

    A. LDAP access

    B. XML access

    C. Fuzzing access

    D. Transitive access

11. Which of the following is a type of smartcard issued by the Department of Defense as a general identification/authentication card for military personnel, contractors, and non-DoD employees?

    A. PIV

    B. POV

    C. DLP

    D. CAC

12. You are working as a security administrator for a small financial institution. You want to use an authentication method that will periodically reauthenticate clients. Which protocol is best suited for this?

    A. PAP

    B. SPAP

    C. KERBEROS

    D. CHAP

13. Which command most likely produced the output shown in the graphic?

    ```
    Interface: 192.168.1.104 --- 0xc
      Internet Address      Physical Address      Type
      192.168.1.1           60-38-e0-6f-c9-d3     dynamic
      192.168.1.110         54-8c-a0-e7-56-ca     dynamic
      192.168.1.120         00-26-ab-bb-27-b8     dynamic
      192.168.1.129         c8-f7-33-1d-ac-d1     dynamic
      192.168.1.130         5c-a3-9d-33-68-a4     dynamic
      192.168.1.135         a4-db-30-bc-88-d5     dynamic
      192.168.1.255         ff-ff-ff-ff-ff-ff     static
      224.0.0.2             01-00-5e-00-00-02     static
      224.0.0.22            01-00-5e-00-00-16     static
      224.0.0.251           01-00-5e-00-00-fb     static
      224.0.0.252           01-00-5e-00-00-fc     static
      224.0.2.3             01-00-5e-00-02-03     static
      239.192.152.143       01-00-5e-40-98-8f     static
      239.255.255.239       01-00-5e-7f-ff-ef     static
      239.255.255.246       01-00-5e-7f-ff-f6     static
      239.255.255.250       01-00-5e-7f-ff-fa     static
      255.255.255.255       ff-ff-ff-ff-ff-ff     static
    ```

    A. `arp -a`

    B. `ping -a`

    C. `netstat`

    D. `nslookup`

14. John is trying to determine the origin of an email. He has captured the email headers and knows the IP address of the originating email server. What command would show John the complete path to that IP address?

    A. `ping -a`

    B. `arp`

    C. `tracert`

    D. `nslookup`

15. Juanita is the security administrator for a large university. She is concerned about copyright issues and wants to ensure that her university does not violate copyrights. What would be her main concern regarding unauthorized software?

A. It might be copyrighted.

B. It might be used to circumvent copyright protection.

C. That should not be a copyright concern.

D. It is not a concern if she has a least one license for the software.

16. Terrance is examining an authentication system that was developed at MIT and uses tickets for authentication. What system is Terrance most likely examining?

A. CHAP

B. MS-CHAP

C. KERBEROS

D. OATH

17. Melissa is planning on implementing biometric authentication on her network. Which of the following should be a goal for any biometric solution she selects?

A. High FRR, low FAR

B. High FAR, low FRR

C. Low CER

D. High CER

18. Jarod is evaluating web-based, single sign-on solutions. Which of the following technologies is most associated with web page authorization?

A. SAML

B. PIV

C. CHAP

D. RBAC

19. You are a network administrator for ACME Corporation. You want to implement a new access control mechanism. The mechanism you are considering takes into account the entire environment/scenario of the access request. What does this describe?

A. MAC

B. DAC

C. RBAC

D. ABAC

20. Dennis has implemented an authentication system that uses a password, a PIN, and the user's birthday. What best describes this system?

A. Single factor

B. Two factor

C. Three factor

D. Strong authentication

Chapter

5

Wireless Network Threats

THE FOLLOWING COMPTIA SECURITY+ EXAM OBJECTIVE IS COVERED IN THIS CHAPTER:

✓ **1.2   Compare and contrast types of attacks.**

- Wireless Attacks: Replay; IV; Evil twin; Rogue AP; Jamming; WPS; Bluejacking; Bluesnarfing; RFID; NFC; Disassociation

Wireless systems, plainly put, create many opportunities for attackers. These systems are intercepted relatively easily, as compared to their wired counterparts.

This chapter discusses various types of wireless threats and attacks that you'll need to be aware of and make certain that you only encounter them in a book, rather than on your systems.

Wireless Threat Terminology

When it comes to wireless threats, acronyms and names that sound like they belong in a Star Wars movie are prominent. In some cases, there can be overlap between terms: an evil twin *is* a rogue AP, for example. The following terms (also found in the online glossary) are those that CompTIA is fond of using and testing on in this category. They are provided in order to make it easier for you to know what each is intended to convey.

Security+ Terminology

802.1x   The IEEE standard that defines port-based security for wireless network access control.

access point (AP)   The point at which access to a network is accomplished. This term is often used in relation to a wireless access point (WAP).

bluejacking   The sending of unsolicited messages over a Bluetooth connection.

bluesnarfing   The gaining of unauthorized access through a Bluetooth connection.

disassociation   An attack in which the intruder sends a frame to the AP with a spoofed address to make it look like it came from the victim and disconnects them from the network.

evil twin   An attack in which a rogue wireless access point poses as a legitimate wireless service provider to intercept information that users transmit.

interference   The byproduct of electrical processes. One common form of interference is Radio Frequency Interference (RFI), which is usually projected across a radio spectrum.

IV attack   An attack that involves looking at repeated results in order to crack the WEP secret key.

jamming   Purposely obstructing or interfering with a signal.

near field communication (NFC)   Technology that enables communication between devices when they're "touched" together. Often used to verify (often through RFID or Wi-Fi) that the device is present.

radio frequency identification (RFID)   A technology that incorporates the use of electromagnetic coupling in the radio frequency (RF) portion of the spectrum to identify items uniquely (object, animal, person, credit cards, door access tokens, antishoplifting devices, and so on).

replay attack   An attack that captures portions of a session to play back later to convince a host that it is still talking to the original connection.

rogue access point   An unauthorized wireless access point on a network.

SSID   The Service Set Identifier (SSID) is used by the access point of a wireless LAN to identify itself and is intended to be unique for a particular area/entity on a network.

Wi-Fi   A wireless network operating in the 2.4 GHz or 5 GHz range.

Wi-Fi Protected Setup (WPS)   An authentication process that requires the user to do something in order to complete the enrollment process. Examples include pressing a button on the router within a short time period, entering a PIN, or bringing the new device close.

Wired Equivalent Privacy (WEP)   A security protocol for 802.11b (wireless) networks that attempts to establish the same security for them as would be present in a wired network.

wireless access point   A connection device used for clients in a radio frequency (RF) network.

Wireless Vulnerabilities to Know

Wireless systems are vulnerable to all of the same attacks as wired networks. However, because these protocols use radio frequency signals for data emanation, they have an additional weakness: all radio frequency signals can be easily intercepted. To intercept 802.11x traffic, all you need is a PC with an appropriate 802.11x card installed. Many networks will regularly broadcast their name (known as an *SSID broadcast*) to announce their presence. Simple software on the PC can capture the link traffic in the wireless AP and then process this data in order to decrypt account and password information.

One method of protecting the network that is often recommended is to disable, or turn off, the SSID broadcast (also known as *cloaking*). The access point is still there, and it is still accessible by those who have been told of its existence by the administrator, but it prevents those who are just scanning from finding it. This is considered a *very weak* form of security because there are still other ways, albeit a bit more complicated, to discover the presence of the access point besides the SSID broadcast.

In Exercise 5.1, we'll show you how to configure Windows to connect to a network not broadcasting an SSID.

EXERCISE 5.1

Configuring a Wireless Connection Not Broadcasting an SSID

To configure the client to connect to a network, even when the SSID is not broadcasting, follow these steps:

1. On a Windows client, right-click the network icon and choose Connect To A Network.

2. Right-click the network to which you are connected and choose Properties.

3. Click the Connection tab, and check the Connect Even If The Network Is Not Broadcasting box.

4. Click OK.

5. Exit the Connect To A Network dialog box.

An additional aspect of wireless systems is the site survey. *Site surveys* involve listening in on an existing wireless network using commercially available technologies. Doing so allows intelligence, and possibly data capture, to be performed on systems in your wireless network. The term *site survey* initially meant determining whether a proposed location was free from *interference*. When used by an attacker, a site survey can determine what types of systems are in use, the protocols used, and other critical information about your network. It's the primary method used to gather information about wireless networks. Virtually all wireless networks are vulnerable to site surveys.

In the following sections, we will focus on the various types of wireless attacks, technologies, and topics that CompTIA wants you to be familiar with for the Security+ exam.

Replay

A *replay attack* is a kind of access or modification attack that has become quite common. They occur when information is captured over a network and then malevolently reused for a purpose other than intended.

As an example, in a distributed environment, logon and password information is sent between the client and the authentication system. The attacker can capture the information and replay it later. This can also occur with security certificates from systems such as Kerberos: the attacker resubmits the certificate, hoping to be validated by the authentication system and circumvent any time sensitivity, thus entering the system.

If this type of attack is successful, the attacker in this example will have all of the rights and privileges from the original certificate. This is the primary reason that most certificates contain a unique session identifier and a time stamp. If the certificate has expired, it will be rejected and an entry should be made in a security log to notify system administrators.

IV (initialization vector) attacks are made possible due to weaknesses in Wired Equivalent Privacy (WEP), a wireless protocol designed to provide a privacy equivalent to that of a wired network. WEP was implemented in a number of wireless devices, including smartphones and other mobile devices, but it is vulnerable because of weaknesses in the way its encryption algorithms (RC4) are employed. These weaknesses allow the algorithm to be cracked potentially in as little as five minutes using available PC software. For this reason, WEP is considered to be one of the more vulnerable security protocols.

The initialization vector (IV) that WEP uses for encryption is 24-bit, which is quite weak and means that IVs are reused with the same key. By examining the repeating result, it was easy for attackers to crack the WEP secret key. This is known as an *IV attack*.

Since the IV is shorter than the key, it must be repeated when used. To put it in perspective, the attack happened because the algorithm used is RC4, the IV is too small, the IV is static, and the IV is part of the RC4 encryption key.

Figure 5.1 shows the configuration settings on a very simple wireless router and sums up the situation best: the only time to use WEP is when you must have compatibility with older devices that do not support new encryption.

FIGURE 5.1   Wireless security settings for a simple router

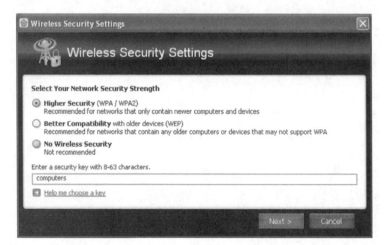

To strengthen WEP encryption, a *Temporal Key Integrity Protocol (TKIP)* was employed. This placed a 128-bit wrapper around the WEP encryption with a key that is based on things such as the MAC address of the destination device and the serial number of the packet. TKIP was designed as a backward-compatible replacement to WEP, and it could work with all existing hardware. Without the use of TKIP, WEP, as mentioned earlier in this chapter, was considered very weak. It is worth noting, however, that even TKIP has been broken.

Rogue APs and Evil Twins

Weak encryption was an issue with earlier access points, but most of the newer wireless APs use special ID numbers (SSIDs) and must be configured in network cards to allow communication. However, using ID number configurations doesn't necessarily prevent wireless networks from being monitored. One particularly mischievous undertaking involves taking advantage of *rogue access points*. Any wireless access point added to your network that has not been authorized is considered a rogue.

The rogue may be added by an attacker, or it could have been innocently added by a user wanting to enhance their environment. The problem with a user doing so is that there is a good chance they will not implement the same level of security that you would, and this could open up the system for a man-in-the-middle attack or evil twin attack. An *evil twin attack* is one in which a rogue wireless access point poses as a legitimate wireless service provider to intercept information that users transmit.

Educate and train users about a wireless network and the need to keep it secure, just as you would train and educate them about any other security topic. They may think that there is no harm in them joining any wireless network they can find as they travel, such as those shown in Figure 5.2, but they should question whether the administrators for all such networks have the best interests of your company data at heart.

FIGURE 5.2   Examples of some questionable wireless networks

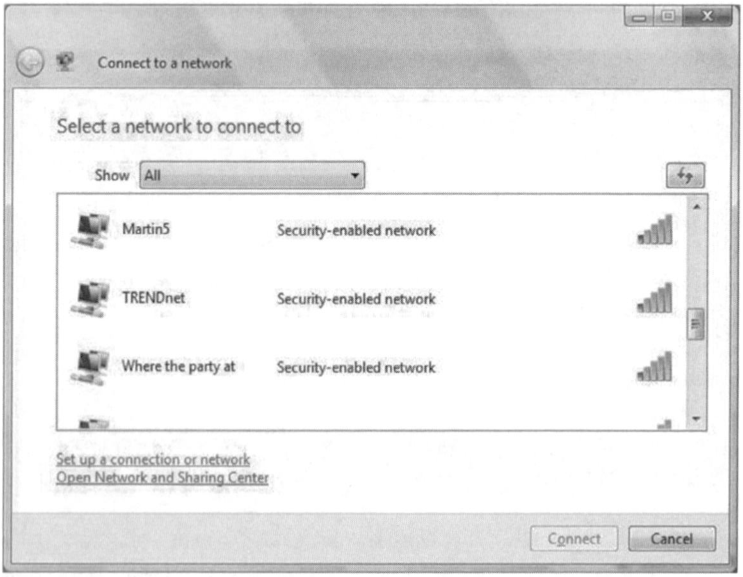

Jamming

Interference can be unintentional (caused by other devices in the vicinity, for example) or intentional. When it is intentional, then it is referred to as *jamming*, as the intent is to jam the signal and keep the legitimate device from communicating. Given the way the jamming attack works, it can be thought of as a type of denial-of-service (DoS) attack and is a violation of federal law in most cases.

Powerful jammers are available that send a constant signal and, if in the right vicinity, can incapacitate a network quickly. Since they are so strong, however, these constant jammers are usually easily detected, and administrators can implement antijamming procedures (such as switching channels) to negate them.

More troublesome to identify are low-powered jammers, some of which hide by sending out signals and then stopping, hiding for a while, and then sending out signals again.

WPS

To simplify network setup, a number of small office and home office (SOHO) routers use a series of EAP (Extensible Authentication Protocol) messages to allow new hosts to join the network and use WPA/WPA2 (Wi-Fi Protected Access versions 1 and 2). Known as *Wi-Fi Protected Setup (WPS)*, this often requires the user to do something in order to complete the enrollment process: press a button on the router within a short time period, enter a PIN, or bring the new device close by (so that near field communication can take place).

Unfortunately, *WPS attacks* have become commonplace because the technology is susceptible to brute-force attacks used to guess the user's PIN. Once an attacker gains access, they are then on the Wi-Fi network. For that reason, we suggest that you disable WPS in devices that allow it (and update the firmware in those where it is a possibility).

Bluejacking

Bluetooth technology is often used for creating personal area networks (PANs or WPANs), and most Bluetooth devices come with a factory-default PIN that you will want to change to more secure values. With the popularity of Bluetooth on the rise, two additional vulnerabilities have been added: bluejacking and bluesnarfing. *Bluejacking* is the sending of unsolicited messages (think spam) over a Bluetooth connection. While annoying, it is basically considered harmless.

Bluesnarfing

Bluesnarfing is the gaining of unauthorized access through a Bluetooth connection. This access can be obtained through a smartphone or any Bluetooth device. Once access has been achieved, the attacker can copy data in the same way that they could with any other type of unauthorized access.

 The Bluetooth standard has addressed weaknesses in the technology, and it continues to become ever more secure. One of the simplest ways to secure Bluetooth devices is not to set their attribute to Discoverable.

NFC and RFID

Near field communication (NFC) is a technology that requires a user to bring the client close to the AP in order to verify—often through *radio frequency identification (RFID)* or Wi-Fi—that the device is present. The popularity of this has grown with phones being used as a part of payment systems, and it can also be used between two phones to "bump" and send data from one to another. Although there is no hardcoded standard defining "near," the industry tends to use 4cm (1.6 inches) as the distance.

NFC is a newer standard, but it is built on the older standards created for RFID, which allows compatible hardware both to supply power to and to communicate with an otherwise unpowered and passive electronic tag using radio waves. RFID is widely used for identification, authentication, and tracking applications.

Disassociation

Just as jamming can be classified as a type of DoS attack, so too can a *disassociation attack* (commonly known as a *deauthentication attack*). With this type of attack, the intruder sends a frame to the AP with a spoofed address to make it look like it came from the victim and disconnects them from the network. Since the victim is unable to keep a connection with the AP, it increases their chances of choosing to use another AP—a rogue one or one in a hotel or other venue that they have to pay for to use. A number of hotels had suits filed against them by the Federal Trade Commission for launching attacks of this type and generating revenue by requiring their guests to pay for "premium" services rather than being able to use the free Wi-Fi.

Wireless Commonsense

Be sure to change the default password settings on all wireless devices. Never assume that a wireless connection is secure. The emissions from a wireless portal may be detectable through walls and for several city blocks from the portal. Interception is easy to accomplish, given that RF is the medium used for communication. Newer wireless devices offer data security, and you should use it. You can set newer APs and wireless routers to non-broadcast in addition to configuring WPA2 and a higher encryption level.

Wireless Attack Analogy

Imagine that you've decided to go to a sandwich shop for lunch and that you want to eat and get back to work as quickly as possible. Problems lurk with the lunch, however, as illustrated by Table 5.1. Not every type of attack fits this scenario, and only those that do are examined.

TABLE 5.1   Sandwich shop attacks

Attack	Analogy
Rogue access point	While standing in line to place your order, an employee who is on a break recognizes you as a regular customer and offers to make you a sandwich from ingredients in the back room rather than making you wait. This will circumvent the cash register and short the owner.
Jamming	While trying to place your order, a co-worker who knows you keeps mimicking what you are saying. Their attempt at humor is keeping the sandwich preparer from correctly hearing your order.
Interference	While trying to place your order, an obnoxious businessman stands behind you in line and shouts into his smartphone. He is so loud that he keeps the sandwich preparer from correctly hearing your order.
Bluejacking	As you're ordering, someone in line behind you keeps anonymously mentioning things to be added to the sandwich, and the sandwich preparer adds them to your order thinking that you are the one who wants them.
Evil twin	Distracted by the rain, you get out of your car and run into what you think is your favorite sandwich shop, only to find out that you went in one door too soon and are in a rival sandwich shop that charges twice as much and gives half as much meat.
Replay attack	The person behind you in line tells the sandwich preparer that they will have the exact same thing you had, and it should be added to your bill.

It would be great if your obnoxious co-workers did not know that the shop existed because you never mentioned it (disable the SSID broadcast), if the sandwich preparer only placed items on the sandwich that they knew for certain you ordered (near field communication), and if they only allowed in new people recommended by current customers (Wi-Fi Protected Setup).

Summary

Wireless systems have become increasingly popular and standardized. Those wireless networks are vulnerable to a number of threats.

Vulnerabilities exist because of weaknesses in the protocols. As an example, WEP is vulnerable because of weaknesses in the way that the encryption algorithms are employed; the initialization vector (IV) that WEP uses for encryption is 24-bit, and IVs are reused with the same key. By examining the repeating result, it is easy for intruders to crack the WEP secret key, known as an IV attack.

Mobile devices use either RF signaling or cellular technologies for communication. If the device uses WAP, several levels of security exist: anonymous authentication (anyone can connect), server authentication (the workstation must authenticate against the server), and two-way authentication (both the client and the server must authenticate with each other).

Exam Essentials

Know that a wireless access point extends the reach of the network.   The wireless access point (AP) sits on the wired network and then acts as the router for the wireless clients. Most wireless access points will work with more than one 802.11 standard. Wireless clients, using a wireless NIC card, and mobile devices connect to the access point.

Know the vulnerabilities of wireless networks.   The primary method of gaining information about a wireless network is a site survey. Site surveys can be accomplished with a PC and an 802.11 card. Wireless networks are subject to the same attacks as wired networks.

Know the wireless security protocols.   The 802.11i standard is often referenced as WPA2 (Wi-Fi Protected Access version 2). It is an enhancement to earlier standards, which were much weaker. WPS (Wi-Fi Protected Setup) often requires the user to do something in order to complete the enrollment process: press a button on the router within a short time period, enter a PIN, or bring the new device close by to increase security.

Review Questions

You can find the answers in the Appendix.

1. An IV attack is usually associated with which of the following wireless protocols?
   - **A.** WEP
   - **B.** WAP
   - **C.** WPA
   - **D.** WPA2

2. What is the size of the initialization vector (IV) that WEP uses for encryption?
   - **A.** 6-bit
   - **B.** 24-bit
   - **C.** 56-bit
   - **D.** 128-bit

3. What is the size of the wrapper TKIP places around the WEP encryption with a key that is based on things such as the MAC address of your machine and the serial number of the packet?
   - **A.** 128-bit
   - **B.** 64-bit
   - **C.** 56-bit
   - **D.** 12-bit

4. What technology is used to send data between phones that are in close proximity to each other?
   - **A.** NFC
   - **B.** IBI
   - **C.** IBJ
   - **D.** IFNC

5. What technology is used to simplify network setup by allowing a router to have the administrator push a button on it to allow a new host to join?
   - **A.** WEP
   - **B.** WPA
   - **C.** WTLS
   - **D.** WPS

6. Which of the following technologies is used to identify and track tags attached to objects?
   - **A.** NFC
   - **B.** RFID
   - **C.** IV
   - **D.** DSC

7. What type of attack captures portions of a session to play back later to convince a host that it is still talking to the original connection?

A. Replay

B. Echo

C. Duplication

D. Reprise

8. Which standard defines port-based security for wireless network access control?

A. 802.1n

B. 802.1g

C. 802.1x

D. 802.1s

9. Which of the following types of attacks involves the sending of unsolicited messages over a Bluetooth connection?

A. Bluesmurfing

B. Bluesnarfing

C. Bluewhaling

D. Bluejacking

10. Karl has checked into a hotel after a long day of travel. He is attempting to check his daily deluge of email messages using the free in-room Wi-Fi, but it keeps losing the connection. When he calls the front desk, they suggest that he might want to use the premium Wi-Fi (which costs more) to get a better connection. What type of attack could this scenario represent?

A. Upselling

B. Cross-selling

C. Disassociation

D. Imitation

11. Frustrated with the low signal that the devices in his cubicle receive, Spencer brings in his own access point and creates his own network. Kristin, a co-worker, tells him that if the boss finds out about this it is grounds for immediate dismissal, and he should read the employee handbook if he has any questions. Setting up your own access point represents which of the following?

A. Degenerate

B. Rogue

C. Corporeal

D. Temporal

12. During the authentication part of setting up his small office access point, Wolfgang was required to enter a PIN within 60 seconds. This process is known as:

A. Wired Equivalent Privacy

B. Wi-Fi Protected Access

C. Wi-Fi Protected Setup

D. Wi-Fi Authentication Protection

13. Which security protocol for wireless networks attempts to establish the same security for them as would be present in a wired network?

A. WEP

B. WEB

C. WELL

D. WALL

14. Evan fears that the tenant in the office next door is using RF interference to try to force his small company to vacate the building in frustration. Purposely obstructing or interfering with a signal is known as which of the following?

A. Shoving

B. Jamming

C. Cramming

D. Blocking

15. What is a disassociation attack more commonly known as?

A. Decertification attack

B. Disconfirmation attack

C. Deauthentication attack

D. Denial attack

16. With near field communication (NFC) technology, the industry tends to use what distance as "near"?

A. 1 inch

B. 1.2 inches

C. 1.6 inches

D. 2 inches

17. With Bluetooth devices suddenly popping up everywhere in your network, you want to secure as many of them as possible. One of the simplest methods of securing these devices is not to set their attribute to:

A. Discoverable

B. Transmit

C. Announce

D. Communicate

18. Which of the following is the gaining of unauthorized access through a Bluetooth connection?

    A. Bluejumping

    B. Bluesnarfing

    C. Bluerunning

    D. Bluelining

19. A client calls you and says that he wants to turn off the SSID broadcast on his small network because he is afraid that those simply scanning for a network are finding it and trying to connect to it. You inform him that this is a *very weak* form of security and suggest some other options, but he is insistent on this being done. What is this form of hiding the router known as?

    A. Veiling

    B. Masking

    C. Shrouding

    D. Cloaking

20. Which of the following is attack in which a rogue wireless access point poses as a legitimate wireless service provider to intercept information that users transmit?

    A. Collision

    B. Evil twin

    C. NFC

    D. WPS

Chapter

6

Securing the Cloud

THE FOLLOWING COMPTIA SECURITY+ EXAM OBJECTIVE IS COVERED IN THIS CHAPTER:

✓ **3.7 Summarize cloud and virtualization concepts.**

- Hypervisor: Type I; Type II
- VM sprawl avoidance
- VM escape protection
- Cloud storage
- Cloud deployment models: SaaS; PaaS; IaaS; Private; Public; Hybrid; Community
- On-premise vs. hosted vs. cloud
- VDI/VDE
- Cloud access security broker
- Security as a Service

If there were such a thing as a word-of-the-day for information technology, the one that would have to be the most popular recently would be "cloud." Vendors have come to embrace the word in their marketing materials for everything from tablets to servers and a lot of odd devices in between. As a security professional, you are likely to be pulled into discussions about the cloud by many who don't fully understand the meaning of what they are saying.

CompTIA has created stand-alone certifications around cloud-based technology. The purpose of this chapter is to define just what the cloud—and its necessary cousin, virtualization—really is and what you need to know about this topic for the Security+ exam and to be able to keep your systems secure.

Cloud-Related Terminology

The cloud means a lot of different things to different individuals. What you care about while you are studying for the Security+ exam is what it means to CompTIA and the sources they use when they create the exam. The following terms (also found in the online glossary) are those that CompTIA is fond of using and testing on in this category. They are provided in order to make it easier for you to know what each is intended to convey.

Security+ Terminology

cloud access security broker On-premise or cloud-based security policy enforcement points.

cloud bursting Moving the execution of an application to the cloud on an as-needed basis.

cloud computing A model for enabling ubiquitous, convenient, on-demand network access to a shared pool of configurable computing resources.

community cloud Cloud delivery model in which the infrastructure is shared by organizations with something in common.

hybrid cloud Any cloud delivery model that combines two or more of the other delivery model types.

hypervisor   The software that allows virtual machines to exist. The machine running the hypervisor is known as a host, while the instances of virtual machines are known as guests.

Infrastructure as a Service (IaaS)   A model of cloud computing that utilizes virtualization; clients pay an outsourcer for the resources used.

National Institute of Standards and Technology (NIST)   An agency (formerly known as the National Bureau of Standards [NBS]) that has been involved in developing and supporting standards for the U.S. government for over 100 years. NIST has become involved in cryptography standards, systems, and technology in a variety of areas. It's primarily concerned with governmental systems, where it exercises a great deal of influence.

Platform as a Service (PaaS)   A cloud service model wherein the consumer can deploy but does not manage or control any of the underlying cloud infrastructure.

private cloud   A cloud delivery model owned and managed internally.

public cloud   A cloud delivery model available to others.

QoS (quality of service)   A collection of technologies that provide the ability to balance network traffic and prioritize workloads.

sandboxing   Isolating applications to keep users of them from venturing to other data.

Security as a Service   A subscription-based business model intended to be more cost effective than smaller individuals/corporations could ever achieve on their own.

Software as a Service (SaaS)   A model of cloud computing in which the consumer can use the provider's applications, but they do not manage or control any of the underlying cloud infrastructure.

Type I hypervisor   Virtualization method that is independent of the operating system and boots before the OS.

Type II hypervisor   Virtualization method that is dependent on the operating system.

VDE   A virtual desktop environment (VDE) stores everything related to the user (wallpaper, folders, windows, and so on) remotely and client software locally simulates the user's desktop environment and capabilities while running them on the host.

VDI   Virtual desktop infrastructure (VDI) is the process of running a user desktop inside a virtual machine that lives on a server in the datacenter. It enables fully personalized desktops for each user yet maintains centralized management and security.

virtualization   Emulating one or more physical computers on the same host.

VM escape   The act of breaking out of one virtual machine into one or more others on the same physical host.

VM sprawl   Growth that occurs on a large number of virtual machines and requires resources—usually administration related—to keep up with.

Working with Cloud Computing

One of the reasons "the cloud" can be so confusing in discussions is that there are many instances in which the phrase has been improperly used in marketing hype. To find a meaning that all can agree on, let's turn to the National Institute of Standards and Technology (NIST). Three service models are defined in Special Publication 800-145: Software as a Service (SaaS), Platform as a Service (PaaS), and Infrastructure as a Service (IaaS). Each of these service models are explored in the sections that follow. Following that, we will take a look at the four possible delivery models: private, public, community, and hybrid.

 So important is NIST when it comes to cloud computing definitions that the objectives for the Cloud+ certification from CompTIA include the phrase "according to NIST" after the first six topics in the first subdomain.

Software as a Service (SaaS)

According to NIST, *Software as a Service (SaaS)* is defined as

> The capability provided to the consumer is to use the provider's applications running on a cloud infrastructure. The applications are accessible from various client devices through either a thin client interface, such as a web browser (e.g., web-based email), or a program interface. The consumer does not manage or control the underlying cloud infrastructure including network, servers, operating systems, storage, or even individual application capabilities, with the possible exception of limited user-specific application configuration settings.

> National Institute of Standards and Technology,
> Special Publication 800-145

Although the description may seem verbose, the words used are very important. The ones to focus on in this definition are that the consumer can "use" the provider's applications and that they do not "manage or control" any of the underlying cloud infrastructure. Figure 6.1 graphically depicts the responsibilities of each party in this model.

Platform as a Service (PaaS)

According to NIST, *Platform as a Service (PaaS)* is defined as:

> The capability provided to the consumer is to deploy onto the cloud infrastructure consumer-created or acquired applications created using programming languages, libraries, services, and tools supported by the provider. The consumer does not manage or control the underlying cloud infrastructure including network, servers, operating systems, or storage, but has control over the deployed applications and possible configuration settings for the application-hosting environment.

> National Institute of Standards and Technology,
> Special Publication 800-145

FIGURE 6.1   The SaaS service model

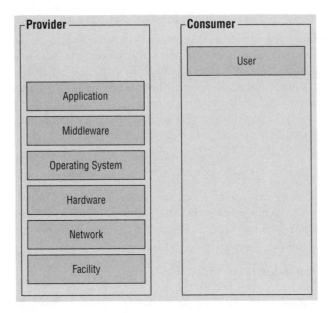

To understand the difference between this model and the others, the key words to focus on in this definition are that the consumer can "deploy," that they do not "manage or control" any of the underlying cloud infrastructure, but that they can have "control over the deployed applications." Figure 6.2 graphically depicts the responsibilities of each party in this model.

FIGURE 6.2   The PaaS service model

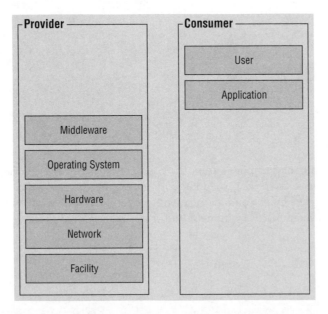

Infrastructure as a Service (IaaS)

The third service model specified by NIST, *Infrastructure as a Service (IaaS)*, is defined as

> The capability provided to the consumer is to provision processing, storage, networks, and other fundamental computing resources where the consumer is able to deploy and run arbitrary software, which can include operating systems and applications. The consumer does not manage or control the underlying cloud infrastructure but has control over operating systems, storage, and deployed applications; and possible limited control of select networking components (e.g., host firewalls).

> **National Institute of Standards and Technology,**
> **Special Publication 800-145**

The relevant wording here is that the consumer can "provision," is able to "deploy and run," but still does not "manage or control" the underlying cloud infrastructure, but now they can be responsible for some aspects. Figure 6.3 graphically depicts the responsibilities of each party in this model.

FIGURE 6.3   The IaaS service model

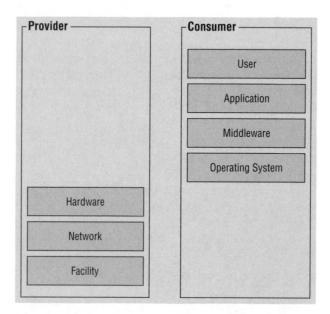

Regardless of the service model used, the characteristics of each are that they must include on-demand self-service, broad network access, resource pooling, rapid elasticity, and measured service. Once you have a service model selected, both CompTIA and NIST recognize four different delivery models, and those are explored in the sections that follow.

When multiple models are combined—mixing IaaS, PaaS, and/or SaaS into a hybrid—this is referred to as *Anything as a Service (XaaS)*.

Private Cloud

According to NIST, a *private cloud* is defined as follows:

> The cloud infrastructure is provisioned for exclusive use by a single organization comprising multiple consumers (e.g., business units). It may be owned, managed, and operated by the organization, a third party, or some combination of them, and it may exist on or off premises.
>
> **National Institute of Standards and Technology,**
> **Special Publication 800-145**

Under most circumstances, a private cloud is owned by the organization, and they act as both the provider and the consumer. They have an advantage in not needing to put their data on the Internet.

Public Cloud

As opposed to a private cloud, the *public cloud* is defined as follows:

> The cloud infrastructure is provisioned for open use by the general public. It may be owned, managed, and operated by a business, academic, or government organization, or some combination of them. It exists on the premises of the cloud provider.
>
> **National Institute of Standards and Technology,**
> **Special Publication 800-145**

Under most circumstances, the cloud provider owns a public cloud, and it will use a pay-as-you-go model. Examples include webmail and online document sharing/collaboration.

Community Cloud

According to NIST, a *community cloud* is defined as follows:

> The cloud infrastructure is provisioned for exclusive use by a specific community of consumers from organizations that have shared concerns (e.g., mission, security requirements, policy, and compliance considerations). It may be owned, managed, and operated by one or more of the organizations in the community, a third party, or some combination of them, and it may exist on or off premises.
>
> **National Institute of Standards and Technology,**
> **Special Publication 800-145**

The key to distinguishing between a community cloud and other types of cloud delivery is that it serves a *similar* group. There must be joint interests and limited enrollment. For an analogy, think of a private cloud as a house (you own it; you're responsible for the maintenance, utilities, and all of it; and so forth), a public cloud as a hotel (you're using only a small part of it; you have very little responsibility for the structure), and a community cloud as a condominium (you own a portion, you share maintenance of common areas, and so on).

Hybrid Cloud

The last of the delivery models, the *hybrid cloud*, is defined as follows:

> The cloud infrastructure is a composition of two or more distinct cloud infrastructures (private, community, or public) that remain unique entities, but are bound together by standardized or proprietary technology that enables data and application portability (e.g., cloud bursting for load balancing between clouds).

> **National Institute of Standards and Technology,**
> **Special Publication 800-145**

Although a hybrid can be any combination of public, private, and community clouds, under most circumstances it is an amalgamation of private and public clouds. When you start mixing in community clouds, it often becomes more of an extension of the community cloud rather than a hybrid cloud.

One common implementation of cloud computing is to take advantage of *cloud bursting*. This means that when your servers become too busy, you offload traffic to resources from a cloud provider. Technologies that make much of the load balancing/prioritizing possible employ the *QoS (Quality of Service)* protocols.

Working with Virtualization

An equally popular (and complementary) buzzword to "the cloud" is *virtualization*. The cost savings promised by virtualization are often offset by the threats to security should the virtual machine (VM) be compromised. One reason for the popularity of virtualization is that in order to have cloud computing, you must have virtualization—this abstraction of the hardware and making it available to the VMs is the foundation on which cloud computing is built. Today, that is being accomplished through the use of hypervisors or containers.

Understanding Hypervisors

At the core of most virtualization is the hypervisor, which is the software/hardware combination that makes it possible. There are two methods of implementation: Type I and Type II.

The *Type I hypervisor* model, also known as *bare metal*, is independent of the operating system and boots before the OS. The *Type II hypervisor* model, also known as *hosted*, is dependent on the operating system and cannot boot until the OS is up and running. It needs the OS to stay up so that it can boot.

Figure 6.4 illustrates the Type I model. From a performance and scalability standpoint, this model is superior to Type II. Type II is considered more complex to manage.

FIGURE 6.4 Type I hypervisor model

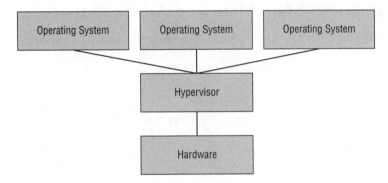

Figure 6.5 illustrates the Type II model. The latest and greatest iteration of ESX would be a type 1 whereas the old VMWare workstation or MS Virtual PC are clear examples of a type 2.

FIGURE 6.5 Type II hypervisor model

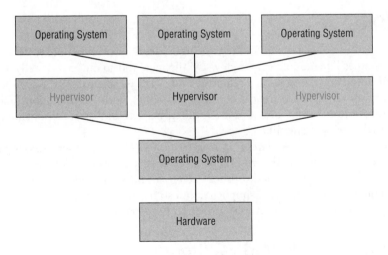

 The machine on which virtualization software is running is known as a *host*, whereas the virtual machines are known as *guests*.

Both proprietary and open source implementations of both types are available, and sometimes it can be confusing as to which type of implementation is in use. Xen, for example, forks into both proprietary and open source solutions. As a general rule, Xen is considered to be both free and open source; ESX, from VMware, is free but not open source (proprietary); KVM is free and open source; and Hyper-V, from Microsoft, is usually free (depending on the implementation) but definitely not open source (proprietary). ESX is a good example of a type 1 installation while VMWare workstation and Microsoft Virtual PC are good examples of type 2.

Understanding Containers and Application Cells

Whereas once it was the case that hypervisors were the only way to have virtualization, *containers* are now thought by most to be their successor. Sometimes referred to as "Docker containers," after the application that introduced the technology, with containers, a piece of software is bundled with everything that it needs to run—code, runtime, system tools, system libraries, and so forth—and deployed without the need to launch an entire VM for each application (which is why *application cells* is another synonym).

Containers are an operating system–level virtualization method for running multiple isolated systems (the containers themselves) on a control host using a single kernel. This method of virtualization provides an isolated environment for applications.

When first introduced, containers were not as secure a method of virtualization as hypervisors, but that quickly changed. Containers now often run as regular users on the host using "unprivileged containers," which are prevented from accessing hardware directly.

VDI/VDE

In a *virtual desktop environment (VDE)*, the user's session is run remotely. While it looks as if the resources like the folders, windows, wallpaper, and so on, exist locally, in reality they are all stored and running on a remote server. VDE is, essentially, the generic term for desktop virtualization. There are lots of reasons for going with VDE solutions, including that fully functioning virtual desktops are less expensive than PCs and application management/licensing is simplified.

Building on this, with *virtual desktop infrastructure (VDI)*, the user's desktop is running inside a virtual machine that resides on a server in a datacenter. VDI is a form of VDE that enables fully personalized desktops for each user and the benefits that come with centralized management: security, simplicity, and so on. In total, there are four main virtualization types: Server, Desktop, Application, and Presentation.

On-Premise vs. Hosted vs. Cloud

The servers used for virtualization can be located just about anywhere. If you choose to locate them within the physical confines of your location, then they are said to be *on-premise*. The benefit of locating them on-premise is that you control physical access to the servers and have an interest in protecting them more than anyone else. Naturally, you assume the risks and responsibilities associated with security when choosing to use an on-premise model as well as the overhead (electricity, depreciation, and so forth).

With a *hosted* model, another provider assumes the responsibility for supplying you with the virtual access you need. You contract with them for a specific period of time, and during that time they bear responsibility for security, overhead, and so on. They may store the server(s) at a single location or multiple locations, but the agreement you have with them spells out their obligations and you are mostly hands-off.

Very similar to hosted is a *cloud* solution. Although they sound very similar in theory, NIST defines the cloud model as differing in that it is centered around five different attributes:

1. *On-demand self-service.* The customer is able to provision new users, services, virtual machines, and so on without involving the provider.

2. *Broad network access.* Services are accessed via the Internet, instead of through an internal network accessible only over private connections.

3. *Resource pooling.* Shared resources are made available so that services can draw from them as needed.

4. *Rapid elasticity.* Needs can expand or contract, and needed service will expand or contract with those needs.

5. *Measured service.* Billing is based on some measured consumption (which could be licenses, CPU cycles, storage consumed, and so forth)—you pay for what you use.

VM Escape Protection

The possibility exists that a crash in another customer's implementation could expose a path by which a user might hop ("server hop") to your data. It is important to know that though this possibility exists—and you should test extensively to keep it from happening—the possibility of it occurring has been greatly exaggerated by some in the media.

Sandboxing involves running apps in restricted memory areas to provide escape protection. By doing so, it is possible to limit the possibility of an app's crash, allowing a user to access another app or the data associated with it. Without sandboxing, the possibility of hopping is increased, but sandboxing greatly diminishes this possibility.

VM Sprawl Avoidance

Virtual machines are like anything else IT-related—they can start small but typically continue to grow in both size and number at alarming rates.

As they grow, so do the licenses, the users, the maintenance, and the overall administration. This growth is known as *sprawl*, and it can quickly catch an organization off-guard when the savings they thought they were getting suddenly leave them with a bigger job than they can manage.

The best way to handle sprawl is to plan for it as you would anything else. If you monitor usage, add resources, and move underutilized VMs from busy machines, you can counter sprawl and keep things running smoothly.

Security and the Cloud

Since this is a certification exam on security and not just on memorization of cloud-based terminology, it is important to recognize the security issues associated with cloud computing. Two you should know for the exam are multitenancy and laws and regulations:

Multitenancy   One of the ways cloud computing is able to obtain cost efficiencies is by putting data from various clients on the same machines. This "multitenant" nature means that workloads from different clients can be on the same system, and a flaw in implementation could compromise security. In theory, a security incident could originate with another customer at the cloud provider and bleed over into your data. Because of this, data needs to be protected from other cloud consumers and from the cloud provider as well.

Laws and Regulations   The consumer retains the ultimate responsibility for compliance. According to NIST:

> The main issue centers on the risks associated with moving important applications or data from within the confines of the organization's computing center to that of another organization (i.e., a public cloud), which is readily available for use by the general public. The responsibilities of both the organization and the cloud provider vary depending on the service model. Reducing cost and increasing efficiency are primary motivations for moving towards a public cloud, but relinquishing responsibility for security should not be. Ultimately, the organization is accountable for the choice of public cloud and the security and privacy of the outsourced service.

> **National Institute of Standards and Technology,**
> **Special Publication 800-144**

Cloud computing holds great promise when it comes to scalability, cost savings, rapid deployment, and empowerment. As with any technology where so much is removed from your control, though, risks are involved. Each risk should be considered carefully in order to identify ways to help mitigate it. Data segregation, for example, can help reduce some of the risks associated with multitenancy. In multitenancy, you have multiple tenants on one machine and the theoretical risk exists for a user to jump from one tenant to another. By segregating the data, you reduce the risk associated with this.

Software and services not necessary for the implementation should be removed or at least disabled. Patches and firmware updates should be kept current, and log files should be carefully monitored. You should find the vulnerabilities in the implementation before others do and work with your service provider(s) to close any holes.

When it comes to data storage on the cloud, encryption is one of the best ways to protect it (keeping it from being of value to unauthorized parties), and VPN routing and forwarding can help. Backups should be performed regularly (and encrypted and stored in safe locations), and access control should be a priority.

For a good discussion of cloud computing and data protection, visit http://whoswholegal.com/news/features/article/18246/cloud-computing-data-protection.

Cloud Access Security Brokers

While they sound like individuals, *cloud access security brokers (CASBs)* are actually on-premise or cloud-based security policy enforcement points. They exist between the cloud service users and the cloud service providers for the purpose of combining (and adding) enterprise security policies as resources are accessed.

The brokers can consolidate lots of different types of security policy enforcement (single sign-on, authorization, credential mapping, encryption, and so forth) while acting like a gatekeeper. They essentially allow the organization to extend the reach of their own security policies beyond the confines of their own infrastructure.

Though it is tempting to think of the broker as a person, know that it is a software tool or service.

Cloud Storage

The trend for both individuals and enterprises has been to collect and store as much data as possible. This has led to large local hard drives—DAS (direct attached storage), NAS (network area storage), SANs (storage area networks), and now the cloud.

Just as the cloud holds such promise for running applications, balancing loads, and a plethora of other options, it also offers the ability to store more and more data on it and to let a provider worry about scaling issues instead of local administrators. From an economic perspective, this can be a blessing, but from a security standpoint, this can be troublesome—and it is from that perspective that we focus throughout this book.

First and foremost, it is imperative that you understand and accept that you are responsible for the protection of your data (legally, morally, and so forth), even if another party hosts it. The SLA needs to spell out how the provider will protect the data (sandboxing and/or other methods) as well as redundancy, disaster recovery, and so on. Make sure that you encrypt the data, back it up, and implement as much control as possible.

Security as a Service

Not to be confused with the NIST deployment models (SaaS, PaaS, and IaaS), *Security as a Service (SECaaS)* is a subscription-based business model intended to be more cost effective than individuals and smaller corporations could ever get on their own. With this model, a large service provider integrates their security services into a corporate infrastructure and makes them available on a subscription basis. Due to economies of scale, the solution is more cost effective when total cost of ownership is factored in.

No on-premise hardware is needed by the subscriber, and the services offered can include such things as authentication, antivirus, antimalware/spyware, and intrusion detection. In this way, SECaaS can serve as a buffer against many online threats.

Summary

Cloud computing holds great promise. It offers the ability to decrease costs, increase efficiency, and make the world a better place. Three service models are available (SaaS, PaaS, and IaaS), and there are four delivery models (private, public, community, and hybrid).

Virtualization is a key component of cloud computing. It makes it possible by abstracting the hardware and making it available to the virtual machines.

The abstraction can be done through the use of a hypervisor, which can be either Type I (bare metal) or Type II (hosted), or through the use of containers. Two big issues with virtualization about which you should be aware are VM sprawl and VM escape. The latter also illustrates that new technologies often introduce new security risks. It is imperative that design considerations not overshadow the need for securing the data and keeping security a priority. Some of the costs for security can be reduced through the economies of scale possible with Security as a Service models.

Exam Essentials

Know the three cloud service models.   NIST (National Institute of Standards and Technology) recognizes three possible cloud service models: Software as a Service (SaaS), Platform as a Service (PaaS), and Infrastructure as a Service (IaaS).

Know the four different cloud delivery models.   NIST recognizes four possible cloud delivery models: private, public, community, and hybrid.

Know the purpose of the hypervisor.   The hypervisor is the element (software/hardware) that allows a virtual machine to exist.

Know the hypervisor types.   A Type I hypervisor is known as bare metal and runs as both hypervisor and operating system. A Type II hypervisor is known as hosted, and it runs on top of another operating system.

Review Questions

You can find the answers in the Appendix.

1. In which cloud service model can the consumer "provision" and "deploy and run"?

   A. SaaS

   B. PaaS

   C. IaaS

   D. CaaS

2. Which cloud delivery model is implemented by a single organization, enabling it to be implemented behind a firewall?

   A. Private

   B. Public

   C. Community

   D. Hybrid

3. Which cloud service model provides the consumer with the infrastructure to create applications and host them?

   A. SaaS

   B. PaaS

   C. IaaS

   D. CaaS

4. Which cloud delivery model could be considered a pool of services and resources delivered across the Internet by a cloud provider?

   A. Private

   B. Public

   C. Community

   D. Hybrid

5. Which cloud service model gives the consumer the ability to use applications provided by the cloud provider over the Internet?

   A. SaaS

   B. PaaS

   C. IaaS

   D. CaaS

6. Which cloud delivery model has an infrastructure shared by several organizations with shared interests and common IT needs?

   A. Private

   B. Public

   C. Community

   D. Hybrid

7. Which cloud delivery model could be considered an amalgamation of other types of delivery models?

   A. Private

   B. Public

   C. Community

   D. Hybrid

8. With which of the following subscription-based models is security more cost effective than individuals or smaller corporations could ever get on their own?

   A. SECaaS

   B. PaaS

   C. XaaS

   D. WaaS

9. Which of the following are on-premise or cloud-based security policy enforcement points?

   A. Feature slugs

   B. Flood guards

   C. VDI/VDEs

   D. Cloud access security brokers

10. Which feature of cloud computing involves dynamically provisioning (or deprovisioning) resources as needed?

   A. Multitenancy

   B. Elasticity

   C. CMDB

   D. Sandboxing

11. What is the term for restricting an application to a safe/restricted resource area?

   A. Multitenancy

   B. Fencing

   C. Securing

   D. Sandboxing

12. Which of the following terms implies hosting data from more than one consumer on the same equipment?

   A. Multitenancy

   B. Duplexing

   C. Bastioning

   D. Fashioning

13. When going with a public cloud delivery model, who is accountable for the security and privacy of the outsourced service?

   A. The cloud provider and the organization

   B. The cloud provider

   C. The organization

   D. No one

14. When your company purchased a virtual datacenter provider, you inherited a mess. The employees working there had to respond regularly to requests to create virtual machines without the disciplines and controls normally found in the physical world. This resulted in machines being over-provisioned (too much CPU, memory, or disk) and consuming resources long after they were no longer required. What type of problem is this?

   A. VM escape

   B. VM digress

   C. VM sprawl

   D. VM Type I

15. Although a hybrid cloud could be any mixture of cloud delivery models, it is usually a combination of which of the following?

   A. Public and community

   B. Public and private

   C. Private and community

   D. Two or more communities

16. Which type of hypervisor implementation is known as "bare metal"?

   A. Type I

   B. Type II

   C. Type III

   D. Type IV

17. Which type of hypervisor implementation is known as "hosted"?

   A. Type I

   B. Type II

   C. Type III

   D. Type IV

18. When your servers become too busy, you can offload traffic to resources from a cloud provider. This is known as which of the following?

   A. Latency

   B. Cloud bursting

   C. Multitenancy

   D. Peaking

19. What protocol is used by technologies for load balancing/prioritizing traffic?

    A. ESX

    B. QoS

    C. IBJ

    D. IFNC

20. What is the machine on which virtualization software is running known as?

    A. Node

    B. Workstation

    C. Host

    D. Server

Chapter

7

Host, Data, and Application Security

THE FOLLOWING COMPTIA SECURITY+ EXAM OBJECTIVES ARE COVERED IN THIS CHAPTER:

✓ **1.3   Explain threat actor types and attributes.**

- Types of actors: Script kiddies; Hacktivist; Organized crime; Nation states/APT; Insiders; Competitors

- Attributes of actors: Internal/external; Level of sophistication; Resources/funding; Intent/motivation

- Use of open-source intelligence

✓ **1.6   Explain the impact associated with types of vulnerabilities.**

- Race conditions

- Vulnerabilities due to: End-of-life systems; Embedded systems; Lack of vendor support

- Improper input handling

- Improper error handling

- Misconfiguration/weak configuration

- Default configuration

- Resource exhaustion

- Untrained users

- Improperly configured accounts

- Vulnerable business processes

- Weak cipher suites and implementations

- Memory/buffer vulnerability: Memory leak; Integer overflow; Buffer overflow; Pointer dereference; DLL injection

- System sprawl/undocumented assets

- Architecture/design weaknesses
- New threats/zero day
- Improper certificate and key management

✓ **2.6 Given a scenario, implement secure protocols.**

- Protocols
  - DNSSEC
  - SSH
  - S/MIME
  - SRTP
  - LDAPS
  - FTPS
  - SFTP
  - SNMPv3
  - SSL/TLS
  - HTTPS
  - Secure POP/IMAP
- Use cases
  - Voice and video
  - Time synchronization
  - Email and web
  - File transfer
  - Directory services
  - Remote access
  - Domain name resolution
  - Routing and switching
  - Network address allocation
  - Subscription services

✓ **3.5 Explain the security implications of embedded systems.**

- SCADA/ICS
- Smart devices/IoT: Wearable technology; Home automation
- HVAC

- SoC
- RTOS
- Printers/MFDs
- Camera systems
- Special purpose: Medical devices; Vehicles;
- Aircraft/UAV

✓ 3.6   Summarize secure application development and deployment concepts.

- Development life-cycle models: Waterfall vs. Agile
- Secure DevOps: Security automation; Continuous integration; Baselining; Immutable systems; Infrastructure as code
- Version control and change management
- Provisioning and deprovisioning
- Secure coding techniques: Proper error handling; Proper input validation; Normalization; Stored procedures; Code signing; Encryption; Obfuscation/camouflage; Code reuse/ dead code; Server-side vs. client-side execution and validation; Memory management; Use of third-party libraries and SDKs; Data exposure
- Code quality and testing; Static code analyzers; Dynamic analysis (e.g., fuzzing); Stress testing; Sandboxing; Model verification
- Compiled vs. runtime code

Computers (servers and clients), data, and applications are best secured by implementing them properly. That is not perfect security, but it is the foundation of security. However, once you start reducing security settings to increase interoperability with other operating systems or applications, you introduce weaknesses that may be exploited. This chapter deals with the process of ensuring that the products you use are as secure as they can be.

In this chapter, we'll begin by discussing the actual actors who are threats to any network. This will provide you with an understanding of the techniques and motivations behind specific attacks. Then we will look at specific vulnerabilities and their impact on your organization.

Next, we will examine embedded systems. This will include SCADA systems, smart systems, printers, medical devices, and other related systems.

We will finish the chapter with how to secure an application. As you'll see, a number of security threats are based on exploiting flaws in applications, particularly web applications. Next, we'll discuss methods to secure the computer, or the host, itself. We explored operating system hardening in Chapter 2, "Monitoring and Diagnosing Networks," so we won't repeat that material here. Finally, we'll discuss methods to protect the data itself.

Threat Actors and Attributes

There are a number of terms associated with host, data, and application security that you need to be aware of for the exam. The following terms (also found in the online glossary) are those that CompTIA is fond of using and testing on in this category. They are provided in order to make it easier for you to know what each is intended to convey.

Security+ Terminology

advanced persistent threats (APTs)   Any sophisticated series of related attacks taking place over an extended period of time.

Agile development   A method of software development meant to be rapid.

baselining   Creating a fundamental, or baseline, security level.

Big Data   Data that is larger than what can be handled with traditional tools and algorithms.

database normalization   The process of removing duplication in a relational database.

embedded system   Operating system in a device, sometimes on a single chip.

fuzzing   A method of testing that intentionally enters invalid input to see if the application can handle it.

hardening   The process of making a server or an application resistant to an attack.

Infrastructure as Code (IaC)   The process of managing and provisioning computer datacenters through machine-readable definition files.

Internet of Things (IoT)   Devices that interact on the Internet, without human intervention.

NoSQL database   Datastores that do not use a relational structure.

Open Web Application Security Project (OWASP)   An online community that develops free articles, documentation, tools, and more on web application security.

prototyping   Creating a version of an application that has only the bare minimum functionality so that it can be evaluated before further development.

sandboxing   Operating in an isolated environment.

script kiddy   An attacker with very minimal skills.

secure coding   Programming in a manner that is secure.

stored procedures   SQL statements written and stored on the database that can be called by applications.

stress testing   Subjecting a system to workloads that are extreme.

Structured Query Language (SQL)   The language used by all relational databases.

waterfall method   A software development method that uses very well-defined sequential phases.

zero-day exploit   A vulnerability that is unknown to the product vendor, and thus there is no patch for it.

A key issue in security is knowing who are the attackers. Understanding the various types of attackers is a fundamental part of cyber-threat intelligence. Much like a police officer, you will be more effective if you understand who is likely to attack your network as well as their motives.

Script Kiddies

The term *script kiddy* is a derogatory term for people who use hacking techniques but have limited skills. Often such attackers may rely almost entirely on automated tools they download from the Internet.

You might think that with their relatively low skill level, script kiddies are not a real security threat. Two issues bely that thought, however. The first issue is the prevalence of hacking tools available on the web. You can readily find tools to automate denial-of-service (DoS) attacks, create viruses, make a Trojan horse, or even distribute ransomware as a service. Personal technical skills are no longer a barrier to attacking a network.

The second issue is the sheer number of script kiddies. There are tens of thousands of such individuals—any one of whom might try an attack on any given network at any given time.

In general, the motivations of script kiddies revolve around trying to prove their skill. In other words, they may attack your network simply because it is there. Secondary school and university networks are common targets of script kiddy attacks, due to the number of script kiddies in their student populations. Fortunately, the number of script kiddies is offset by their lack of skill and lack of resources. These individuals tend to be rather young, they work alone, and they have very few resources. And by resources, we mean time as well as money. A script kiddy cannot attack your network 24 hours a day. He or she must work a job or go to school and attend to other life functions.

It is not common for a script kiddy to be an insider. The reason for this is that if an insider is behind an attack and has minimal skills, they usually get caught rather quickly. Note, however, that though it is not common, it still does occur sometimes.

Hacktivist

Hacktivists use hacking techniques to accomplish some activist goal. They might deface the website of a company whose policies they disagree with. Or a hacktivist might attack a network due to some political issue. The defining characteristic of hacktivists is that they believe they are doing something ethical, even if illegal.

This motivation means that measures that might deter other attackers will be less likely to deter a hacktivist. Because they believe that they are engaged in a just crusade, they will, at least in some instances, even risk getting caught to accomplish their goals. However, unlike a script kiddy, the skill levels of hacktivists vary widely. Some are only script kiddies, whereas others are quite skilled. The more skilled hacktivist can be a danger to any network.

The resources of hacktivists also vary somewhat. Many are working alone and have very limited resources. However, some are part of organized efforts. The hacking group Anonymous has engaged in hacktivism. A collective group will always have more time and other resources than a lone attacker. Anonymous is a loose organization of hackers who have engaged in a variety of high-profile attacks. Due to their very nature, it is difficult to identify who is and who is not in Anonymous. As far as can be determined, they don't have a definitive structure or hierarchy but operate as a loose collective.

Hacktivists tend to be external attackers, but in some cases, internal employees who disagree strongly with their company's policies engage in hacktivism. In those instances, it is more likely that the hacktivist will attack the company by releasing confidential information. This has occurred among various government employees.

Organized Crime

Organized crime groups have been involved in cyber-crime now for many years. There have been cases involving the Mafia, outlaw motorcycle gangs, Russian organized crime, and other groups engaging in cyber-crime. The common thread among these groups is motive and intent. The motive is simply illegal profits. There is no political issue or cause, and the criminal acts are not out to prove anything. The goal is simply to steal.

Organized crime tends to have attackers who range from moderately skilled to highly skilled. It is rare for script kiddies to be involved in these crimes, and if they are, they tend to be caught rather quickly. The other defining factor is that organized crime groups tend to have more resources, both in terms of time and money, than do hacktivists or script kiddies.

Nation-States/APT

In recent years, a great deal of attention has been given to nation-states hacking into either foreign governments or corporations. The security company Mandiant first traced multiple attacks to the Chinese army. These attacks where defined as *advanced persistent threats (APTs)*. The name tells you a great deal about the attacks themselves. First, they used advanced techniques, not simply tools downloaded from the Internet. Second, the attacks continued for a significant period of time. In some cases, the attacks continued for years.

The APT attacks that Mandiant reported are emblematic of *nation-state attacks*. They tend to be characterized by highly skilled attackers with significant resources. A nation has the manpower, time, and money to finance ongoing, sophisticated attacks.

The motive can be political or economic. In some cases, the attack is done for traditional espionage goals: to gather information about the targets defense capabilities. In other cases, the attack might be targeting intellectual property or other economic assets.

Insiders

Insiders are a rather different problem. The first issue is skill level. An insider might be of any skill level. He or she could be a script kiddy or very technically skilled. The second issue is motivation. Insiders' reasons and goals can span the range of motivations. Some are motivated by certain activist goals, whereas others are motivated by financial gain. Still others may simply be upset that they were passed over for a promotion or slighted in some other manner.

Regarding resources, an insider will usually be working alone and have limited financial resources and time. However, the fact that they are insiders gives them an automatic advantage. They already have some access to your network and some level of knowledge. Depending on the insider's job role, he or she might have significant access and knowledge.

Competitors

Corporate espionage is a widely known, but little discussed, problem. Although most companies are ethical and would not engage in such tactics, clearly some companies do. The fact is that corporate espionage is a problem that has been around for a long time. The motives are clear: financial gain. The skill level can vary, but it tends to be moderate to highly skilled, and the resources are usually extensive.

In some cases, competitors will use a disgruntled insider to get information from your company. Another related phenomenon relates to dark web markets that actively traffic in stolen information. Figure 7.1 shows an actual dark web market with corporate information for sale.

FIGURE 7.1 Dark web market

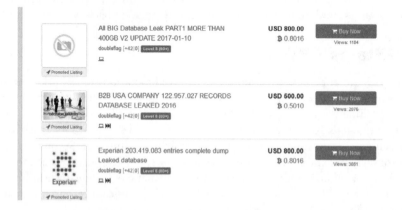

These markets don't care how they get the information: their only concern is selling it. In some cases, hackers break into a network and then sell the information to a dark web market. In other cases, insiders sell confidential information on the dark web. In fact, some dark web markets are advertising that they wish to buy confidential data from corporate insiders. This provides a ready resource for competitors to purchase your company's information on the dark web.

Use of Open Source Intelligence

When considering threats, it is important to be able to conduct cyber-threat intelligence gathering. Fortunately, open source intelligence provides a number of options in this area. Websites and tools are available that allow you to gather information on current threats or even on specific issues.

ThreatCrowd is a search engine that enables you to find information about the latest threats. Figure 7.2 shows the main page for threatcrowd.org.

You can use this website to search for a specific virus or attack, or even search for an IP address to determine if that IP address has been connected to attacks.

FIGURE 7.2   ThreatCrowd

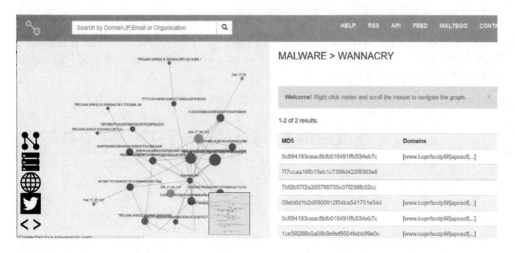

Another important open source intelligence source is https://openphish.com/. This site will give you up-to-the-minute information on the current phishing schemes. You can see the web page and search results in Figure 7.3.

FIGURE 7.3   OpenPhish

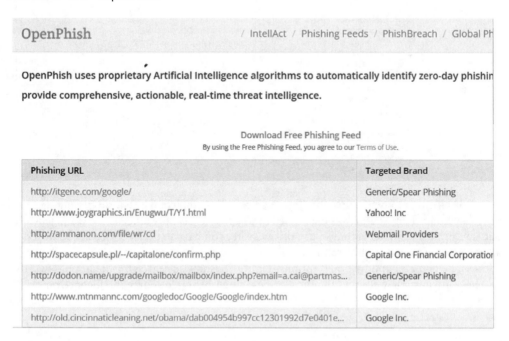

Once you have identified a threat source, open source tools are available that allow you to investigate that threat. For example, if you believe that an email address is the source of a virus or phishing attempt, or if you believe a specific IP address or URL is the source of an attack, you can investigate that source. One open source resource available to you on the web is http://osintframework.com. This website allows you to search a wide range of open source resources; see Figure 7.4.

FIGURE 7.4   OSINT framework

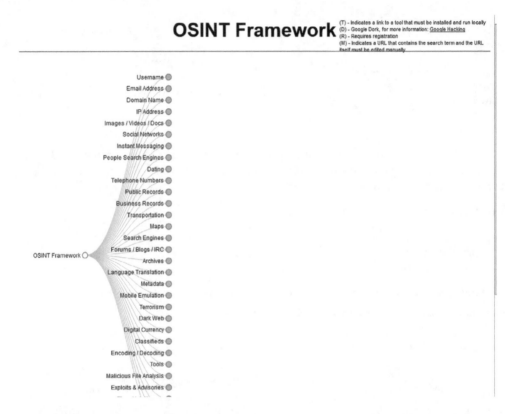

No discussion of open source intelligence would be complete without discussing www.shodan.io. This website was mentioned in Chapter 4, "Identity and Access Management," but is worth mentioning again. To use this website, you have to create a free account. It allows you to search for vulnerabilities. You can search in a given geographic area, by IP address, by domain, and by other options. Figure 7.5 shows a search for default passwords.

These are just a few sources that you can use to gather open source intelligence on current threats.

FIGURE 7.5 Shodan

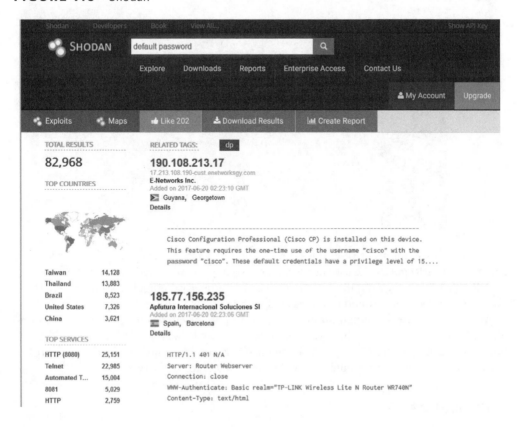

Types of Vulnerabilities

A wide range of vulnerabilities could affect your system. Being aware of what vulnerabilities you are attempting to mitigate is an important aspect of cybersecurity.

Configuration Issues

The systems you have, and the security those systems support, are of little use without proper configuration. This can be as simple as failing to change default settings or default passwords. Or it can be a matter of not having the appropriate training for a given piece of equipment and thus leaving it configured improperly.

Related to misconfiguration is the issue of weak configuration. Many devices can be configured with strong or weak security. Consider your web browser. Whether you use Firefox, Edge, Chrome, Opera, Safari, or some other browser, you can select the security settings. If you select weak security, then you have undermined the security of your entire computer. You can see basic security settings for Firefox in Figure 7.6.

FIGURE 7.6 Firefox

As you can see, the security settings (for example, "Warn you when sites try to install add-ons") are selected. If the user deselects these settings, then there is a weak configuration. Related to weak configuration is the issue of improperly configured accounts. All accounts on all systems should be configured with least privileges.

Also related to weak configuration is the issue of poor cryptography selection. For example, all wireless access points have the option of using WEP, WPA, or WPA2. Only WPA2 fully implements the 802.11i security requirements. If you implement WEP, then you are implementing a weak cipher suite that will be inadequate for security.

User Issues

The weakest point in security for many organizations is the end user. This issue is best addressed by training and education. An untrained user cannot possibly adhere to good security practices because he or she is not aware of them. Security training is just as important as any technology that you can purchase or policy that you can implement.

Of course, in addition to proper configuration and user training, there needs to be vendor support. For security purposes, this means a vendor that promptly patches any vulnerabilities that are discovered. Poor vendor support undermines system security. The unfortunate fact is that vulnerabilities will be discovered in almost any technology. The question is, however, how quickly does the vendor respond and correct those vulnerabilities?

Zero-Day Exploits

When a hole is found in a web browser or other software and attackers begin exploiting it the very day it is discovered, bypassing the one-to-two-day response time that many software providers need to put out a patch once a hole has been found, this is known as a *zero-day exploit*. This exploit can occur before the vendor is even aware of the vulnerability. Responding to a zero-day exploit can be very difficult. If attackers learn of the weakness the same day as the developer, then they have the ability to exploit it until a patch is released.

Often, the only thing that you as a security administrator can do, between the discovery of the exploit and the release of the patch, is to turn off the service. Although this can be a costly undertaking in terms of productivity, it is the only way to keep your network safe.

Secure Protocols

Transport Layer Security was originally used to encrypt web traffic. HTTP (Hyper Text Transfer Protocol) was secured with TLS to become HTTPS. This process was invented by Netscape, though at the time they used SSL rather than TLS. If web traffic involves sensitive information such as credit card numbers, then the HTTP should be encrypted with TLS. All banking websites and e-commerce websites use HTTPS to protect sensitive information.

Transport layer security can be used to secure many different protocols. TLS adds encryption and authentication to the protocol. For example, email protocol SMTP (Simple Mail Transfer Protocol), POP3 (Post Office Protocol v3), and IMAP (Internet Message Access Protocol) can all be secured with TLS. Each of these becomes SMTPS, POP3S, IMAPS. The "S" is for secure. In general, the use of secured email is recommended in almost all cases. If you fail to secure your email, then anyone running a packet sniffer between your machine and the email server can see the content of your email and possibly passwords as well. Most email services today insist on using TLS to secure the email protocols.

FTP (File Transfer Protocol) can also be secured with TLS to become FTPS. If you are transferring files with sensitive information, then you should use FTPS rather than FTP. As an alternative to FTPS there is SFTP, and SCP. Secure File Transfer Protocol and Secure Copy both secure file transfer but they secure with SSH (Secure Shell) rather than SSL/TLS. The use of SFTP, SCP, or FTPS is always recommended if any sensitive files are being transferred.

Domain Name System Security Extensions (DNSSEC) are security specifications for security DNS (Domain Name System). DNSSEC involves many security features such as digitally signed DNS responses. These mechanisms are meant to mitigate the risk of DNS attacks such as DNS poisoning. This is also related to DNS resolution. When the DNS resolution process is sent in clear text, that leaves it vulnerable to packet sniffing. Therefore, DNS resolution should also be secured/encrypted.

SNMP (Simple Network Management Protocol) is used to manage networks. Each managed device has a software agent installed that reports issues and problems to a centralized SNMP management server. Versions 1 and 2 of SNMP sent all data as clear text. SNMP v3 encrypts all data. In all cases, SNMPv3 should be used. The detailed network information being sent by SNMP is sensitive enough that it should never be sent in clear text.

Lightweight Directory Access Protocol (LDAP) is a directory protocol that contains literally all the information about your network. It lists all directory services, servers, workstations, users, etc. An attacker would find this information very useful. Therefore, it is recommended that you encrypt this traffic with TLS. Anytime you have a concern about any attacker enumerating your network, you should use LDAPS.

Voice and video calls are established with session initiation protocol (SIP). The data is transmitted with realtime transfer protocol (RTP). Clearly some voice calls can be sensitive. If you want secure voice calls, then you must use sRTP (secure realtime transfer protocol). You can also use sRTP to secure video, particularly for confidential video conferences.

Remote access, whether it uses RADIUS, TACACS+, or Diameter should be secured. During remote connection, there is an authentication process that transmits user credentials. If this process is not encrypted then anyone can see the login credentials. In fact, any communication that could reveal sensitive information should be encrypted. In addition to the previously discussed protocols this includes time synchronization, routing and switching, subscribing to a service (subscription service), network address allocation via DHCP, should all be encrypted. TLS is not the only way to encrypt traffic, but it is an effective and widely supported method.

Other Issues

Several other vulnerabilities do not fit neatly into one of the preceding categories. Each of these will be briefly discussed in this section.

System sprawl is a common problem for many networks. As the network grows, it becomes more difficult to track all the equipment and software on the network. This can lead to undocumented assets. These become a problem because their security configuration is unknown. For example, an undocumented Wi-Fi access point might be using default passwords, have weak encryption, or simply be unpatched.

Improper certificate management or cryptographic key management is another issue. In Chapter 8, "Cryptography," we will discuss, in some detail, the facets of digital certificates. For now, you merely need to be aware that failure to store private keys and symmetric keys properly is a security vulnerability. Also, having expired digital certificates in use on the network is another, related vulnerability.

Older systems can also represent a security vulnerability. There is a point at which vendors no longer patch older systems. These end-of-life systems can be quite vulnerable. For example, the wannacry ransomware initially spread during the writing of this book. Among other issues was the fact that those using Windows XP had no patch for the vulnerability wannacry exploited. In this case, Microsoft did release an emergency patch for Windows XP. Nevertheless, this situation illustrates the vulnerabilities associated with end-of-life systems.

In some cases, the business processes themselves can be vulnerabilities. Failure to perform background checks properly or to verify vendors are vulnerabilities. Acquiring software from suspect sources is a vulnerability. It would be quite a challenge to list all the possible business process vulnerabilities in a single chapter of a single book. However, you should be aware that the processes of any organization are every bit as important to security as the technology that is implemented.

Related to poor business processes is the issue of architecture and design weaknesses. When the manner in which a network is designed is itself insecure, this presents a vulnerability. An example of this would be a network that does not use a DMZ between the internal network and the external, or a network that is not segmented. These are design weaknesses that lead to security vulnerabilities.

Embedded Systems Security

An *embedded system* is a computer system with a dedicated function within a larger mechanical or electrical system. These can be chips within Internet of Things (IoT) devices or controllers in manufacturing equipment. A variety of embedded systems are in use today.

To some extent, the security concerns with these devices is the same as it is with other computer devices. That includes the use of robust authentication, patch management, encrypting data, and similar security measures.

The *Internet of Things (IoT)* is a growing issue. At first, this encompassed primarily automated industrial devices. However, it has even spread to private homes. As more people embrace technologies such as smart thermostats and similar devices, the security issues become a greater concern.

On August 7, 2016, the first ever ransomware for smart thermostats was reported (http://motherboard.vice.com/read/internet-of-things-ransomware-smart-thermostat). Fortunately, in this case, this was not ransomware found in the wild but rather the creation of two security researchers. They designed it to illustrate a flaw in smart home technology. They demonstrated their proof of concept at the famous Defcon conference in Las Vegas.

Wearable technology comes in many forms. This can be exercise related devices or medical devices. In either case, sensitive personal information is stored on the device. In some cases, the device synchronizes with a computer. The data stored on the device should be encrypted on the device, and any data sent should be encrypted in transit. TLS is an excellent solution for encrypting in transit.

In addition to smart home technology, industrial systems have long used smart technology in heating, ventilation, and air conditioning (HVAC). These systems use smart technology to regulate air flow and temperature.

Printers have presented a security issue for as long as networked printers have existed. Most modern printers of any significant capability have programmed embedded chips. Furthermore, many offer the ability to access the printer remotely using telnet, SSH, or some similar technology. These remote access technologies are quite convenient, but they also provide a means of access to an attacker, particularly if these protocols use default settings.

In Chapter 1, "Managing Risk," we discussed various industry standards. Recall that NIST 800-82, Special Publication 800-82, Revision 2, "Guide to Industrial Control System (ICS) Security," is specific to industrial control systems. Industrial systems include SCADA (Supervisor Control and Data Acquisition) and PLCs (primary logic controllers).

One of the most fundamental security steps that you can take with a SCADA system is to implement account usage and monitoring. This will provide details on who is using the system, how, and when.

Real-time operating systems (RTOSs) are another issue. These operating systems are designed to process data as quickly as possible. Note that we are talking about real-time operating systems, not just software that operates in real time. RTOSs were developed originally for military applications. These systems are designed to have zero latency, or as near to that as possible.

Another relatively new technology is system-on-a-chip (SoC). These devices are completely self-contained systems on a single chip.

Medical devices are also a growing concern. Barnaby Jack, a famous hacker, was able to hack into an insulin pump and cause the device to dispense all 300 units of the insulin it contained. The device had wireless capability in order to synchronize data with a doctor's computer. That wireless communication was insecure, however. Yes, *this means that someone could have been actually killed via hacking*, although there are no documented cases of this occurring. Encrypted communications and strong authentication are the appropriate countermeasures for this.

More and more, vehicles have sophisticated computers and even wireless capabilities. This makes these vehicles susceptible to attack. This is not limited to automobiles, however—unmanned aerial vehicles (UAVs, or drones) and even manned aircraft are vulnerable.

Security cameras are another issue. Many such cameras are digital with wireless capabilities. This makes them potentially vulnerable to attack. An attacker could breach the device and use it to surveil the victim.

While there are a host of new devices to secure, many more than existed 10 years ago, the security concerns are not truly that different. Regardless of the device in question, the same security questions must be asked: Does the device have robust authentication? Is the data encrypted, both at rest and in transit? Has the device's software/firmware been patched? All of the same issues that you would address in your network are now extended to other devices. Moreover, it seems a safe bet that there will be even more devices in the coming years than there are today.

All of these security technologies discussed in this chapter (as well as elsewhere in this book) can be quite complicated to manage. This brings up very important aspects of security. The first is security automation. As much as possible, security should be an automatic feature of technology. For example, you don't have to manually tell your browser to encrypt traffic. The HTTPS protocol handles that for you.

In addition to security automation, security must always be integrated into technology. Continuous integration requires that security be in product design, development, implementation, and maintenance. Security cannot simply be added as an afterthought.

Application Vulnerabilities

So many of the vulnerabilities and even breaches that we hear about are due to programming flaws. Application flaws provide a way for an attacker to exploit the system. Some application flaws enable an attacker to gain access, whereas others just make the system less stable. Before we discuss hardening and security coding, you should understand the vulnerabilities at issue.

Input Vulnerabilities

A number of attacks, such as SQL injection and cross-site scripting, depend on input not being properly checked. All input should be validated. This means that when a user enters data into a text field, it is checked at the client side in order to ensure that it is of the proper data type and size. Other checks, such as looking for common SQL injection symbols, are also done at this time. This also means, however, that when data is moved from one system to another, it is checked again. When data moves from the client to a server-side component, the server-side component should validate the data. When data is read in from a database or service, do not assume it—validate it.

A number of attacks, including those already mentioned, would be almost impossible if all applications utilized proper *input validation*. This includes validating input before it is even used in a specific function in a program.

Buffer overflows involve attempting to load more data into an array than the array can hold. If you have a 10-byte array and 15 bytes is loaded into it, that additional 5 bytes is loaded into memory, overwriting something. By simply checking the boundaries of input, buffer overflows, and the related integer, the overflow would never occur.

This can be summarized by stating that all data should be validated on both the client side and the server side. Doing so provides a robust validation mechanism that can eliminate many vulnerabilities.

Related to input validation is error handling. Every function that has any meaningful functionality should have appropriate error handling. Put another way, whenever a program crashes, it is a good bet that proper error handling was not involved. If a program has appropriate, robust error handling, then in the event of a problem, the user will simply see an error message box.

Memory Vulnerabilities

Memory leaks are the most common issue in memory management. Many modern programming languages (C# and Java, for example) don't allow the programmer to directly allocate or deallocate memory. Therefore, those programming languages are not prone to memory leaks.

However, certain programming languages, most notably C and C++, give the programmer a great deal of control over memory management. Memory leaks are usually caused by failure to deallocate memory that has been allocated. A static code analyzer can check to see if all memory allocation commands (`malloc`, `alloc`, and others) have a matching deallocation command.

Pointers are another sophisticated method for manipulating memory. C and C++ have the concept of a pointer. This is a variable that, rather than store data, points to the memory address of another variable. This can lead to the problem of pointer dereferencing. This attack consists of finding null references in the target program and dereferencing them, causing an exception to be generated.

Another issue is resource exhaustion. When an application continuously allocates additional resources (such as memory), eventually the finite resources of the host machine are exhausted, leading the system to hang or crash. This can be a form of denial-of-service attack when executed intentionally.

All of these attacks involve memory management. Applications must make effective use of memory management. That means handling pointers, memory allocation, and any related tasks effectively.

Windows programs frequently make use of dynamic linked libraries (DLLs) that are loaded into the memory space of the application that is using the DLL. DLL injection is a situation in which the malware tries to inject code into the memory process space of a library. In other words, a DLL is compromised, and it is used to attempt to compromise the program calling the DLL. DLL injection is a rather sophisticated attack.

Race conditions are a vulnerability related to multithreaded applications. When a multithreaded application does not properly handle various threads accessing a common value, this can lead to unpredictable values for that variable. This is called a *race condition*.

Secure Programming

To program securely, you must have some idea of how code is written. Software is complex, and there are specific models that detail how to develop an application.

Programming Models

The *waterfall method* has these steps: requirements gathering, design, implementation (also called coding), testing (also called verification), deployment, and maintenance. Each stage is completely self-contained. Once one stage is completed, then you move on to the next stage. This approach is appropriate for situations wherein the requirements are clearly defined well in advance.

Agile development works in cycles, with each cycle producing specific deliverables. This means that phases like design and development get repeated. Agile programming is a type of *prototyping*. All such methods use a general approach such as prototype code ➤ test ➤ deploy ➤ gather feedback. This process is repeated, each time getting closer to the final goal. The process is shown in Figure 7.7.

FIGURE 7.7   Prototyping

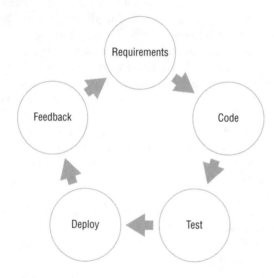

There are many Agile methods, including these:

- Agile Modeling
- Scrum
- Adaptive Software Development
- Crystal
- Feature-Driven Development
- Dynamic Systems Development Method
- Lean Software Development
- XP (Extreme Programming)

Software Testing

Most applications that are written to accept input expect a particular type of data—string values, numerical values, and so on. Sometimes, it is possible to enter unexpected values and cause the application to crash. When that happens, the user may be left with elevated privileges or access to values they should not have. *Fuzzing* is the technique of providing unexpected values as input to an application in order to make it crash. This is a type of dynamic testing, purposefully testing with unexpected values to find security vulnerabilities. Those values can be random, invalid, or just unexpected. A common method is to flood the input with a stream of random bits.

In addition to dynamic testing, there are static testing techniques. Static code analyzers are tools that simply read through the source code trying to document vulnerabilities. This can include inadequate error handling, missing memory deallocation, or other problems.

Both dynamic and static testing are methods to test the code quality. One of the most fundamental aspects of secure coding is first to assure code quality. Flaws in a program's coding are often exploited as security vulnerabilities, as you have already seen in this chapter.

Stress testing is another aspect of software testing. This involves subjecting the target system to a workload far in excess of what it would normally encounter. This can uncover defects in the software, including security vulnerabilities. So, for example, if you expect 1,000 visitors a day to your website, simulate 10,000 or even 100,000 a day to test how the system responds to this stress.

Many forms of testing are, at their core, simulation. Stress testing simulates some extraordinary conditions; fuzzing simulates incorrect input. Whenever you are using any simulation to test your applications, you must verify the model. It is important to verify that all aspects of a simulation model are accurate. If the model has any inaccurate data or settings, then the results will not be accurate.

Specific Types of Testing

In addition to the general approaches to testing described previously in this section, there are five forms of testing that must be done during the software development life cycle, regardless of the software model being used. Each of these forms of testing is briefly described here:

Unit Testing   When a functioning unit is complete, whether it is a module, programming class, or complete application, it should be tested. This is usually done by the programmer(s). The testing can be either dynamic, static, or both.

Integration Testing   When two or more units are connected, they should be tested to ensure that they function together. This is usually done by the programmer(s). This testing is usually dynamic testing.

System Testing   When you have a complete functioning system, it should be tested. This is often done by a separate testing team. This testing is usually dynamic testing.

User Acceptance Testing   This is often called beta testing. A test group of users is given access to the system to test it. They are usually testing to see if the system meets their needs.

Regression Testing   Once a system is deployed, whenever a change is made, not only must the change be tested, but all of the systems that might be affected by that change should also be tested.

Clearly secure programming, which will be discussed next, is about concrete steps taken to make more secure software. Some sources recommended simple obfuscation/camouflage of the vulnerabilities. However, the obfuscation is not security. No matter how you camouflage a security vulnerability, an attacker can find it. Therefore, direct mitigation of security risks is the appropriate approach. You should not rely on obfuscation/camouflage.

Secure Coding Standards

Secure coding can best prevent many of the attacks discussed in this chapter. Cross-site scripting and SQL injection are discussed in detail in this chapter, and proper/secure coding is the only prevention for these attacks. Buffer overflows are examined elsewhere in this book, but again, secure coding is the only real defense against this attack.

General Secure Coding Guidelines

Before examining some secure coding standards, it is important to consider a few simple security measures that are applicable to all programming.

The first is encryption. For all data in transit, you should at least consider encrypting that data; this is particularly true for web applications. In Chapter 8, we will look at SSL/TLS as the primary means of encrypting data.

For all code that will be installed on third-party machines, code signing is recommended. By digitally signing code, such as ActiveX components in web pages or device drivers, the end user who is installing the software can be confident as to the software's origin.

Version control and change management is another concept common to all programming. Source code control tools, some of which are open source (such as Subversion and Git), are available that allow you to control versions of software. It is also important that changes to software be subjected to the same rigorous change management procedures that you might use in any other network change. This includes a request for changes (RFC) that will be evaluated by a change approval board (CAB).

It will also be important to determine the type of program with which you are working. Is it a compiled program, such as C or C++, or is it runtime program, such as Java or .NET? In the case of runtime programs, potential vulnerabilities exist in the runtime environment. For example, when using Java, you need to check the version of the Java virtual machine (JVM) you are using to ensure that it does not have any vulnerabilities.

Secure Coding Standards

Secure coding is a broad area, but for the Security+ exam you only need to know the general concepts. If you are a programmer or if you supervise application security, we recommend that you delve deeper into this topic through the URLs that are provided in this section.

OWASP

The *Open Web Application Security Project (OWASP)* (https://www.owasp.org/index.php/OWASP_Secure_Coding_Practices_-_Quick_Reference_Guide) is a voluntary group dedicated to forming secure coding practices for web-based applications, mobile and client applications, and backend design issues. The focus on web-based applications is important since they are among the most vulnerable to attack. This organization offers a range of coding standards. The most fundamental (and the most critical for the Security+ exam) is input validation.

As you will see later in this chapter, some attacks, such as SQL injection, depend entirely on unfiltered input being sent through a web application. OWASP recommends that all data input by a user be validated before it is processed. As mentioned earlier, there are two primary ways to do input validation: client-side validation and server-side validation.

Client-side validation usually works by taking the input that a user enters into a text field and, on the client side, checking for invalid characters or input. This process can be as simple as verifying that the input does not exceed the required length, or it can be a complete check for SQL injection characters. In either case, the validation is accomplished on the client web page before any data is sent to the server.

Server-side validation involves validating data after the server has received it. This process can include checking business logic to see if the data sent conforms to expected parameters. It is unusual to have just server-side validation. You may have systems with only client-side validation, but server-side validation is normally done in conjunction with client-side validation.

CERT Secure Coding Standards

The *Computer Emergency Response Team (CERT)* at Carnage Mellon University (`www.cert.org/secure-coding/`) also details standards for secure coding. CERT standards cover many of the same issues as OWASP, but they also have complete language-specific standards for Java, Perl, C, and C++.

One item that CERT addresses is the issue of exception handling. The fact is that programs encounter errors. How those errors are handled is critical to security. For example, some programmers present detailed error information to the end user. Not only is this not very helpful for most end users, it might actually provide information useful to a hacker. A better idea is to have a simple but helpful message displayed to the end user and just to log the detailed information.

Application Configuration Baselining

Baselining always involves comparing performance to a metric. That metric is a historical measurement that you can point to and identify as coming before a configuration change, before the site became busy, before you added new services, and so on. Baselining can be done with any metric, such as network performance or CPU usage, as well as with applications.

It is advisable to do baselining with key applications prior to major configuration changes. Make certain that applications have proper settings to work at their optimal values and to provide security protection as well.

Operating System Patch Management

In Chapter 2, we discussed patches. There are three types of operating system patches, each with a different level of urgency:

Hotfix   A *hotfix* is an immediate and urgent patch. In general, these represent serious security issues and are not optional; they must be applied to the system.

Patch   A *patch* provides some additional functionality or a non-urgent fix. These are sometimes optional.

Service Pack   *Service packs* are a cumulative assortment of the hotfixes and patches to date. These should always be applied but tested first to be sure that no problems are caused by the update.

Application Patch Management

Just as you need to keep operating system patches current, since they often fix security problems discovered within the OS, you need to do the same with application patches. Once an exploit in an application becomes known, an attacker can take advantage of it to enter or harm a system. Most vendors post patches on a regular basis, and you should routinely scan for any available ones.

A large number of attacks today are targeted at client systems for the simple reason that clients do not always manage application patching well. When you couple that with the fact that most clients have many applications running, the odds of being able to find a weakness to exploit are increased dramatically.

Other Application Security Issues

A variety of application-related security issues do not neatly fit into any of the previous categories, so they are discussed in this section.

Databases and Technologies

One key reason why computers are installed is for their ability to store, access, and modify data. The primary tool for data management is the database. Databases have become increasingly sophisticated, and their capabilities have grown dramatically over the last 10 years. This growth has created opportunities to view data in new ways; it has also created problems for both designers and users of these products.

This section briefly discusses database technologies and some of the common issues associated with vulnerabilities in database systems.

The *relational database* has become the most common approach to database implementation. This technology allows data to be viewed in dynamic ways based on the user's or administrator's needs. The most common language used to speak to databases is *Structured Query Language (SQL)*. SQL allows queries to be configured in real time and passed to database servers. This flexibility causes a major vulnerability when it isn't implemented securely.

Don't confuse the acronym *SQL* with Microsoft's database product *SQL Server*. SQL Server implements Structured Query Language, or SQL, as do most other databases.

For example, you might want to get the phone numbers of all of the customers who live in a certain geographic area and have purchased products from your company in the last two years. In a manual system, you would first need to determine which customers live in the area you want to research. You would perform a manual search of customer records, and then you would identify which customers have made purchases. This type of process could be very involved and time-consuming.

In a relational database environment, you could query the database to find all of the records that meet your criteria and then print them. The command to do this might be a single line of code, or it might require thousands of instructions. Obviously, the increase in productivity is a worthwhile investment.

Corporate or organizational data is one of an organization's most valuable assets. It usually resides either in desktop systems or in large centralized database servers. This information makes the servers tempting targets for industrial espionage and damage.

Database servers suffer from all of the vulnerabilities that we've discussed up to this point. Additionally, the database itself is a complex set of programs that work together to provide access to data.

Early database systems connected the end user directly to the data through applications programs. These programs were intended to allow easy data access and to permit transactions to be performed against the database. In a private network, physical security was usually all that was needed to protect the data.

As the Internet has grown, businesses have allowed customers access to such data as tracking orders, reviewing purchases, wiring funds, and virtually any other capabilities they wanted. This increased interoperability has added more coding, more software, and more complexity to databases.

Software manufacturers work hard to keep up with customer demands. Unfortunately, they frequently release software that is prone to security problems. The increase in demand for database-oriented systems and the security problems introduced by software developers and manufacturers have been the biggest areas of vulnerability for database servers.

Databases need patching just like other applications. You should configure them to use access controls and provide their own levels of security.

To improve system performance, as well as to augment the security of databases, companies have implemented the tiered systems model. Three different models are explained here:

One-Tier Model   In a *one-tier model*, or *single-tier environment*, the database and the application exist on a single system. This is common on desktop systems running a stand-alone database. Early Unix implementations also worked in this manner; each user would sign on to a terminal and run a dedicated application that accessed the data.

Two-Tier Model   In a *two-tier model*, the client workstation or system runs an application that communicates with the database that is running on a different server. This is a common implementation, and it works well for many applications.

Three-Tier Model   The *three-tier model* effectively isolates the end user from the database by introducing a *middle-tier server*. This server accepts requests from clients, evaluates them, and then sends them on to the database server for processing. The database server sends the data back to the middle-tier server, which then sends the data to the client system. This approach is becoming common in business today. The middle server can also control access to the database and provide additional security.

These three models provide increased capability and complexity. You must manage each system and keep it current in order for it to provide security.

NoSQL

NoSQL is a relatively new concept. Most commercial relational database management systems (Oracle, Microsoft SQL Server, MySQL, PostGres, and others) use SQL. A *NoSQL database* is not a relational database and does not use SQL. These databases are less common than relational databases but are often used where scaling is important. Table 7.1 compares NoSQL and SQL databases.

TABLE 7.1   NoSQL databases vs. SQL databases

Feature	NoSQL database	SQL database
Database type	Nonrelational/distributed	Relational
Schema type	Dynamic	Predefined
Data storage	Stores everything in a single nested document, often in XML format (document-based)	Individual records are stored as rows in tables (table-based)
Benefits	Can handle large volumes of structured, semi-structured, and unstructured data	Widely supported and easy to configure for structured data
Typical scaling model	Horizontal: Add more servers	Vertical: Beef up the server
Popular vendors/ implementations	MongoDB, CouchDB, and others	Oracle, Microsoft, MySQL, and others
Susceptible to SQL injection attacks?	No, but susceptible to similar injection-type attacks	Yes

Big Data

Increasingly, organizations have to store extremely large amounts of data, often many terabytes. This is sometimes referred to simply as *Big Data*. This data normally cannot fit on a single server, and it is instead stored on a storage area network (SAN), which is discussed next. One of the issues with Big Data is that it reaches a size where it becomes difficult to search, store, share, back up, and truly manage.

Database Security

The first step in database security is a stable database configuration. One of the most elementary aspects of database configuration is *database normalization*. Normalization is the process of removing redundant entries from a database. There are typically four levels of normalization, ranging from 1N at the lowest (the most duplication) to 4N at the highest (the least duplication).

Once you have a secure database configuration, the next issue is how SQL queries are executed. This is normally accomplished with stored procedures. *Stored procedures* are commonly used in many database management systems to contain SQL statements. The database administrator, or someone designated by the DBA, creates the various SQL statements that are needed in that business, and then programmers can simply call the stored procedures.

This approach prevents each programmer from writing his or her own SQL commands. When diverse people are writing SQL statements, there is the potential for poorly written SQL. Also, having the SQL statements in a single location, the stored procedures, makes maintenance much easier.

Secure Configurations

One method of securely configuring a system is an immutable system. As the name suggests, this is a system that is, in effect, frozen. Nothing can be added to or changed on the system. In some situations, this is necessary to prevent configuration changes.

Another secure configuration approach is *Infrastructure as Code (IaC)*, which is the process of managing and provisioning computer datacenters through machine-readable definition files, rather than physical hardware configuration or interactive configuration tools. Whether the datacenter (or datacenters) uses physical machines or virtual machines, this is an effective way to manage the datacenters.

Sandboxing is an increasingly popular way to provide secure applications. If the application is operating in isolation from the host environment, it is highly unlikely that any security breach of the application can affect the host operating system. Sandboxing can be accomplished by simply running the application in a virtual machine. This approach is used in a wide range of situations, but it is particularly useful for legacy applications that might require an outdated version of an operating system.

All of these methods, and the other recommendations that you have seen in this chapter, are about secure DevOps. This is just a term for security development operations. It means that security is integrated into all of your development operations, which includes database design, programming, and infrastructure.

Code Issues

Code reuse is quite common, but it can lead to security vulnerabilities. In a code reuse attack, the attacker executes code that is meant for some other purposes. In many cases, this can be old code that is no longer used (dead code), even if that code is in a third-party library.

Code reuse is related to the use of third-party libraries or software development kits (SDKs). Although this is a very common practice, it can lead to security vulnerabilities. In 2014, there was a vulnerability in a specific version of WordPress (a web development tool) that led to thousands of sites being vulnerable to SQL injection. This is one example of how a vulnerability in an SDK can be widespread, affecting every application developed with that SDK.

Summary

This chapter introduced you to the concept of hardening, the process of making a server or an application resistant to an attack. To secure a network, each of the elements in its environment must be individually evaluated. Remember, your network is no more secure than its weakest link. One of the major methods of hardening is to disable anything that isn't needed in the system. Keeping systems updated also helps improve security.

Product updates are often used to improve security and to fix errors. The three primary methods of upgrading systems are hotfixes, service packs, and patches. Hotfixes are usually meant as immediate fixes, whereas service packs usually contain multiple fixes. Patches are used to fix a program temporarily until a permanent fix can be applied.

Application hardening helps to ensure that vulnerabilities are minimized. Make sure that you run only the applications and services that are needed to support your environment. Attackers can target application protocols. Many of the newer systems offer a rich environment for end users, and each protocol increases your risk.

Database technologies are vulnerable to attacks because of the nature of the flexibility they provide. Make sure that database servers and applications are kept up to date. To provide increased security, many environments have implemented multitiered approaches to data access.

Exam Essentials

Be able to discuss the weaknesses and vulnerabilities of the various applications that run on a network. Web, email, and other services present unique security challenges that must be considered. Turn off services that aren't needed. Make sure that applications are kept up to date with security and bug fixes. Implement these services in a secure manner as the manufacturer intended. This is the best method for securing applications.

Understand secure programming. Input validation, error handling, programming models, and software testing are all important on the Security+ exam. You should be familiar with all of these.

Be familiar with new technologies. The Security+ exam will ask basic questions regarding SCADA, IoT, medical devices, and other technologies. Make sure that you are familiar with the security issues associated with these technologies.

Review Questions

You can find the answers in the Appendix.

1. Which of the following terms refers to the process of establishing a standard for security?

    A. Baselining

    B. Security evaluation

    C. Hardening

    D. Methods research

2. You've been chosen to lead a team of administrators in an attempt to increase security. You're currently creating an outline of all the aspects of security that will need to be examined and acted on. Which of the following terms describes the process of improving security in a network operating system (NOS)?

    A. Common criteria

    B. Hardening

    C. Encryption

    D. Networking

3. John is responsible for application security at his company. He is concerned that the application reacts appropriately to unexpected input. What type of testing would be most helpful to him?

    A. Unit testing

    B. Integration testing

    C. Stress testing

    D. Fuzzing

4. Myra is concerned about database security. She wants to begin with a good configuration of the database. Which of the following is a fundamental issue with database configuration?

    A. Normalization

    B. Input validation

    C. Fuzz testing

    D. Stress testing

5. Which of the following is the technique of providing unexpected values as input to an application to try to make it crash?

    A. DLP

    B. Fuzzing

    C. Stress testing

    D. HSM

6. Mary is responsible for website security in her company. She wants to address widely known and documented web application vulnerabilities. Which resource would be most helpful?

A. OWASP

B. CERT

C. NIST

D. ISO

7. You're redesigning your network in preparation for putting the company up for sale. The network, like all aspects of the company, needs to perform at its best in order to benefit the sale. Which model is used to provide an intermediary server between the end user and the database?

A. One-tiered

B. Two-tiered

C. Three-tiered

D. Relational database

8. The administrator at MTS was recently fired, and it has come to light that he didn't install updates and fixes as they were released. As the newly hired administrator, your first priority is to bring all networked clients and servers up to date. What is a bundle of one or more system fixes in a single product called?

A. Service pack

B. Hotfix

C. Patch

D. System install

9. Your company does electronic monitoring of individuals under house arrest around the world. Because of the sensitive nature of the business, you can't afford any unnecessary downtime. What is the process of applying a repair to an operating system while the system stays in operation?

A. Upgrading

B. Service pack installation

C. Hotfix

D. File update

10. Juan has just made a minor change to the company's e-commerce application. The change works as expected. What type of testing is most important for him to perform?

A. Unit testing

B. Regression testing

C. Static testing

D. Stress testing

11. Your company has grown at a tremendous rate, and the need to hire specialists in various IT areas has become apparent. You're helping to write an online advertisement that will be used to recruit new employees, and you want to make certain that applicants possess the necessary skills. One knowledge area in which your organization is weak is database intelligence. What is the primary type of database used in applications today that you can mention in the ads?

    A. Hierarchical

    B. Relational

    C. Network

    D. Archival

12. What is the process of applying manual changes to a program called?

    A. Hotfix

    B. Service pack

    C. Patching

    D. Replacement

13. You want to assign privileges to a user so that she can delete a file but not be able to assign privileges to others. What permissions should you assign?

    A. Full Control

    B. Delete

    C. Administrator

    D. Modify

14. Ahmed is responsible for security of a SCADA system. If availability is his biggest concern, what is the most important thing for him to implement?

    A. SIEM

    B. IPS

    C. Automated patch control

    D. Log monitoring

15. Gerard is concerned about SQL injection attacks on his company's e-commerce server. What security measure would be most important for him to implement?

    A. Stress testing

    B. Input validation

    C. IPS

    D. Agile programming

16. Elizabeth works for a company that manufactures portable medical devices, such as insulin pumps. She is concerned about security for the device. Which of the following would be the most helpful in securing these devices?

    A. Ensure that all communications with the device are encrypted.

    B. Ensure that the devices have FDE.

    C. Ensure that the devices have been stress tested.

    D. Ensure that the devices have been fuzz tested.

17. Vincent is a programmer working on an e-commerce site. He has conducted a vulnerability scan and discovered a flaw in a third-party module. There is an update available for this module that fixes the flaw. What is the best approach for him to take to mitigate this threat?

    A. Submit an RFC.

    B. Immediately apply the update.

    C. Place the update on a test server; then if it works, apply it to the production server.

    D. Document the issue.

18. Which of the following would be the most secure way to deploy a legacy application that requires a legacy operating system?

    A. Sandboxing

    B. Stress testing

    C. Dynamic testing

    D. Placing it on an encrypted drive

19. Denish is testing an application that is multithreaded. Which of the following is a specific concern for multithreaded applications?

    A. Input validation

    B. Memory overflow

    C. Race conditions

    D. Unit testing

20. Gertrude is managing a new software project. The project has very clearly defined requirements that are not likely to change. Which of the following is the most appropriate development model for her?

    A. Agile

    B. XP Programming

    C. Waterfall

    D. Scrum

Chapter

8

Cryptography

THE FOLLOWING COMPTIA SECURITY+ EXAM OBJECTIVES ARE COVERED IN THIS CHAPTER:

✓ **1.2 Compare and contrast types of attacks.**

- Cryptographic attacks: Birthday; Known plain text/cipher text; Rainbow tables; Dictionary; Brute force—Online vs. offline— Collision; Downgrade; Replay; Weak implementations

✓ **6.1 Compare and contrast basic concepts of cryptography.**

- Symmetric algorithms
- Modes of operation
- Asymmetric algorithms
- Hashing
- Salt, IV, nonce
- Elliptic curve
- Weak/deprecated algorithms
- Key exchange
- Digital signatures
- Diffusion
- Confusion
- Collision
- Steganography
- Obfuscation
- Stream vs. block
- Key strength
- Session keys
- Ephemeral key
- Secret algorithm
- Data-in-transit
- Data-at-rest

- Data-in-use

- Random/pseudo-random number generation

- Key stretching

- Implementation vs. algorithm selection: Crypto service provider; Crypto modules

- Perfect forward secrecy

- Security through obscurity

- Common use cases: Low power devices; Low latency; High resiliency; Supporting confidentiality; Supporting integrity; Supporting obfuscation; Supporting authentication; Supporting non-repudiation; Resource vs. security constraints

✓ **6.2 Explain cryptography algorithms and their basic characteristics.**

- Symmetric algorithms: AES; DES; 3DES; RC4; Blowfish/Twofish

- Cipher modes: CBC; GCM; ECB; CTM; Stream vs. block

- Asymmetric algorithms: RSA; DSA; Diffie-Hellman—Groups; DHE; ECDHE—Elliptic curve; PGP/GPG

- Hashing algorithms: MD5; SHA; HMAC; RIPEMD

- Key stretching algorithms: BCRYPT; PBKDF2

- Obfuscation: XOR; ROT13; Substitution ciphers

✓ **6.3 Given a scenario, install and configure wireless security settings.**

- Cryptographic protocols: WPA; WPA2; CCMP; TKIP

- Authentication protocols: EAP; PEAP; EAP-FAST; EAP-TLS; EAP-TTLS; IEEE 802.1x; RADIUS Federation

- Methods: PSK vs. Enterprise vs. Open; WPS; Captive portals

✓ **6.4 Given a scenario, implement public key infrastructure.**

- Components: CA; Intermediate CA; CRL; OCSP; CSR; Certificate; Public key; Private key; Object identifiers (OID)

- Concepts: Online vs. offline CA; Stapling; Pinning; Trust model; Key escrow; Certificate chaining

- Types of certificates: Wildcard; SAN; Code signing; Self-signed; Machine/computer; Email; User; Root; Domain validation; Extended validation

- Certificate formats: DER; PEM; PFX; CER; P12

There is often overlap between terms used to define certain threats and attacks, but it is important to be as specific as possible when discussing them to be able to understand and report them as unambiguously as possible. The following terms (also found in the online glossary) are those that CompTIA is fond of using and testing on in this category. They are provided in order to make it easier for you to know what each is intended to convey.

Security+ Terminology

asymmetric cipher   Cryptographic algorithms that use two different keys—one key to encrypt and another to decrypt. Also called public key cryptography.

Challenge Handshake Authentication Protocol (CHAP)   An authentication protocol that periodically reauthenticates.

collision   When two different inputs into a cryptographic hash produce the same output, this is known as a collision.

cryptographic hash   A function that is one-way (nonreversible), has a fixed length output, and is collision resistant.

PRNG   A pseudo-random number generator is an algorithm used to generate a number that is sufficiently random for cryptographic purposes.

rainbow table   A table of precomputed hashes used to guess passwords by searching for the hash of a password.

salt   Bits added to a hash to make it resistant to rainbow table attacks.

symmetric cipher   Any cryptographic algorithm that uses the same key to encrypt and decrypt. DES, AES, and Blowfish are examples.

X.509   The X.509 standard is the most widely used standard for digital certificates.

Cryptography is the science of altering information so that it cannot be decoded without a key. It is the practice of protecting information through encryption and transformation. As data becomes more valuable, it is an area of high interest to governments, businesses, and, increasingly, individuals.

People want privacy when it comes to their personal and other sensitive information. Corporations want—and need—to protect financial records, trade secrets, customer lists, and employee information. The government uses cryptography to help ensure the safety and well-being of its citizens. Entire governmental agencies have been created to help ensure secrecy, and millions of dollars have been spent trying to protect national secrets and attempting to learn the secrets of other countries.

The study of cryptographic algorithms is called *cryptography*. The study of how to break cryptographic algorithms is called *cryptanalysis*. The two subjects taken together are generally referred to as *cryptology*. All of these disciplines require a strong mathematics background, particularly in number theory.

NOTE   Many people, even many textbooks, tend to use the terms *cryptography* and *cryptology* interchangeably.

An Overview of Cryptography

Cryptography is a field almost as old as humankind. The first recorded cryptographic efforts occurred 4,000 years ago. These early efforts included translating messages from one language into another or substituting characters. Since that time, cryptography has grown to include a plethora of possibilities. Ultimately, all cryptography seeks to obfuscate the plain text so that it is not readily readable. Classic methods used relatively simple techniques that a human being could usually break in a reasonable amount of time. The obfuscation used in modern cryptography is much more sophisticated and can be unbreakable within a practical period of time.

Historical Cryptography

Historical methods of cryptography predate the modern computer age. These methods did not depend on mathematics, as many modern methods do, but rather on some technique for scrambling the text.

A *cipher* is a method used to scramble or obfuscate characters to hide their value. *Ciphering* is the process of using a cipher to do that type of scrambling to a message. The two primary types of nonmathematical cryptography, or ciphering methods, are *substitution* and *transposition*. We will discuss both of these methods in this section.

Substitution Ciphers

A *substitution cipher* is a type of coding or ciphering system that changes one character or symbol into another. Character substitution can be a relatively easy method of encrypting information. One of the oldest known substitution ciphers is called the *Caesar cipher*. It was purportedly used by Julius Caesar. The system involves simply shifting all letters a certain number of spaces in the alphabet. Supposedly, Julius Caesar used a shift of three to the right. He was working in Latin, of course, but the same thing can be done with any language, including English. Here is an example:

I will pass the Security plus test.

If you shift each letter three to the right, you get the following:

L zloo sdvv wkh Vhfxulwb soxv whvw.

Substitution ciphers are not adequate for modern uses, and a computer would crack one almost instantly. The issue involved is letter and word frequency. All languages have certain words and letter combinations that appear more often than others. In English, if you see a three-letter word, it is most likely to be *the* or *and*. If you see a single-letter word, it is most likely to be *I* or *a*. So using this information, you can guess that the first *L* is really an *I*, that the *wkh* is actually the word *the*, and then use that information to decrypt the rest of the message. The more cipher text you have to work with, the easier it is to decrypt.

Atbash is another ancient substitution cipher. Hebrew scribes copying the book of Jeremiah used this substitution cipher. Applying the Atbash cipher is fairly simple—just reverse the order of the letters of the alphabet. This is, by modern standards, a very primitive and easy-to-break cipher. For example, in English:

A becomes Z, B becomes Y, C becomes X, and so forth.

Of course, the Hebrews used a different alphabet, with aleph being the first letter and tav the last letter. However, I will use English examples to demonstrate this:

Attack at dawn

becomes

Zggzxp zg wzdm

Multi-alphabet Substitution

One of the problems with substitution ciphers is that they did not change the underlying letter and word frequency of the text. One way to combat this was to have multiple substitutions. For example, you might shift the first letter by three to the right, the second letter by two to the right, and the third letter by one to the left; then repeat this formula with the next three letters. The most famous example of a multi-alphabet substitution from historical times was the *Vigenère cipher*. It used a keyword to look up the cipher text in a table. The user would take the first letter in the text that they wanted to encrypt, go to the Vigenère table, and match that with the letter from the keyword in order to find the cipher text letter. This would be repeated until the entire message was encrypted. Each letter in the keyword generated a different substitution alphabet.

Transposition Ciphers

A *transposition cipher* involves transposing or scrambling the letters in a certain manner. Typically, a message is broken into blocks of equal size, and each block is then scrambled.

In the simple example shown in Figure 8.1, the characters are transposed by changing the order of the group. In this case, the letters are rotated three places in the message. You could change the way Block 1 is transposed from Block 2 and make it a little more difficult, but it would still be relatively easy to decrypt.

FIGURE 8.1   A simple transposition cipher in action

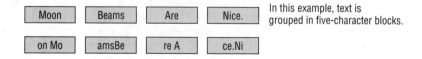

Moon beams are nice.

| Moon | Beams | Are | Nice. |

In this example, text is grouped in five-character blocks.

| on Mo | amsBe | re A | ce.Ni |

In this example, each character (including the spaces) is moved to the right three positions.

The Rail Fence Cipher is a classic example of a transposition cipher. With this cipher, you write message letters out diagonally over a number of rows and then read off cipher row by row. For example, you write the message out as:

m e m a t r h t g p r y
e t e f e t e o a a t

yielding the cipher text:

MEMATRHTGPRYETEFETEOAAT

 Real World Scenario

Working with rot13

One very common substitution cipher is *ROT13*, and it is also one commonly asked about on the Security+ exam. This simple algorithm rotates every letter 13 places in the alphabet. Thus an *A* becomes an *N*, a *B* becomes an *O*, and so forth. The same rotation of 13 letters that is used to encrypt the message is also used to decrypt the message. Many newsgroups offer a ROT13 option that allows you to encrypt or decrypt postings.

See if you can solve these encryptions:

1. Neg snve qrohgf urer Fngheqnl.

2. Gevcyr pbhcbaf ng Xebtre!

3. Gel lbhe unaq ng chmmyrf.

One of the easiest ways to solve ROT13 text messages is to take a sheet of paper and write the letters from *A to M* in one column and from *N to Z* in a second. To decipher, replace the letter in the encrypted message with the one that appears beside it in the other column.

Here are the answers:

1. Art fair debuts here Saturday.

2. Triple coupons at Kroger!

3. Try your hand at puzzles.

The Enigma Machine

No discussion of the history of cryptography would be complete without discussing the Enigma machine. The *Enigma machine* was essentially a typewriter that implemented a multi-alphabet substitution cipher. When each key was hit, a different substitution alphabet was used. The Enigma machine used 26 different substitution alphabets. Prior to computers, this was extremely hard to break.

Contrary to popular misconceptions, the Enigma is not a single machine, but rather a family of machines. The first version was invented by German engineer Arthur Scherbius toward the end of World War I. It was also used by the military of several different countries, not just Nazi Germany.

The core of the Enigma machine were the rotors. These were disks arranged in a cycle with 26 letters on them. The rotors where lined up. Essentially each rotor represented a different single substitution cipher. You can think of the Enigma as a sort of mechanical poly-alphabet cipher.

Steganography

Steganography is the process of hiding a message in a medium such as a digital image, audio file, or other file. In theory, doing this prevents analysts from detecting the real message. You could encode your message in another file or message and use that file to hide your message.

The most common way this is done today is called the *least significant bit (LSB) method*. As you know, everything on a computer is stored in bits that are organized into bytes. For example, a single pixel on a Windows computer screen is stored in 3 bytes/24 bits. If you changed the very last bit (the least significant bit in each byte), then that would not make a noticeable change in the image. In other words, you could not tell that anything had been changed. Using this fact, you can store data by putting it in the least significant bits of an image file. Someone observing the image would see nothing out of the ordinary.

It is also possible to hide data in audio files, video files, or literally any digital file type. There are even programs available on the Web for doing steganography. QuickStego (`http://quickcrypto.com`) is a free and easy-to-use program. Invisible Secrets (`www.invisiblesecrets.com`) is fairly inexpensive and quite robust.

Steganography can also be used to accomplish *electronic watermarking*. Mapmakers and artists have used watermarking for years to protect copyrights. If an image contains a watermark placed there by the original artist, proving that copyright infringement has occurred in a copy is relatively easy.

In Exercise 8.1, we will show you how to encrypt a filesystem in SuSE Linux.

EXERCISE 8.1

Encrypting a Filesystem in Linux

This lab requires access to a server running SuSE Linux Enterprise Server or OpenSuSE. To encrypt a filesystem, follow these steps:

1. Log in as root and start YaST.

2. Choose System ➢ Partitioner.

3. Answer Yes to the prompt that appears. Select a filesystem and click Edit.

4. Select the Encrypt File System check box and click OK.

Modern Cryptography

With the advent of computers, older methods of cryptography are no longer viable. A computer can quickly and easily crack substitution and transposition ciphers. Even Vigenère and the Enigma machine are not able to withstand modern cryptographic attacks.

Modern cryptography is divided into three major areas: symmetric cryptography, asymmetric cryptography, and hashing algorithms. All three of these are covered extensively on the Security+ certification exam and are discussed in detail in this section.

Before we begin with modern symmetric ciphers, we should discuss the exclusive OR (XOR) operation. It is a very simple mathematical operation that is a part of all symmetric ciphers. *XOR* (as it is usually termed) is a simple but powerful binary math operation. Consider two binary numbers, 1011 and 1001. To XOR these numbers, you start at the least significant bit (LSB) and ask a simple question: is there a 1 in the top or bottom number, but not both (that is, not and/or, but exclusively or)? If so, then the resultant is a 1; if not the resultant is a 0.

$$
\begin{array}{c}
1011 \\
\underline{1001} \\
0010
\end{array}
$$

Now that may not look particularly interesting, until you realize that the XOR operation is reversible. If I take the resultant (0010) and XOR it with either of the other two numbers, I get back the other. So, for example:

$$
\begin{array}{c}
0010 \\
\underline{1001} \\
1011
\end{array}
$$

At some point, all symmetric ciphers use an XOR operation as a part of their algorithm. By itself, XOR would be a very weak encryption algorithm—so weak, in fact, that it would probably not be accurate to consider it encryption, at least not by modern standards. However, it is a part of symmetric ciphers and combined with a number of other operations.

Working with Symmetric Algorithms

Symmetric algorithms require both the sender and receiver of an encrypted message to have the same key and processing algorithms. Symmetric algorithms generate a secret key that must be protected. A *symmetric key*, sometimes referred to as a *secret key* or *private key*, is a key that isn't disclosed to people who aren't authorized to use the encryption system. The disclosure of this secret key breaches the security of the encryption system. If a key is lost or stolen, the entire process is breached. These types of systems are common, but the keys require special handling. Figure 8.2 illustrates a symmetric encryption system; in this example, the keys are the same on each end.

FIGURE 8.2   Symmetric encryption system

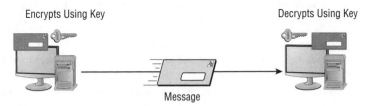

Encrypts Using Key   Decrypts Using Key

Message

The other issue surrounding symmetric cryptography is key distribution. If you wish to encrypt messages with a friend in another city, how do you exchange keys?

> A few basic facts to know about symmetric cryptography for the test are that symmetric cryptographic algorithms are always faster than asymmetric, and they can be just as secure with a smaller key size. For example, RSA (an asymmetric algorithm) uses keys of a minimum length of 2,048 bits, whereas AES (a symmetric algorithm) uses key sizes of 128, 192, or 256 bits.

Symmetric methods use either a block or stream cipher. As the name implies, with a *block cipher*, the algorithm works on chunks of data, encrypting one and then moving to the next. With a *stream cipher*, the data is encrypted one bit, or byte, at a time.

Before we examine specific symmetric algorithms, there are some general principles of symmetric cryptography of which we should take note. Two terms, in particular, are of interest. These terms are diffusion and confusion. These terms come from information theory. *Diffusion* means that a change in a single bit of input changes more than one bit of the output. With classic ciphers (Caesar, Vigenère, and others) that we examined earlier, this is not the case. However, modern symmetric ciphers are structured so that if one changes a single bit of input, multiple output bits are changed.

The other concept that is relevant to symmetric ciphers is confusion. This term is not a reference to how you might feel after reading a chapter on cryptography. It is instead the concept that the relationship between the plain text, cipher text, and key are very difficult to see. This can best be understood by examining the opposite. Consider the XOR operation previously described. In that operation, the relationship between plain text, cipher text, and the key is very easy to see. There is virtually no confusion at all. Modern symmetric ciphers are structured so that they have a great deal of confusion.

Several successful encryption systems use symmetric algorithms. A strong algorithm can be difficult to break. Here are some of the common standards that use symmetric algorithms:

Data Encryption Standard   The *Data Encryption Standard (DES)* has been used since the mid-1970s. It was the primary standard used in government and industry until it was replaced by AES. It's based on a 56-bit key, and it has several modes that offer security and integrity. It is now considered insecure because of the small key size. Note that DES actually generates a 64-bit key, but 8 of those bits are just for error correction and only the 56 bits are the actual key.

Triple-DES   *Triple-DES (3DES)* is a technological upgrade of DES. 3DES is still used, even though AES is the preferred choice for government applications. 3DES is considerably harder to break than many other systems, and it's more secure than DES. It increases the key length to 168 bits (using three 56-bit DES keys).

Advanced Encryption Standard   *Advanced Encryption Standard (AES)* has replaced DES as the current standard, and it uses the Rijndael algorithm. AES was developed by Joan Daemen and Vincent Rijmen. AES is the current product used by U.S. governmental agencies. It supports key sizes of 128, 192, and 256 bits, with 128 bits being the default.

For more background/historical information about Rijndael (AES), visit this website: http://csrc.nist.gov/archive/aes/index.html.

CAST   *CAST* is an algorithm developed by Carlisle Adams and Stafford Tavares (hence the name). It's used in some products offered by Microsoft and IBM. CAST uses a 40-bit to 128-bit key, and it's very fast and efficient. Two additional versions, CAST-128 and CAST-256, also exist.

GOST   *GOST* is a DES-like algorithm developed by the Soviets in the 1970s. It was classified but released to the public in 1994. It uses a 64-bit block and a key of 256 bits. It is a 32-round Feistel cipher. GOST is an acronym for *gosudarstvennyy* standard, which translates into English as "state standard." The official designation is GOST 28147-89. It was meant as an alternative to the U.S. DES algorithm and has some similarities to DES.

Feistel ciphers, also called Feistel networks, and Feistel functions are specific algorithm types developed originally by Horst Feistel and first used in DES. The process is to split the block of plain text into two halves. One half is put through a round function (repeated each round) and the other is not. Next the half that was not put through the round function is XOR'd with the output of the half that was put through the round function and the two are swapped. This process is repeated each round of the algorithm. DES, for example, goes for 16 rounds.

Ron's Cipher   RC is an encryption family produced by RSA laboratories. RC stands for *Ron's Cipher* or *Ron's Code*. (Ron Rivest is the author of this algorithm.) The current levels are RC4, RC5, and RC6. RC5 uses a key size of up to 2,048 bits. It's considered to be a strong system.

RC4 is popular with wireless and WEP/WPA encryption. It is a streaming cipher that works with key sizes between 40 and 2,048 bits, and it is used in SSL and TLS. It is also popular with utilities used for downloading BitTorrent files, since many providers limit the download of these. By using RC4 to obfuscate the header and the stream, it makes it more difficult for the service provider to realize that they are indeed BitTorrent files being moved about.

Blowfish and Twofish   *Blowfish* is an encryption system invented by a team led by Bruce Schneier that performs a 64-bit block cipher at very fast speeds. It is a symmetric block cipher that can use variable-length keys (from 32 bits to 448 bits). *Twofish* is quite similar, and it works on 128-bit blocks. The distinctive feature of the latter is that it has a complex key schedule.

International Data Encryption Algorithm   *International Data Encryption Algorithm (IDEA)* was developed by a Swiss consortium. It's an algorithm that uses a 128-bit key. This product is similar in speed and capability to DES, but it's more secure. IDEA is used in Pretty Good Privacy (PGP), a public domain encryption system used by many for email. Currently, Ascom AG holds the right to market IDEA.

One-Time Pads   *One-time pads* are the only truly completely secure cryptographic implementations. They are so secure for two reasons. First, they use a key that is as long as a plain-text message. This means that there is no pattern in the key application for an attacker to use. Also, one-time pad keys are used only once and then discarded. So even if you could break a one-time pad cipher, that same key would never be used again, so knowledge of the key would be useless.

The Vernam cipher is a type of one-time pad. The concept behind a one-time pad is that the plain text is somehow altered by a random string of data so that the resulting cipher text is truly random. Gilbert Vernam proposed a stream cipher that would be used with teleprinters. It would combine a prepared key, character by character, which was stored on a paper tape, with the characters of the plain text to produce the cipher text. The recipient would again apply the key to get back the plain text.

In 1919, Vernam patented his idea (U.S. Patent 1,310,719). Vernam's method used the binary XOR (Exclusive OR) operation applied to the bits of the message.

Symmetric Ciphers Issues

An important issue in symmetric ciphers is the latency. In cryptography, *latency* refers to the difference between the time you input plain text and the time get out cipher text. You might think that it would be good simply to keep churning away at input, scrambling it more and more. However, low latency is a goal of any cipher. This is particularly important in low-power devices. The longer it takes to encrypt data, the more power is consumed.

Another issue is *high resiliency.* The concern is various rather advanced attacks that can "leak" a portion of the secret key, such as with side-channel attacks. The nature of these attacks is beyond the scope of this text. Nonetheless, the concept of high resiliency is that algorithms that are resilient are less prone to leaking bits of data. The Security+ exam will, at most, mention this in passing. It is a complex topic that requires some background in cryptography.

Key Exchange

Key exchange is an important topic in relation to symmetric cryptography. There are two primary approaches to key exchange: in-band key exchange and out-of-band key exchange. *In-band key exchange* essentially means that the key is exchanged within the same communications channel that is going to be encrypted. IPSec, which will be discussed later in this chapter, uses in-band key exchange. *Out-of-band key exchange* means that some other channel, other than the one that is going to be secured, is used to exchange the key.

Forward secrecy is a property of any key exchange system, which ensures that if one key is compromised, subsequent keys will not also be compromised. *Perfect forward secrecy* occurs when this process is unbreakable. A common approach uses ephemeral keys, discussed later in this chapter.

Symmetric Cipher Modes

Symmetric ciphers can be executed in several different modes of operation. The easiest is *Electronic Code Book (ECB).* This simply means to use the algorithm without any modification at all. Essentially, you implement the algorithm exactly as it is designed.

The second mode, quite commonly used, is *cipher-block chaining (CBC).* Block ciphers (for example, DES, AES, Blowfish, GOST, and others) divide the plain text into blocks (often 64-bit or 128-bit) and encrypt each block, one at a time. What CBC does is that when one block is finished encrypting, before the second block is started, the output of the first block is XOR'd with the plain text of the next block. This causes two interesting improvements in the cipher. The first is that it introduces even more diffusion. The second is that it makes known plain-text attacks totally ineffective. The reason for the second improvement is simply that with CBC, even if every single block of plain text were identical, the outputs would be different.

Counter mode (CTM or CTR) is used to convert a block cipher into a stream cipher. It basically works by generating a keystream block by encrypting sequential values of some counter. This counter can be any function that produces a sequence that has a long period with no repetition.

Another mode, *Galois Counter Mode (GCM),* is a bit more complex than either ECB or CBC. This mode uses a hash function of a binary Galois field to provide encryption that is authenticated. In normal counter mode, each block is encrypted with a cipher in a sequential manner to produce a stream cipher. The GCM uses a Galois field with a hash to have an authenticated cipher. The details of Galois fields are beyond the scope of the Security+ exam.

PRNG

The cipher key used with symmetric algorithms should be a random number. However, this poses a problem. Orderly algorithms don't produce truly random numbers. So instead, cryptographers use pseudo-random number generators. These are algorithms that produce numbers that are random enough. There are many applications for PRNGs. We already mentioned using them to generate keys for symmetric ciphers.

Another use of PRNGs is to generate initialization vectors (IVs). IVs are numbers that should be used only once and are added to a key to make the algorithm stronger. In fact, the term used in cryptography is nonce (number used only once). As one example, 64-bit WEP (which we will discuss later in this chapter) uses a 40-bit RC4 key that will be used for some period of time, perhaps months. However, with each 40-bit key is a 24-bit IV that is only used one time. This means that even if someone should crack the 40-bit RC4 key, they would still not be able to decrypt the message.

Working with Asymmetric Algorithms

Asymmetric algorithms use two keys to encrypt and decrypt data. These asymmetric keys are referred to as the *public key* and the *private key*. The sender uses the public key to encrypt a message, and the receiver uses the private key to decrypt the message; what one key does, the other one undoes. As you may recall, symmetrical systems require the key to be private between the two parties.

The public key may be truly public or it may be a secret between the two parties. The private key is kept private, and only the owner (receiver) knows it. If someone wants to send you an encrypted message, they can use your public key to encrypt the message and then send you the message. You can use your private key to decrypt the message. The private key is always kept protected. If both keys become available to a third party, the encryption system won't protect the privacy of the message.

The real "magic" of these systems is that the public key cannot be used to decrypt a message. If Bob sends Alice a message encrypted with Alice's public key, it does not matter if everyone else on Earth has Alice's public key, which cannot decrypt the message. Only Alice's private key can do that, as illustrated in Figure 8.3. All asymmetric algorithms are based on number theory.

FIGURE 8.3   A two-key system in use

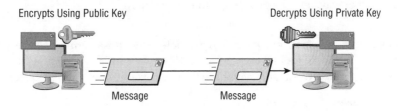

Encrypts Using Public Key   Decrypts Using Private Key

Message   Message

Two-key systems are referred to as *public key cryptography (PKC)*. Don't confuse this with public key infrastructure (PKI), which uses PKC as a part of the process.

Four popular asymmetric systems are in use today:

RSA   *RSA* is named after its inventors Ron Rivest, Adi Shamir, and Leonard Adleman. The RSA algorithm is an early public key encryption system that uses large integers as the basis for the process. It's widely implemented, and it has become a de facto standard. RSA works with both encryption and digital signatures, which are discussed later in the chapter. RSA is used in many environments, including Secure Sockets Layer (SSL), and it can be used for key exchange.

The RSA Cryptographic Algorithm

The Security+ exam does not require you to know the details of any cryptographic algorithms. However, many people are confused by the concept of asymmetric cryptography, and the RSA algorithm is rather simple, so we present it here for your edification.

Key generation is actually pretty simple, as shown in the following example:

1. Generate two large random primes, *p* and *q*, of approximately equal size such that their product, $n = pq$, is of the required bit length (such as 2,048 bits, 4,096 bits, and so forth).

Let n = pq

Let m = (p-1)(q-1)

2. Choose a small number *e*, co-prime to *m*. (Note: Two numbers are co-prime if they have no common factors.)

3. Find *d*, such that

de mod m ≡ 1

4. Publish *e* and *n* as the public key. Keep *d* and *n* as the secret key. Encrypt as follows:

C= M^e mod n

or, put another way, compute the cipher text:

c = m^e mod n

5. Decrypt as follows:

P = C^d mod n

or, put another way, use this private key (*d*,*n*) to compute:

m = c^d mod n

To make this even more clear, let's look at an example. Now this example uses very small prime numbers—too small for real cryptography. However, this is exactly how RSA is really done; only for real-world applications are much larger prime numbers used:

1. Select primes: $p = 17$ and $q =1 1$

2. Compute $n = pq =17×11 = 187$

3. Compute $\emptyset(n) = (p-1)(q-1) = 16 \times 10 = 160$

4. Select $e = 7$

5. Find d, such that de mod m $\equiv$ 1, d = 23

6. Since $23 \times 7 = 161$ mod M (160) = 1

7. Publish public key 7,187

8. Keep secret private key 23,187

Now let's use these keys. Use the number 3 as the plain text. Remember e = 7, d = 23, and n = 187.

> Cipher text = Plaintext^e mod n or
> Cipher text = 3^7 mod 187
> Cipher text = 2187 mod 187
> Cipher text = 130

Decrypt

> Plaintext = Cipher text^d mod n
> Plaintext = 130^{23} mod 187
> Plaintext = 4.1753905413413116367045797e+48mod 187
> Plaintext = 3

The purpose of this example is to provide you with a deeper understanding of the RSA algorithm in particular, and by extrapolation, asymmetric cryptography in general.

Diffie-Hellman   Whitfield Diffie and Martin Hellman conceptualized the *Diffie-Hellman key exchange*. They are considered the founders of the public/private key concept. This algorithm is used primarily to generate a shared secret key across public networks. The process isn't used to encrypt or decrypt messages; it's used merely for the creation of a symmetric key between two parties.

An interesting twist is that the method had actually been developed a few years earlier by Malcolm J. Williamson of the British Intelligence Service, but it was classified.

> On the Security+ exam, if you are asked about an algorithm for exchanging keys over an insecure medium, unless the context is IPsec, the answer is always Diffie-Hellman.

Elliptic Curve Cryptography   *Elliptic Curve Cryptography (ECC)* provides similar functionality to RSA but uses smaller key sizes to obtain the same level of security. ECC encryption systems are based on the idea of using points on a curve combined with a point at infinity and the difficulty of solving discrete logarithm problems.

Many vendors have implemented, or are implementing, the ECC system for security. The National Security Agency has also recommended several implementations of ECC. You can expect that ECC will be commonly implemented in mobile devices in the near future.

There are many variations of Elliptic Curve, including:

- Elliptic Curve Diffie-Hellman (ECC-DH)
- Elliptic Curve Digital Signature Algorithm (ECC-DSA)

ElGamal   *ElGamal* was developed by Taher Elgamal in 1984. It is an asymmetric algorithm, and several variations of ElGamal have been created, including Elliptic Curve ElGamal. ElGamal and related algorithms use what is called an ephemeral key. An *ephemeral key* is simply a key that exists only for that session. Essentially, the algorithm creates a key to use for that single communication session, and it is not used again.

Not as many asymmetric algorithms have been discussed here as have symmetric encryption algorithms, but it can still be difficult keeping all of them straight. Table 8.1 provides an alphabetic list of the most popular asymmetric algorithms, and it should be useful for Security+ exam preparation.

TABLE 8.1   Asymmetric algorithms

Algorithm	Common use
Diffie-Hellman	Key agreement.
ElGamal	Transmitting digital signatures and key exchanges.
Elliptic Curve (ECC)	An option to RSA that uses less computing power than RSA and is popular in smaller devices like smartphones.
RSA	The most commonly used public key algorithm, RSA is used for encryption and digital signatures.

Cryptography Concepts

There are some general concepts that are applicable to all algorithms, including both symmetric and asymmetric cryptographic algorithms.

What Cryptography Should You Use?

Whether you are using asymmetric or symmetric cryptography, it is important to use only proven cryptography technologies. In cryptology, one of the key principles is called Kerckhoffs' principle. This principle was first stated by Auguste Kerckhoffs in the nineteenth century. Essentially, *Kerckhoffs' principle* states that the security of an algorithm should depend only on the secrecy of the key and not on the secrecy of the algorithm itself.

This literally means that the algorithm can be public for all to examine, and the process will still be secure as long as you keep the specific key secret.

Allowing the algorithm to be public might seem counterintuitive. Nevertheless, all of the major algorithms discussed in this chapter are public, and the entire set of algorithms is published in many books and articles and on numerous websites. This allows researchers to examine the algorithm for flaws.

Usually, secret algorithms have not been properly vetted. The cryptology community has not been given the opportunity to examine the algorithm for flaws. This all leads to a basic principle: you should only use proven cryptography technology—that is, avoid new and "secret" methods.

Keeping a cryptographic method secret not only makes it impossible for it to be tested by the cryptographic community, it is something that security experts term *security through obscurity*. This means that something is not particularly secure, just that the details are hidden and you hope that no attacker finds them. This is a very bad approach to security.

Implementation

This also brings us to implementation issues. Yes, selecting a strong algorithm (such as AES 256 bit) is a good idea for cryptography. However, the algorithm must also be implemented properly. This includes aspects such as how the key is generated (using a good PRNG), not reusing keys, and key exchange. It is just as important to be concerned about proper implementation as it is the choice of algorithm.

Part of implementation is the selection of cryptographic modules and cryptographic providers. It is very unlikely that you will program your own cryptography solutions, and frankly you should not try to do so unless you have a significant cryptography background. Therefore, you will use some third-party cryptographic modules and providers. One of the goals of your learning more about cryptography is that you can ask the right questions of such vendors. For example, you should ask about their key generation and key storage methods.

Other issues include time and power consumption. A cryptographic module that is slow might not be useful for commercial solutions. A cryptographic module that requires significant power won't be useful for low-power devices. This is essentially a comparison of resources versus security. Clearly security is critical, but the cryptographic solution should not be a strain on system resources.

Hashing Algorithms

The hashes used to store data, such as hash tables, are very different from cryptographic hashes. In cryptography, a hash function must have three characteristics:

1. *It must be one-way.* This means that it is not reversible. Once you hash something, you cannot unhash it.

2. *Variable-length input produces fixed-length output.* This means that whether you hash two characters or two million, the hash size is the same.

3. *The algorithm must have few or no collisions.* This means that hashing two different inputs does not give the same output.

The following sections discuss hashing algorithms and related concepts with which you should become familiar.

Secure Hash Algorithm

The *Secure Hash Algorithm (SHA)* was designed to ensure the integrity of a message. SHA is a one-way hash that provides a hash value that can be used with an encryption protocol. This algorithm produces a 160-bit hash value. SHA-2 has several sizes: 224, 256, 334, and 512 bit. SHA-2 is the most widely used, but SHA-3 has been released. Although SHA-3 is now a standard, there simply are no known issues with SHA-2, so it is still the most widely used and recommended hashing algorithm. The algorithm was originally named *Keccak* and designed by Guido Bertoni, Joan Daemen, Michaël Peeters, and Gilles Van Assche.

The SHA-3 standard was published in 2012, but it is still not widely used. This is not due to any problem with SHA-3, but rather the fact that SHA-1 is perfectly fine. It should also be noted that in 2016, issues with SHA-1 were discovered and it is recommended that you use SHA-2 instead.

Message Digest Algorithm

The *Message Digest Algorithm (MD)* also creates a hash value and uses a one-way hash. The hash value is used to help maintain integrity. There are several versions of MD; the most common are MD5, MD4, and MD2. MD4 was used by NTLM (discussed in a moment) to compute the NT Hash.

MD5 is the newest version of the algorithm. It produces a 128-bit hash, but the algorithm is more complex than its predecessors and offers greater security. Its biggest weakness is that it does not have strong collision resistance, and thus it is no longer recommended for use. SHA (1 or 2) are the recommended alternatives.

RIPEMD

The *RACE Integrity Primitives Evaluation Message Digest (RIPEMD)* algorithm was based on MD4. There were questions regarding its security, and it has been replaced by RIPEMD-160, which uses 160 bits. There are versions in existence that use 256 and 320 bits (RIPEMD-256 and RIPEMD-320, respectively), but all versions of RIPEMD remain.

GOST

GOST is a symmetric cipher developed in the old Soviet Union that has been modified to work as a hash function. GOST processes a variable-length message into a fixed-length output of 256 bits.

LANMAN

Prior to the release of Windows NT, Microsoft's operating systems used the *LANMAN protocol* for authentication. While functioning only as an authentication protocol, LANMAN used LM Hash and two DES keys. It was replaced by the NT LAN Manager (NTLM) with the release of Windows NT.

NTLM

Microsoft replaced the LANMAN protocol with *NTLM (NT LAN Manager)* with the release of Windows NT. NTLM uses MD4/MD5 hashing algorithms. Several versions of this protocol exist (NTLMv1, *NTLMv2*), and it is still in widespread use despite the fact that Microsoft has pointed to Kerberos as being its preferred authentication protocol. Although LANMAN and NTLM both employ hashing, they are used primarily for the purpose of authentication.

Collision

A *collision* occurs when two different inputs to a hashing algorithm produce the same output. Modern hashing algorithms are designed to make this less likely. However, basic logic should tell you that if a given hash has a 160-bit output (like SHA1) and you put in 2^{160} +1 separate inputs, the last one must have a collision with one of the preceding inputs. Now don't be too concerned; 2^{160} is a very large number: 1.4615016373309029182036848327163e+48.

Rainbow Tables and Salt

Since a hashing algorithm is not reversible, you might think it is impossible to break a hash. However, there are methods to do so. This is particularly important since passwords are often stored as a hash. Rainbow tables are one such method.

With a *rainbow table,* all of the possible hashes are computed in advance. In other words, you create a series of tables; each has all the possible two-letter, three-letter, four-letter, and so forth combinations and the hash of that combination, using a known hashing algorithm like SHA-2. Now if you search the table for a given hash, the letter combination in the table that produced the hash must be the password that you are seeking.

Popular password cracking tools, such as OphCrack, use rainbow tables. A counter-measure, called *Salt*, refers to the addition of bits at key locations, either before or after the hash. So if you type in the password letmein, bits are added by the operating system before it is hashed. Using Salt, should someone apply a rainbow table attack, the hash they search for will yield a letter combination other than what you actually typed in.

Key Stretching

Key stretching refers to processes used to take a key that might be a bit weak and make it stronger, usually by making it longer. The key (or password/passphrase) is input into an algorithm that will strengthen the key and make it longer and thus less susceptible to brute-force attacks. There are many methods for doing this—here's two:

PBKDF2   *PBKDF2 (Password-Based Key Derivation Function 2)* is part of PKCS #5 v. 2.01. It applies some function (like a hash or HMAC) to the password or passphrase along with Salt to produce a derived key.

Bcrypt   *bcrypt* is used with passwords, and it essentially uses a derivation of the Blowfish algorithm converted to a hashing algorithm to hash a password and add Salt to it.

Cryptanalysis Methods

If time has taught us anything, it is that people frequently do things that other people thought were impossible. Every time a new code or process is invented that is thought to be unbreakable, someone comes up with a method of breaking it.

Let's look at some common code-breaking techniques.

Brute Force

This method simply involves trying every possible key. It is guaranteed to work, but it is likely to take so long that it is simply not usable. For example, to break a Caesar cipher, there are only 26 possible keys, which you can try in a very short time. But even DES, which has a rather weak key, would take 2^{56} different attempts. That is 72,057,594,037,927,936 possible DES keys. To put that in perspective, if you try 1 million keys per second, it would take you just a bit over 46,190,765 years to try them all.

Frequency Analysis

Frequency analysis involves looking at the blocks of an encrypted message to determine if any common patterns exist. Initially, the analyst doesn't try to break the code but looks at the patterns in the message. In the English language, the letters *e* and *t* and words like *the*, *and*, *that*, *it*, and *is* are very common. Single letters that stand alone in a sentence are usually limited to *a* and *I*.

A determined cryptanalyst looks for these types of patterns and, over time, may be able to deduce the method used to encrypt the data. This process can sometimes be simple, or it may take a lot of effort. This method works only on the historical ciphers that we discussed at the beginning of this chapter. It does not work on modern algorithms.

Known Plain Text

This attack relies on the attacker having pairs of known plain text along with the corresponding cipher text. This gives the attacker a place to start attempting to derive the key. With modern ciphers, it would still take many billions of such combinations to have a chance at cracking the cipher. This method was, however, successful at cracking the German Naval Enigma. The code breakers at Bletchley Park in the UK realized that all German Naval messages ended with *Heil Hitler*. They used this known plain-text attack to crack the key.

Chosen Plain Text

In this attack, the attacker obtains the cipher texts corresponding to a set of plain texts of their own choosing. This allows the attacker to attempt to derive the key used and thus decrypt other messages encrypted with that key. This can be difficult, but it is not impossible. Advanced methods such as differential cryptanalysis are types of chosen plain-text attacks.

Related Key Attack

This is like a chosen plain-text attack, except the attacker can obtain cipher texts encrypted under two different keys. This is actually a useful attack if you can obtain the plain text and matching cipher text.

Birthday Attack

This is an attack on cryptographic hashes, based on something called the *birthday theorem*. The basic idea is this:

> How many people would you need to have in a room to have a strong likelihood that two would have the same birthday (month and day, but not year)?

Obviously, if you put 367 people in a room, at least 2 of them must have the same birthday, since there are only 365 days in a year, plus one more in a leap year. The paradox is not asking how many people you need to guarantee a match—just how many you need to have a strong probability.

Even with 23 people in the room, you have a 50 percent chance that 2 will have the same birthday. The probability that the first person does not share a birthday with any previous person is 100 percent, because there are no previous people in the set. That can be written as 365/365.

The second person has only one preceding person, and the odds that the second person has a birthday different from the first are 364/365. The third person might share a birthday with two preceding people, so the odds of having a birthday from either of the two preceding people are 363/365. Because each of these is independent, we can compute the probability as follows:

$$365/365 * 364/365 * 363/365 * 362/365 \ldots * 342/365$$

(342 is the probability of the 23rd person shares a birthday with a preceding person.) When we convert these to decimal values, it yields (truncating at the third decimal point):

$$1 * 0.997 * 0.994 * 0.991 * 0.989 * 0.986 * \ldots 0.936 = 0.49, \text{ or } 49 \text{ percent}$$

This 49 percent is the probability that 23 people will not have any birthdays in common; thus, there is a 51 percent (better than even odds) chance that 2 of the 23 will have a birthday in common.

The math works out to about $1.7 \sqrt{n}$ to get a collision. Remember, a collision is when two inputs produce the same output. So for an MD5 hash, you might think that you need $2^{128} + 1$ different inputs to get a collision—and for a guaranteed collision you do. That is an exceedingly large number: 3.40282366920938463463374607431177e+38.

But the Birthday paradox tells us that to just have a 51 percent chance of there being a collision with a hash you only need $1.7 \sqrt{n}$ (n being 2^{128}) inputs. That number is still very large: 31,359,464,925,306,237,747.2. But it is much smaller than the brute-force approach of trying every possible input.

Other Methods

Some other methods are not truly cryptanalysis, but rather means to get at passwords that someone might have used when they encrypted something. For example, when someone encrypts a hard drive, the user must select a password for later decrypting the password. If the user selected a weak password, then it could be vulnerable to a dictionary attack. A dictionary attack involves attempting common words (such as words in a dictionary) that might be used as a password, hoping one will work.

A *downgrade attack* is sometimes used against secure communications such as TLS in an attempt to get the user to shift to less secure modes. The idea is to trick the user into shifting to a less secure version of the protocol, one that might be easier to break.

An older method was the *replay attack*. When a user sends their login information, even if it is encrypted, the attacker captures it and later sends the same information. The user never decrypted that login information; they simply replayed it. Modern authentication methods make this highly unlikely.

There are also scenarios in which someone is using a good cryptographic algorithm (like AES) but has it implemented in a weak manner—for example, using weak key generation. A classic example, which we will review later in this chapter, is Wireless Equivalent Privacy (WEP), which uses RC4, a good algorithm. But it was implemented improperly, making it weak.

Password cracking can be done online or offline. For example, the rainbow tables mentioned earlier in this book can be done online on a live system. Or someone can capture the password hash and then use offline methods to try to find a match. Offline methods can use more resources and take as long as needed. Online methods have to be executed quite quickly.

Exploiting Human Error

Human error is one of the major causes of encryption vulnerabilities. If an email is sent using an encryption scheme, someone else may send it *in the clear* (unencrypted). If a cryptanalyst gets ahold of both messages, the process of decoding future messages will be considerably simplified. A code key might wind up in the wrong hands, giving insights into what the key consists of. Many systems have been broken into as a result of these types of accidents.

A classic example involved the transmission of a sensitive military-related message using an encryption system. Most messages have a preamble that informs the receiver who the message is for, who sent it, how many characters are in the message, the date and time it was sent, and other pertinent information. In this case, the preamble was sent in clear text, and this information was also encrypted and put into the message. As a result, the cryptanalysts gained a key insight into the message contents. They were given approximately 50 characters that were repeated in the message in code. This error caused a relatively secure system to be compromised.

Another error is to use weak or deprecated algorithms. Over time, some algorithms are no longer considered appropriate. This may be due to some flaw found in the algorithm. It can also be due to increasing computing power. For example, in 1976 DES was considered very strong. But advances in computer power have made its key length too short. Although the algorithm is sound, the key size makes DES a poor choice for modern cryptography, and that algorithm has been deprecated.

Wi-Fi Encryption

Wi-Fi encryption requires a short discussion of its own. In such an environment, the clients and the access point share the same key, using symmetric encryption; RC4 was mentioned for this purpose earlier in this chapter. Since all of the clients and the access point share the same key, this is known as a *preshared key*.

WEP (Wired Equivalent Privacy) encryption was an early attempt to add security, but it fell short because of weaknesses in the way the encryption algorithms are employed. The *Wi-Fi Protected Access (WPA)* and *Wi-Fi Protected Access 2 (WPA2)* technologies were designed to address the core problems with WEP.

WPA couples the RC4 encryption algorithm with TKIP (Temporal Key Integrity Protocol). Essentially, TKIP mixes a root key with an initialization vector. This key mixing means that there is effectively a new key for each packet.

WPA2 favors *Counter Mode with Cipher Block Chaining Message Authentication Code Protocol (CCMP)*. CCMP uses 128-bit AES. The most important thing to recall about WPA2 is that it fully implements the 802.11i Wi-Fi security standards.

Many wireless routers also provide the option of using Wi-Fi protected setup (WPS) to establish an initial connection. WPS uses a PIN to connect to the wireless access point. This means that for the first connection, you only need the PIN in order to connect. This is quite convenient, but it does open up a system to a particular attack. The WPS attack attempts to intercept that PIN in transmission, connect to the WAP, and then steal the WPA2 password.

When setting up Wi-Fi encryption, there are two modes you can use. There is *pre-shared key (PSK)* mode and *enterprise* mode. In enterprise mode, a server handles distribution of cryptographic keys and/or digital certificates. In PSK mode, the client and the wireless access point must negotiate and share a key prior to initiating communications. A third mode, sometimes called *open*, is simply unsecure. This is sometimes used for public Wi-Fi that has no access to any sensitive data, but it is simply a portal to access the Internet.

It is also common to launch a web page when users first connect. The web page may list acceptable use policies or require some authentication. This page must be navigated before full access to network resources is granted. The term for this web page is a *captive portal*.

 The Security+ exam, as well as other security-related tests, addresses the fact that WPA2 uses counter mode with cipher block chaining, but it doesn't address exactly what cipher block chaining is. Though it was covered earlier in this chapter, it bears repeating. It is actually simple, but effective.

As you encrypt text with any block cipher (including AES), if you encrypt the same block in different places in the message, it is likely to come out exactly the same in the cipher text. AES 128 uses a 128-bit block that is 16 characters. So, if the same 16 characters appear more than once in your plain text, they may come out exactly the same in the cipher text, giving attackers a clue that they can use.

The answer to this is to take the output of block *i-1* and exclusively OR (XOR) it with the plain text of block *i* before encrypting it. Basically, the output of each block is combined with the plain text of the next block before that next block is encrypted. This guarantees that, even if you have the same plain text in various places in your text, it won't come out the same in the cipher text.

Using Cryptographic Systems

A *cryptographic system* is a system, method, or process that is used to provide encryption and decryption. It may be a hardware, software, or manually performed process. Cryptographic systems exist for the same reasons that security exists: to provide confidentiality, integrity, authentication, nonrepudiation, and access control. The following sections discuss these issues within the framework of cryptographic systems.

Confidentiality, integrity, and availability are the three most important concepts in security. You should know and understand them well before taking the Security+ certification exam. Confidentiality and integrity are discussed here. Availability relates to disaster recovery and system redundancy.

Confidentiality and Strength

One of the major reasons to implement a cryptographic system is to ensure the confidentiality of the information being used. Confidentiality may be intended to prevent the unauthorized disclosure of information in a local network or to prevent the unauthorized disclosure of information across a network. A cryptographic system must do this effectively in order to be of value.

The need to keep records secure from internal disclosure may be just as great as the need to keep records secure from outside attacks. The effectiveness of a cryptographic system in preventing unauthorized decryption is referred to as its *strength*. A strong cryptographic system is difficult to crack. Strength is also referred to as the algorithm's *work factor*: the work factor describes an estimate of the amount of time and effort that would be necessary to break a system.

The system may be considered weak if it allows weak keys, has defects in its design, or is easily decrypted. Many systems available today are more than adequate for business and personal use, but they are inadequate for sensitive military or governmental applications.

Integrity

The second major reason for implementing a cryptographic system involves providing assurance that a message wasn't modified during transmission. Modification may render a message unintelligible or, even worse, inaccurate. Imagine the consequences if record alterations weren't discovered in medical records involving drug prescriptions. If a message is tampered with, the encryption system should have a mechanism to indicate that the message has been corrupted or altered.

Integrity can be accomplished by adding information such as redundant data that can be used as checked using a hashing algorithm. Essentially, a hash of the message is generated and appended to the end of the message. The receiving party calculates the hash of the message they received and compares it to the hash they received. If something changed in transit, the hashes won't match.

Hashing is an acceptable integrity check for many situations. However, if an intercepting party wishes to alter a message intentionally and the message is not also encrypted, then a hash is ineffective. The intercepting party can see that there is a 160-bit value, for example, attached to the message. Since SHA-1 produces a 160-bit digest, they can assume that this is a SHA-1 digest. Then the interceptor can simply alter the message as they wish, delete the original SHA-1 hash, and recalculate a hash from the new, altered message. Note that the terms hash, digest, message digest, and hash value are used interchangeably.

A common method of verifying integrity involves adding a *message authentication code (MAC)* to the message. A MAC is calculated by using a symmetric cipher in *cipher block chaining mode (CBC)* with only the final block being produced. Essentially, the output of the CBC is being used like the output of a hashing algorithm. However, unlike a hashing algorithm, the cipher requires a symmetric key that is exchanged between the two parties in advance. Someone attempting to intercept the message and alter it would not have the key and would not be able to re-create the MAC value (see Figure 8.4).

FIGURE 8.4   The MAC value is calculated by the sender and receiver using the same algorithm.

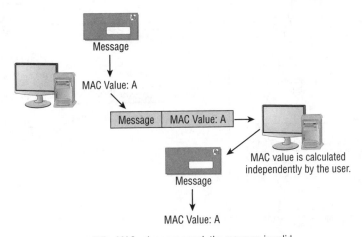

HMAC value is calculated independently by the user.

If the MAC values are equal, the message is valid.

HMAC (hash-based message authentication code) uses a hashing algorithm along with a symmetric key. Thus, for example, two parties agree to use an MD5 hash. Once the hash is computed, it is exclusively or'd (XOR) with the digest, and that resultant value is the HMAC. Again, should someone intercept the message and attempt to alter the message and the associated HMAC, that party would not have the key and would not be able to duplicate the HMAC.

When to Encrypt

Another issue in using cryptographic systems is when you should encrypt the data. There are three primary times when data might be encrypted. The first is when the data is simply stored—for example, on a hard drive. This is referred to as *data at rest*. The second is when data is being transmitted from point A to point B. This is called *data in transit*. Finally, should data be encrypted when it is actually being used? This is referred to as *data in use*.

As a general rule, if it is possible to encrypt data in any of these three states, without unduly interfering with the ability of legitimate users to use the data, then it should be encrypted. Encrypting data at rest is very common, and there is really no compelling reason to not do so. We will be discussing SSL/TLS later in this chapter, which is very commonly used to encrypt data in transit.

Digital Signatures

A *digital signature* is similar in function to a standard signature on a document. It validates the integrity of the message and the sender. The message is encrypted using the encryption system, and a second piece of information, the digital signature, is added to the message. Figure 8.5 illustrates this concept.

FIGURE 8.5   Digital signature processing steps

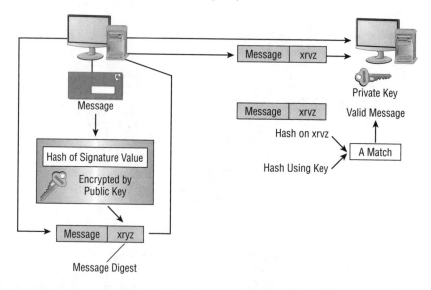

Let's say that the sender in Figure 8.5 wants to send a message to the receiver. It's important that this message not be altered. The sender uses the private key to create a digital signature. The message is, in effect, signed with the private key. The sender then sends the message to the receiver. The receiver uses the public key of the sender to validate the digital signature. If the values match, the receiver knows that the message is authentic.

The receiver uses a key provided by the sender—the public key—to decrypt the message. Most digital signature implementations also use a hash to verify that the message has not been altered, intentionally or accidently, in transit. In fact, what is normally signed is the hash of the message.

The receiver compares the signature area referred to as a *message digest* in the message with the calculated value. If the values match, the message hasn't been tampered with and the originator is verified as the person they claim to be. This process provides message integrity, nonrepudiation, and authentication. Since this process provides nonrepudiation, the receiver can be confident the message was sent by the sender, not someone pretending to be the sender. In some cases, digital signatures are also part of authentication. For example, a user logs in and provides their username and password, but that login information is digitally signed.

Digital signatures are also used for code signing. When code is distributed over the Internet, be it some device driver or ActiveX web component, it is essential that the user be able to trust that it was really produced by the claimed sender. An attacker would very much like to produce a fake device driver or web component that purported to be from some major vendor but was really malware. Using code signing mitigates this danger.

Authentication

Authentication is the process of verifying that the sender is who they say they are. This is critical in many applications. A valid message from an invalid source isn't authentic.

One of the common methods of verifying authenticity is the addition of a digital signature. This is the most common method used today. In fact, most device drivers are digitally signed by the vendor.

Nonrepudiation

Nonrepudiation prevents one party from denying actions that they carried out. To use an analogy, imagine coming home to find your home's picture window broken. All three of your kids say they didn't do it, and the babysitter says it must have been broken when she arrived. All of the parties who could be guilty are "repudiating" the fact that they did it, and it's their word against common sense. Now, imagine that you had a nanny-cam running and were able to review the video and see who actually broke it. The video cancels out their saying that they knew nothing about the broken window and offers "nonrepudiation" of the facts.

In the electronic world, a similar type of proof can be achieved in a two-key system. The problem is that anyone can claim to be a legitimate sender, and if they have access to this type of system, they can send you a public key. So, although you have received the message, you would have no way of verifying that the sender is really who they say they are, and you need nonrepudiation to verify that the sender is who they say they are.

Third-party organizations called *certificate authorities (CAs)* manage public keys and issue certificates verifying the validity of a sender's message. The verifying aspect serves as nonrepudiation, as a respected third party vouches for the individual. The goal of any effective cryptography system must include nonrepudiation. However, the implementation is a little more difficult than the concept.

Key Features

Key escrow addresses the possibility that a cryptographic key may be lost. The concern is usually with symmetric keys or with the private key in asymmetric cryptography. If that occurs, then there is no way to get the key back, and the user cannot decrypt messages. Companies that implement encryption throughout their organization often establish key escrows in order to be able to recover lost keys.

A *key recovery agent* is an entity that has the ability to recover a key, key components, or plain-text messages as needed. Obviously, a key recovery agent is a sensitive position. This person could potentially access all of the keys for a given key escrow. This is an excellent place to implement separation of duties so that no one person can independently access the key escrow account.

Key registration is the process of providing certificates to users, and a registration authority (RA) typically handles this function when the load must be lifted from a CA.

There is also the issue of keys that are no longer to be used. A key may have expired, it may have been canceled due to some breach of security, or it may have been replaced. In any case, there must be some mechanism to find out if a key is still valid. The most widely used method is the *certificate revocation list (CRL)*. This is literally a list of certificates that a specific CA states should no longer be used. CRLs are now being replaced by a real-time protocol called *Online Certificate Status Protocol (OCSP)*.

Stapling is a method used with OCSP, which allows a web server to provide information on the validity of its own certificate rather than needing to go to the certificate vendor. This is done by the web server essentially downloading the OCSP response from the certificate vendor in advance and providing that to browsers.

When a key is compromised, a revocation request should be made to the CA—immediately. It may take a day or longer for the CRL to be disseminated to everyone using that CA.

Trust models exist in PKI implementations and come in a number of types. A *trust model* is simply a model of how different certificate authorities trust each other and consequently how their clients will trust certificates from other certificate authorities. The four main types of trust models that are used with PKI are bridge, hierarchical, hybrid, and mesh.

Understanding Cryptography Standards and Protocols

Numerous standards are available to establish secure services. Some of the standards that will be presented in the following sections have already been discussed in greater detail in earlier chapters. Here we will remind you of them and introduce you to a few more standards.

The movement from proprietary governmental standards toward more unified global standards is a growing trend that has both positive and negative implications. Higher interoperability between disparate systems will also mean that these standards will be widely used. The more that standards are used, the more that attackers will focus on them to try to break them.

As a security administrator, you have to weigh the pros and cons of the various standards and evaluate them against your organization's needs. The following sections introduce you to the major standards, discuss their focus, and describe how they were developed.

The Origins of Encryption Standards

As mentioned at the beginning of the chapter, early cryptography standards were primarily designed to secure communications for the government and the military. Many different standards groups exist today, and they often provide standards that are incompatible with the standards of other groups. These standards are intended to address the specific environments in which these groups exist.

The following sections describe key U.S. government agencies, a few well-known industry associations, and public-domain cryptography standards.

The Role of Government Agencies

Several U.S. government agencies are involved in the creation of standards for secure systems. They either directly control specific sectors of government or provide validation, approval, and support to government agencies. We'll look at each of these agencies in the following sections.

National Security Agency

The *National Security Agency (NSA)* is responsible for creating codes, breaking codes, and coding systems for the U.S. government. The NSA was chartered in 1952. It tries to keep a low profile; for many years, the government didn't publicly acknowledge its existence.

The NSA is responsible for obtaining foreign intelligence and supplying it to the various U.S. government agencies that need it. It's said to be the world's largest employer of mathematicians. The NSA's missions are extremely classified, but its finger is in everything involving cryptography and cryptographic systems for the U.S. government, government contractors, and the military.

The NSA's website is www.nsa.gov.

National Security Agency/Central Security Service

The *National Security Agency/Central Security Service (NSA/CSS)* is an independently functioning part of the NSA. It was created in the early 1970s to help standardize and support Department of Defense (DoD) activities. The NSA/CSS supports all branches of the military. Each branch of the military used to have its own intelligence activities. Frequently, these branches didn't coordinate their activities well. NSA/CSS was created to help coordinate their efforts.

National Institute of Standards and Technology

The *National Institute of Standards and Technology (NIST)*, which was formerly known as the National Bureau of Standards (NBS), has been involved in developing and supporting standards for the U.S. government for over 100 years. NIST has become involved in cryptography standards, systems, and technology in a variety of areas. It's primarily concerned with governmental systems, and it exercises a great deal of influence on them. NIST shares many of its findings with the security community because business needs are similar to government needs.

NIST publishes information about known vulnerabilities in operating systems and applications. You'll find NIST helpful in your battle to secure your systems.

    You can find NIST on the web at www.nist.gov.

Industry Associations and the Developmental Process

The need for security in specific industries, such as the banking industry, has driven the development of standards. Standards frequently begin as voluntary or proprietary efforts.

The *request for comments (RFC)*, originated in 1969, is the mechanism used to propose a standard. It's a document-creation process with a set of practices. An RFC is categorized as standard (draft or standard), best practice, informational, experimental, or historic.

Draft documents are processed through a designated RFC editor, who makes sure that the document meets publication standards. Editors play a key role in the RFC process; they are responsible for making sure that proposals are documented properly, and they manage the discussion. The RFC is then thrown open to the computer-user community for comments and critique. This process ensures that all interested parties have the opportunity to comment on an RFC.

The RFC process allows open communications about the Internet and other proposed standards. Virtually all standards relating to the Internet that are adopted go through this process.

Several industrial associations have assumed roles that allow them to address specific environments. The following sections briefly discuss some of the major associations and the specific environments they address.

Internet Engineering Task Force

The *Internet Engineering Task Force (IETF)* is an international community of computer professionals that includes network engineers, vendors, administrators, and researchers. The IETF is mainly interested in improving the Internet; it's also very interested in computer security issues. The IETF uses working groups to develop and propose standards.

IETF membership is open to anyone. Members communicate primarily through mailing lists and public conferences.

You can find additional information about the IETF on its website at www.ietf.org.

Institute of Electrical and Electronics Engineers

The *Institute of Electrical and Electronics Engineers (IEEE)* is an international organization focused on technology and related standards. Pronounced "I Triple-E," the IEEE is organized into several working groups and standards committees. IEEE is actively involved in the development of PKC, wireless, and networking protocol standards.

You can find information on the IEEE at www.ieee.org.

Public Key Infrastructure X.509/Public Key Cryptography Standards

The *Public Key Infrastructure X.509 (PKIX)* is the working group formed by the IETF to develop standards and models for the PKI environment. The PKIX working group is responsible for the X.509 standard, which is discussed in the next section.

The *Public Key Cryptography Standards (PKCS)* is a set of voluntary standards created by RSA and security leaders. Early members of this group included Apple, Microsoft, DEC (now HP), Lotus, Sun, and MIT.

Currently, there are 15 published PKCS standards:

PKCS #1: RSA Cryptography Standard
PKCS #2: Incorporated in PKCS #1
PKCS #3: Diffie-Hellman Key Agreement Standard
PKCS #4: Incorporated in PKCS #1
PKCS #5: Password-Based Cryptography Standard
PKCS #6: Extended-Certificate Syntax Standard
PKCS #7: Cryptographic Message Syntax Standard
PKCS #8: Private-Key Information Syntax Standard
PKCS #9: Selected Attribute Types
PKCS #10: Certification Request Syntax Standard
PKCS #11: Cryptographic Token Interface Standard
PKCS #12: Personal Information Exchange Syntax Standard
PKCS #13: Elliptic Curve Cryptography Standard
PKCS #14: Pseudorandom Number Generators
PKCS #15: Cryptographic Token Information Format Standard

These standards are coordinated through RSA; however, experts worldwide are welcome to participate in the development process.

X.509

The *X.509 standard* defines the certificate formats and fields for public keys. It also defines the procedures that should be used to distribute public keys. The current version of X.509 certificates is version 3, and it comes in two basic types:

End-Entity Certificate   The most common is the *end-entity certificate*, which is issued by a CA to an end entity. An *end entity* is a system that doesn't issue certificates but merely uses them.

CA Certificate   The *CA certificate* is issued by one CA to another CA. The second CA, in turn, can then issue certificates to an end entity.

All X.509 certificates have the following:

- Signature of the issuer.

- Version.

- Serial number.

- Signature algorithm ID.

- Issuer name.

- Validity period.

- Subject name.

- Subject public key information.

- Issuer unique identifier (relevant for versions 2 and 3 only).

- Subject unique identifier (relevant for versions 2 and 3 only).

- Extensions (in version 3 only).

- Object identifiers, or OIDs, are used in X.509 certificate extensions (and are thus optional). These are values that help identify objects. They are dot separated numbers usually. For example, OID 2.5.4.6 might correspond to the country-name value.

Certificate Formats

There are numerous formats for certificates. A few are described here:

DER   The DER extension is used for binary DER-encoded certificates. These files may also bear the CER or the CRT extension.

PEM   The PEM extension is used for different types of X.509v3 files that contain ASCII (Base64) armored data prefixed with a `-- BEGIN ...` line.

PFX   This is an archive file for PKCS#12 standard certificate information.

CER   This is an alternate form of `.crt` (Microsoft Convention). You can use Microsoft crypto API to convert `.crt` to `.cer` (both DER-encoded `.cer`, or base64 [PEM]-encoded `.cer`). The `.cer` file extension is also recognized by IE as a command to run an MS cryptoAPI command (specifically `rundll32.exe cryptext.dll, CryptExtOpenCER`).

P12   This refers to the use of PKCS#12 standard.

P7b: These are base 64 encoded ASCII files. They actually include several variations: P7b, P7C, etc.

Certificate Concepts

Certificate chaining refers to the fact that certificates are handled by a chain of trust. You purchase a digital certificate from a certificate authority (CA), so you trust that CA's certificate. In turn, that CA trusts a root certificate. In this example, the CA's certificate is an intermediate CA, and the ultimate trust is the root certificate.

It is also possible to generate a *self-signed certificate*. In fact, this is an easy task to perform using Microsoft Internet Information Services (IIS). The certificate will be X.509, but it will be digitally signed by you. This means that although it can be used to transmit your public key, it won't be trusted by browsers. It will instead generate a certificate error message.

Pinning is a method designed to mitigate the use of fraudulent certificates. Basically, once a public key or certificate has been seen for a specific host, that key or certificate is pinned to the host. Should a different key or certificate be seen for that host, that might indicate an issue with a fraudulent certificate.

Certificate authorities can be online or offline. Online certificate authorities are the most common. They are always connected and always accessible. Offline is usually for a root certificate authority that has been isolated from network access. It is brought online for specific purposes. The concept is that, since it is isolated, the chances of it being compromised are reduced. That is one reason why this is usually only done with root certificate authorities.

Types of Certificates

There are several types of X.509 certificates, each for a slightly different purpose. The general structure will be the same, but the application is different.

Wildcard certificates, as the name suggests, can be used more widely, usually with multiple subdomains of a given domain. So rather than have a different X.509 certificate for each subdomain, you would use a wildcard certificate for all subdomains.

Subject Alternative Name (SAN) is not so much a type of certificate as a special field in X.509. It allows you to specify additional items (IP addresses, domain names, and so on) to be protected by this single certificate.

Code signing certificates were mentioned earlier in this chapter. These are X.509 certificates used to digitally sign some type of computer code.

Machine/computer certificates are X.509 certificates assigned to a specific machine. These are often used in authentication schemes. For example, in order for the machine to sign in to the network, it must authenticate using its machine certificate.

Email certificates are used for securing email. Secure Multipurpose Internet Mail Extensions (S/MIME) uses X.509 certificates to secure email communications.

User certificates are used for individual users. Like machine/computer certificates, these are often used for authentication. Users must present their certificate to authenticate prior to accessing some resource.

Root certificates are used for root authorities. These are usually self-signed by that authority.

Domain validation certificates are among the most common certificates. These are used to secure communication with a specific domain. This is a low-cost certificate that website administrators use to provide TLS for a given domain.

Extended validation certificates, as the name suggests, require more validation of the certificate holder; thus, they provide more security.

Public Key Infrastructure

Many aspects of PKI have been introduced already in this chapter. In this section, we will expand some of those concepts. The *public key infrastructure (PKI)* is intended to offer a means of providing security to messages and transactions on a grand scale. The need for universal systems to support e-commerce, secure transactions, and information privacy is one aspect of the issues being addressed with PKI.

Certificate authorities have been mentioned previously. However, a more thorough description is given here. A *certificate authority (CA)* is an organization that is responsible for issuing, revoking, and distributing certificates. A *certificate* is nothing more than a mechanism that associates the public key with an individual. It contains a great deal of information about the user. Each user of a PKI system has a certificate that can be used to verify their authenticity. One of the first steps in getting a certificate is to submit a *certificate-signing request (CSR)*. This is a request formatted for the CA. This request will have the public key that you wish to use and your fully distinguished name (often a domain name). The CA will then use this to process your request for a digital certificate.

CAs can be either private or public, with companies like DigiCert, Verisign, and others providing certificates to the general public. Many operating system providers allow their systems to be configured as CA systems. These CA systems can be used to generate internal certificates that are used within a business or in large external settings.

The process of providing certificates to users, although effective in helping to ensure security, requires a server. Over time, the server can become overloaded and need assistance. An additional component, the registration authority, is available to help offload work from the CA.

A *registration authority (RA)* offloads some of the work from a CA. An RA system operates as an intermediary in the process: it can distribute keys, accept registrations for the CA, and validate identities. The RA doesn't issue certificates; that responsibility remains with the CA.

Pretty Good Privacy

Pretty Good Privacy (PGP) is a freeware email encryption system. As mentioned earlier in the chapter, PGP was introduced in the early 1990s, and it's considered to be a very good system. It's widely used for email security.

PGP uses both symmetrical and asymmetrical systems as a part of its process; it is this serial combination of processes that makes it so competent. Figure 8.6 provides an overview of how the various components of a PGP process work together to provide security. During the encryption process, the document is encrypted with the public key and also a session key, which is a one-use random number, to create the cipher text. The session key is encrypted into the public key and sent with the cipher text.

FIGURE 8.6   The PGP encryption system

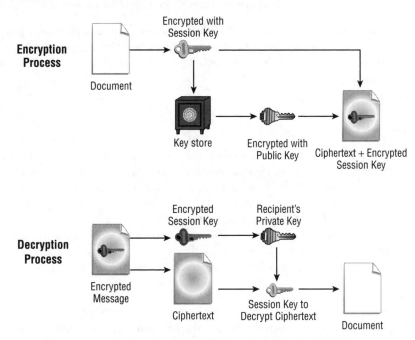

On the receiving end, the private key is used to ascertain the session key. The session key and the private key are then used to decrypt the cipher text back into the original document.

An alternative to the freeware PGP is *GPG (GNU Privacy Guard)*. It is part of the GNU project by the Free Software Foundation, and it is interoperable with PGP. Like its alternative, PGP, it is considered a hybrid program since it uses a combination of symmetric and public key cryptography. This free replacement for PGP can be downloaded from www.gnupg.org.

⊕ Real World Scenario

Securing Unix Interactive Users

You've been asked to examine your existing Unix systems and evaluate them for potential security weaknesses. Several remote users need to access Telnet and FTP capabilities in your network. Telnet and FTP connections send the logon and password information in the clear. How could you minimize security risks for Telnet and FTP connections?

You should consider using a VPN connection between these remote connections and your corporate systems. One workable solution might be to provide SSH to your clients and install it on your Unix servers. Doing so would allow FTP and Telnet connectivity in a secure environment.

SSL and TLS

Secure Sockets Layer (SSL) is used to establish a secure communication connection between two TCP-based machines. This protocol uses the handshake method of establishing a session. The number of steps in the handshake depends on whether steps are combined and/or mutual authentication is included. The number of steps is always between four and nine, inclusive, based on who is doing the documentation.

One of the early steps will always be to select an appropriate cipher suite to use. A *cipher suite* is a combination of methods, such as an authentication, encryption, and message authentication code (MAC) algorithms used together. Many cryptographic protocols such as TLS use a cipher suite.

 Netscape originally developed the SSL method, which has gained wide acceptance throughout the industry. SSL establishes a session using asymmetric encryption and maintains the session using symmetric encryption.

Regardless of which vendor's implementation is being discussed, the steps can be summarized as illustrated in Figure 8.7. Here is the complete handshake process:

1. The client sends the server the client's SSL version number, cipher settings, session-specific data, and other information that the server needs to communicate with the client using SSL.

2. The server sends the client the server's SSL version number, cipher settings, session-specific data, and other information that the client needs to communicate with the server over SSL. The server also sends its own certificate, and if the client is requesting a server resource that requires client authentication, the server requests the client's certificate.

FIGURE 8.7   The SSL connection process

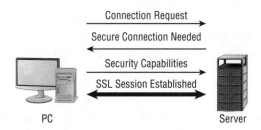

Connection Request

Secure Connection Needed

Security Capabilities

SSL Session Established

PC

Server

3. The client uses the information sent by the server to authenticate the server—for example, in the case of a web browser connecting to a web server, the browser checks whether the received certificate's subject name actually matches the name of the server being contacted, whether the issuer of the certificate is a trusted certificate authority, whether the certificate has expired, and, ideally, whether the certificate has been revoked. If the server cannot be authenticated, the user is warned of the problem and informed that an encrypted and authenticated connection cannot be established. If the server can be successfully authenticated, the client proceeds to the next step.

4. Using all of the data generated in the handshake thus far, the client (with the cooperation of the server, depending on the cipher in use) creates the pre-master secret for the session, encrypts it with the server's public key (obtained from the server's certificate, sent in step 2), and then sends the encrypted pre-master secret to the server.

5. If the server has requested client authentication (an optional step in the handshake), the client also signs another piece of data that is unique to this handshake and known by both the client and server. In this case, the client sends both the signed data and the client's own certificate to the server along with the encrypted pre-master secret.

6. If the server has requested client authentication, the server attempts to authenticate the client. If the client cannot be authenticated, the session ends. If the client can be successfully authenticated, the server uses its private key to decrypt the pre-master secret, and then performs a series of steps (which the client also performs, starting from the same pre-master secret) to generate the master secret.

7. Both the client and the server use the master secret to generate the session keys, which are symmetric keys used to encrypt and decrypt information exchanged during the SSL session and to verify its integrity (that is, to detect any changes in the data between the time it was sent and the time it is received over the SSL connection).

8. The client sends a message to the server informing it that future messages from the client will be encrypted with the session key. It then sends a separate (encrypted) message indicating that the client portion of the handshake is finished.

9. The server sends a message to the client informing it that future messages from the server will be encrypted with the session key. It then sends a separate (encrypted) message indicating that the server portion of the handshake is finished.

This session will stay open until one end or the other issues a command to close it. The command is typically issued when a browser is closed or another URL is requested.

As a security administrator, you will occasionally need to know how to configure SSL/TLS settings for a website running on your operating system. You should also know that, in order for SSL/TLS to work properly, the clients must be able to accept the level of encryption that you apply. Modern browsers can work with 128-bit encrypted sessions/certificates. Earlier browsers often needed to use 40- or 56-bit SSL encryption. As an administrator, you should push for the latest browsers on all clients.

Verisign used a clever advertising strategy that makes this point readily comprehensible: It mailed flyers in a clear bag with the lines "Sending sensitive information over the Web without the strongest encryption is like sending a letter in a clear envelope. Anyone can see it." This effectively illustrates the need for the strongest SSL possible.

Transport Layer Security (TLS) is a security protocol that expands on SSL. Though many people still say "SSL," it is highly unlikely you are actually using SSL, as TLS has been around since 1999. Figure 8.8 illustrates the connection process in the TLS network.

FIGURE 8.8 The TLS connection process

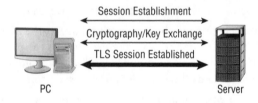

Session Establishment

Cryptography/Key Exchange

TLS Session Established

PC   Server

Think of TLS as an updated version of SSL. TLS is based on SSL, and it is intended to supersede it.

In Exercise 8.2, we will show you how to configure the TLS port in Windows Server 2016.

EXERCISE 8.2

TLS Settings in Windows Server 2016

This lab requires a test machine (nonproduction) running Windows Server 2016, but it will also work on Windows Server 2012. To configure the SSL port setting, follow these steps:

1. Open Internet Information Services Manager by choosing Start ➢ Administrative Tools ➢ Internet Information Services (IIS) Manager.

2. Expand the left pane entries until your website becomes an option. Right-click the website, and choose Properties from the context menu.

3. Select the Web Site tab. Check whether the port number for SSL is filled in. If it isn't, enter a number here.

4. Click OK and exit Internet Information Services Manager.

Notice that the TLS port field is blank by default, and any port number can be entered here—this differs from the way some previous versions of IIS worked. The default SSL/ TLS for HTTP traffic port is 443; if you enter a number other than that in this field, then clients must know and request that port in advance in order to connect.

Using Public Key Infrastructure

In addition to understanding the essentials of cryptography algorithms and techniques, you should understand the implementation of cryptography. Cryptography is implemented as part of your network infrastructure.

Hardware-Based Encryption Devices

In addition to software-based encryption, hardware-based encryption can be applied. Within the advanced configuration settings on some BIOS configuration menus, for example, you can choose to enable or disable TPM. A *trusted platform module (TPM)* can be used to assist with cryptographic key generation. TPM is the name assigned to a chip that can store cryptographic keys, passwords, or certificates. TPM can be used to protect smartphones and devices other than PCs as well. It can also be used to generate values used with whole disk encryption such as BitLocker. BitLocker can be used with or without TPM. It is much more secure when coupled with TPM (and is preferable) but does not require it.

The TPM chip may be installed on the motherboard; when it is, in many cases it is set to off in the BIOS by default. More information on TPM can be found at the Trusted Computing Group's website: https://www.trustedcomputinggroup.org/.

In addition to TPM, *HSM (hardware security module)* is also a cryptoprocessor that can be used to enhance security. HSM is commonly used with PKI systems to augment security with CAs. As opposed to being mounted on the motherboard like TPMs, HSMs are traditionally PCI adapters.

Data Encryption

Data encryption, mentioned earlier in relation to mobile devices, allows data that has been stolen to remain out of the eyes of the intruders who took it as long as they do not have the proper passwords. One of the newest security features that is available on only the Pro and Enterprise version of Windows 8.1 (and the Ultimate version of Windows 7) is BitLocker. *BitLocker* is a *full disk encryption* feature that can encrypt an entire volume with 128-bit encryption. When the entire volume is encrypted, the data is not accessible to someone who might boot another operating system in an attempt to bypass the computer's security. Full disk encryption is sometimes referred to as *hard drive encryption*.

BitLocker to Go allows you to apply the same technology to removable media. This often means encrypting USB devices, but it can also mean any removable media. By encrypting removable hard drives and USB flash drives, you also prevent them from being so destructive when intercepted by the wrong hands.

There are several other data encryption technologies beyond BitLocker including the widely used *VeraCrypt*. Both tools allow you to encrypt either the entire disk or just portions. For example, one might use individual file encryption. A related concept is *database encryption*. Many relational database systems, such as Microsoft SQL Server, have the option to encrypt the database.

Authentication

Cryptographic algorithms also play a role in various authentication methods.

Extensible Authentication Protocol (EAP) is a framework frequently used in wireless networks and point-to-point connections. It was originally defined in RFC 3748, but it has been updated since then. It handles the transport of key's and related parameters. There are several versions of EAP, which we will look at briefly:

LEAP   Lightweight Extensible Authentication protocol was developed by Cisco and has been used extensively in wireless communications. LEAP is supported by many Microsoft operating systems, including Windows 7. LEAP uses a modified version of MS-CHAP.

Extensible Authentication Protocol – Transport Layer Security   This protocol utilizes TLS in order to secure the authentication process. Most implementations of EAP-TLS utilize X.509 digital certificates to authenticate the users.

Protected Extensible Authentication Protocol   This protocol encrypts the authentication process with an authenticated TLS tunnel. PEAP was developed by a consortium including Cisco, Microsoft, and RSA Security. It was first included in Microsoft Windows XP.

EAP – FAST or Flexible Authentication via Secure Tunneling   This protocol was proposed by Cisco as a replacement for the original EAP. EAP-FAST establishes a TLS tunnel for authentication, but it does so using a Protected Access Credential (PAC).

EAP-TTLS (Tunneled Transport Layer Security)   This protocol extends TLS. It was first supported natively in Windows with Windows 8. There are currently two versions of EAP-TTLS: EAP-TTLS v0 and EAP-TTLSv1.

EAP (and its variations) are widely used in a number of other protocols. For example, the remote access protocols RADIUS (Remote Authentication Dial-In User Service) and Diameter both support EAP for authentication.

EAP is also used with 802.1.x. 802.1x is the IEEE standard for port-based network access control. It can be used on a LAN or a WLAN. 802.1x allows you to secure a port so that only authenticated users can connect to it.

Radius Federation is a federation that is using RADIUS to authenticate between the various entities within the federation. Radius is Remote Authentication Dial In User Service. It was developed in 1991 and is still used today. It operates at layer 7 of the OSI model.

Summary

This chapter focused on the basic elements of cryptography and the PKI implementation. There are three primary methods of encryption:

- Symmetric
- Asymmetric
- Hashing

Symmetric systems require that each end of the connection have the same key. Asymmetric systems use a two-key system. In public key cryptography, the receiver has a private key known only to them; a public key corresponds to it, which it makes known to others. The public key can be sent to all other parties; the private key is never divulged. Hashing refers to performing a calculation on a message and producing a fixed length hash value.

The five main considerations in implementing a cryptography system are as follows:

1. *Confidentiality* means that the message retains its privacy.

2. *Integrity* means that the message can't be altered without detection.

3. *Authentication* is used to verify that the person who sent the message is actually who they say they are.

4. *Nonrepudiation* prevents the sender from denying it was sent.

5. *Access controls* are the methods, processes, and mechanisms of preventing unauthorized access systems.

In this chapter, you also learned about the standards, agencies, and associations that are interested in cryptography. Several government agencies have been specifically charged with overseeing security and encryption. The NSA and NIST are both concerned with government encryption standards. NIST is primarily concerned with nonmilitary standards; NSA/CSS is concerned with military applications.

Exam Essentials

Be able to describe the process of a hashing algorithm.   Hashing algorithms are used to generate a fixed-length value mathematically from a message. The most common hashing standards for cryptographic applications are the SHA and MD algorithms.

Know the principles of a symmetric algorithm.   A symmetric algorithm requires that receivers of the message use the same private key. Symmetric algorithms can be extremely secure. This method is widely implemented in governmental applications.

Be able to describe the process of asymmetric algorithms.   Asymmetric algorithms use a two-key method of encryption. The message is encrypted using the public key and decrypted using a second key or private key. The key is derived from the same algorithm.

Know the primary objectives for using cryptographic systems.   The main objectives for these systems are confidentiality, integrity, authentication, and nonrepudiation. Digital signatures can be used to verify the integrity and provide nonrepudiation of a message.

Understand the process used in PKI.   PKI is an encryption system that uses a variety of technologies to provide confidentiality, integrity, authentication, and nonrepudiation. PKI uses certificates issued from a CA to provide this capability as well as encryption. PKI is being widely implemented in organizations worldwide.

Review Questions

You can find the answers in the Appendix.

1. Which of the following does not apply to a hashing algorithm?

    A. One-way

    B. Long key size

    C. Variable-length input with fixed-length output

    D. Collision resistance

2. During a training session, you want to impress upon users the serious nature of security and, in particular, cryptography. To accomplish this, you want to give them as much of an overview about the topic as possible. Which government agency should you mention is primarily responsible for establishing government standards involving cryptography for general-purpose government use?

    A. NSA

    B. NIST

    C. IEEE

    D. ITU

3. You are responsible for e-commerce security at your company. You want to use the most widely implemented asymmetric algorithm available today. Which of the following is the most widely used asymmetric algorithm today?

    A. RSA

    B. AES

    C. 3DES

    D. SHA

4. You're a member of a consortium wanting to create a new standard that will effectively end all spam. After years of meeting, the group has finally come across a solution and now wants to propose it. The process of proposing a new standard or method on the Internet is referred to by which acronym?

    A. WBS

    B. X.509

    C. RFC

    D. IEEE

5. Mary claims that she didn't make a phone call from her office to a competitor and tell them about developments at her company. Telephone logs, however, show that such a call was placed from her phone, and time clock records show that she was the only person working at the time. What do these records provide?

    A. Integrity

    B. Confidentiality

    C. Authentication

    D. Nonrepudiation

6. Mercury Technical Solutions has been using SSL in a business-to-business environment for a number of years. Despite the fact that there have been no compromises in security, the new IT manager wants to use stronger security than SSL can offer. Which of the following protocols is similar to SSL but offers the ability to use additional security protocols?

    A. TLS

    B. SSH

    C. RSH

    D. X.509

7. MAC is an acronym for what as it relates to cryptography?

    A. Media access control

    B. Mandatory access control

    C. Message authentication code

    D. Multiple advisory committees

8. You've been brought in as a security consultant for a small bicycle manufacturing firm. Immediately, you notice that they're using a centralized key-generating process, and you make a note to dissuade them from that without delay. What problem is created by using a centralized key-generating process?

    A. Network security

    B. Key transmission

    C. Certificate revocation

    D. Private key security

9. You need to encrypt your hard drive. Which of the following is the best choice?

    A. DES

    B. RSA

    C. AES

    D. SHA

10. As the head of IT for MTS, you're explaining some security concerns to a junior administrator who has just been hired. You're trying to emphasize the need to know what is important and what isn't. Which of the following is *not* a consideration in key storage?

    A. Environmental controls

    B. Physical security

    C. Hardened servers

    D. Administrative controls

11. What is the primary organization for maintaining certificates called?

    A. CA

    B. RA

    C. LRA

    D. CRL

12. Due to a breach, a certificate must be permanently revoked, and you don't want it to ever be used again. What is often used to revoke a certificate?

   A. CRA

   B. CYA

   C. CRL

   D. PKI

13. Which organization can be used to identify an individual for certificate issue in a PKI environment?

   A. RA

   B. LRA

   C. PKE

   D. SHA

14. Kristin from Payroll has left the office on maternity leave and won't return for at least six weeks. You've been instructed to suspend her key. Which of the following statements is true?

   A. In order to be used, suspended keys must be revoked.

   B. Suspended keys don't expire.

   C. Suspended keys can be reactivated.

   D. Suspending keys is a bad practice.

15. What document describes how a CA issues certificates and for what they are used?

   A. Certificate policies

   B. Certificate practices

   C. Revocation authority

   D. CRL

16. Your company has implemented email encryption throughout the enterprise. You are concerned that someone might lose their cryptographic key. You want to implement some mechanism for storing copies of keys and recovering them. What should you implement?

   A. Key escrow

   B. Key archival

   C. Key renewal

   D. Certificate rollover

17. The CRL takes time to be fully disseminated. Which protocol allows a certificate's authenticity to be immediately verified?

   A. CA

   B. CP

   C. CRC

   D. OCSP

18. John is concerned about message integrity. He wants to ensure that message integrity cannot be compromised no matter what the threat. What would best help him accomplish this goal?

   A. SHA2

   B. MD5

   C. AES

   D. MAC

19. Which of the following is similar to Blowfish but works on 128-bit blocks?

   A. Twofish

   B. IDEA

   C. CCITT

   D. AES

20. Your IT manager has stated that you need to select an appropriate tool for email encryption. Which of the following would be the best choice?

   A. MD5

   B. IPSEC

   C. TLS

   D. PGP

Chapter

9

Threats, Attacks, and Vulnerabilities

THE FOLLOWING COMPTIA SECURITY+ EXAM OBJECTIVES ARE COVERED IN THIS CHAPTER:

✓ **1.1 Given a scenario, analyze indicators of compromise and determine the type of malware.**

- Viruses
- Crypto-malware
- Ransomware
- Worm
- Trojan
- Rootkit
- Keylogger
- Adware
- Spyware
- Bots
- RAT
- Logic bomb
- Backdoor

✓ **1.2 Compare and contrast types of attacks.**

- Application/service attacks: DoS; DDoS; Man-in-the-middle; Buffer overflow; Injection; Cross-site scripting; Cross-site request forgery; Privilege escalation; ARP poisoning; Amplification; DNS poisoning; Domain hijacking; Man-in-the-browser; Zero day; Replay; Pass the hash; Hijacking and related attacks (Clickjacking; Session hijacking; URL hijacking; Typo squatting); Driver manipulation (Shimming; Refactoring); MAC spoofing; IP spoofing

As we discussed in Chapter 1, "Managing Risk," everywhere you turn there are risks. They begin the minute you first turn on a computer, and they grow exponentially the moment a network card becomes active. Whereas Chapter 1 discussed how to measure and weigh risks, this chapter will focus on two particular types of risks: malware and attacks. We will then discuss tools that you can use to combat them.

In the case of malware, you are exposed to situations because of software that is running on your system—vulnerabilities not intentionally created but that are there nevertheless. In the case of attacks, someone is purposely targeting your system(s) and trying to do you harm.

In this chapter, we'll look at some of the reasons why your network may be vulnerable. This list is far from complete because attackers create new variants of each vulnerability on a regular basis. The list is thorough, however, on two counts: It includes everything CompTIA expects you to know for the exam, and many of the new malware and attack variants are simply newer modifications, or implementations, of those discussed here.

Threat and Attack Terminology

There is often overlap between terms used to define certain threats and attacks, but it is important to be as specific as possible when discussing them to be able to understand and report them as unambiguously as possible. The following terms (also found in the online glossary) are those that CompTIA is fond of using and testing on in this category. They are provided in order to make it easier for you to know what each is intended to convey.

Security+ Terminology

Address Resolution Protocol (ARP)   Protocol used to map known IP addresses to unknown physical addresses.

Address Resolution Protocol (ARP) poisoning   An attack that convinces the network that the attacker's MAC (Media Access Control) address is the one associated with an allowed address so that traffic is wrongly sent to attacker's address.

adware   Software that gathers information to pass on to marketers or that intercepts personal data such as credit card numbers and makes it available to third parties.

antivirus software   Software that identifies the presence of a virus and is capable of removing or quarantining the virus.

armored virus   A virus that is protected in a way that makes disassembling it difficult. The difficulty makes it "armored" against antivirus programs that have trouble getting to, and understanding, its code.

ARP spoofing   More commonly known as ARP poisoning, this involves the MAC (Media Access Control) address of the data being faked.

attack   Any unauthorized intrusion into the normal operations of a computer or computer network. The attack can be carried out to gain access to the system or any of its resources.

attack surface   The area of an application that is available to users—those who are authenticated and, more importantly, those who are not.

attack surface reduction (ASR)   Minimizing the possibility of exploitation by reducing the amount of code and limiting potential damage.

backdoor   An opening left in a program application (usually by the developer) that allows additional access to data. Typically, a backdoor is created for debugging purposes and is not documented. Before the product ships, the backdoors are closed; when they aren't closed, security loopholes exist.

bot   An automated software program (network robot) that collects information on the web. In its malicious form, a bot is a compromised computer being controlled remotely.

buffer overflow   A type of denial-of-service (DoS) attack that occurs when more data is put into a buffer than it can hold, thereby overflowing it (as the name implies).

clickjacking   Using multiple transparent or opaque layers to trick a user into clicking a button or link on another page when they had intended to click on the top page.

companion virus   A virus that creates a new program that runs in the place of an expected program of the same name.

cross-site request forgery (XSRF)   A form of web-based attack in which unauthorized commands are sent from a user that a website trusts.

cross-site scripting (XSS)   Running a script routine on a user's machine from a website without their permission.

denial-of-service (DoS)   A type of attack that prevents any users—even legitimate ones—from using a system.

dictionary attack   The act of attempting to crack passwords by testing them against a list of dictionary words. With today's powerful computers, an attacker can combine one of many available automated password-cracking utilities with several large dictionaries or "wordlists" and crack huge numbers of passwords in a matter of minutes. Any password based on any dictionary word is vulnerable to such an attack.

distributed denial-of-service (DDoS)   A derivative of a DoS attack in which multiple hosts in multiple locations all focus on one target to reduce its availability to the public. This can be accomplished through the use of compromised systems, botnets, and other means.

DNS poisoning   An attack method in which a daemon caches DNS reply packets, which sometimes contain other information (data used to fill the packets). The extra data can be scanned for information useful in a break-in or man-in-the-middle attack.

DNS spoofing   The DNS server is given information about a name server that it thinks is legitimate when it isn't.

Domain Name System (DNS)   The network service used in TCP/IP networks that translates hostnames to IP addresses.

integer overflow   Putting too much information into too small of a space that has been set aside for numbers.

IP spoofing   Making the data look as if it came from a trusted host when it didn't (thus spoofing the IP address of the sending host).

least privilege   A permission method in which users are granted only the privileges necessary to perform their job function.

least privilege policy   The policy of giving a user only the minimum permissions needed to do the work that must be done.

logic bomb   Any code that is hidden within an application and causes something unexpected to happen based on some criteria being met. For example, a programmer could create a program that always makes sure her name appears on the payroll roster; if it doesn't, then key files begin to be erased.

macro virus   A software exploitation virus that works by using the macro feature included in many applications, such as Microsoft Office.

malicious code   Any code that is meant to do harm.

malicious insider threat   A threat from someone inside the organization intent on doing harm.

man-in-the-middle   An attack that occurs when someone/something that is trusted intercepts packets and retransmits them to another party. Man-in-the-middle attacks have also been called TCP/IP hijacking in the past.

multipartite virus   A virus that attacks a system in more than one way.

password attacks   Attempting to ascertain a password that you should not know.

phage virus   A virus that modifies and alters other programs and databases.

ping of death   A large Internet Control Message Protocol (ICMP) packet sent to overflow the remote host's buffer. A ping of death usually causes the remote host to reboot or hang.

polymorphic   An attribute of some viruses that allows them to mutate and appear differently each time they crop up. The mutations make it harder for virus scanners to detect (and react) to the viruses.

privilege escalation   The result when a user obtains access to a resource that they wouldn't normally be able to access. Privilege escalation can be done inadvertently by running a program with Set User ID (SUID) or Set Group ID (SGID) permissions or by temporarily becoming another user (via su or sudo in Unix/Linux or RunAs in Windows). It can also be done purposefully by an attacker seeking full access.

ransomware   Software that demands payment before restoring the data or system infected.

replay attack   An attack that captures portions of a session to play back later to convince a host that it is still talking to the original connection.

retrovirus   A virus that attacks or bypasses the antivirus software installed on a computer.

rogueware   A form of malware that tries to convince the user to pay for a fake threat.

rootkit   Software program that has the ability to obtain root-level access and hide certain things from the operating system.

scareware   Software that tries to convince unsuspecting users that a threat exists.

shim   A small library that is created to intercept API calls transparently.

spoofing   An attempt by someone or something to masquerade as someone/something else.

spyware   Software programs that work—often actively—on behalf of a third party.

stealth virus   A virus that attempts to avoid detection by masking itself from applications.

Trojan horse   Any application that masquerades as one thing in order to get past scrutiny and then does something malicious. One of the major differences between Trojan horses and viruses is that Trojan horses tend not to replicate themselves.

typo squatting   Creating domains that are based on the misspelling of another.

URL hijacking   Registering domains that are similar to those for a known entity but based on a misspelling or typographical error.

virus   A program intended to damage a computer system.

watering hole attack Identifying a site that is visited by those whom they are targeting, poisoning that site, and then waiting for the results.

Xmas attack An advanced attack that tries to get around detection and send a packet with every single option enabled.

zero-day exploit An attack that begins the very day an exploit is discovered.

zombie Any system taking directions from a master control computer. Zombies are often used in distributed denial-of-service (DDoS) and botnet attacks.

Living in a World of Viruses

A *virus* is a piece of software designed to infect a computer system. Under the best of circumstances, a virus may do nothing more than reside on the computer, but it may also damage the data on your storage devices, destroy your operating system, and possibly spread to other systems. Viruses get into your computer in one of three ways:

- On contaminated media (DVD, USB drive, or other)
- Through email and social networking sites
- As part of another program

Because so many other types of malware are misclassified as viruses, or accompany viruses, we will spend more time discussing them than some of the other entities.

 Estimates for losses due to viruses are in the billions of dollars. These losses include financial loss as well as losses in productivity.

The following sections introduce the general symptoms of a virus infection, explain how a virus works, and describe the types of viruses that you can expect to encounter and how they generally behave. You'll also see how a virus is transmitted through a network.

Symptoms of a Virus Infection

Many viruses will announce that you're infected as soon as they gain access to your system. They may take control of your system and flash annoying messages on your screen or destroy your hard disk. When this occurs, you'll know that you're a victim. Other viruses will cause your system to slow down, cause files to disappear from your computer, or take over disk space.

You should look for some of the following symptoms when determining if a virus infection has occurred:

- The programs on your system start to load more slowly. This happens because the virus is spreading to other files in your system or is taking over system resources.

- Unusual files appear on your hard drive, or files start to disappear from your system. Many viruses delete key files in your system to render it inoperable.

- Program sizes change from the installed versions. This occurs because the virus is attaching itself to these programs on your disk.

- Your browser, word processing application, or other software begins to exhibit unusual operating characteristics. Screens or menus may change.

- The system mysteriously shuts itself down or starts itself up and does a great deal of unanticipated disk activity.

- You mysteriously lose access to a disk drive or other system resources. The virus has changed the settings on a device to make it unusable.

- Your system suddenly doesn't reboot or gives unexpected error messages during startup.

This list is by no means comprehensive, but it is a good start to determining if your computer has been infected.

How Viruses Work

A virus, in most cases, tries to accomplish one of two things: render your system inoperable or spread to other systems. Many viruses will spread to other systems given the chance and then render your system unusable. This is common with many of the newer viruses.

If your system is infected, the virus may try to attach itself to every file in your system and spread each time you send a file or document to other users. Figure 9.1 shows a virus spreading from an infected system, either through a network or by removable media. When you give removable media to another user or put it into another system, you then infect that system with the virus.

FIGURE 9.1   Virus spreading from an infected system using the network or removable media

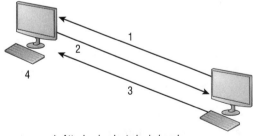

1. Attacker implants logic bomb.
2. Victim reports installation.
3. Attacker sends attack message.
4. Victim does as logic bomb indicates.

Many viruses spread using email. The infected system attaches a file to any email that you send to another user. The recipient opens this file, thinking it's something that you legitimately sent them. When they open the file, the virus infects the target system. The virus might then attach itself to all of the emails that the newly infected system sends, which in turn infects the recipients of the emails. Figure 9.2 shows how a virus can spread from a single user to literally thousands of users in a very short time using email.

FIGURE 9.2   An email virus spreading geometrically to other users

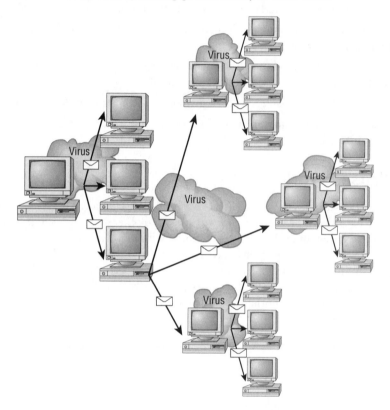

Quite a few viruses can spread through contaminated USB thumb drives. An employee may see one lying about, think it lost from a co-worker, and plug it into a machine without realizing that it contains a virus. This is such a problem that the U.S. Department of Defense has banned the use of thumb drives.

For more information on thumb drives and viruses, see www.tomshardware.com/news/usb-flash-virus-secure,6564.html.

Types of Viruses

Viruses take many different forms. The following sections briefly introduce these forms and explain how they work. These are the most common types, but this list isn't comprehensive.

The best defense against a virus attack is up-to-date antivirus software that is installed and running. The software should be on all workstations as well as the server. A whitelist of allowed applications should also be created and adhered to.

Armored Virus   An *armored virus* is designed to make itself difficult to detect or analyze. Armored viruses cover themselves with protective code that stops debuggers or disassemblers from examining critical elements of the virus. The virus may be written in such a way that some aspects of the programming act as a decoy to distract from analysis while the actual code hides in other areas in the program.

From the perspective of the creator, the more time it takes to deconstruct the virus, the longer it can live. The longer it can live, the more time it has to replicate and spread to as many machines as possible. The key to stopping most viruses is to identify them quickly and educate administrators about them—the very things that the armor intensifies the difficulty of accomplishing.

Companion Virus   A *companion virus* attaches itself to legitimate programs and then creates a program with a different filename extension. This file may reside in your system's temporary directory. When a user types the name of the legitimate program, the companion virus executes instead of the real program. This effectively hides the virus from the user. Many of the viruses that are used to attack Windows systems make changes to program pointers in the Registry so that they point to the infected program. The infected program may perform its dirty deed and then start the real program.

Macro Virus   A *macro virus* exploits the enhancements made to many application programs that are used by programmers to expand the capability of applications such as Microsoft Word and Excel. Word, for example, supports a mini-BASIC programming language that allows files to be manipulated automatically. These programs in the document are called *macros*. For example, a macro can tell your word processor to spell-check your document automatically when it opens. Macro viruses can infect all of the documents on your system and spread to other systems via email or other methods.

Multipartite Virus   A *multipartite virus* attacks your system in multiple ways. It may attempt to infect your boot sector, infect all of your executable files, and destroy your application files. The hope here is that you won't be able to correct all of the problems and this will allow the infestation to continue.

Phage Virus   A *phage virus* modifies and alters other programs and databases. The virus infects all of these files. The only way to remove this virus is to reinstall the programs that are infected. If you miss even a single incident of this virus on the victim system, the process will start again and infect the system once more.

Polymorphic Virus   *Polymorphic viruses* and *polymorphic malware* of any type—though viruses are the only ones truly prevalent—change form in order to avoid detection. These types of viruses attack your system, display a message on your computer, and delete files on your system. The virus will attempt to hide from your antivirus software. Frequently, the virus will encrypt parts of itself to avoid detection. When the virus does this, it's referred to as *mutation*. The mutation process makes it hard for antivirus software to detect common characteristics of the virus. It is common for a virus to change a signature to try to fool antivirus software.

Retrovirus A *retrovirus* attacks or bypasses the antivirus software installed on a computer. You can consider a retrovirus to be an anti-antivirus. Retroviruses can directly attack your antivirus software and potentially destroy your virus definition database file. Destroying this information without your knowledge would leave you with a false sense of security. The virus may also directly attack an antivirus program to create bypasses for itself.

Stealth Virus A *stealth virus* attempts to avoid detection by masking itself from applications. It may attach itself to the boot sector of the hard drive. When a system utility or program runs, the stealth virus redirects commands around itself in order to avoid detection. An infected file may report a file size different from what is actually present in order to avoid detection. Stealth viruses may also move themselves from fileA to fileB during a virus scan for the same reason.

An updated list of the most active viruses and spyware is on the Panda Software site at www.pandasecurity.com/homeusers/security-info/default.aspx?lst=ac.

Present Virus Activity

New viruses and threats are released on a regular basis to join the cadre of those already in existence. From an exam perspective, you need only be familiar with the world as it existed at the time the questions were written. From an administration standpoint, however, you need to know what is happening today. This book is current for virus activity up to the date of publication, but you should stay up-to-date on what has happened since then.

To find out this information, visit the CERT/CC Current Activity web page at www.us-cert.gov/current/current_activity.html. Here you'll find a detailed description of the most current viruses as well as links to pages on older threats.

Managing Spam to Avoid Viruses

Although spam is not truly a virus or a hoax, it is one of the most annoying things with which an administrator must contend. *Spam* is defined as any unwanted, unsolicited email, and not only can the sheer volume of it be irritating, but it can also often open the door to larger problems. For instance, some of the sites advertised in spam may be infected with viruses, worms, and other unwanted programs. If users begin to respond to spam by visiting those sites, then viruses and other problems will multiply in your system.

Numerous antispam programs are available, and users as well as administrators can run them. False positives are one of the biggest problems with many of these applications: they will occasionally flag legitimate email as spam and stop it from being delivered. You should routinely check your spam folders and make sure that legitimate email is not being inadvertently flagged as junk and held there.

Just as you can, and must, install good antivirus software programs, you should also consider similar measures for spam. Filtering the messages out and preventing them from ever entering the network is the most effective method of dealing with the problem. Recently, the word *spam* has found its way into other forms of unwanted messaging beyond email, giving birth to the acronyms *SPIM* (spam over instant messaging) and *SPIT* (spam over Internet telephony).

Antivirus Software

The primary method of preventing the propagation of malicious code involves the use of *antivirus software*. Antivirus software is an application that is installed on a system to protect it and to scan for viruses as well as worms and Trojan horses. Most viruses have characteristics that are common to families of virus. Antivirus software looks for these characteristics, or fingerprints, to identify and neutralize viruses before they impact you. Most of the newer antivirus packages now look for problems with cookies as well.

Thousands of known viruses, worms, logic bombs, and other malicious code have been defined. New ones are added all the time. Your antivirus software manufacturer will usually work very hard to keep the definition database files current. The definition database file contains all the known viruses and countermeasures for a particular antivirus software product. You probably won't receive a virus that hasn't been seen by one of these companies. If you keep the virus definition database files in your software up-to-date, you probably won't be overly vulnerable to attacks.

The best method of protection is to use a layered approach. Antivirus software should be at the gateways, at the servers, and at the desktop. If you want to go one step further, you can use software at each location from different vendors to make sure that you're covered from all angles.

The second method of preventing viruses is user education. Teach your users not to open suspicious files and to open only those files that they're reasonably sure are virus-free. They need to scan every disk, email, and document they receive before they open them. You should also verify that the security settings are high within the applications that your users are using.

Real World Scenario

How to Stop a Virus or Worm That Is Out of Control

A large private university has over 30,000 students taking online classes. These students use a variety of systems and network connections. The instructors at this university are being routinely hit with the Klez32 virus. Klez32 (specifically, in this case, the W32/Klez. mm virus) is a well-known and documented virus. It uses Microsoft Outlook to spread. It grabs a name randomly from the address book, and it uses that name in the header. The worm part of it then uses a mini-mailer and mails the virus to all the people in the address book. When one of these users opens the file, the worm attempts to disable their antivirus software and spread to other systems. Doing so opens the system to an attack from other viruses, which might follow later.

You've been appointed to the IT department at this school, and you've been directed to solve this problem. Take a moment to ponder what you can do about it.

If you think the best solution would be to install antivirus software that scans and blocks all emails that come through the school's servers, you are right. You should also inspect outgoing email and notify all internal users of the system when they attempt to send a virus-infected document using the server.

These two steps—installing antivirus scanners on the external and internal connections and notifying unsuspecting senders—would greatly reduce the likelihood that the virus could attack either student or instructor computers.

Malware and Crypto-Malware

The term *malware* is used to refer to software that does harm—intentionally (such as a virus) or unintentionally (such as poorly written code). If the malware incorporates cryptography, then it can be referred to as *crypto-malware*, which is simply a subset of malware.

The term *software exploitation* refers to attacks launched against applications and higher-level services. They include gaining access to data using weaknesses in the data access objects of a database or a flaw in a service or application. This section briefly outlines common exploitations that have been successful in the past. The following exploitations can be introduced by using viruses or access attacks:

Ransomware   With *ransomware*, software—often delivered through a Trojan (discussed in a moment)—takes control of a system and demands that a third party be paid. The "control" can be accomplished by encrypting the hard drive, by changing user password information, or via any of a number of other creative ways. Users are usually assured that by paying the extortion amount (the ransom), they will be given the code needed to revert their systems to normal operations.

Worm   A *worm* can do various roguish things once it is on a system, but its primary purpose is to replicate. It functions as a stand-alone piece of software in that it can spread without intervention by another program (or human), and it focuses on spreading from an infected system to as many unaffected systems as possible, placing that objective above all others. A piece of malware can act as a Trojan, as spyware, as a worm, and so forth. As long as it has a primary focus on spreading and can function as a stand-alone entity, it is classified as a worm.

Trojan   A *Trojan*, or *Trojan horse*, is a program that enters a system or network under the guise of another program. A Trojan horse may be included as an attachment or as part of an installation program. The Trojan horse could create a backdoor or replace a valid program during installation. It would then accomplish its mission under the guise of another program. Trojan horses can be used to compromise the security of your system, and they can exist on a system for years before they're detected.

Trojans Today

One area in which Trojan horses have been cropping up is with social networking. The Boonana Trojan began cropping up in Facebook and affecting both macOS and Windows-based systems. A message would appear asking the user if they appeared in certain a video and including a link. Clicking the link to run the video triggered a Java applet that would then redirect legitimate requests to known malware servers.

The best preventive measure for Trojan horses is not to allow them to enter your system. Immediately before and after you install a new software program or operating system, back it up! If you suspect a Trojan horse, you can reinstall the original programs, which should delete the Trojan horse. A port scan may also reveal a Trojan horse on your system. If an application opens a TCP or UDP port that isn't regularly used in your network, you may notice this and begin corrective action.

Is a Trojan horse also a virus? A *Trojan horse* is anything that sneaks in under the guise of something else. Given that general definition, it's certainly possible that a virus can (and usually does) sneak in, but this description most often fits the definition of a companion virus. The primary distinction, from an exam perspective, is that with a Trojan horse you always intentionally obtained something (usually an application) and didn't know an unpleasant freeloader was hidden within. An example is spyware, which is often installed (unknown to you) as part of another application.

One of the most important measures you can take to combat software attacks proactively is to know common file extensions and the applications with which they're associated. For example, the .scr filename extension is used for screensavers, and viruses are often distributed through the use of these files. No legitimate user should be sending screensavers via email to your users, and all attachments with the .scr filename extension should be banned from entering your network. Files with other extensions aren't often so clear cut. Compressed files with the .zip extension, for example, are often necessary for sending large attachments, yet encrypted .zip files also serve as the primary distribution method for ransomware.

Table 9.1, while not comprehensive, contains the most common filename extensions for files that should and should not, as a general rule, be allowed into your network as email attachments.

TABLE 9.1   Common filename extensions for email attachments

Should be allowed	Should *not* be allowed
.doc/docx	.bat
.pdf	.com
.txt	.exe
.xls/xlsx	.hlp
	.pif
	.scr

Rootkits   Recently, rootkits have become the software exploitation program du jour. *Rootkits* are software programs that have the ability to hide certain things from the operating system. With a rootkit, a number of processes may be running on a system that do not show up in Task Manager or connections established or available that do not appear in a netstat display—the rootkit masks the presence of these items. The rootkit is able to do this by manipulating function calls to the operating system and filtering out information that would normally appear. Theoretically, rootkits could hide anywhere that there is enough memory to reside: video cards, PCI cards, and the like. In Exercise 9.1, we'll show you how to view running processes on a Windows-based machine, and in Exercise 9.2, we'll do the same on a Linux-based machine.

Unfortunately, many rootkits are written to get around antivirus and antispyware programs that are not kept up-to-date. The best defense that you have is to monitor what your system is doing and catch the rootkit in the process of installation.

EXERCISE 9.1

Viewing Running Processes on a Windows-Based Machine

As an administrator, you need to know what processes are running on a machine at any given time. In addition to the programs that a user may be running, there are always many others that are required by the operating system, network, or other applications.

All recent versions of Windows include Task Manager, which allows you to see what is running. To access this information, follow these steps:

1. Right-click an empty location in the Windows Taskbar.

2. Choose either Task Manager or Start Task Manager (depending on the Windows version you are running) from the pop-up menu that appears.

3. The Task Manager opens to Applications by default and shows what the user is actually running. Click the Processes tab. Information about the programs that are needed for the running applications is shown, as well as all other processes that are currently running.

4. If the Show Processes From All Users check box appears beneath this tab, click it. Many of the names of the processes appear cryptic, but definitions for most (good and bad) can be found with a Google search.

5. Examine the list and look for anything out of the ordinary. After doing this a few times, you will become familiar with what is normally there and will be able to spot oddities quickly.

6. Notice the values in the CPU column. Those values will always total 100, with System Idle Processes typically making up the vast majority. High numbers on another process can indicate that there is a problem with it. If the numbers do not add up to 100, it can be a sign that a rootkit is masking some of the display.

7. If you are running a newer version of Windows, click the button Show Processes From All Users. User Account Control (UAC) will ask you to confirm the action; click Continue.

8. Click the top of the second column where it says User Name to order the list alphabetically by this field.

9. Scroll to where the SYSTEM entries begin and look for anything suspicious there.

10. Close Task Manager.

EXERCISE 9.2

Viewing Running Processes on a Linux-Based Machine

Most versions of Linux include a graphical utility to allow you to see the running processes. Those utilities differ based on the distribution of Linux in use and the desktop that you have chosen.

All versions of Linux, however, do offer a command line and the ability to use the ps utility. Because of that, this method is employed in this exercise. To access this information, follow these steps:

1. Open a shell window or otherwise access a command prompt.

2. Enter **ps -ef | more**.

EXERCISE 9.2 *(continued)*

3. The display shows the processes running for all users. The names of the processes appear in the rightmost column, and the processor time will be in the column closest to it. The names are cryptic, but definitions for most can be found using the man command followed by the name of the process. Those that are application specific can usually be found through a web search.

   Examine the list and look for anything out of the ordinary. After doing this a few times, you will become familiar with what is normally there and will be able to spot oddities quickly.

4. Pay particular attention to those processes associated with the root user (the user appears in the first column). Because the root user has the power to do anything, only necessary daemons and processes should be associated with that user. You can look only at those running that are associated with the root user by entering **ps -u root**.

5. Exit the shell.

 As these new threats have developed, so too have some excellent programs for countering them. Within any search engine, you can find a rootkit analyzer for your system, including Spybot, Spyware Doctor, and Ad-Aware. There are also a number of products that specialize in integrity verification, such as those from Tripwire (www.tripwire.com).

Keylogger   A *keylogger* is a piece of software that records keystrokes pressed into a log file and then allows that log file to be viewed so that passwords and other sensitive data can be seen. The log file is often encrypted so that it isn't easily seen or accessed by anyone other than the troublemaker who placed the keylogger on the machine.

Although some keyloggers exist as software only, many are installed on devices such as keyboard adapters that can be placed on a system and retrieved at a later date. These hardware devices store the log file and operate as hidden drives until unlocked using their unlock code.

Adware   If the primary purpose of the malware application is to deliver ads, then it is classified as *adware*. Adware can have the same qualities as spyware, but the primary purpose of adware is to display ads and generate revenue for the creator. Because spyware and adware share similar features, Windows Defender can be used as a first line of defense.

Spyware   *Spyware* differs from other malware in that it works—often actively—on behalf of a third party. Rather than self-replicating, like viruses and worms, spyware is spread to machines by users who inadvertently ask for it. The users often do not know that they have asked for it, but they have acquired it by downloading other programs, visiting infected sites, and so on.

The spyware program monitors the user's activity and reports it to another party without informing the user that it is doing so. Often, it is gathering information about the user to pass on to marketers, or intercepting personal data such as credit card numbers. One thing separating spyware from most other malware is that it almost always exists to provide commercial gain. The operating systems from Microsoft are the ones most affected by spyware.

 One of the reasons why spyware is so prevalent is that there are many legal uses for it, such as monitoring children's or employees' online habits. It is the implementation of spyware in an illegal manner that makes it a problem.

Bots   Software running on infected computers called *zombies* is often known as a *bot* or *botnet*. Bots, by themselves, are but a form of software that runs automatically and autonomously. (For example, Google uses the Googlebot to find web pages and bring back values for the index.) Botnet, however, has come to be the word used to describe malicious software running on a zombie and under the control of a *bot-herder*.

Denial-of-service attacks—DoS and DDoS—can be launched by botnets, as can many forms of adware, spyware, and spam (via *spambots*). Most bots are written to run in the background with no visible evidence of their presence. Many malware kits can be used to create botnets and modify existing ones.

There is no universal approach to dealing with botnets, but knowing how to deal with various botnet types (all of which are described here) is important for exam preparation. Some can be easily detected by looking at a database of known threats, whereas others have to be identified through analysis of their behavior.

RAT   A *remote administration tool (RAT)* is one that, as the name implies, allows a remote user to access the system for the purpose of administering it. Although this can be extremely valuable for legitimate administration, improperly accessed it offers the opportunity to exploit powerful features of the operating system. One of the most dangerous exploits was Ghost Rat (or GhostRat), which took advantage of the complex features built into Adobe Acrobat PDF files to allow attackers to record audio and video remotely in Windows-based operating systems.

Logic Bomb   *Logic bombs* are programs or code snippets that execute when a certain predefined event occurs. A bomb may send a note to an attacker when a user is logged on to the Internet and is using a word processor. This message informs the attacker that the user is ready for an attack.

Figure 9.3 shows a logic bomb in operation. Notice that this bomb doesn't begin the attack, but it tells the attacker that the victim has met the needed criteria or state for an attack to begin. Logic bombs may also be set to go off on a certain date or when a specified set of circumstances occurs.

FIGURE 9.3 A logic bomb being initiated

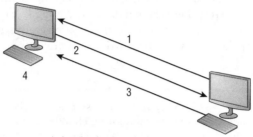

1. Attacker implants logic bomb.
2. Victim reports installation.
3. Attacker sends attack message.
4. Victim does as logic bomb indicates.

In the attack depicted in Figure 9.3, the logic bomb sends a message back to the attacking system that it has loaded successfully. The victim system can then be used to initiate an attack, such as a DDoS attack, or it can grant access at the time of the attacker's choosing.

Backdoor   The term *backdoor attack* (known also as *backdoor*) can have two different meanings. The original term backdoor referred to troubleshooting and developer hooks into systems that often circumvented normal authentication. During the development of a complicated operating system or application, programmers add backdoors or maintenance hooks. Backdoors allow them to examine operations inside the code while the code is running. The backdoors are stripped out of the code when it's moved into production. When a software manufacturer discovers a hook that hasn't been removed, it releases a maintenance upgrade or patch to close the backdoor. These patches are common when a new product is initially released.

The second type of backdoor refers to gaining access to a network and inserting a program or utility that creates an entrance for an attacker. The program may allow a certain user ID to log on without a password or to gain administrative privileges. Figure 9.4 shows how a backdoor attack can be used to bypass the security of a network. In this example, the attacker is using a backdoor program to utilize resources or steal information.

A backdoor attack is usually either an access or modification attack. A number of tools exist to create backdoor attacks on systems. Two popular ones are Back Orifice and NetBus. Fortunately, most conventional antivirus software will detect and block these types of attacks.

Back Orifice and NetBus are remote administration tools used by attackers to take control of Windows-based systems. These packages are typically installed using a Trojan horse program. Back Orifice and NetBus allow a remote user to take full control of systems on which they are installed. They run on all of the current Windows operating systems.

FIGURE 9.4   A backdoor attack in progress

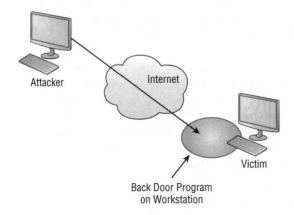

New Attacks on the Way

The discussion of attacks in this chapter isn't comprehensive. New methods for dealing with and counteracting attacks are being developed even as you read this book. Your first challenge when confronting an attack is to recognize that you're fighting the battle on two fronts:

- The first front involves the inherent open nature of TCP/IP and its protocol suite. TCP/IP is a robust and rich environment. This richness allows many opportunities to exploit the vulnerabilities of the protocol suite.

- The second front of this battle involves the implementation of TCP/IP by various vendors. A weak TCP/IP implementation will be susceptible to all forms of attacks, and there is little that you'll be able to do about it except to complain to the software manufacturer.

Fortunately, most of the credible manufacturers are now taking these complaints seriously and doing what they can to close the holes that they have created in your systems. Keep your updates current because this is where most of the corrections for security problems are implemented.

This section looked at all of the types of malware that you need to know for the CompTIA Security+ exam. Know that viruses come in many forms and can be far more complicated than other forms or malware.

Understanding Various Types of Application/Service Attacks

In computing, a lot of the terminology used comes from other fields, such as the military. That seems to be particularly true when it comes to security. Using that line of logic, an *attack* occurs when an unauthorized individual or group of individuals attempts to access, modify, or damage your systems or environment. These attacks can be fairly simple and unfocused, or they can appear to be almost blitzkrieg-like in their intensity.

One main reason for the differences in attacks is that they occur in many ways and for different reasons. Attackers have various reasons for initiating an attack. Here are a few:

- They might be doing it for the sheer fun of it.

- They might be criminals attempting to steal from you.

- They might be individuals or groups who are using the attack to make a political statement or commit an act of terrorism.

Regardless of their motive, your job is to protect the people you work with from these acts of aggression. You are, in many cases, the only person in your organization charged with the responsibility of repelling these attacks.

The following sections deal with the general types of attacks that you'll experience.

Identifying Denial-of-Service and Distributed Denial-of-Service Attacks

Denial-of-service (DoS) attacks prevent access to resources by users authorized to use those resources. An attacker may attempt to bring down an e-commerce website to prevent or deny usage by legitimate customers. Most simple DoS attacks occur from a single system, and a specific server or organization is the target.

> There isn't a single type of DoS attack. Rather, there are a variety of similar methods that have the same purpose. It's easiest to think of a DoS attack by imagining that your servers are so busy responding to false requests that they don't have time to service legitimate ones. Not only can the servers be physically busy, but the same result can also occur if the attack consumes all of the available bandwidth.

Several types of attacks can occur in this category. These attacks can do the following:

- Deny access to information, applications, systems, or communications.

- Bring down a website while the communications and systems continue to operate.

- Crash the operating system (a simple reboot may restore the server to normal operation).

- Fill the communications channel of a network and prevent access by authorized users.

- Open as many TCP sessions as possible. This type of attack is called a TCP SYN flood DoS attack.

Two of the most common types of DoS attacks are the *ping of death* and the *buffer overflow*. The ping of death crashes a system by sending Internet Control Message Protocol (ICMP) packets (think echoes) that are larger than the system can handle. Buffer overflow attacks, as the name implies, attempt to put more data (usually long input strings) into the buffer than it can hold. Code Red, Slapper, and Slammer are all attacks that took advantage of buffer overflows, and sPing is an example of a ping of death.

A *distributed denial-of-service (DDoS)* attack is similar to a DoS attack. A DDoS attack amplifies the concepts of a DoS attack by using multiple computer systems (often through botnets) to conduct the attack against a single organization. These attacks exploit the inherent weaknesses of dedicated networks such as DSL and cable. These permanently attached systems usually have little, if any, protection. An attacker can load an attack program onto dozens or even hundreds of computer systems that use DSL or cable modems. The attack program lies dormant on these computers until they get an attack signal from a master computer. The signal triggers the systems, which launch an attack simultaneously on the target network or system. DDoS attacks are common on the Internet, where they have hit large companies, and such attacks are often widely publicized in the media.

Figure 9.5 shows an attack occurring and the master controller orchestrating the attack. The master controller may be another unsuspecting user. The systems taking direction from the master control computer are referred to as *zombies* or *nodes*. These systems merely carry out the instruction they've been given by the master computer.

FIGURE 9.5   Distributed denial-of-service attack

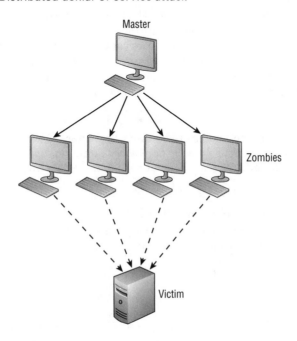

Remember that the difference between a DoS attack and a DDoS attack is that the latter uses multiple computers—all focused on one target. DDoS is far more common—and effective—today than DoS.

The nasty part of this type of attack is that the machines used to carry out the attack belong to normal computer users. The attack gives no special warning to those users. When the attack is complete, the attack program may remove itself from the system or infect the unsuspecting user's computer with a virus that destroys the hard drive, thereby wiping out the evidence.

Can You Prevent Denial Attacks?

In general, there is little that you can do to prevent DoS or DDoS attacks. Many operating systems are particularly susceptible to these types of attacks. Fortunately, most operating system manufacturers have implemented updates to minimize their effects. Make sure that your operating system and the applications you use are up-to-date.

Man-in-the-Middle Attacks

Man-in-the-middle attacks clandestinely place something (such as a piece of software or a rouge router) between a server and the user about which neither the server's administrators nor the user is aware. The man-in-the-middle attack intercepts data and then sends the information to the server as if nothing is wrong. The server responds to the software, thinking it's communicating with a legitimate client. The attacking software continues sending information on to the server, and so forth.

If communication between the server and user continues, what's the harm of the software? The answer lies in whatever else the software is doing. The man-in-the-middle software may be recording information for someone to view later, altering it, or in some other way compromising the security of your system and session.

A man-in-the-middle attack is an active attack. Something is actively intercepting the data and may or may not be altering it. If it's altering the data, the altered data masquerades as legitimate data traveling between the two hosts.

Figure 9.6 illustrates a man-in-the-middle attack. Notice how both the server and client assume that the system they're talking to is the legitimate system. The man in the middle appears to be the server to the client, and it appears to be the client to the server.

FIGURE 9.6   A man-in-the-middle attack occurring between a client and a web server

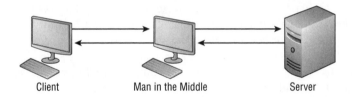

Client   Man in the Middle   Server

In recent years, the threat of man-in-the-middle attacks on wireless networks has increased. Because it's no longer necessary to connect to the wire, a malicious rogue can be outside the building intercepting packets, altering them, and sending them on. A common solution to this problem is to enforce a secure wireless authentication protocol such as WPA2.

An older term generically used for all man-in-the-middle attacks is *TCP/IP hijacking*.

TCP/IP hijacking involves the attacker gaining access to a host in the network and logically disconnecting it from the network. The attacker then inserts another machine with the same IP address. This happens quickly, and it gives the attacker access to the session and to all the information on the original system. The server won't know that this has occurred, and it will respond as if the client is trusted—the attacker forces the server to accept its IP address as valid. The hijacker will hope to acquire privileges and access to all the information on the server. You can do little to counter this threat, but fortunately these attacks require fairly sophisticated software and are harder to engineer than a simple DoS attack.

Buffer Overflow

Buffer overflows occur when an application receives more data than it's programmed to accept. This situation can cause an application to terminate or to write data beyond the end of the allocated space. Termination may leave the system sending the data with temporary access to privileged levels in the attacked system, while overwriting can cause important data to be lost. This exploitation is usually the result of a programming error in the development of the software.

Buffer overflows, though a less common source of exploitation than in the past, are still quite common and continue to represent a large problem.

Injection

Many types of injection attacks can occur, including those involving SQL, LDAP, XML, and other commands. We will take a look at each of these possibilities.

SQL Injection

SQL (Structured Query Language) is the de facto language used for communicating with online (and other relational) databases. With a *SQL injection attack* (also known as a *SQL insertion attack*), an attacker manipulates the database code to take advantage of a weakness in it. For example, if the interface is expecting the user to enter a string value but it is not specifically coded that way, the attacker could enter a line of code and that code would then execute instead of being accepted as a string value.

Various types of exploits use SQL injection, and the most common fall into the following categories:

▪ Escape characters not filtered correctly

▪ Type handling not properly done

▪ Conditional errors

▪ Time delays

The way to defend against this attack is always to filter input. This means that the website code should check to see if certain characters are in the text fields and, if so, to reject that input.

 Although the Security+ test won't ask you for details about this attack, it is useful for security professionals to know exactly how an attack is executed. Since SQL injection is such a common attack, this is an excellent one to understand.

SQL is used to communicate with a database, so it is common to have SQL statements executed when someone clicks a logon button. The SQL statements take the username and password entered, and they query the database to see if they are correct.

The problem begins with the way websites are written. They are written in some scripting, markup, or programming language, such as HTML (Hypertext Markup Language), PHP (PHP: Hypertext Preprocessor), ASP (Active Server Pages), and others. These languages don't understand SQL, so the SQL statements are usually put into a string and whatever the user inputs in the username and password boxes is appended to that string. Here is an example:

```
"SELECT * FROM tblUSERS WHERE UserName ='" + txtUserName + "'"AND ↵
Password = '"+password +"'"
```

Notice that single quotes are inserted into the text so that whatever the user types into username and password text fields is enclosed in quotes within the SQL query string, like this:

```
SELECT * FROM tblUSERS WHERE UserName ='admin' AND Password = 'password'';
```

Now the attacker will put a SQL statement into the username and password fields that is always true, like this:

```
' or '1' ='1
```

This results in a SQL query like this:

```
'SELECT * FROM tblUSERS WHERE UserName ='' or '1' ='1' AND Password = ''
or '1' ='1''
```

So now it says to get all entries from table = tblUsers if the username is '' (blank) OR IF 1 =1. Since 1 always equals 1, the user is logged in.

LDAP Injection

Just as SQL injection attacks take statements that are input by users and exploit weaknesses within, an *LDAP injection attack* exploits weaknesses in LDAP (Lightweight Directory Access Protocol) implementations. This can occur when the user's input is not properly filtered, and the result can be executed commands, modified content, or results returned to unauthorized queries.

The best way to prevent LDAP injection attacks is to filter the user input and to use a validation scheme to make certain that queries do not contain exploits.

 Real World Scenario

LDAP Injection in Action

One of the most common uses of LDAP is associated with user information. Numerous applications exist—such as employee directories—where users find other users by typing in a portion of their name. These queries are looking at the cn value or other fields (those defined for department, home directory, and so on).

Someone attempting LDAP injection could feed unexpected values to the query to see what results are returned. All too often, finding employee information equates to finding usernames and values about those users that could be portions of their passwords.

XML Injection

When web users take advantage of a weakness with SQL by entering values that they should not, it is known as a *SQL injection attack*. Similarly, when users enter values that query XML (known as XPath) with values that take advantage of exploits, it is known as an *XML injection attack*. XPath works in a similar manner to SQL, except that it does not have the same levels of access control, and taking advantage of weaknesses within can return entire documents.

The best way to prevent XML injection attacks is to filter the user's input and sanitize it to make certain that it does not cause XPath to return more data than it should.

Directory Traversal/Command Injection

If an attacker is able to gain access to restricted directories (such as the root directory) through HTTP, it is known as a *directory traversal attack*. If the attacker can gain access to the root directory of a system (which is limited from all but administrative users), they can essentially gain access to everything on the system. Bear in mind that the root directory of a website is far from the true root directory of the server; an absolute path to the site's root directory is likely to be something in IIS (Internet Information Services), such as C:\inetpub\wwwroot. If an attacker can get out of this directory and get to C:\windows, the possibility for inflicting harm is increased exponentially.

One of the simplest ways to perform directory traversal is by using a *command injection attack* that carries out the action. For example, exploiting a weak IIS implementation by calling up a web page along with the parameter cmd.exe?/c+dir+c:\ would call the command shell and execute a directory listing of the root drive (C:\). With Unicode support, entries such as %c%1c and %c0%af can be translated into / and \, respectively.

The ability to perform command injection is rare these days. Most vulnerability scanners will check for weaknesses with directory traversal/command injection and inform you of their presence. To secure your system, you should run such a scanner and keep the web server software patched.

Cross-Site Scripting and Request Forgery

Using a client-side scripting language, it is possible for an attacker to trick a user who visits the site into having code execute locally. When this is done, it is known as *cross-site scripting (XSS)*. Let's look at an example. UserA gets a message telling him that he needs to make changes to his XYZ account, but the link in the message is not really to the XYZ site (a phishing ploy). When he visits the site, a script routine begins to run on his machine with his permissions and can begin doing such things as running malevolent routines to send, delete, or alter data.

In this attack, the perpetrator finds some place on a website where users can interact with each other. A product review section is ideal. Rather than put a comment in the input text field, the attacker types in some script, such as JavaScript. The next time a user visits that section of the website, the script is executed. The way to prevent this attack is to filter input, much like with SQL injection.

Cross-site request forgery—also known as *XSRF*, session riding, and one-click attack—involves unauthorized commands coming from a trusted user to the website. This is often done without the user's knowledge, and it employs some type of social networking to pull it off.

For example, assume that Evan and Spencer are chatting through Facebook. Spencer sends Evan a link to what he purports is a funny video that will crack him up. Evan clicks the link, but it actually brings up Evan's bank account information in another browser tab, takes a screenshot of it, closes the tab, and sends the information to Spencer. The reason the attack is possible is because Evan is a trusted user with his own bank. In order for it to work, Evan would need to have recently accessed that bank's website and have a cookie that had yet to expire.

The best protection against cross-site scripting is to disable the running of scripts (and browser profiles).

Privilege Escalation

Privilege escalation involves a user gaining more privileges than they should have. With their elevated permissions, they can perform tasks they should not be allowed to do (such as delete files or view data). This condition is often associated with bugs left in software. When creating a software program, developers will occasionally leave a backdoor in the program that allows them to become a root user should they need to fix something during the debugging phase.

After debugging is done and before the software goes live, these abilities are removed. If a developer forgets to remove the backdoor in the live version and the method of accessing it gets out, it leaves the ability for an attacker to take advantage of the system.

To understand privilege escalation, think of cheat codes in video games. Once you know the game's code, you can enter it and become invincible. Similarly, someone might take advantage of a hidden cheat in a software application in order to become root.

 Real World Scenario

Responding to an Attack

As a security administrator, you know all about the different types of attacks that can occur, and you're familiar with the value assigned to the data on your system. Now imagine that the log files indicate that an intruder entered your system for a lengthy period last week while you were away on vacation.

The first thing that you should do is to make a list of questions that you should begin asking to deal with the situation, using your network as a frame of reference. The following list includes some of the questions you should consider:

1. How can you show that a break-in really occurred?

2. How can you determine the extent of what was done during the entry?

3. How can you prevent further entry?

4. Whom should you inform in your organization?

5. What should you do next?

Answers to these questions will be addressed throughout this book. The most important question on the list, though, is who you should inform in your organization. It's important to know the escalation procedures without hesitation and to be able to act quickly.

ARP Poisoning

With *ARP poisoning* (also known as *ARP spoofing*), the MAC (Media Access Control) address of the data is faked. By faking this value, it is possible to make it look as if the data came from a network that it did not. This fake address can be used to gain access to the network, to fool the router into sending data here that was intended for another host, or to launch a DoS attack. In all cases, the address being faked is an address of a legitimate user, and that makes it possible to get around such measures as allow/deny lists.

Amplification

Amplification attacks are usually employed as a part of a DDoS attack. The goal of the attacker is to get a response to their request in a greater than 1:1 ratio so that the additional bandwidth traffic works to congest and slow the responding server down. The ratio achieved is known as the *amplification factor*, and high numbers are possible with UDP-based protocols such as NTP, CharGen, and DNS.

As an example, the command `monlist` can be used with an NTP amplification attack to send details of the last 600 people who have requested the time from that computer back to the requester, resulting in more than 550 times the amount of data that was requested to be sent back to a spoofed victim. Bots can be used to send requests with the same spoofed IP source address from lots of different zombies and cause the servers to send a massive amount of data back to the victim; for this reason, it is also referred to as reflected DoS.

DNS Poisoning

With *DNS poisoning*, the DNS server is given information about a name server that it thinks is legitimate when it isn't. This can send users to a website other than the one to which they wanted to go, reroute mail, or do any other type of redirection in which data from a DNS server is used to determine a destination. Another name for this is *DNS spoofing*, and fast flux is one of the most popular techniques.

> Another DNS weakness is *domain name kiting*. When a new domain name is issued, there is technically a five-day grace period before you must pay for it. Those engaged in kiting can delete the account within the five days and re-register it, allowing them to have accounts that they never have to pay for.

Domain Hijacking

As the name implies, *domain hijacking* involves an individual changing the domain registration information for a site without the original registrant's permission. Once hijacked, often the website is replaced by one that looks identical but that records private information (passwords) or spreads malware.

Man-in-the-Browser

A *man-in-the-browser* attack (abbreviated as MITB, MitB, MIB, and MiB) is a type of man-in-the-middle attack in which a Trojan horse manipulates calls between the browser and its security mechanisms, sniffing or modifying transactions as they are formed on the browser yet still displaying back the user's intended transaction.

Zero-Day Exploits

When a hole is found in a web browser or other software and attackers begin exploiting it the very day it is discovered by the developer (bypassing the one-to-two-day response time that many software providers need to put out a patch once the hole has been found), it is known as a *zero-day exploit*. It is very difficult to respond to a zero-day exploit. If attackers learn of the weakness the same day as the developer, then they have the ability to exploit it until a patch is released. Often, the only thing that you as a security administrator can do, between the discovery of the exploit and the release of the patch, is to turn off the service. Although this can be a costly undertaking in terms of productivity, it is the only way to keep the network safe.

Several years ago, Stuxnet was found to be using a total of four zero-day vulnerabilities to spread:

```
www.symantec.com/connect/blogs/stuxnet-using-three-additional-zero-day-
vulnerabilities
```

Replay Attacks

Replay attacks are becoming quite common. They occur when information is captured over a network. A *replay attack* is a kind of access or modification attack. In a distributed environment, logon and password information is sent between the client and the authentication system. The attacker can capture the information and replay it later. This can also occur with security certificates from systems such as Kerberos: the attacker resubmits the certificate, hoping to be validated by the authentication system and circumvent any time sensitivity.

Figure 9.7 shows an attacker presenting a previously captured certificate to a Kerberos-enabled system. In this example, the attacker gets legitimate information from the client and records it. Then the attacker attempts to use the information to enter the system. The attacker later relays information to gain access.

If this attack is successful, the attacker will have all of the rights and privileges from the original certificate. This is the primary reason that most certificates contain a unique session identifier and a time stamp. If the certificate has expired, it will be rejected, and an entry should be made in a security log to notify system administrators.

FIGURE 9.7 A replay attack occurring

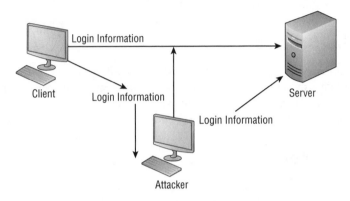

Login Information

Client

Login Information

Login Information

Server

Attacker

Pass the Hash

Due to a weakness in NTLM and LanMan, it is possible for an attacker to send an authenticated copy of the password hash value (along with a valid username) and authenticate to any remote server (Windows, Unix, or any other operating system) that is accepting LM or NTLM authentication. This attack takes advantage of a weakness in the authentication protocol in which the password hash remains static from session to session until the password is changed.

Hijacking and Related Attacks

Hijacking has already been discussed as it relates to domain hijacking, but this is far from the only type that exists. Whenever someone takes over an entity other than the responsible party, it can be considered hijacking. There are a number of other types that CompTIA wants you to know—all of which are discussed in the following sections.

Clickjacking

Clickjacking involves an attacker using multiple transparent or opaque layers to trick a user into clicking a button or link on another page when they were intending to click on the top-level page. In this way, the attacker is "hijacking" clicks meant for one page and routing them to another page associated with another application, domain, or both.

An example would be a legitimate web page that includes a Click For More Info link that a miscreant places a transparent button over. When an innocent user thinks that they are clicking on the link, they are actually activating the invisible button, which takes them to a completely different site—often then asking information that is collected by the miscreant for future malevolent purposes.

Session Hijacking

The term *session hijacking* describes when the item used to validate a user's session, such as a cookie, is stolen and used by another to establish a session with a host that thinks it is still communicating with the first party. To use an overly simplistic analogy, imagine that you just finished a long phone conversation with a family member and then accidentally left your smartphone in the room while stepping outside. If Jim were to pick up that phone and press redial, the family member would see the caller ID, know that they had just been talking with you, and falsely assume that you were calling back. If Jim could imitate your voice, he could rattle off numerous nasty comments that would jeopardize your relationship with that family member. This same premise could be true if someone could fool a host into thinking it was still talking to your computer rather than theirs.

Numerous types of attacks use session hijacking, including man-in-the-middle and sidejacking. A weakness in a Firefox extension made news when it became known that an exploit made it possible for public Wi-Fi users to fall prey to this type of attack. (Firesheep was an extension created to take advantage of the weakness.)

Some of the best ways to prevent session hijacking are to encrypt the sessions, encourage users to log out of sites when finished, and perform secondary checks on the identity of the user.

Typo Squatting and URL Hijacking

Typo squatting (also spelled *typosquatting*) and *URL hijacking* are one and the same. Difficult to describe as an attack, this is the act of registering domains that are similar to those for a known entity but based on a misspelling or typographical error. As an example, a reader wanting to go to Sybex.com to find out additional information about this book would be visiting the publisher's site (hosted beneath Wiley, incidentally), but someone intending on doing harm could register Sybecks.com in the hopes that the same reader would misspell the word. Instead of arriving at the safe site of the publisher, they would end up at the other site, which could download Trojans, worms, and viruses—oh, my!

The best defense against typo squatting is to register those domains around yours for which a user might intentionally type in a value when trying to locate you. This includes top-level domains as well (`.com`, `.biz`, `.net`, and so on) for all reasonable deviations of your site.

Driver Manipulation

Within an operating system or application, one way to inflict harm is to change the data with which the driver is working. This manipulation causes the driver(s) to be bypassed altogether *or* to do what it was programmed to do—just not with the values that it should be receiving. Two popular methods of driver manipulation are shimming and refactoring.

Shimming

A *shim* is a small library that is created to intercept API calls transparently and do one of three things: handle the operation itself, change the arguments passed, or redirect the request elsewhere. Often, shims are written to support old APIs and give them functionality which they weren't originally written to have (such as run on OS versions for which they weren't developed). Conversely, shims can be written to support a new API in an older environment as well, but this is less common.

In terms of malware, shimming involves creating a library—or modifying an existing one—to bypass a driver and perform a function other than the one for which the API was created.

Refactoring

Refactoring is the name given to a set of techniques used to identify the flow and then modify the internal structure of code without changing the code's visible behavior. In the non-malware world, this is done in order to improve the design, to remove unnecessary steps, and to create better code. In the malware world, this is often done to look for opportunities to take advantage of weak code and look for holes that can be exploited.

MAC and IP Spoofing Attacks

A *spoofing* attack is an attempt by someone or something to masquerade as someone else. This type of attack is usually considered an access attack. A common spoofing attack that was popular for many years on early Unix and other timesharing systems involved a programmer writing a fake logon program. It would prompt the user for a user ID and password. No matter what the user typed, the program would indicate an invalid logon attempt and then transfer control to the real logon program. The spoofing program would write the logon and password into a disk file, which was retrieved later.

Figure 9.8 shows a spoofing attack occurring as part of the logon process on a computer network. The attacker in this situation impersonates the server to the client attempting to log in. No matter what the client attempts to do, the impersonating system will fail the login. When this process is finished, the impersonating system disconnects from the client. The client then logs into the legitimate server. In the meantime, the attacker now has a valid user ID and password.

FIGURE 9.8 A spoofing attack during logon

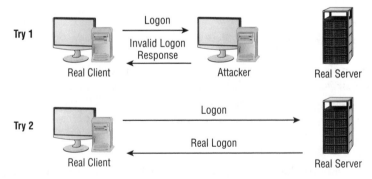

Attacker now has logon and password.

When it comes to spoofing, the important point to remember is that an attack involving it tricks something or someone into thinking that something legitimate is occurring when it is not. As mentioned in the discussion of ARP poisoning, with ARP spoofing the MAC address of the data is faked. With *IP spoofing*, the goal is to make the data look as if it came from a trusted host when it didn't (thus spoofing the IP address of the sending host).

 Always think of spoofing as fooling. Attackers are trying to fool the user, system, and/or host into believing they're something that they are not. Because the word *spoof* can describe any false information at any level, spoofing can occur at any level of the network.

Summary

This chapter focused on the various threats and vulnerabilities you'll encounter. We covered:

- Types of malware
- Types of viruses
- Types of application attacks

Some of the attacks discussed are denial-of-service, distributed denial-of-service, backdoor attacks, spoofing attacks, man-in-the-middle attacks, and replay attacks. These are just some of the attacks you may encounter. Each takes advantage of inherent weaknesses in the network technologies most commonly used today.

Malicious code describes an entire family of software that has nefarious intentions about your networks and computers. This includes viruses, Trojan horses, logic bombs, and worms. Viruses and worms are a major problem on the Internet.

Exam Essentials

Be able to describe the various types of attacks to which your systems are exposed.   Your network is vulnerable to DoS attacks caused by either a single system or multiple systems. Multiple-system attacks are called DDoS. Your systems are also susceptible to access, modification, and repudiation attacks.

Be able to describe the methods used to conduct a backdoor attack.   Backdoor attacks occur using either existing maintenance hooks or developmental tools to examine the internal operations of a program. These hooks are usually removed when a product is prepared for market or production. Backdoor attacks also refer to inserting into a machine a program or service that allows authentication to be bypassed and access gained.

Know how a spoofing attack occurs.   Spoofing attacks occur when a user or system masquerades as another user or system. Spoofing allows the attacker to assume the privileges and access rights of the real user or system.

Be able to describe a man-in-the-middle attack.   Man-in-the-middle attacks are based on the principle that a system can be placed between two legitimate users to capture or exploit the information being sent between them. Both sides of the conversation assume that the man in the middle is the other end and communicate normally. This creates a security breach and allows unauthorized access to information.

Be able to describe a replay attack.   A replay attack captures information from a previous session and attempts to resend it to gain unauthorized access. This attack is based on the premise that if it worked once, it will work again. This is especially effective in environments where a user ID and password are sent in the clear across a large network.

Know the characteristics and types of viruses used to disrupt systems and networks. Several different types of viruses are floating around today. The most common ones are polymorphic viruses, stealth viruses, retroviruses, multipartite viruses, and macro viruses.

Be able to explain the characteristics of Trojan horses and logic bombs.   Trojan horses are programs that enter a system or network under the guise of another program. Logic bombs are programs or snippets of code that execute when a certain predefined event occurs.

Be able to describe how antivirus software operates.   Antivirus software looks for a signature in the virus to determine what type of virus it is. The software then takes action to neutralize the virus based on a virus definition database. Virus definition database files are regularly made available on vendor sites.

Review Questions

You can find the answers in the Appendix.

1. As the security administrator for your organization, you must be aware of all types of attacks that can occur and plan for them. Which type of attack uses more than one computer to attack the victim?

   A. DoS

   B. DDoS

   C. Worm

   D. UDP attack

2. An alert signals you that a server in your network has a program running on it that bypasses authorization. Which type of attack has occurred?

   A. DoS

   B. DDoS

   C. Backdoor

   D. Social engineering

3. An administrator at a sister company calls to report a new threat that is making the rounds. According to him, the latest danger is an attack that attempts to intervene in a communications session by inserting a computer between the two systems that are communicating. Which of the following types of attacks does this constitute?

   A. Man-in-the-middle attack

   B. Backdoor attack

   C. Worm

   D. TCP/IP hijacking

4. You've discovered that an expired certificate is being used repeatedly to gain logon privileges. Which type of attack is this most likely to be?

   A. Man-in-the-middle attack

   B. Backdoor attack

   C. Replay attack

   D. TCP/IP hijacking

5. Which type of attack denies authorized users access to network resources?

   A. DoS

   B. Worm

   C. Logic bomb

   D. Social engineering

6. Your system has just stopped responding to keyboard commands. You noticed that this occurred when a spreadsheet was open and you connected to the Internet. Which kind of attack has probably occurred?

    A. Logic bomb

    B. Worm

    C. Virus

    D. ACK attack

7. You're explaining the basics of security to upper management in an attempt to obtain an increase in the networking budget. One of the members of the management team mentions that they've heard of a threat from a virus that attempts to mask itself by hiding code from antivirus software. What type of virus is she referring to?

    A. Armored virus

    B. Malevolent virus

    C. Worm

    D. Stealth virus

8. What kind of virus could attach itself to the boot sector of your disk to avoid detection and report false information about file sizes?

    A. Trojan horse virus

    B. Stealth virus

    C. Worm

    D. Polymorphic virus

9. What is it known as when an attacker manipulates the database code to take advantage of a weakness in it?

    A. SQL tearing

    B. SQL manipulation

    C. SQL cracking

    D. SQL injection

10. What term describes when the item used to validate a user's session, such as a cookie, is stolen and used by another to establish a session with a host that thinks it is still communicating with the first party?

    A. Patch infiltration

    B. XML injection

    C. Session hijacking

    D. DTB exploitation

11. Which of the following involves unauthorized commands coming from a trusted user to the website?

A. ZDT

B. HSM

C. TT3

D. XSRF

12. When a hole is found in a web browser or other software, and attackers begin exploiting it before the developer can respond, what type of attack is it known as?

A. Polymorphic

B. Xmas

C. Malicious insider

D. Zero-day

13. Which of the following is a small library that is created to intercept API calls transparently?

A. Chock

B. Wedge

C. Refactor

D. Shim

14. The new head of software engineering has demanded that all code be tested to identify the design flow and then modified, as needed, to clean up routines without changing the code's visible behavior. What is this process known as?

A. Straightening

B. Sanitizing

C. Refactoring

D. Uncluttering

15. Karl from Accounting is in a panic. He is convinced that he has identified malware on the servers—a type of man-in-the-middle attack in which a Trojan horse manipulates calls between the browser and yet still displays back the user's intended transaction. What type of attack could he have stumbled on?

A. Man-in-the-browser

B. Man-in-the-castle

C. Man-in-the-code

D. Man-in-the-business

16. Pass-the-hash attacks take advantage of a weak encryption routine associated with which protocols?

   A. NetBEUI and NetBIOS

   B. NTLM and LanMan

   C. Telnet and TFTP

   D. Chargen and DNS

17. The command `monlist` can be used with which protocol as part of an amplification attack?

   A. SMTP

   B. NTP

   C. SNMP

   D. ICMP

18. An attacker has placed an opaque layer over the Request A Catalog button on your web page. This layer tricks visitors into going to a form on a different website and giving their contact information to another party when their intention was to give it to you. What type of attack is this known as?

   A. Clickjacking

   B. Man-in-the-middle

   C. XSRF

   D. Zero-day

19. With which of the following is the DNS server given information about a name server that it thinks is legitimate when it isn't?

   A. DNS tagging

   B. DNS kiting

   C. DNS poisoning

   D. DNS foxing

20. It has been brought to your attention that a would-be attacker in Indiana has been buying up domains based on common misspellings of your company's name with the sole intent of creating websites that resemble yours and prey on those who mistakenly stumble onto these pages. What type of attack is this known as?

   A. Watering hole

   B. Poisoned well

   C. Faulty tower

   D. Typo squatting

Chapter

10

Social Engineering and Other Foes

THE FOLLOWING COMPTIA SECURITY+ EXAM OBJECTIVES ARE COVERED IN THIS CHAPTER:

✓ **1.2 Compare and contrast types of attacks.**

- Social engineering: Phishing; Spear phishing; Whaling; Vishing; Tailgating; Impersonation; Dumpster diving; Shoulder surfing; Hoax; Watering hole attack; Principles (reasons for effectiveness): Authority; Intimidation; Consensus; Scarcity; Familiarity; Trust; Urgency

✓ **3.9 Explain the importance of physical security controls.**

- Lighting; Signs; Fencing/gate/cage; Security guards; Alarms; Safe; Secure cabinets/enclosures; Protected distribution/ Protected cabling; Airgap; Mantrap; Faraday cage; Lock types; Biometrics; Barricades/Bollards; Tokens/cards; Environmental controls (HVAC; Hot and cold aisles; Fire suppression); Cable locks; Screen filters; Cameras; Motion detection; Logs; Infrared detection; Key management

✓ **5.7 Compare and contrast various types of controls.**

- Deterrent; Preventive; Detective; Corrective; Compensating; Technical; Administrative; Physical

✓ **5.8 Given a scenario, carry out data security and privacy practices.**

- Data destruction and media sanitation: Burning; Shredding; Pulping; Pulverizing; Degaussing; Purging; Wiping

- Data sensitivity labeling and handling: Confidential; Private; Public; Proprietary; PII; PHI

- Data roles: Owner; Steward/custodian; Privacy officer

- Data retention

- Legal and compliance

Keeping computers and networks secure involves more than just the technical aspects of the systems and networks. In many cases, the weakest link is the user who has access to data and a less-than-complete understanding of the security problems that they may encounter.

As a security professional, you must address the issue of users' lack of security expertise using a balanced response from both a technical and business perspective. It is your responsibility to keep the data safe, and if that means training users in addition to implementing tighter network security, then, as Lady Macbeth so eloquently put it, "Screw your courage to the sticking-place, and we'll not fail."

This chapter will help you understand the complexities of managing security and the issues involved with social engineering, physical security, and data policies.

Social Engineering and Physical Security Terminology

Just as was the case with the preceding chapters, there are a number of definitions and nomenclatures that you must know when it comes to social engineering and physical security. The following terms (also found in the online glossary) are those CompTIA is fond of using and testing on in this category. They are provided in order to make it easier for you to know what each is intended to convey.

Security+ Terminology

administrative control   A control implemented through administrative policies or procedures.

cable lock   A physical security deterrent used to protect a computer.

cold aisles   Server room aisles that blow cold air from the floor.

compensating controls   Gap controls that fill in the coverage between other types of vulnerability mitigation techniques. (Where there are holes in coverage, we compensate for them.)

control   Processes or actions used to respond to situations or events.

control types   Technical, physical, or administrative measures in place to assist with resource management.

data disposal   Getting rid of/destroying media no longer needed.

detective control   Controls that are intended to identify and characterize an incident in progress (for example, sounding the alarm and alerting the administrator).

dumpster diving   Looking through trash for clues—often in the form of paper scraps—to find users' passwords and other pertinent information.

Faraday cage   An electrically conductive wire mesh or other conductor woven into a "cage" that surrounds a room and prevents electromagnetic signals from entering or leaving the room through the walls.

fire suppression   The act of stopping a fire and preventing it from spreading.

hoax   Typically, an email message warning of something that isn't true, such as an outbreak of a new virus. A hoax can send users into a panic and cause more harm than the virus.

hot aisles   A server room aisle that removes hot air.

impersonation   Pretending to be another person to gain information.

information classification   The process of determining what information is accessible, to what parties, and for what purposes.

mantrap   A device, such as a small room, that limits access to one or a few individuals. Mantraps typically use electronic locks and other methods to control access.

PASS method   The correct method of extinguishing a fire with an extinguisher: Pull, Aim, Squeeze, and Sweep.

perimeter security   Security set up on the outside of the network or server to protect it.

Personal Identity Verification (PIV)   Card required of federal employees and contractors to gain access (physical and logical) to government resources.

personally identifiable information (PII)   Information that can be uniquely used to identify, contact, or locate a single person. Examples include Social Security number, driver's license number, fingerprints, and handwriting.

phishing   A form of social engineering in which you simply ask someone for a piece of information that you are missing by making it look as if it is a legitimate request. Commonly sent via email.

physical controls   Controls and countermeasures of a tangible nature intended to minimize intrusions.

preventive controls   Controls intended to prevent attacks or intrusions.

privacy   A state of security in which information isn't seen by unauthorized parties without the express permission of the party involved.

privacy filters   Screens that restrict viewing of monitors to only those sitting in front of them.

PTZ   Cameras that can pan, tilt, and zoom.

restricted information   Information that isn't made available to all and to which access is granted based on some criteria.

shoulder surfing   Watching someone when they enter their username, password, or sensitive data.

social engineering   An attack that uses others by deceiving them. It does not directly target hardware or software, but instead it targets and manipulates people.

spear phishing   A form of phishing in which the message is made to look as if it came from someone you know and trust as opposed to an informal third party.

tailgating   Following someone through an entry point.

technical controls   Controls that rely on technology.

vishing   Combining phishing with Voice over IP (VoIP).

watering hole attack   Identifying a site that is visited by those that they are targeting, poisoning that site, and then waiting for the results.

wetware   Another term for social engineering.

whaling   Phishing only large accounts.

Understanding Social Engineering

Social engineering is the process by which intruders gain access to your facilities, your network, and even your employees by exploiting the generally trusting nature of people. A social engineering attack may come from someone posing as a vendor, or it could take the form of an email from a (supposedly) traveling executive who indicates that they have forgotten how to log on to the network or how to get into the building over the weekend. It's often difficult to determine whether the individual is legitimate or has bad intentions.

Occasionally, social engineering is also referred to as *wetware*. This term is used because it is a form of hacking that does not require software or hardware but rather the gray matter of the brain.

Social engineering attacks can develop subtly. They're also hard to detect. Let's look at some classic social engineering attacks.

Someone enters your building wearing a white lab jacket with a logo on it. He also has a toolkit. He approaches the receptionist and identifies himself as a copier repairman from a major local copier company. He indicates that he's here to do preventive service on your copier. In most cases, the receptionist will let him pass and tell him the location of the copier. Once the "technician" is out of sight, the receptionist probably won't give him a second thought. Your organization has just been the victim of a social engineering attack. The attacker has now penetrated your first and possibly even your second layer of security. In many offices, including security-oriented offices, this individual would have access to the entire organization and would be able to pass freely anywhere he wanted. This attack didn't take any particular talent or skill other than the ability to look like a copier repairman. *Impersonation* can go a long way in allowing access to a building or network.

Another social engineering attack actually happened at a high-security government installation. Access to the facility required passing through a series of manned checkpoints. Professionally trained and competent security personnel staffed these checkpoints. An employee decided to play a joke on the security department: he took an old employee badge, cut his picture out of it, and pasted in a picture of Mickey Mouse. He was able to gain access to the facility for two weeks before he was caught.

Social engineering attacks like these are easy to accomplish in most organizations. Even if your organization uses biometric devices, magnetic card strips, or other electronic measures, social engineering attacks are still relatively simple.

Famed hacker Kevin Mitnick wrote a book called *The Art of Deception: Controlling the Human Element of Security* (Wiley, 2002) in which 14 of the 16 chapters are devoted to social engineering scenarios that have played out. If nothing else, the fact that one of the most notorious hackers—who could write on any security subject he so desired—chose to write a book on social engineering should make the importance of this topic abundantly clear.

More recently, Christopher Hadnagy wrote a book on the topic called *Social Engineering: The Art of Human Hacking* (Wiley, 2010). It is highly recommended reading for any administrator, security or otherwise.

Types of Social Engineering Attacks

As an administrator, one of your responsibilities is to educate users on how to avoid falling prey to social engineering attacks. They should know the security procedures that are in place and follow them to a tee. You should also have a high level of confidence that the correct procedures are in place, and one of the best ways to obtain that confidence is to check on your users occasionally.

Preventing social engineering attacks involves more than just providing training on how to detect and prevent them. It also involves making sure that people stay alert. Here's a list of some of the most common attacks:

Phishing *Phishing* is a form of social engineering in which you ask someone for a piece of information that you are missing by making it look as if it is a legitimate request. An email might look as if it is from a bank and contain some basic information, such as the user's name. In the email, it will often state that there is a problem with the person's account or access privileges. The user will be told to click a link to correct the problem. After they click the link—which goes to a site other than the bank's—they are asked for their username, password, account information, and so on. The person instigating the phishing can then use the values entered there to access the legitimate account.

One of the best counters to phishing is simply to mouse over the Click Here link and read the URL. Almost every time it is pointing to an adaptation of the legitimate URL as opposed to a link to the real thing.

Spear Phishing *Spear phishing* is a unique form of phishing in which the message is made to look as if it came from someone you know and trust as opposed to an informal third party. For example, in a phishing attack, you would get a message that appears to be from Giant Bank XYZ telling you that there is a problem with your account and that you need to log in to rectify this right away. Such a message from someone you've never heard of would run a high risk of raising suspicion and thus generate a lower than desired rate of return for the phishers. With spear phishing, you might get a message that appears to be from your boss telling you that there is a problem with your direct deposit account and that you need to access this HR link right now to correct it.

Spear phishing works better than phishing because it uses information that it can find about you from email databases, friends lists, and the like.

Whaling *Whaling* is nothing more than phishing or spear phishing, but for big users. Instead of sending out a To Whom It May Concern message to thousands of users, the whaler identifies one person from whom they can gain all of the data they want—usually a manager or owner—and targets the phishing campaign at them.

Vishing When you combine phishing with Voice over IP (VoIP), it becomes known as *vishing*, an elevated form of social engineering. Although crank calls have been in existence since the invention of the telephone, the rise in VoIP now makes it possible for someone to call you from almost anywhere in the world without worrying about tracing, caller ID, and other landline-related features. They then pretend to be someone they are not in order to get data from you. Figure 10.1 shows an example of vishing in action.

Tailgating A favorite method of gaining entry to electronically locked systems is to follow someone through the door they just unlocked, a process known as *tailgating*. Many people don't think twice about this event—it happens all the time—as they hold the door open for someone behind them who is carrying heavy boxes or is disabled in some way (see Figure 10.2).

FIGURE 10.1   An example of vishing

FIGURE 10.2   An example of tailgating

Impersonation   As mentioned at the beginning of the chapter, *impersonation* involves any act of pretending to be someone you are not. This can be a service technician, a pizza delivery driver, a security guard, or anyone else who might be allowed unfettered access to the grounds, network, or system. Impersonation can be done in person, over the phone, by email, and so forth.

Dumpster Diving   *Dumpster diving*, illustrated in Figure 10.3, is a common physical access method. Companies normally generate a huge amount of paper, most of which eventually winds up in dumpsters or recycle bins. Dumpsters may contain information that is highly sensitive in nature. In high-security and government environments, sensitive papers are either shredded or burned. Most businesses don't do this. In addition, the advent of "green" companies has created an increase in the amount of recycled paper, which can often contain all sorts of juicy information about a company and its employees.

FIGURE 10.3   An example of dumpster diving

Shoulder Surfing   One popular form of social engineering is known as *shoulder surfing*, and it involves nothing more than watching someone "over their shoulder" when they enter their sensitive data (as illustrated in Figure 10.4). They can see you entering a password, typing in a credit card number, or entering any other pertinent information. The best defense against this type of attack is to survey your environment before entering personal data. It is a good idea for users not to have their monitors positioned in ways that make it easy for this act to occur, but they also need to understand and appreciate that such an attack can occur away from the desk as well: in any public location where they sit with their laptops, at business travel centers in hotels, at ATMs, and so on.

FIGURE 10.4   An example of shoulder surfing

Passwords entered on Apple products by default display the last letter entered as convenience to the user. Unfortunately, this increases the dangers posed by shoulder surfing. *Privacy filters*, which go over the screen and restrict the viewing angle to straight on, can be used to decrease the success of shoulder surfing.

Hoax   Network users have plenty of real viruses to worry about. Yet some people find it entertaining to issue phony threats to keep people on their toes. Some of the more popular *hoaxes* (as illustrated in Figure 10.5) that have been passed around are the Good Time and Irina viruses. Millions of users received emails about these two viruses, and the symptoms sounded just awful.

Both of these viruses claimed to do things that are impossible to accomplish with a virus. When you receive a virus warning, you can verify its authenticity by looking on the website of the antivirus software you use, or you can go to several public systems. One of the more helpful sites to visit to get the status of the latest viruses is that of the CERT organization (www.cert.org). CERT monitors and tracks viruses and provides regular reports on this site.

Though the site names are similar, there is a difference between www.cert .org and https://www.us-cert.gov/. The latter is a government site for the United States Computer Emergency Readiness Team, and the former is a federally funded research and development center at Carnegie Mellon University.

FIGURE 10.5   Falsely sounding an alarm is a type of hoax.

When you receive an email that you suspect is a hoax, check the CERT site before forwarding the message to anyone else. The creator of the hoax wants to spread panic, and if you blindly forward the message to co-workers and acquaintances, you're helping the creator accomplish this task. For example, any email that says "forward to all your friends" is a candidate for hoax research. Disregarding the hoax allows it to die a quick death and keeps users focused on productive tasks. Any concept that spreads quickly through the Internet is referred to as a *meme*.

> Symantec and other vendors maintain pages devoted to bogus hoaxes (www.symantec.com/business/security_response/threatexplorer/ risks/hoaxes.jsp). You can always check there to verify whether an email you've received is indeed a hoax.

Watering Hole Attack   A *watering hole attack* can sound a lot more complicated than it really is. The strategy the attacker takes is simply to identify a site that is visited by those they are targeting, poisoning that site, and then waiting for the results.

As an example, suppose an attacker wants to gain unauthorized access to the servers at Spencer Industries, but Spencer's security is really good. The attacker discovers that

Spencer does not host its own email but instead outsources it to a big cloud provider. Thus, they focus their attention on the weaker security of the cloud provider. On the cloud provider's email site, they install the malware du jour, wait until a Spencer employee gets infected, and suddenly have the access they coveted.

The best defense against a watering hole attack is to make certain that all of your partners are secure. Identify weak links, and bring them up to the same level of security as the rest of your infrastructure.

From an exam perspective, one of the best things about most of these types of attacks is that the name telegraphs the predicament. As an IT administrator, you have no way of preventing someone from trying these tactics against your company, but educating users about them is the best way to prevent them from being successful. The more people are aware of their presence and potential harm, the more likely they can help thwart such attacks since the ultimate objective is to gain unauthorized access to information.

From a real-world perspective, a number of tools are available that can help limit the success of social engineering attacks. Most browsers include a feature allowing them to check websites that a user wishes to visit against a database of known questionable sites and warns them if they find a match.

What Motivates an Attack?

Social engineering is easy to do, even with all of today's technology to prevent it. Education is the key. Educate users on the reasons why someone would attempt to gain access to data and how the company can be negatively affected by it. Educate them on the simple procedures in which they can engage, such as stopping tailgating to increase security. It is surprising how helpful users can be once they understand the reasons why they're being asked to follow certain procedures.

Don't overlook the most common personal motivator of all: greed. It may surprise you, but people can be bribed to give away information, and one of the toughest challenges is someone on the inside who is displeased with the company and eager to profit from it. This is known as a *malicious insider threat,* and it can be far more difficult to contend with than any outside threat since they already have access—both physical and login access—to your systems.

 It is often a comforting thought to think that we cannot be bought. We look to our morals and standards and think that we are above being bribed. The truth of the matter, though, is that almost everyone has a price. Your price may be so high that for all practical purposes you don't have an amount that anyone in the market would pay, but can the same be said for the other administrators in your company?

Social engineering can have a hugely damaging effect on a security system. Always remember that a social engineering attack can occur over the phone, by email, or by a visit. The intent is to acquire access information, such as user IDs and passwords.

Always think of a social engineering attack as one that involves people who are unwitting.

The Principles Behind Social Engineering

A number of principles, or elements, allow social engineering attacks to be effective. Most of these are based on our nature to be helpful, to trust others in general, and to believe that there is a hierarchy of leadership that should be followed. For the exam, be familiar with the following reasons for its effectiveness:

Authority   If it is possible to convince the person you are attempting to trick that you are in a position of authority, they may be less likely to question your request. That position of authority could be upper management, tech support, HR, or law enforcement.

Intimidation   Although authority can be a source of intimidation, it is possible for intimidation to occur in its absence as well. This can be done with threats, with shouting, or even with guilt.

Consensus   Putting the person being tricked at ease by putting the focus on them—listening intently to what they are saying, validating their thoughts, charming them—is the key to this element. The name comes from a desire that we all have to be told that we are right, attractive, intelligent, and so forth, and we tend to be fond of those who confirm this for us. By being so incredibly nice, the social engineer convinces the other party that there is no way their intentions could possibly be harmful.

Discussions at home with a spouse, or casual conversations with associates where we are bragging or trying to impress others, can lead to sharing more information than we should.

Scarcity   Convincing the person who is being tricked that there is a limited supply of something can often be effective if carefully done. For example, convincing them that there are only 100 vacation requests that will be honored for the entire year and that they need to go to a fictitious website now and fill out their information (including username and password, of course) if they want to take a vacation anytime during the current year can dupe some susceptible employees.

Familiarity   Mental guards are often lowered, many times subconsciously, when we are dealing with other individuals that we like. The "like" part can be gained by someone having, or pretending to have, the same interests as we do, be engaged in the same activities, or otherwise working to gain positive attention.

Trust   One of the easiest ways to gain trust is through reciprocation. When someone does something for you, there is often a feeling that you owe that person something. For example, to gain your trust, someone may help you out of a troublesome situation or buy you lunch.

Urgency   The secret for successfully using the urgency element is for the social engineer to convince the individual whom they are attempting to trick that time is of the essence. If they don't do something right away, money will be lost, a nonexistent intruder will get away, the company will suffer irreparable harm, or a plethora of other negative possibilities may occur.

> More than one principle can be used in any given attack. It is not uncommon, for example, to see both scarcity and urgency used together.

Social Engineering Attack Examples

Social engineering attacks are relatively low tech and are more akin to con jobs. Here are a few examples.

Your help desk gets a call at 4 a.m. from someone purporting to be a vice president at your company. She tells the help desk personnel that she is out of town to attend a meeting, that her computer just failed, and that she is sitting in a Kinko's trying to get a file from her desktop computer back at the office. She can't seem to remember her password and user ID. She tells the help desk representative that she needs access to the information right away or the company could lose millions of dollars. Your help desk rep believes the caller and gives the vice president her user ID and password over the phone instead of calling IT. You've been hit!

Another common approach is initiated by a phone call or email from someone claiming to be one of your software vendors, telling you that they have a critical fix that must be installed on your computer system. If this patch isn't installed right away, your system will crash and you'll lose all your data. For some reason, you've changed your maintenance account password, and they can't log on. Your systems operator gives the password to the person instead of calling IT. You've been hit again.

> Users are bombarded with emails and messages on services such as PayPal asking them to confirm their password. These attacks appear to come from the administrative staff of the network. The attacker already has the user ID or screen name, and all that they need to complete the attack is the password. Make sure that your users never give out their user IDs or passwords. Either case potentially completes an attack.

With social engineering, the villain doesn't always have to be seen or heard to conduct the attack. The use of email was mentioned earlier, and in recent years the frequency of attacks via instant messaging has also increased thanks to social media. Attackers can send infected files over *instant messaging (IM)* as easily as they can over email, and this can occur in Facebook, LinkedIn, or anywhere else that IM is possible. A recent virus on the scene accesses a user's IM client and uses the infected user's friend's list to send messages to other users and infect their machines as well.

In Exercise 10.1, we'll show you how to test social engineering in your environment.

EXERCISE 10.1

Test Social Engineering

In this exercise, you'll test your users to determine the likelihood of a social engineering attack. The following are suggestions for tests; you might need to modify them slightly to be appropriate at your workplace. Before doing any of them, make certain that your manager knows that you're conducting such a test and approves of it:

1. Call the receptionist from an outside line. Say that you're a new salesperson and that you didn't write down the username and password that the sales manager gave you last week. Tell the receptionist that you need to get a file from the email system for a presentation tomorrow. Does the receptionist direct you to the appropriate person?

2. Call the human resources department from an outside line. Don't give out your real name, but instead say that you're a vendor who has been working with this company for years. You'd like a copy of the employee phone list to be emailed to you, if possible. Does HR agree to send you the list, which would contain information that could be used to try to guess usernames and passwords?

3. Pick a user at random. Call the user and identify yourself as someone who works for the company. Say that you're supposed to have some new software ready for the user by next week and that you need to know the user's password in order to finish configuring it. Does the user do the right thing?

4. Look on Facebook for people who work for the company and see what information they are posting. Are they talking about co-workers? About clients? Are there pictures posted from inside the workplace where it is possible to see doors, locks, or servers?

The best defense against any social engineering attack is education. Make certain that the employees of your company know how to react to requests like these.

The only preventive measure in dealing with social engineering attacks is to educate your users and staff never to give out passwords and user IDs over the phone or via email or to anyone who isn't positively verified as being who they say they are. Social engineering is a recurring topic that will appear several times throughout this book as it relates to the topic being discussed.

 Real World Scenario

A Security Analogy

In this chapter, we discussed a number of access methods. Sometimes it can be confusing to keep them all straight. To put the main ones somewhat into perspective, think of the problem in terms of a stranger who wants to gain access to your house. Any number of types of individuals may want to get in your house without your knowing it:

- A thief who wants to steal your valuables

- Teenagers itching to do something destructive on a Saturday night

- Homeless people seeking to get in out of the cold and find some food

- A neighbor who has been drinking and accidentally pulls in the wrong driveway and starts to come in, thinking it is his or her house

- A professional hitman waiting for you to come home

There are many more, but these represent a good cross-section of individuals, each of whom has different motives and motivational levels for trying to get in.

To keep the thief out, you could post security signs all around your house and install a home alarm. He might not know if you have ABC Surveillance active monitoring, as the signs say, but he might not want to risk it and will go away looking for an easier target. In the world of computer security, encryption acts like your home alarm and monitoring software, alerting you (or your monitoring company) to potential problems as they arise.

The teenagers just want to do damage somewhere, and your house is as good as the next one. Installing motion lights above the doors and around the side of the house is all you need to make them drive farther down the road. In the world of computer security, good passwords—and policies that are enforced—will keep these would-be intruders out.

The homeless also have no particular affection for your home as opposed to the next. You can keep them out by using locks on your doors and windows and putting a fence around your yard. If they can't get in the fence, they can't approach the house—and if they do manage that, the locks confront them. Firewalls serve this purpose in the world of computer security.

The neighbor just made a legitimate error. That happens. This author once went into the wrong person's tent when camping because they all looked the same. To make yours look different, you can add banners and warnings to the login routines stating, for example, that this is ABC server and that you must be an authorized user to access it.

This leaves the hitman. He has been paid to do a job, and that job entails gaining access to your home. No matter how good the locks are on your house, no matter how many motion lights you put up, if someone's sole purpose in life is to gain access to your house, they will find a way to do it. The same is true of your server. You can implement measures to keep everyone else out, but if someone spends their entire existence dedicated to getting access to that server, they will do so if it entails putting on a heating and air-conditioning uniform and walking past the receptionist, pointing two dozen computers to hashing routines that will crack your passwords, or driving a tank through the side of the building. Your job is to handle all of the reasonable risks that come your way. Some, however, you have to acknowledge have only a slim chance of ever truly being risks, and some, no matter what precautions you take, will not go away.

Understanding Physical Security

Access control is a critical part of physical security, and it can help cut down the possibility of a social engineering or other type of attack from succeeding. Systems must operate in controlled environments in order to be secure. These environments must be, as much as possible, safe from intrusion. Computer system consoles can be a vital point of vulnerability because many administrative functions can be accomplished from the system console. These consoles, as well as the systems themselves, must be protected from physical access.

A key aspect of access control involves *physical barriers*. The objective of a physical barrier is to prevent access to computers and network systems. The most effective physical barrier implementations require that more than one physical barrier be crossed to gain access. This type of approach is called a *multiple barrier system* or *defense in depth*.

Ideally, your systems should have a minimum of three physical barriers:

- The external entrance to the building, referred to as a *perimeter*, which is protected by burglar alarms, external walls, fencing, surveillance, and so on. This should be used with an *access list*, which identifies who can enter a facility and who can be verified by a guard or someone in authority.

- A locked door protecting the computer center; you should also rely on such items as ID badges, proximity readers, fobs, or keys to gain access.

- The entrance to the computer room itself. This should be another locked door that is carefully monitored. Although you try to keep as many intruders out with the other two barriers, many who enter the building could be posing as someone they are not—heating technicians, representatives of the landlord, and so on. Although these pretenses can get them past the first two barriers, the locked computer room door should still stop them.

Any temporary access individual, such as a vending machine repair person or HVAC technician, should be escorted at all times and never left alone in secure areas.

Each of these entrances can be individually secured, monitored, and protected with alarm systems. Figure 10.6 illustrates this concept.

Proximity reader is a catchall term for any ID or card reader capable of reading *proximity cards*. Proximity cards go by a number of different titles, but they are just RFID (radio frequency identification) cards that can be read when close to a reader and truly never need to touch anything. The readers work with 13.56 MHz smart cards and 125 kHz proximity cards, and they can open turnstiles, gates, and any other physical security safeguards once the signal is read.

Although these three barriers won't always stop intruders, they will potentially slow them down enough so that law enforcement can respond before an intrusion is fully developed. Once inside, a truly secure site should be dependent on a physical token (something you have) or biometrics (something you are) for access to the actual network resources.

FIGURE 10.6   The three-layer security model

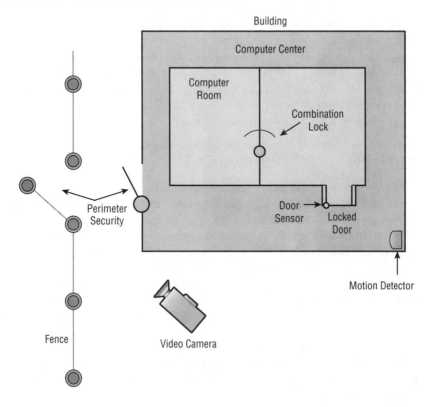

Lighting

Lighting can play an important role in the security of any facility. Poor lighting can lead to a variety of unwanted situations: someone sneaking in a door that is not well lit, an individual passing a checkpoint and being mistaken for another person, or a biometric reading failure. The latter is particularly true with facial recognition, and proper lighting needs to be in place for both the face and the background.

 Lighting can also serve as a deterrent. Bright lighting in a parking lot, access way, or storage area, for example, can help reduce the risk of theft.

Signs

One of the least expensive physical security tools that can be implemented is a *sign*. Signs can be placed around secure areas telling those who venture by that only authorized access is allowed, that trespassers will be prosecuted, and so on. There is a story told of a couple of magicians who drove across country while on tour, and to prevent anyone from breaking into their car, they put a sign on it identifying the car as a transport vehicle for the Centers for Disease Control. Supposedly, it worked, and no one ever broke into the vehicle.

Within Microsoft Windows, you have the ability to put signs (in the form of onscreen pop-up banners) that appear before the login telling similar information—authorized access only, violators will be prosecuted, and so forth. Such banners convey warnings or regulatory information to the user that they must "accept" in order to use the machine or network.

In Windows, the banner is turned on in the Registry through an entry beneath `HKEY_ LOCAL_MACHINE\SOFTWARE\Microsoft\Windows\CurrentVersion\Policies\System`. You can configure `legalnoticecaption` as the caption of the sign that you want to appear and `legalnoticetext` as the text that will show up, which will need to be dismissed before the user can move on. Both are string values accepting any alphanumeric combination.

Fencing, Gates, and Cages

Perimeter security, whether physical or technological, is the first line of defense in your security model. In the case of a physical security issue, the intent is to prevent unauthorized access to resources inside a building or facility.

Physical perimeter security is intended to accomplish for a network what perimeter security does for a building. How do you keep intruders from gaining access to systems and information in the network through the network? In the physical environment, perimeter security is accomplished through fencing, gates, cages, locks, doors, surveillance systems, and alarm systems. This isn't functionally any different from a network, which uses border routers, intrusion detection systems, and firewalls to prevent unauthorized access.

Few security systems can be implemented that don't have weaknesses or vulnerabilities. A determined intruder can, with patience, overcome most security systems. The task may not be easy, and it may require careful planning and study; however, a determined adversary can usually figure out a way. This is why deterrence is so important.

If you want to deter intruders from breaking into your building, you can install improved door locks, coded alarm systems, and magnetic contacts on doors and windows. Remember that you can't always keep an intruder out of your building; however, you can make an intrusion riskier and more likely to be discovered if it happens.

Don't overlook the obvious. Adding a security guard at the front door will go a long way toward keeping an intruder out.

 **Real World Scenario**

Circumventing Security

Recently, a small business noticed that the level of network traffic seemed to be very high in the late evening and early morning. The business couldn't find a network-related reason why this was happening. Upon investigation, the security consultant found that a part-time employee had established a multiuser game server in his office. The game server was set to turn on after 10 p.m. and turn off at 5:30 a.m. This server was hidden under a desk, and it supported some 30 local game players. The part-time employee didn't have a key to the building, so an investigation was conducted to determine how he gained access to the building after hours. The building had electronic locks on its outside entrances, and a passcard was needed to open the doors. The door locks, however, were designed to unlock automatically when someone was leaving the building.

The investigation discovered that the employee and a friend had figured out a way to slide a piece of cardboard under one of the external doors, which activated the door mechanisms and unlocked the doors. The intruders took advantage of this weakness in the doors to gain access after hours without using a passcard and then used the server to play games in his office.

Security Guards

As opposed to signs, one of the most expensive physical security tools that can be implemented is a *guard*. A guard can respond to a situation and be intimidating, but a guard is also fallible and comes at a considerable cost.

Alarms

An *alarm* is used to draw attention to a breach, or suspected breach, when it occurs. This alarm can be sounded in many ways—through the use of a siren, a series of lights (flashing or solid), or an email or voice message. However, it is always intended to draw attention to the event.

A *security zone* is an area in a building where access is individually monitored and controlled. A large network, such as the ones found in a big physical plant, may have many areas that require restricted access. In a building, floors, sections of floors, and even offices can be broken down into smaller areas. These smaller zones are referred to as security zones. In the physical environment, each floor is broken down into separate zones. An alarm system that identifies a zone of intrusion can inform security personnel about an intruder's location in the building; zone notification tells security where to begin looking when they enter the premises.

The concept of security zones is as old as security itself. Most burglar alarms allow the creation of individual zones within a building or residence; these zones are then treated separately by the security staff. In a residence, it would be normal for the bedroom to be assigned a zone of its own so that movement here can occur while other parts of the house may be scanned by a motion detector.

Safe

A *safe* provides a secure, physical location where items can be stored. Those items can include hard copies of your data, backup media, or almost anything else vital to your firm. It is important that access to the safe be tightly governed and that the safe be fireproof and sturdy enough to reduce threats of burglary, robbery, and internal theft. Commercial safes come in many varieties including those that require biometric authentication to open. Be sure to choose a safe that is suited for your purpose.

Secure Cabinets and Enclosures

Hardware security involves applying physical security modifications to secure the system(s) and preventing them from leaving the facility. Don't spend all of your time worrying about intruders coming through the network wire while overlooking the obvious need for physical security.

When it comes to desktop models, adding a lock to the back cover can prevent an intruder with physical access from grabbing the hard drive or damaging the internal components. The lock that connects through a slot on the back of the computer can also go to a cable that then connects to a desk or other solid fixture to keep the entire PC from being carried away. An example of this type of configuration is shown in Figure 10.7.

FIGURE 10.7   A cable can be used to keep a desktop machine from easily being taken.

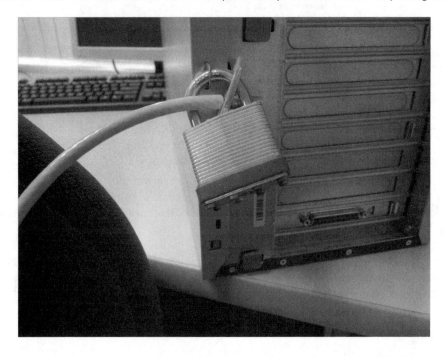

In addition to running a cable to the desk, you can choose to run an end of it up to the monitor if theft of peripherals is a problem in your company. An example of this type of physical security is shown in Figure 10.8.

FIGURE 10.8   If theft of equipment is a possibility, run one end of the cable from the monitor to the desktop computer through a hole in the work desk.

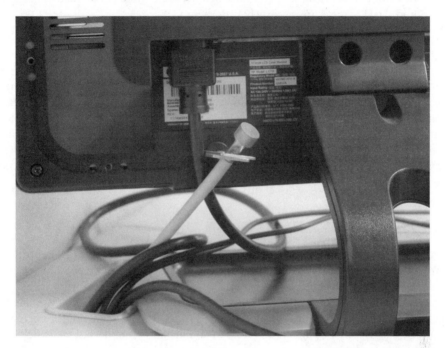

You should also consider using a *safe* and *locking cabinets* to protect backup media, documentation, and any other physical artifacts that could do harm if they fell into the wrong hands. Server racks should lock the rack-mounted servers into the cabinets to prevent someone from simply pulling one and walking out the front door with it.

 Although this discussion relates to physical security, don't overlook encryption as a means of increasing data security should a desktop or laptop machine be stolen. You can also consider removing the hard drives in areas that are difficult to monitor and forcing all data to be stored on the network.

Protected Distribution

A *protected distribution system (PDS)* is one in which the network is secure enough to allow for the transmission of classified information in unencrypted format—in other words, where physical network security has been substituted for encryption security. In a small office, for example, you could ban the use of wireless devices and require that all such devices be connected to a bus topology network that is clearly visible as it runs through the space.

Moving forward from this overly simplistic scenario, it is possible to create a much larger network that uses fiber, various topologies, and so on, as long as you still have the ability to monitor and control the span of it. Such networks were once called "approved circuits," and the U.S. government largely uses them.

Protected Cabling

A secure system is only as secure as its weakest link, and sometimes that weak link can be the cabling. Closely associated with protected distribution systems, protected cabling involves using locked wiring closets, locked spare jacks, conduit, and cable trays to prioritize the protection of the cabling. Physical security safeguards are put in place to prevent accidental damage, disruption, and physical tampering with the cabling, as well as to help prevent eavesdropping or "in-transit modification" of transmissions (NIST 800-53r4).

Airgap

An *airgap* (or, more commonly, *air gap*) is a network security measure used to ensure that a secure computer network is physically isolated from unsecured networks. Those "unsecured networks" include both the Internet and any unsecured local area networks.

Airgapping is commonly used in environments where networks or devices are rated to handle different levels of classified information (classified and unclassified, for example). When moving data from one system to another, confidentiality models (such as Bell–LaPadula) are commonly used.

Mantrap

High-security installations use a type of intermediate access control mechanism called a *mantrap* (also occasionally written as *man-trap*). Mantraps require visual identification, as well as authentication, to gain access. A mantrap makes it difficult for a facility to be accessed by large numbers of individuals at once because it allows only one or two people into a facility at a time. It's usually designed to contain an unauthorized, potentially hostile person physically until authorities arrive. Figure 10.9 illustrates a mantrap. Notice in this illustration that the visual verification is accomplished using a security guard. A properly developed mantrap includes bulletproof glass, high-strength doors, and locks. After a person is inside the facility, additional security and authentication may be required for further entrance.

FIGURE 10.9   A mantrap in action

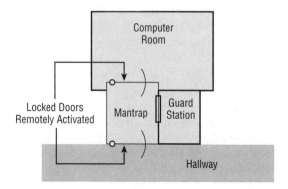

 Some mantraps even include scales to weigh the person. Weight can be used to help identify a person, and the scales are often used to make sure that no one is sneaking in. If the weight of the scale appears too high, an officer can check to make sure that two people haven't crowded in who are attempting to bypass security.

Faraday Cage

Shielding refers to the process of preventing electronic emissions from your computer systems from being used to gather intelligence and preventing outside electronic emissions from disrupting your information-processing abilities. In a fixed facility, such as a computer center, surrounding the computer room with a *Faraday cage* can provide electronic shielding. A Faraday cage usually consists of an electrically conductive wire mesh or other conductor woven into a "cage" that surrounds a room. The conductor is then grounded. Because of this cage, few electromagnetic signals can either enter or leave the room, thereby reducing the ability to eavesdrop on a computer conversation. To verify the functionality of the cage, radio frequency (RF) emissions from the room are tested with special measuring devices.

Lock Types

Locks come in many different sizes, shapes, types, and designs. Likewise, they offer many different levels of security and/or ease/difficulty of operation. Some locks look impressive but can be easily broken or circumvented. Others are quite simplistic in design yet are next to impossible to thwart.

As an administrator, you need to make sure that the lock being used for a purpose is able to fulfill that purpose. You can rarely go wrong by using a lock that provides a higher level of security than you need for the job, but you can fail horribly by using a lock that fails to provide the needed level of security for the task.

A friend once locked his keys in his vehicle in a retail parking lot and did not discover this until he was done shopping. Sure enough, when he looked through the rolled-up window of the driver's door, the keys were still visible in the ignition. He tried to conjure up a way to get the door open without setting off the vehicle's alarm system, but—after more than 30 minutes of plotting, scheming, and trying—he couldn't come up with a way to do so and called a locksmith. The locksmith arrived and walked self-assuredly around the car one time and then reached through the already rolled-down passenger window and flipped the button to unlock all the doors electronically.

The point of the story is that any lock is only as good as its use. There are many incidents where complicated locking mechanisms are sidestepped because they weren't active at the moment of an incident and a perpetrator bypassed them altogether.

A good overview of the various types of locks can be found on the Security Blogger site at www.thesecurityblogger.com/the-many-different-types-of-locks/.

Biometrics

Biometric systems use some kind of unique biological trait to identify a person, such as fingerprints, patterns on the retina, and handprints. Some methods that are used include hand scanners, retinal scanners, facial recognition applications, and keystroke recognition programs, which can be used as part of the access control mechanisms. These devices should be coupled into security-oriented computer systems that record all access attempts. They should also be under surveillance in order to prevent individuals from bypassing them.

These technologies are becoming more reliable, and they will become widely used over the next few years. Many laptops sold now have a fingerprint reader built in. The costs associated with these technologies have fallen dramatically in recent years. One of the best independent sources of information on development in the field of biometrics is BiometricNews.net, where you can find links to publications and their blog. From a reference standpoint, be sure to visit www.nist.gov/itl/biometrics/index.cfm.

Real World Scenario

Installing Biometric Devices

Problem

You've been asked to solve the problem of people forgetting smartcards that give them access to the computer center. Hardly a day goes by that an employee doesn't forget to bring their card. This causes a great deal of disruption in the workplace because someone has to reissue smartcards constantly. The company has tried everything it could think of short of firing people who forget their cards. What would you recommend to the company?

Solution

Investigate whether biometric devices (such as hand scanners) or number access locks can be used in lieu of smartcards for access. These devices will allow people who forget their smartcards to enter areas to which they should have access.

Barricades/Bollards

To stop someone from entering a facility, barricades or gauntlets can be used. These are often used in conjunction with guards, fencing, and other physical security measures, but they can be used as stand-alones as well.

Tokens/Cards

Physical tokens or *FOBs* are anything that a user must have on them to access network resources, and they are often associated with devices that enable the user to generate a one-time password authenticating their identity. SecurID, from RSA, is one of the best-known examples of a physical token. No matter how secure you think your system is, you'll never be able to stop everyone. But your goal is to stop most attempts and, at the very least, slow down the most sophisticated. As an analogy, the front door of your home may contain a lock and a deadbolt. This minimal security is enough to convince most burglars to try somewhere less secure. A professional who is bent on entering your home, however, could always take the appropriate lock-defeating tools to the door.

Environmental Controls

The location of your computer facility is critical to its security. Computer facilities must be placed in a location that is physically possible to secure. Additionally, the location must have the proper capabilities to manage temperature, humidity, and other environmental factors necessary to the health of your computer systems. The following sections look at various environmental elements about which you must be aware.

HVAC

If the computer systems for which you're responsible require special environmental considerations, you'll need to establish cooling and humidity control. Ideally, systems are located in the middle of the building, and they're ducted separately from the rest of the HVAC (heating, ventilation, and air-conditioning) system. It's a common practice for modern buildings to use a zone-based air-conditioning environment, which allows the environmental plant to be turned off when the building isn't occupied. A computer room will typically require full-time environmental control.

> In the event of power failure, HVAC for the server room should be on the uninterruptable power supply (UPS) in order to keep it cool.

Hot and Cold Aisles

There are often multiple rows of servers located in racks in server rooms. The rows of servers are known as aisles, and they can be cooled as *hot aisles* and *cold aisles*. With a hot aisle, hot air outlets are used to cool the equipment, whereas with cold aisles, cold air intake is used to cool the equipment. Combining the two, you have cold air intake from below the aisle and hot air outtake above it, providing constant circulation.

It is important that the hot air exhausting from one aisle of racks not be the intake air pulled in by the next row of racks or overheating will occur. Air handlers must move the hot air out, whereas cold air, usually coming from beneath a raised floor, is supplied as the intake air. Figure 10.10 shows an example of a hot and cold aisle design.

FIGURE 10.10   A hot and cold aisle design

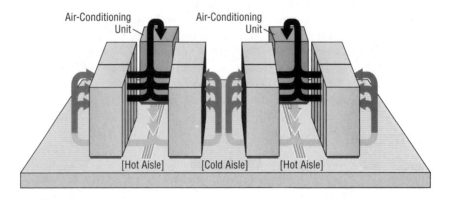

Fire Suppression

Fire suppression is a key consideration in computer-center design. Fire suppression is the act of extinguishing a fire versus preventing one. Two primary types of fire-suppression systems in use are fire extinguishers and fixed systems.

Fire Extinguishers

Fire extinguishers are portable systems. The selection and use of fire extinguishers is critical. Four primary types of fire extinguishers are available, classified by the types of fires they put out: A, B, C, and D. Table 10.1 describes the four types of fires and the capabilities of various extinguishers.

TABLE 10.1   Fire extinguisher ratings

Type	Use	Retardant composition
A	Wood and paper	Largely water or chemical
B	Flammable liquids	Fire-retardant chemicals
C	Electrical	Nonconductive chemicals
D	Flammable metals	Varies; type specific

A type K extinguisher that is marketed for use on cooking oil fires can also be found in stores. In actuality, this is a subset of class B extinguishers.

Several multipurpose extinguishers combine several extinguisher capabilities in a single bottle. The more common multipurpose extinguishers are A-B, B-C, and ABC.

The recommended procedure for using a fire extinguisher is called the *PASS method*: Pull, Aim, Squeeze, and Sweep. Fire extinguishers usually operate for only a few seconds—if you use one, make sure that you don't fixate on a single spot. Most fire extinguishers have a limited effective range of between 3 and 8 feet.

A major concern with electrical fires is that they can recur quickly if the voltage isn't removed. Make sure that you remove voltage from systems when a fire occurs.

Most fire extinguishers require an annual inspection. This is a favorite area of citation by fire inspectors. You can contract with services to do this on a regular basis: They will inspect or replace your fire extinguishers according to a scheduled agreement.

Fixed Systems

Fixed systems are usually part of the building systems. The most common fixed systems combine fire detectors with fire-suppression systems, where the detectors trigger either because of a rapid temperature change or because of excessive smoke. The fire-suppression system uses either water sprinklers or fire-suppressing gas. Water systems work with overhead nozzles, as illustrated in Figure 10.11. These systems are the most common method in modern buildings. Water systems are reliable and relatively inexpensive, and they require little maintenance.

FIGURE 10.11   Water-based fire-suppression system

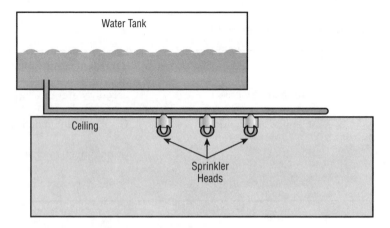

The one drawback of water-based systems is that they cause extreme damage to energized electrical equipment such as computers. These systems can be tied into relays that terminate power to computer systems before they release water into the building.

Gas-based systems were originally designed to use carbon dioxide and later halon gas. Halon gas isn't used anymore because it damages the ozone layer. Environmentally acceptable substitutes are now available, with FM200 being one of the most common. The principle of a gas system is that it displaces the oxygen in the room, thereby removing this essential component of a fire.

WARNING   Evacuate the room immediately in the event of a fire. Halon-based systems work by removing oxygen from the fire, and this can suffocate anyone in the room as well.

The major drawback of gas-based systems is that they require sealed environments to operate. Special ventilation systems are usually installed in gas systems to limit air circulation when the gas is released. Gas systems are also expensive, and they're usually implemented only in computer rooms or other areas where water would cause damage to technology or other intellectual property.

EMI Shielding

Electromagnetic interference (EMI) and *radio frequency interference (RFI)* are two additional environmental considerations. Motors, lights, and other types of electromechanical objects cause EMI, which can cause circuit overload, spikes, or electrical component failure. Making sure that all signal lines are properly shielded and grounded can minimize EMI. Devices that generate EMI should be as physically distant from cabling as is feasible because this type of energy tends to dissipate quickly with distance.

Figure 10.12 shows a motor generating EMI. In this example, the data cable next to the motor is picking up the EMI. This causes the signal to deteriorate, and it might eventually cause the line to be unusable. The gray area in the illustration is representative of the interference generated by the motor.

FIGURE 10.12   Electromagnetic interference (EMI) pickup in a data cable

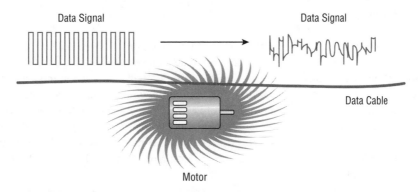

RFI is the byproduct of electrical processes, similar to EMI. The major difference is that RFI is usually projected across a radio spectrum. Motors with defective brushes can generate RFI, as can a number of other devices. If RF levels become too high, it can cause the receivers in wireless units to become deaf. This process is called *desensitizing*, and it occurs because of the volume of RF energy present. This can occur even if the signals are on different frequencies.

Figure 10.13 demonstrates the desensitizing process occurring with a wireless access portal (WAP). The only solution to this problem is to move the devices farther apart or to turn off the RFI generator.

In 1985, Dutch researcher Wim van Eck proposed that it is possible to eavesdrop on CRT and LCD displays by detecting their electromagnetic emissions. Known as *Van Eck phreaking*, this problem/possibility made the news because of potential problems with electronic voting machines. Commonly associated countermeasures recommended by TEMPEST include shielding.

FIGURE 10.13 RF desensitization occurring as a result of cell phone interference

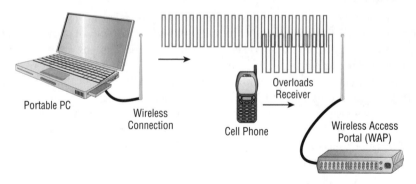

Portable PC

Wireless Connection

Cell Phone

Overloads Receiver

Wireless Access Portal (WAP)

Project TEMPEST

TEMPEST is the name of a project authorized by the U.S. government in the late 1950s. TEMPEST was concerned with reducing electronic noise from devices that would divulge intelligence about systems and information. This program has become a standard for computer systems certification. *TEMPEST shielding protection* means that a computer system doesn't emit any significant amounts of EMI or RFI. For a device to be approved as TEMPEST-compliant, it must undergo extensive testing done to exacting standards dictated by the U.S. government. Today, control zones and white noise are used to accomplish the shielding. TEMPEST-certified equipment frequently costs twice as much as non-TEMPEST equipment.

Environmental Monitoring

Environmental concerns include considerations about water and flood damage as well as fire suppression. Computer rooms should have fire and moisture detectors. Most office buildings have water pipes and other moisture-carrying systems in the ceiling. If a water pipe bursts (which is common in minor earthquakes), the computer room could become flooded. Water and electricity don't mix. Moisture monitors would automatically kill power in a computer room if moisture were detected, so the security professional should know where the water cutoffs are located.

Fire, no matter how small, can cause damage to computer systems. Apart from the high heat, which can melt or warp plastics and metals, the smoke from the fire can permeate the computers. Smoke particles are large enough to lodge under the read/write head of a hard disk, thereby causing data loss. In addition, the fire-suppression systems in most buildings consist of water under pressure, and the water damage from putting out even a small fire could wipe out an entire datacenter.

The three critical components of any fire are heat, fuel, and oxygen. If any component of this trilogy is removed, a fire isn't possible. Most fire-suppression systems work on this concept.

Temperature and Humidity Controls

Many computer systems require *temperature and humidity control* for reliable service. Large servers, communications equipment, and drive arrays generate considerable amounts of heat; this is especially true of mainframe and older minicomputers. An environmental system for this type of equipment is a significant expense beyond the actual computer system costs. Fortunately, newer systems operate in a wider temperature range. Most new systems are designed to operate in an office environment.

Environmental systems should be monitored to prevent the computer center's humidity level from dropping below 50 percent. Electrostatic damage is likely to occur when humidity levels get too low.

Humidity control prevents the buildup of static electricity in the environment. If the humidity drops much below 50 percent, electronic components are extremely vulnerable to damage from electrostatic shock. Most environmental systems also regulate humidity; however, a malfunctioning system can cause the humidity to be extracted almost entirely from a room. Make sure that environmental systems are regularly serviced.

Cable Locks

Adding a *cable lock* between a laptop and a desk prevents someone from picking it up and walking away with a copy of your customer database. All laptop cases include a built-in security slot in which a cable lock can be inserted to prevent it from easily being removed from the premises (see Figure 10.14).

FIGURE 10.14 A cable in the security slot keeps the laptop from easily being removed.

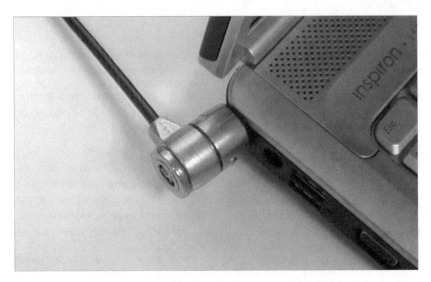

Screen Filters

Screen filters, also known as *privacy filters*, go over the screen and restrict the viewing angle to straight on. These prevent individuals standing at the periphery from being able to see data on the screen and are intended to be used to decrease the success of shoulder surfing.

Cameras

In high-security and military environments, an armed guard as well as *security cameras* or *video surveillance* would be placed at the mantrap. Beyond mantraps, you can combine guards with cameras (or even the threat of cameras) to create a potent deterrent. The cameras can send signals to a room where they are monitored by a guard capable of responding to a situation when the need arises.

Camera vs. Guard

The camera versus guard debate is an old one. You must decide what is best for your own environment. The benefit of a camera (also known as *closed-circuit television*, or *CCTV*) is that it is always running and can record everything it sees, creating evidence that can be admissible in court if necessary. On the other hand, it is stationary, lacks any sort of intelligence, is possible to avoid, and needs someone to monitor the feed or review the tape to be effective, which many times does not happen until a problem has been discovered.

The benefit of a guard is that the person can move about, apply intelligence to situations, and collect evidence. The guard, however, is not always recording, can be avoided, and has more downtime.

 Real World Scenario

Evaluating Your Security System

You've been asked to evaluate your building's security system. The president chose you because you understand computers and, after all, these new alarm systems are computerized.

In evaluating the environment, you notice that there is a single control panel for the whole building. A few motion detectors are located in the main hallway. Beyond that, no additional security components are installed.

This situation is fairly normal in a small building. You could recommend enhancing the system by adding motion detectors in each major hallway. You could also install video monitoring (also known as surveillance) cameras, such as closed-circuit television (CCTV), at all of the entrances. Most security/surveillance CCTV cameras have *PTZ* (Pan, Tilt, and Zoom) capabilities too, and they can often do so based on sound or motion. You should also consider recommending that they upgrade the perimeter security by adding contact sensors on all the doors and ground-floor windows.

Always evaluate the building from a multitiered approach. Incorporate as many different elements as you can where needed: perimeter security, security zones, and surveillance.

Motion Detection

A *motion detection* system can monitor a location and signal an alarm if it picks up movement. Systems are commonly used to monitor homes, and the same technology can be used to protect server rooms, office buildings, or any other location. The motion detection can be accomplished with sensors that are infrared, microwave, or sonic, or that utilize a variety of hybrid sensors.

In Exercise 10.2, we'll walk you through the evaluation of your environment.

EXERCISE 10.2

Security Zones in the Physical Environment

As a security administrator, you'll need to evaluate your workplace and consider physical zones that should exist in terms of the different types of individuals who might be present. If your workplace is already divided into zones, forget that this has been done and start from scratch. Answer the following questions:

1. What areas represent the physical dimension of your workplace (buildings, floors, offices, and so on)?

2. Which areas are accessible by everyone from administrators to visitors? Can a visitor ever leave the reception area without an escort and, if so, go to a restroom, meeting room, break room, and so forth?

3. In what areas are users allowed to move about freely? Are you certain that no visitors or guests can enter those areas?

4. What areas are administrators allowed to enter that users cannot—server room? Wiring closets? How do you keep users out and verify that only administrators enter?

5. Are wall jacks, network access, or Wi-Fi available in areas where visitors are located?

6. Do other areas need to be secured for entities beyond the user/administrator distinction (such as groups)?

Once you're armed with this information, you should look for ways to address the weaknesses. Evaluate your environment routinely to make certain that the zones that exist within your security plan are still relevant. Always start from scratch and pretend that no zones exist; then verify that the zones that do exist are the same as those that you've created in this exercise.

Logs

Log files record events that have occurred and under what circumstances. Logging functions should provide sufficient information about the nature of the attack to help administrators determine what has happened and to assist in evaluating the threat. This information can then be used to devise methods to counter the threat, investigate it further, or serve as evidence in legal proceedings.

Infrared Detection

Just as motion detectors work by identifying changes in motion, *infrared detectors* work by detecting changes in infrared radiation—traditionally thermal heat. Once changes outside of the set threshold are detected, an alarm or alert can be triggered and responded to according to whatever established protocols are in place.

Key Management

Key management is an area of importance that continues to grow as PKI services increase and expand to mobile. Chapter 8, "Cryptography," focuses on cryptography and the issues associated with managing keys.

Various Control Types

One of the most generic terms in security is *control*. The word is used in so many different ways that its meaning can become blurred. The best thing to do is to equate the word with whatever entity is charged with the task at the moment. That task can be preventing something from happening, logging when something does, responding to it, or any variety of other possibilities. For the exam, CompTIA has categorized controls into eight types as follows:

Deterrent   A *deterrent control* is anything intended to warn a would-be attacker that they should not attack. This could be a posted warning notice that they will be prosecuted to the fullest extent of the law, locks on doors, barricades, lighting, or anything that can delay or discourage an attack.

Preventive   As the name implies, the purpose of *preventive controls* is to stop something from happening. These controls can include locked doors that keep intruders out, user training on potential harm (to keep them vigilant and alert), or biometric devices and guards that deny access until authentication has occurred.

Detective   The purpose of a *detective control* is to uncover a violation. The only time that they would be relevant is when a preventive control has failed and they need to sound an alarm. A detective control can range from a checksum on a downloaded file, an alarm that sounds when a door has been pried open, or an antivirus scanner that actively looks for problems. It could also be a sonic detector, motion sensor, or anything that would detect that an intrusion is under way.

Corrective   *Corrective controls* are, as the name implies, those intended to correct a situation: to prevent the recurrence of errors. Corrective controls typically begin when improper outcomes are detected. Some examples of corrective controls in the administrative world include quality circle teams and budget variance reports.

Compensating   *Compensating controls* are backup controls that come into play only when other controls have failed. An office building may have a complex electronic lock on the door (preventive control) and a sign that you will be arrested if you enter (deterrent control), but it is a safe bet that they will also have an alarm that sounds (a compensating control) when the door is jimmied as well as a backup generator (another compensating control) to keep that electronic lock active when the power goes out.

Technical *Technical controls* are those controls implemented through technology. They may be deterrent, preventive, detective, or compensating (but not administrative), and include such things as firewalls, IDS, and IPS.

Administrative An *administrative control* is one that comes down through policies, procedures, and guidelines. An example of an administrative control is the escalation procedure to be used in the event of a break-in: who is notified first, who is called second, and so on. Another example of an administrative control is the list of steps to be followed when a key employee is terminated: disable their account, change the server password, and so forth.

Physical *Physical controls* are those put in place to reduce the risk of harm coming to physical property, information, computer systems, or other assets. These typically include cameras, guards, fences, barricades, and other items discussed earlier in this chapter related to physical security.

An Analogy of Control Types

To prepare for the certification exam, it often helps to use analogies to put topics in context. In light of that, consider a residential home this author owns in the middle of town. I grow prized tomato plants in the backyard, and it is very important to me that no one goes back there for fear that they might do something to harm the tomatoes. Thus, I implement the following controls:

- *Administrative:* I establish a number of policies to keep the tomatoes safe:
  - *Preventive:* I instruct every member of my family that they are not to go into the backyard and they are not to let anyone else go back there either.
  - *Deterrent:* I tell the kids that if I ever hear of any of them—or their friends—being the backyard, I will take away their allowance for month.
  - *Detective:* As a matter of routine, I want each member of the family to look out the window on a regular basis to see if anyone has wandered into the yard.
  - *Compensating:* Every member of the family is instructed on how to call the police the minute they see anyone in the yard.
- *Technical:* Not trusting that the administrative controls will do the job without fail, I implement a number of technical controls:
  - *Preventive/Physical:* I put up a fence around the yard, and the door that leads out from the garage is locked.
  - *Deterrent:* "Beware of Dog" signs are posted all over the fence (although I have no dog).
  - *Detective:* Sensors are placed on the gate to trigger an alarm if the gate is opened.
  - *Compensating:* Triggered alarms turn on the backyard sprinklers at full volume to douse any intruder who wanders in.

These controls work in conjunction with one another to help keep individuals who should not be there out of the backyard and away from my tomatoes. Naturally, as the owner/administrator, I have the ability to override all of them as needed. I can ignore the warning signs, turn off physical controls such as the sprinklers, and get full access to the garden when I desire. The controls are not in place to hinder my access, but only to obstruct and prevent others from accessing the yard.

Data Security and Privacy Practices

One of the risks of working with data is that it can be difficult to secure. It can be seen not only by the intended parties but by others as well. Some of the dangers can come about as a routine part of using the data, whereas others can be introduced when you no longer need the data and are ready to get rid of it.

Regardless of whether the harms are the result of daily access or end-of-life destruction, you are responsible for safeguarding and protecting that data. Some of the issues associated with this role are discussed in the following sections.

Data Destruction and Media Sanitation

As an example of the need for such a policy, consider that the capacity of flash drives (also known as thumb drives, memory sticks, jump drives, and USB drives) has grown significantly, as has their popularity. Many users now store all of their files on a flash drive that they transport with them everywhere, rather than save files to hard drives on one or more computers (work, home, and so on). The technology is stable enough so that this scenario works well, and there are no problems until you need to erase all traces of a file.

Imagine that your flash drive has one or more files on it that, if found, could get you into serious hot water. The files could be inappropriate nonbusiness pictures, tax returns, Social Security numbers, or almost anything else that you would not want to fall into the wrong hands. Deleting these files isn't a good solution since what actually is deleted is the pointer to the file—the content still remains until it is overwritten. Someone armed with the right tools (many shareware ones are available) and knowledge could recover the file with little trouble.

A number of programs can be found online that purport to delete the files permanently by wiping the free space. Trust them if you wish, but according to Dan Goodin, IT Security Editor at the technology news and information website, *Ars Technica*:

> ...as much as 67 percent of data stored in a file remained even after it was deleted from an SSD (Solid State Drive) using the secure erase feature ... Other overwrite operations, which securely delete files by repeatedly rewriting the data stored in a particular disk location, failed by similarly large margins when used to erase a single file on an SSD.

For more information, see www.theregister.co.uk/2011/02/21/flash_drive_erasing _peril/.

Burning   Controlled incineration, or *burning*, is a good method for destroying hard copies of data (paper) and some media (ancient floppy disks, for example), but its use is often limited as a disposal method due to environmental concerns. Some media, such as DVDs and CDs, can give off toxic fumes when burned, and thus you should use this method of disposal very sparingly.

Shredding   *Shredding* reduces the size of objects with the intent of making them no longer usable. The most common type of shredding is done with a paper shredder (many of which will also shred CDs and DVDs), and a number of different types and qualities of shredders are available. Strip shredders are usually the fastest because they cut the paper in only one direction; the size of strips they produce is important since smaller strips are harder for a troublemaker to reassemble than are larger strips.

A cross-cut shredder cuts the paper in more than one direction, and it is usually more secure than a strip shredder. Micro shredders are types of cross-cut shredders that produce very small pieces. Naturally, they take longer than strip shredders since they are doing more, and this can be a big disadvantage. To make up for the time element, many companies contract with commercial shredding firms to handle large loads.

Where it can be used, shredding has an advantage over most other methods of destruction in that the equipment used is portable, inexpensive, and easily available.

Pulping   Instead of shredding paper, another option is *pulping* it. Pulping reduces paper to liquid slurry before making it available for reuse in post-consumer products. Although it is a great solution for minimizing waste, the disadvantages include transportation to a pulping facility and the danger of trusting that documents will be secure until pulped. A more secure possibility is to shred the documents first and render them "unreadable" before pulping.

When "trusting" another firm—whether it be a shredding service, a pulping operation, or other—always insist on receiving a Certificate of Destruction. This document should be kept on record for some time in case an audit is done to discover what became of certain files.

Pulverizing   With *pulverizing*, media (usually documents) are fed into a pulverizer that uses hydraulic or pneumatic action to reduce the materials to loose fibers and shards. By destroying it so completely, the big advantage is that readability is assuredly gone. The disadvantages are the cost and the availability; very few commercial disposers use this method.

Degaussing   The process of *degaussing* is used to remove data from magnetic storage media such as hard drives and magnetic tapes. In it, a large magnet—known as a degausser—is used to destroy the data held on the magnetic storage device so that it can no longer be recovered. Because the data is irretrievably lost, degaussing is often referred to as erasure as well.

Purging   *Purging* data is simply removing it and the traces of it. This is usually done with storage devices, such as hard drives, and is often referred to as *sanitation*. Not only would you delete files, for instance, but you would also remove traces of them from the trash bin with the intent that the data could not be reconstructed by any known technique.

Wiping   *Wiping* goes further than purging and is also known as *overwriting* or *shredding*. With wiping, the data that was there is first replaced with something else and then removed. That way, if the data is somehow recovered, what comes back is the overwritten data rather than the original data. The simplest overwrite technique writes a pattern of zeros over the original data.

Data Sensitivity Labeling and Handling

Many different classifications can be placed on data. The classification is important because it should determine how the data is protected and handled. The sections that follow discuss some of the most common data sensitivity labels and the differences between them.

Confidential

This classification is used to identify low-level secrets; it's generally the lowest level of classification used by the military. It's used extensively to prevent access to sensitive information. Information that is lower than Confidential is generally considered Unclassified. The Confidential classification, however, allows information to be restricted for access under the Freedom of Information Act. The maintenance requirements for a machine gun may be classified as Confidential; this information would include drawings, procedures, and specifications that disclose how the weapon works.

Private

Private information is intended only for internal use within the organization. This type of information could potentially embarrass the company, disclose trade secrets, or adversely affect personnel. Private information may also be referred to as *working documents* or *work product*. It's important that private information not be disclosed because it can potentially involve litigation if the disclosure is improper.

Internal information includes personnel records, financial working documents, ledgers, customer lists, and virtually any other information that is needed to run a business. This information is valuable and must be protected. In the case of personnel and medical records, disclosure to unauthorized personnel creates liability issues. Many organizations are unwilling to do anything more than to verify employment because of the fear of unauthorized disclosure.

A school views student information as internal. Schools can't release information about students without specific permission from the student.

Restricted information could seriously damage the organization if disclosed. It includes proprietary processes, trade secrets, strategic information, and marketing plans. This information should never be disclosed to an outside party unless senior management gives specific authorization. In many cases, this type of information is also placed on a *need-to-know basis*—unless you need to know, you won't be informed.

Public

Public information is primarily made available either to the larger public or to specific individuals who need it. Financial statements of a privately held organization might be information that is available publicly but only to individuals or organizations that have a legitimate need for it.

The important thing to keep in mind is that an organization needs to develop policies about what information is available and for what purposes it will be disseminated. It's also helpful to make sure that members of the organization know who has authorization to make these kinds of disclosures. Some organizations gather competitive data for a fee; they often use social engineering approaches to gain information about a business. Good policies help prevent the accidental dissemination of sensitive information.

Limited distribution information isn't intended for release to the public. This category of information isn't secret, but it's private. If a company is seeking to obtain a line of credit, the information provided to a bank is of a private nature. This information, if disclosed to competitors, might give them insight into the organization's plans or financial health. If disclosed to customers, it might scare them and cause them to switch to a competitor.

Some EULAs now limit the information that users can disclose about problems with their software. These new statements have not yet been challenged in court. Try to avoid being the test case for this new and alarming element of some software licenses; read the EULA before you agree to it.

These types of disclosures are usually held in confidence by banks and financial institutions. These institutions typically have privacy and confidentiality regulations as well as policies that must be followed by all employees of the institution.

Software manufacturers typically release early versions of their products to customers who are willing to help evaluate functionality. Early versions of software may not always work properly, and they often have features that aren't included in the final version. This version of the software is a *beta test*. Before beta testers are allowed to use the software, they're required to sign a nondisclosure agreement (NDA). The NDA tells the tester what privacy requirements exist for the product. The product being developed will change, and any problems with the beta version probably won't be a great secret. However, the NDA reminds the testers of their confidentiality responsibilities.

NDAs are common in the technology arena. Make sure that you read any NDA thoroughly before you sign it. You don't have to sign an NDA to be bound by it: if you agree that you'll treat the information as private and then receive the information, you have, in essence, agreed to an NDA. In most cases, this form of verbal NDA is valid for only one year.

Statements indicating privacy or confidentiality are common on limited-access documents. They should indicate that disclosure of the information without permission is a breach of confidentiality. This may help someone remember that the information isn't for public dissemination.

Instead of limited distribution, marketing materials are examples of information that should be available for *full distribution*. Annual reports to stockholders and other information of a public relations nature are also examples of full-distribution materials.

The key element of the full-distribution classification involves decision-making responsibility. Who makes the decision about full disclosure? Larger organizations have a corporate communications department that is responsible for managing this process. If you aren't sure, it's a good idea to ask about dissemination of information. Don't assume that you know; that is the purpose of an information classification policy.

Proprietary

The *proprietary* label is often used with data related to business operations. As such, it is usually synonymous with confidential and should be treated with the same attention and care.

PII

Personally identifiable information (PII) is a catchall for any data that can be used to uniquely identify an individual. This data can be anything from the person's name to a fingerprint (think biometrics), credit card number, or patient record. The term became mainstream when the NIST (National Institute of Standards and Technology) began issuing guides and recommendations regarding it.

NIST defines PII as follows:

> Any information about an individual maintained by an agency, including (1) any information that can be used to distinguish or trace an individual's identity, such as name, social security number, date and place of birth, mother's maiden name, or biometric records; and (2) any other information that is linked or linkable to an individual, such as medical, educational, financial, and employment information.
>
> NIST published Special Publication 800-122, Guide to Protecting the Confidentiality of Personally Identifiable Information (PII)

Users within your organization should understand PII and the reasons to safeguard their own data as well as respect the records of customers and other users. Also, according to NIST:

> For PII protection, awareness methods include informing staff of new scams that are being used to steal identities, providing updates on privacy items in the news such as government data breaches and their effect on individuals and the organization, providing examples of how staff members have been held accountable for inappropriate actions, and providing examples of recommended privacy practices.
>
> NIST published Special Publication 800-122, Guide to Protecting the Confidentiality of Personally Identifiable Information (PII)

To help users understand the significance of PII, explain that the SIM (Subscriber Identification Module) card in their smartphone contains PII information about them and that they would not want it to fall into the wrong hands.

PHI

What CompTIA refers to as *personal health information (PHI)* is more commonly known as *protected* health information and should be thought of as a subset of PII that is protected by law. Under U.S. law, for example, PHI is any information about health status, provision of health care, or payment for health care that is created or collected by a "Covered Entity" that can be linked to a specific individual.

Data Roles

There are any number of roles that an individual can play in relation to a data file. Computer operating systems and network operating systems offer many different choices, but for the exam you should know these three key data roles:

Owner   When it comes to data, the *owner* is the person (or people) identified (by law, contract, or policy) with the responsibility for granting access to users and ensuring appropriate use of the information. Usually, this is the person who created the file, but that need not always be the case. FERPA (the Family Educational Rights and Privacy Act), for example, requires there to be an "information authority" (owner) for student academic records.

Steward/Custodian   The *steward*, or *custodian*, is the person (or people) who has operational responsibility for the physical and electronic security of the data. Typically, this is the systems administrator, database administrator, or programmer/analyst. In most large companies, administrative employees share the role of information steward, whereas a small business unit might have the role fulfilled by an IT person who has a handful of other responsibilities as well.

Privacy Officer   The *privacy officer*, or *chief privacy officer (CPO)*, is the person within an organization charged with safeguarding personal information. In medical organizations, the individual is charged with protection of patient medical records to stay in compliance with HIPAA (the Health Insurance Portability and Accountability Act), whereas in financial organizations, they safeguard consumer financial and banking transactions in compliance with the Fair Credit Reporting Act and the Gramm-Leach-Bliley Act, among others.

Data Retention

A significant portion of this chapter discussed disposing of data, but the question of how long data needs to be kept must factor in as well. You should take into account government regulations on data storage for your business as well as company policies. A *data retention* policy should exist within each organization to outline the guidelines for retaining information for operational use while ensuring adherence to the laws and regulations concerning them.

Legal and Compliance

A number of legal statutes and/or acts govern various aspects of data security, privacy, retention, and disposal. Earlier, this chapter mentioned the Health Insurance Portability and Privacy Act, which applies to medical records, and FERPA, which applies to educational records. There is also the Fair Credit Reporting Act and the Gramm-Leach-Bliley Act for financial institutions. There are dozens of others that apply to particular sectors and not others.

The most important thing is to uncover which laws and policies govern your organization and then make certain you fully understand and comply with them. Know what controls and safeguards you must have in place and regularly audit them to make sure you are conforming fully. Remember that ignorance of the law is never a justifiable defense, and the legal obligation is on you to comply.

Summary

This chapter covered the key elements of physical security and environmental controls and monitoring. Physical security measures include access controls, physical barriers, and environmental systems. Environmental considerations include electrical, fire suppression, and interference issues.

This chapter also examined hardware security, data policies, and social engineering. By employing social engineering, attackers are able to gain access to data or the workplace through employees. Many different types of social engineering attacks can occur, and this chapter examined those as well. As a security professional, your job includes keeping up-to-date on current issues as well as informing affected parties about new threats.

Exam Essentials

Be able to describe the process of social engineering.   Social engineering occurs when an unauthorized individual uses human or nontechnical methods to gain information or access to security information. Individuals in an organization should be trained to watch for these types of attempts, and they should report them to security professionals when they occur.

Know the importance of security awareness and training.   Security awareness and training are critical to the success of a security effort. They include explaining policies, procedures, and current threats to both users and management.

Be able to discuss aspects of environmental systems and functions.   Environmental systems include heating, air-conditioning, humidity control, fire suppression, and power systems. All of these functions are critical to a well-designed physical plant.

Know the purposes of shielding in the environment.   Shielding primarily prevents interference from EMI and RFI sources. Most shielding is attached to an effective ground, thereby neutralizing or reducing interference susceptibility.

Be able to describe the types of fire-suppression systems in use today.   Fire-suppression systems can be either fixed or portable. Portable systems are most commonly fire extinguishers. Fixed systems are part of the building, and they're generally water- or gas-based. Gas-based systems are usually found only in computer rooms or other locations where water-based systems would cause more damage than is warranted. Gas systems work only in environments where airflow can be limited; they remove oxygen from the fire, causing the fire to go out. Water systems usually remove heat from a fire, causing the fire to go out.

Know the six types of controls.   CompTIA has categorized controls into six types: deterrent (warning), preventive (stopping), detective (uncovering), compensating (backup), technical (using technology), and administrative (using policies).

Review Questions

You can find the answers in the Appendix.

1. As part of your training program, you're trying to educate users on the importance of security. You explain to them that not every attack depends on implementing advanced technological methods. Some attacks take advantage of human shortcomings to gain access that should otherwise be denied. What term do you use to describe attacks of this type?

    A. Social engineering

    B. IDS system

    C. Perimeter security

    D. Biometrics

2. Which of the following is another name for social engineering?

    A. Social disguise

    B. Social hacking

    C. Wetware

    D. Wetfire

3. Which of the following is the best description of tailgating?

    A. Following someone through a door they just unlocked

    B. Figuring out how to unlock a secured area

    C. Sitting close to someone in a meeting

    D. Stealing information from someone's desk

4. What is the form of social engineering in which you simply ask someone for a piece of information that you want by making it look as if it is a legitimate request?

    A. Hoaxing

    B. Swimming

    C. Spamming

    D. Phishing

5. When you combine phishing with Voice over IP, it is known as:

    A. Spoofing

    B. Spooning

    C. Whaling

    D. Vishing

6. Which of the following is the best description of shoulder surfing?

    A. Following someone through a door they just unlocked

    B. Figuring out how to unlock a secured area

    C. Watching someone enter important information

    D. Stealing information from someone's desk

7. Which of the following is an intermediate access control mechanism used in a high-security installation that requires visual identification, as well as authentication, to gain access?

   A. Mantrap

   B. Fencing

   C. Proximity reader

   D. Hot aisle

8. You've been drafted for the safety committee. One of your first tasks is to inventory all the fire extinguishers and make certain that the correct types are in the correct locations throughout the building. Which of the following categories of fire extinguisher is intended for use on electrical fires?

   A. Type A

   B. Type B

   C. Type C

   D. Type D

9. Which of the following will not reduce EMI?

   A. Physical shielding

   B. Humidity control

   C. Physical location

   D. Overhauling worn motors

10. Which of the following is the best example of perimeter security?

    A. Chain link fence

    B. Video camera

    C. Elevator

    D. Locked computer room

11. You're the leader of the security committee at ACME Company. After a move to a new facility, you're installing a new security monitoring system throughout. Which of the following categories best describes a motion detector mounted in the corner of a hallway?

    A. Perimeter security

    B. Partitioning

    C. Security zone

    D. IDS system

12. Which technology uses a physical characteristic to establish identity?

    A. Biometrics

    B. Surveillance

    C. Smart card

    D. CHAP authenticator

13. The process of reducing or eliminating susceptibility to outside interference is called what?

    A. Shielding

    B. EMI

    C. TEMPEST

    D. Desensitization

14. You work for an electronics company that has just created a device that emits less RF than any competitor's product. Given the enormous importance of this invention and of the marketing benefits it could offer, you want to have the product certified. Which certification is used to indicate minimal electronic emissions?

    A. EMI

    B. RFI

    C. CC EAL 4

    D. TEMPEST

15. Due to growth beyond current capacity, a new server room is being built. As a manager, you want to make certain that all the necessary safety elements exist in the room when it's finished. Which fire-suppression system works best when used in an enclosed area by displacing the air around a fire?

    A. Gas-based

    B. Water-based

    C. Fixed system

    D. Overhead sprinklers

16. Type K fire extinguishers are intended for use on cooking oil fires. This type is a subset of which other type of fire extinguisher?

    A. Type A

    B. Type B

    C. Type C

    D. Type D

17. Proximity readers work with which of the following? (Choose all that apply.)

    A. 15.75 fob card

    B. 14.32 surveillance card

    C. 13.56 MHZ smart card

    D. 125 kHz proximity card

18. In a hot and cold aisle system, what is the typical method of handling cold air?

    A. It is pumped in from below raised floor tiles.

    B. It is pumped in from above through the ceiling tiles.

    C. Only hot air is extracted, and cold air is the natural result.

    D. Cold air exists in each aisle.

19. If RF levels become too high, it can cause the receivers in wireless units to become deaf. This process is called:

   A. Clipping

   B. Desensitizing

   C. Distorting

   D. Crackling

20. RFI is the byproduct of electrical processes, similar to EMI. The major difference is that RFI is usually projected across which of the following?

   A. Network medium

   B. Electrical wiring

   C. Radio spectrum

   D. Portable media

Chapter

11

Security Administration

THE FOLLOWING COMPTIA SECURITY+ EXAM OBJECTIVES ARE COVERED IN THIS CHAPTER:

✓ **2.5 Given a scenario, deploy mobile devices securely.**

- Connection methods: Cellular; Wi-Fi; SATCOM; Bluetooth; NFC; ANT; Infrared; USB

- Mobile device management concepts: Application management; Content management; Remote wipe; Geofencing; Geolocation; Screen locks; Push notification services; Passwords and pins; Biometrics; Context-aware authentication; Containerization; Storage segmentation; Full device encryption

- Enforcement and monitoring for: Third-party app stores; Rooting/jailbreaking; Sideloading; Custom firmware; Carrier unlocking; Firmware OTA updates; Camera use; SMS/MMS; External media; USB OTG; Recording microphone; GPS tagging; Wi-Fi direct/ad hoc; Tethering; Payment methods

- Deployment models: BYOD; COPE; CYOD; Corporate-owned; VDI

✓ **4.4 Given a scenario, differentiate common account management practices.**

- Account types: User account; Shared and generic accounts/credentials; Guest accounts; Service accounts; Privileged accounts

- General Concepts: Least privilege; Onboarding/offboarding; Permission auditing and review; Usage auditing and review; Time-of-day restrictions; Recertification; Standard naming convention; Account maintenance; Group-based access control; Location-based policies

- Account policy enforcement: Credential management; Group policy; Password complexity; Expiration; Recovery; Disablement; Lockout; Password history; Password reuse; Password length

Wireless connections and portable devices have become ubiquitous in our society. This means that securing these devices is critical to network security. Along with the important topic of portable device security, this chapter will explore a fundamental part of security: account management.

A number of terms are associated with security administration that you should know for the exam. The following terms (also found in the online glossary) are those that CompTIA is fond of using and testing on in this category. They are provided in order to make it easier for you to know what each is intended to convey.

Security+ Terminology

bluejacking   Involves sending unsolicited messages to Bluetooth devices when they are in range.

bluesnarfing   Attack that involves getting data from a Bluetooth device.

BYOD   Stands for Bring Your Own Device.

COPE   Stands for Company-Owned and -Provided Equipment.

CYOD   Stands for Choose Your Own Device.

EDGE   Stands for Enhanced Data Rates for GSM Evolution. This does not fit neatly into the 2G/3G/4G spectrum. It is technically considered pre-3G, but it was an improvement on GSM (2G). So, we could consider it a bridge between 2G and 3G technology developed by the European Telecommunications Standards Institute (ETSI).

evil twin   A rogue wireless access point that mimics the SSID of a legitimate access point.

GSM   Global system for mobile communications. This is commonly known as 2G.

LTE   Stands for Long-Term Evolution. This is a standard for wireless communication of high-speed data for mobile devices. It is what is commonly called 4G.

UMTS   Stands for Universal Mobile Telecommunications Systems. This is a 3G standard based on GSM. It is essentially an improvement over GSM.

Connection Types

There are a variety of ways to connect to a network, particularly with wireless/mobile connections. Each of these presents its own security issues. The various methods of connecting are discussed in this section.

Cellular

Cellular network technology has evolved. Currently the 5G standard is done, but it is not widely available. The available standards are listed here:

GSM: Global System for Mobile Communications   This is a standard developed by the European Telecommunications Standards Institute (ETSI). Basically, GSM is the 2G network.

EDGE: Enhanced Data Rates for GSM Evolution   This standard does not fit neatly into the 2G/3G/4G spectrum. It is technically considered pre-3G, but it was an improvement over GSM (2G). So, we could consider it a bridge between 2G and 3G technology.

UMTS: Universal Mobile Telecommunications Systems   This is a 3G standard based on GSM. It is essentially an improvement over GSM.

LTE: Long-Term Evolution   This is a standard for wireless communication of high-speed data for mobile devices. It is what is commonly called 4G.

Bluetooth

Bluetooth is a short-range, wireless system that is designed for limited distances. Typical Bluetooth devices have an effective range of about 10 meters, or a little over 30 feet. This technology is often used to sync devices.

Bluetooth has its own security issues. Most of these can be remediated by setting the Bluetooth device so that it only connects to other devices, if those are trusted devices.

Two of the most common Bluetooth security issues are bluejacking and bluesnarfing. *Bluejacking* involves sending unsolicited messages to Bluetooth devices when they are in range. *Bluesnarfing* involves getting data from the Bluetooth device. Bluesnarfing is illustrated in Figure 11.1.

FIGURE 11.1   Bluesnarfing

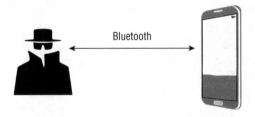

Wi-Fi

Wireless technology consists of several standards. These standards are presented in chronological order in this section.

Early Standards

802.11a was the first wireless standard. It is unlikely that you would encounter this anywhere today. The 802.11a standard operates at the 5-GHz frequency and has a maximum data rate of 54 Mbps.

802.11b was the next standard. This is another older standard, presented here for historical context only. The maximum data rate for 802.11b was 11 Mbps.

The *IEEE 802.11g* standard operates in the frequency range of 2.4 GHz. This makes it downward-compatible with 802.11b devices. When communicating with 802.11b devices, the maximum data rate is reduced to 11 Mbps. The maximum throughput for the 802.11g standard is 54 Mbps.

802.11n

The 802.11n standard operates at 5 GHz, and it can also operate at 2.4 GHz. An 802.11n device is compatible with 802.11a, 802.11b, and 802.11g, but it may not support MIMO technology when paired with these devices. *Multiple-input, multiple-output (MIMO)* is a wireless networking technology that uses two or more streams of data transmission to increase data throughput.

IEEE 802.11n-2009

This technology gets bandwidth of up to 600 Mbit/s with the use of four spatial streams at a channel width of 40 MHz. It uses MIMO, which uses multiple antennas to resolve more information coherently than possible using a single antenna.

802.11ax

There have been several iterations of 802.11ax, each with its own advantages. They are briefly described here.

IEEE 802.11ac   This standard was approved in January 2014. It has a throughput of up to 1 gbps with at least 500 mbps. It uses up to 8 MIMO.

IEEE 802.11ad   This standard was developed by the Wireless Gigabyte Alliance. It supports data transmission rates up to 7 Gbps—more than ten times faster than the highest 802.11n rate.

IEEE 802.11af,   This standard, also referred to as "White-Fi" and "Super Wi-Fi," was approved in February 2014. It allows WLAN operation in the TV white space spectrum in the VHF and UHF bands between 54 and 790 MHz.

Wireless Security

Because much of this was discussed in Chapter 8, "Cryptography," it is simply summarized here. There are three primary methods for security traffic to flow between a device and the wireless access point:

Wired Equivalent Privacy (WEP)   *WEP* stands for *Wired Equivalent Privacy.* You can see by its name that the WEP protocol was intended to make a wireless network as secure as a wired network. However, it was flawed, and it is now recommended you don't use it.

WPA Wi-Fi Protected Access (WPA)   WPA uses Temporal Key Integrity Protocol (TKIP), which is a 128-bit per-packet key, meaning that it dynamically generates a new key for each packet. WPA was introduced in Windows XP Service Pack 1, and it combined the authentication method with encryption. Both features are incorporated into one protocol. An additional improvement to encryption is that it is more difficult to crack than WEP encryption. This is because WPA automatically changes the encryption key with each packet exchanged on the network.

WPA2   WPA2 is based on the IEEE 802.11i standard. It provides the Advanced Encryption Standard (AES) using the Counter Mode-Cipher Block Chaining (CBC)-Message Authentication Code (MAC) Protocol (CCMP) that delivers data confidentiality, data origin authentication, and data integrity for wireless frames.

What you must know for now is that there are three different methods of wireless security: WEP, WPA, and WPA2. WEP should be avoided if at all possible; and if at all possible, always use WPA2.

802.11 Channels

Today you are probably using some variation of the 802.11ax standard. But regardless of what wireless standard you are using, when deploying wireless access points, the channel you use is also important. The 802.11 standard defines 14 channels. The channels that can be used are determined by the host nation. In the United States, a WAP can only use channels 1 through 11. Channels tend to overlap, so nearby WAPs should not use close channels.

Wi-Fi Attacks

Many attacks affect wireless connections, and each has its own security countermeasures. We will briefly examine some of these attacks in this section.

Disassociation   In a *disassociation* attack, the attacker sends a deauthentication packet to the wireless access point, spoofing the user's IP address. This causes the access point to think that the user is logging off and to deauthenticate the user. The defense against this is mutual authentication. That makes it difficult for an attacker to spoof a user.

NFC *Near field communications* (NFC) is a radio wave transmission that automatically connects when in range. While done with radio waves, it can also be made with Bluetooth. If the traffic is not encrypted, then it is susceptible to *sniffing*. Near field communications are often used in very short distances. The most obvious security countermeasure for NFC is to ensure that all transmissions are encrypted. TLS (described in Chapter 8) is one choice for encrypting NFC communications.

Rogue Access Point A *rogue access point* occurs when someone puts up an unauthorized access point. If users connect to it, then all of their traffic goes through this access point. A variation on this is the evil twin. An *evil twin* is a rogue access point that copies the SSID of a legitimate access point. Again, mutual authentication can mitigate this risk. If the access point must authenticate to the user, rogue access points are far more difficult to implement. An evil twin rogue access point is illustrated in Figure 11.2.

FIGURE 11.2 Evil twin rogue access point

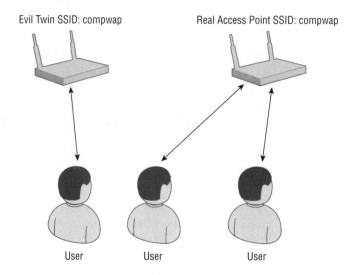

ANT

ANT is a proprietary wireless network technology that provides low power modes, and it is used in Wi-Fi settings. It has been used in sports-related technologies. It provides wireless connectivity using less power. ANT is a proprietary technology developed by a subsidiary of Garmin. It uses the 2.4 GHz frequency. It has a range of about 30 meters. Incidentally, ANT is not an acronym.

Infrared

Infrared was one of the early attempts to create wireless communications, but it is not widely used today. It used light in the infrared spectrum just out of the range that humans can see. That made it an interesting method for transmitting data. However, it suffered from line-of-sight issues. This means that if anything stood between the sender and the receiver, the transmission was blocked. This proved to be a fatal flaw of infrared technology.

SATCOM

As the name suggests, *SATCOM* is an acronym for satellite communications. In the past, such technology was limited to various militaries. Now, however, anyone can purchase a satellite phone. The advantage to the user is that he or she no longer needs to be concerned with being in range of a Wi-Fi, or even a cellular tower. Instead, the phone can be used anywhere on Earth.

However, by its very nature, SATCOM can be a security issue. A person can connect to a satellite without ever going through your company network. Therefore, you have no idea what data might have gone through that phone to some out-of-network device or service.

Mobile Devices

Mobile devices, such as laptops, tablet computers, and smartphones, provide security challenges above those of desktop workstations, servers, and such in that they leave the office, which increases the odds of their theft.

 Real World Scenario

Laptop Theft Nightmare

In 2010, AvMed Health Plans, a Florida-based company, had two laptop computers stolen. Together, over one million personal customer records were on those computers, and this is but one of many similar stories that happen on a regular basis.

At a bare minimum, the following security measures should be in place on mobile devices:

Screen Lock   The display should be configured to time out after a short period of inactivity and the screen locked with a password. To be able to access the system again, the user must provide the password. After a certain number of attempts, the user should not be allowed to attempt any additional logons; this is called *lockout*.

Strong Password   Passwords are always important, but even more so when you consider that the device could be stolen and in the possession of someone who has unlimited access and time to try various values.

Strong passwords can also be augmented with biometrics. Using a fingerprint or even facial recognition is quite popular with today's smartphones. Access control is at least as important for mobile devices as it is for any other device on your network.

Context-Aware Authentication   Context-aware authentication takes into account the context in which the authentication attempt is being made. Context-aware authentication still requires a username and password, but in addition to those criteria it examines the user's location, time of day at which they are logging in, the computer from which they are logging in, what they are trying to do, and so on.

Device Encryption   Data should be encrypted on the device so that if it does fall into the wrong hands, it cannot be accessed in a usable form without the correct passwords. We recommend that you use Trusted Platform Module (TPM), discussed in Chapter 8, for all laptops where possible.

Remote Wipe/Sanitation   Many programs, such as Microsoft Exchange Server 2016 or Google Apps, allow you to send a command to a phone that will remotely clear the data on that phone. This process is known as a *remote wipe*, and it is intended to be used if the phone is stolen or going to be reassigned to another user.

Voice Encryption   Voice encryption can be used with mobile phones and similar devices to encrypt transmissions. This is intended to keep the conversation secure, and it works by adding cryptography (discussed in Chapter 8) to the digitized conversation.

GPS Tracking   Should a device be stolen, GPS (global positioning system) tracking can be used to identify its location and allow authorities to find it. Note that removable storage can circumvent GPS. For example, if a device has GPS tracking but it also has removable storage, thieves can simply remove the data they want and leave the device. This is often related to geotagging, wherein the geographic location of the device is being tagged (tracked).

Geofencing   Geofencing relies on GPS tracking, but it goes a step further. With *geofencing*, the device will only function if it is within certain geographical locations. So, if a mobile device is stolen, that device will not work when taken outside the company perimeter. This concept is illustrated in Figure 11.3.

Application Control   Application control is primarily concerned with controlling what applications are installed on the mobile device. Most viruses that are found on Android phones stem from bad applications being installed. Related to application control is disabling unused services. If you do not need a service, turn it off.

Storage Segmentation   By segmenting a mobile device's storage, you can keep work data separate from personal or operating system data. You can even implement whole-device encryption or just encrypt the confidential data. This can be augmented with *containerization*. Data is contained within specific portions of the device. Particularly if both company data and user data are on the same device, then containing data in separate areas becomes very important.

FIGURE 11.3 Geofencing

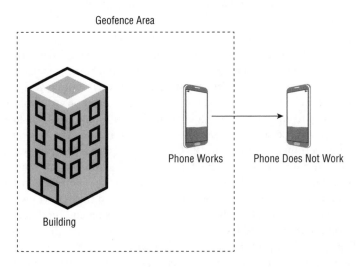

Asset Tracking   You must have a method of asset tracking. It can be as simple as a serial number etched in the device or as complex as a GPS locator. Related to this is inventory control. A complete and accurate list of all devices is an integral part of mobile device management.

Device Access Control   Device access control, in this context, refers to controlling who in the organization has a mobile device. Not every employee should have one. Limiting access to such devices reduces risk.

Content Management   Content management involves multiple topics. The first is controlling what applications are installed on a mobile device. Many applications can pose a security threat to your network. Even benign applications might contain some security flaw that can be exploited to compromise your network. Along with managing applications is the issue of patch management. Using notifications to push out new updates—that is, *push notifications*—is an important aspect of content management.

BYOD Issues

BYOD (Bring Your Own Device) refers to employees bringing their personal devices into the corporate network environment. This is a common issue in the modern workplace, and it can pose substantial security risks.

The first risk involves those devices connecting to the company network. If an employee has a personal smartphone, for example, and they bring it to work and connect it to the company's Wi-Fi network, then any virus, spyware, or other malware that may have infected their phone can spread to the company network. One way to address this is to have a second Wi-Fi network—not connected to the main corporate network, but simply a guest network—and only allow personal devices to connect to that Wi-Fi network and not to the main network.

Another risk involves compromising confidential data. Modern mobile devices are complex computer systems. An employee could use a smartphone to photograph sensitive documents, record conversations, and acquire a great deal of sensitive data. Some Department of Defense contractors do not allow phones in certain sensitive areas of their buildings. This may be more restrictive than at most civilian companies, but at least you should be aware of this potential issue and have a policy to address it. That policy could be as simple as all employees agreeing that if they bring a mobile device onto company property, it is subject to random search.

Data ownership becomes an issue with BYOD. If the device is personally owned but used for company business, who owns the data on the device? The company or the individual? Related to that is the issue of support ownership. Is the individual responsible for support or the company? Patch management is closely related to support ownership. Who will be responsible for ensuring that the personal device has patches updated? Antivirus management is yet another related issue. What antivirus software will be used? How will it be updated? These are all important questions that will need to be answered.

Adherence to corporate policies is an obvious issue. If individuals own their own devices, which they have purchased with their own funds, ensuring that the user and the device adhere to corporate policies will be a challenge. Related to that issue are legal concerns. When a device is owned by the individual but used for company business, a number of legal issues arise. As just one example, what if the device is used to send spam? Is the company responsible? Another example involves the employee leaving the company. How does the organization verify that the device does not have any proprietary data on it? Forensics is still another legal issue. If there is, for example, litigation against the company, usually computer records are subpoenaed, but the data that might reside on a personal device is a legal gray area.

Then there are purely technical concerns. Architecture and infrastructure considerations are critical. Will the personal device be compatible with the organizational infrastructure? On-board cameras and video also pose a challenge. Some organizations forbid the use of cameras within the company, or at least within secure areas. And finally, there is the issue of acceptable use policies. Companies generally have acceptable use policies regarding how computers can be used within the organization. How will that be implemented with devices that don't belong to the company?

None of this is meant to indicate you cannot use BYOD devices in your organization. However, you do need to address the issues mentioned in this section before allowing BYOD devices to connect to your network. Some organizations simply opt to forbid such devices, but in our modern world of ubiquitous devices, that approach may not be feasible in your organization.

There are two other variations on BYOD that are used by some organizations. The first is *Choose Your Own Device (CYOD)*. With this approach, the company creates a list of approved devices that meet the company's minimum security standards. Employees then can select from among this list of preapproved devices. This approach does help in mitigating security risks associated with BYOD, since all employees will be using devices that have a minimum level of security.

The second approach is *Company-Owned and -Provided Equipment (COPE)*. Using COPE, the company has complete control of the devices, and thus it can ensure a higher level of security. However, this approach has its own issues. The first is the issue of cost. It is expensive to provide portable devices to your entire staff, or even a significant portion of the staff. The second issue is personal use of these devices leads to personal data on company-owned equipment.

Another option is using Virtual Desktop Infrastructure (VDI) for mobile phones. VDI has been used to provide a desktop to users on any machine they wish. The desktop itself is actually virtualized, and it contains all of the user's applications, files, settings, and so forth. The same process can be applied to mobile devices, so the user has a VDI for company activity. This provides the company with more control over the deployment of phone apps, updates, and security configurations.

Enforcement

There are a variety of security concerns and countermeasures for mobile devices, many of which were described in the previous sections. However, certain things must be enforced in order to maintain the security of your mobile devices and your network. In the following sections, we will discuss these issues.

Customizing

No matter how secure your device starts out, that security can be significantly compromised by the user altering the configuration of the system. One of the most common methods for doing this with the iPhone has been jailbreaking. By *jailbreaking* the phone, the user takes administrative/root control. This allows the user to install any application they wish, thus circumventing the security controls of the iTunes store. Jailbreaking should be strictly forbidden for any device that will connect to your network.

This issue is comparable to sideloading with Android devices. The term *sideloading* in general means to transfer data between two devices. More specifically with mobile devices, it most often is associated with installing Android apps from places other than Google Play. This, like jailbreaking for iPhones, should be forbidden for any device that will connect to your network. Essentially, any third-party apps from nonapproved sources should be prohibited.

Another related issue with Android phones is rooting. *Root* is the term for an administrator in Linux, and Android phones use Linux. So, rooting means to get root level, or administrative, privileges on an Android phone. This will allow the user to make any modification he or she wishes.

With any device, the loading of custom or nonstandard firmware must also be forbidden. The firmware is the heart of the device, and any nonstandard firmware is very likely to undermine the security of the device. However, the official firmware must be updated. One way to ensure this is *Over-the-Air (OTA) updates*. Whenever a device connects to your wireless network, the device is updated if needed.

Finally, *carrier unlocking* is a security concern. This is the process of moving the phone from the carrier that issued it to another carrier, usually temporarily. This is not the same as simply switching phone service providers.

Physical Control

In some instances, a mobile device is being used in a stationary location. For example, a tablet is set up at a kiosk for general public use. In such cases, tethering the device is important. *Tethering* is the process of literally attaching some cable from the device to some immobile structure.

The device itself can be a security risk. Phones all have microphones that can record. There are apps that turn a phone into a monitoring device, using the phone's own microphone to record conversations within range. The phone's camera is also such a device.

Remember that any phone or tablet can be a USB storage device. This is referred to as *USB OTG* (On the Go). This means that any portable device carried into your network could be used to exfiltrate files and data from your network.

Many portable devices can be readily turned into mobile hotspots. This also presents a security risk. Using a mobile device, it would be possible for someone to begin broadcasting an SSID that is similar to the one used by your actual corporate wireless access point and thus trick users into connecting to the rogue device rather than one of your company's real wireless access points.

A related issue is ad hoc networking. An ad hoc network is done without centralized control, just various devices communicating with each other. That can be a security issue, as there is no means to control security centrally.

Connecting media to a portable device must be done with caution. External media attached to a portable device can be a way to exfiltrate data or to introduce malware to the device and thus to the network.

Payment Methods

It is becoming increasingly common to use the phone itself as a payment method. This often means mobile wallets that can be used to pay for goods and services. It can also include billing the phone carrier for items purchased, and then the cost is added to the user's phone bill. In some cases, Near Field Communication (NFC) can be used with mobile phone pay.

All of these methods provide extremely convenient payment methods, but they also introduce security risks. The most obvious risk is now the phone itself becomes a payment method, making a lost, stolen, or compromised phone a greater security issue.

Account Management Concepts

One of the most fundamental aspects of network security is *account management*. All authorized users must have accounts with the appropriate access level to allow those users to access the resources on the network. At the same time, attackers are always seeking to compromise an account so that they can also access the network resources.

Account Types

The first step in creating secure accounts is to make certain that you have different account types for different uses. Regardless of the type of account, which we will discuss in this section, all accounts should have some of the same properties. Those properties include things such as password complexity, age, and history. These concepts have been mentioned elsewhere in this book but bear revisiting here.

Password complexity refers to requiring capital letters, numbers, and symbols as part of a password. This can be just as important as password length in thwarting at least some attacks. *Password age* relates to how long you can have a password before it expires and a new password is generated. *Password history* determines how many old passwords the system will remember, thus preventing the user from simply repeating previous passwords when it comes time to change his or her password.

In addition to password complexity, there will be related issues such as *password length*. The rule is the longer, the better. *Passphrases* are becoming more common. Beyond using a series of words or other text to control access, passphrases are generally longer in order to provide additional security.

Then there is the issue of *account lockout*. How many times can the user enter the incorrect password before the account is locked? If the account is locked, how will it be recovered? For example, you might have the lockout automatically recover after 24 hours, or it might require an administrator to reset it.

There are no absolute answers to these issues. What is appropriate for one organization might not be right for another. In a low-security environment, you might have passwords that are 8 characters long, expire after 6 months, don't lock out until 6 failed attempts, and then automatically recover in 2 hours. For a high-security environment, you might have 14+ character passwords that are changed every 30 days and lock out after 3 failed attempts. Then, they can only be recovered by an administrator. The specific decisions that you make on these issues will depend on the security needs of your company.

The most obvious type of account is the *user account*. These will be assigned to human users of your network. Each user account should have certain properties. This will include an expiration date as well as the type of user. For example, *administrator accounts* are special user accounts with a great deal of privileges. Administrator accounts should be granted sparingly and monitored closely.

The topic of administrator accounts naturally leads to the broader topic of privileged accounts. By definition, any account that has significant rights on the network is a *privileged account*. The root account in Linux is a classic example. In Windows, the administrator account and power user accounts are good examples. The main issue with such accounts is that they should be given only when absolutely necessary.

The most important account is the *domain admin account*. A local admin account (or root in Linux) gives the user unfettered control of a single machine. But domain admin accounts provide the user with complete and total control of your network. The ultimate goal of any attacker is to get domain admin privileges. For this reason, domain admin accounts must be very closely controlled.

In some cases, you may wish to use a shared account for several uses. This is sometimes called a *generic account*. Using a generic account is usually not recommended. The preferred method is to have individual accounts for individual users. However, in some limited situations, it may be acceptable to use very low-privileged accounts that are shared. For example, for a lab on a college campus that only has access to the lab systems and no other resources, you might have a generic account labuser, which can be used by any student in the lab.

In most organizations of any significant size, you will eventually have outsiders who need to access your network. This could include clients or business partners who are visiting your facilities for a brief period of time. Guests in a hotel are another classic example. These accounts are usually called *guest accounts*. They should have bare minimum privileges. It is possible to have individual accounts for each guest. In fact, hotels often have the guest log in by room number and last name, thus creating an individual account for an individual guest. However, in some situations, hotels may use a shared account for guests. For example, guest Wi-Fi often uses a single "guest" login that every guest shares.

The concept of privileged accounts and guest accounts is part of the larger topic of group-based access control. Any sizable network quickly becomes difficult to manage, and trying to administer privileges individually for a few thousand employees is a daunting task. It is often better to place users into groups based on their job roles and then to manage privileges for those groups. So rather than needing to manage privileges for all sales personnel, you can simply administer the privileges of the Sales group.

Humans are not the only entities that may require access to network resources. You might have software that needs to access your network, separately from human involvement. As one example, database services usually start when the machine they are on boots up. These services require their own accounts. One mistake that is all too common is simply to assign these services to a domain administration account. This violates the principle of least privileges that you have read about repeatedly in this book. The proper approach is to create service accounts with just enough privileges for the service to accomplish its required tasks.

General Concepts

The most important concept in account management that has been mentioned in this chapter, as well as previously in this book, is *least privileges*. This means that each account is given only the privileges that entity (user or service) needs to do their job. This is not a question of lack of trust or lack of skill of that user. The user in question may be very technically skilled and could be someone you would literally trust with your life. However, their user account is only granted just enough privileges to do their job and nothing more.

Once you have assessed the needs of each user and service and then assigned the appropriate privileges to those accounts, the next step is to audit those accounts periodically. Two types of audits are relevant to accounts: usage audits and privilege audits.

Whatever the account type or use, credential management is an important concept. This means the complete management of credentials. For example, how will passwords be stored and where will they be stored? When will accounts expire, and how long can passwords be used? These are all part of credential management. Such management is usually accomplished via policies. That will require account policy enforcement. If your organization has a policy that passwords must be at least 12 characters long and should be changed every 90 days, then there must be a mechanism to enforce that account policy.

Usage Audits

Usage audits literally audit what the account is doing. For users, this is designed to ensure that the account is being used in accordance with company security policies and is only being used for legitimate, work-related purposes. This is an elementary type of security audit that should be conducted on a regular basis.

Privilege Audits

Privilege audits are a bit different. Over time, users change job roles. It is possible that a given user has privileges that they no longer need. This can occur when the user's job role changes, and their new privileges are simply added to the old privileges. It can also be the case that the user was initially assigned more privileges than their job role actually required. A privilege audit is meant to detect any situation where an account has more privileges than is required for his or her job tasks. This is simply enforcing the concept of least privileges.

Privilege audits are closely related to recertification. *Recertification* is the process whereby you determine if given accounts still require the privileges that they have.

Account management is an ongoing process that every company must address on a regular basis. However, the two most important times to be concerned about account management are during onboarding and offboarding of personnel.

Onboarding

Onboarding simply refers to the process that at a very early point after a person has been hired, that person must be informed of the company network policies, particularly security policies. His or her account should then be set up with least privileges.

Offboarding

Offboarding is a bit simpler. When someone leaves the company, for any reason, that user's accounts must all be immediately suspended. It does not matter if this is the most trusted employee who is retiring after 30 years of wonderful service to the organization. While he or she is enjoying cake at the retirement party, their accounts should be getting disabled.

It is important to disable them for a period of time before deleting them. Issues may arise after an employee leaves the company. If you delete their account, you may not be able to access files that they encrypted, and you might even lose some logs associated with that account.

Remember, the cardinal rule of account management is least privileges. Keeping that concept in mind leads one to two other ideas. The first is *time-of-day restrictions*. If a given employee generally works from 8 a.m. to 5 p.m., why is their account accessible at 1 a.m.?

Of course, people fluctuate a bit, so you might wish to set up this hypothetical account such that it is operational from 7 a.m. to 7 p.m. Not all accounts can be locked down by time restrictions. But for those employees who work a relatively consistent schedule, this is an excellent way to improve security.

Related to time-of-day restrictions are *computer restrictions*. As an example, if Elizabeth works in the Accounting department, which is located on the 4th floor, why allow her account also to work on the 10th floor in software development? Limiting accounts only to those machines that user should be using is a natural extension of least privileges. Again, not all accounts can be locked down like this. For example, technical support personnel need to work from almost any computer on the network.

Machine-based restrictions are a special type of location-based controls. *Location-based controls* are any type of controls that limit accounts based on where the person is attempting to sign in. For example, an account might work fine in the Chicago office but not work at all from the Houston office.

These concepts are all related to standard account maintenance. In addition to the items already discussed, there are other issues. One such issue concerns *naming conventions*. Account names should not reveal the job role. As mentioned earlier, attackers want to compromise administrative accounts. If your network has 1,000+ accounts, it can be challenging just to figure out which are the administrator accounts. But if you named your administrator accounts dmnadmin001, it doesn't take Sherlock Holmes to deduce that this is a domain admin account.

Summary

In this chapter, we examined a variety of mobile connectivity methods and security issues associated with each. We also discussed the issues associated with mobile devices in the corporate environment. Finally, we reviewed account management concepts.

Exam Essentials

Be able to describe the wireless security standards.   Understand and be able to articulate details of the 802.11, WEP, WPA, and WPA2 standards. Each of these is of particular importance on the Security+ certification test.

Understand the security issues associated with mobile devices.   As mobile devices become increasingly ubiquitous, so too do the security concerns associated with them. For the Security+ certification test, you must understand the various issues, particularly with BYOD devices as well as variations such as CYOD and COPE.

Be able to explain account management.   Account management is a significant topic on the Security+ certification. You must understand the issues associated with account management and be able to explain how to mitigate relevant security concerns.

Review Questions

You can find the answers in the Appendix.

1. John is looking for a solution for his company that will give the company the most control over mobile devices, while still having the employees purchase their own devices. Which of the following solutions should he select?

   A. BYOD

   B. COPE

   C. CYOD

   D. BBBA

2. Employees in your company are provided smartphones by the company. Which of the following best describes this?

   A. BYOD

   B. CYOD

   C. COPE

   D. BYOE

3. Which of the following would be most effective in preventing a thief from using a mobile device stolen from your company?

   A. GPS tracking

   B. WPA2

   C. COPE

   D. Geofencing

4. Ahmed is a network administrator for an insurance company. He is concerned about users storing company data on their smartphones to exfiltrate that data. Which of the following best describes this?

   A. BYOD

   B. Bluejacking

   C. USB OTG

   D. CYOD

5. Using Bluetooth to extract data from a victim's phone is best described as which of the following?

   A. Bluesnarfing

   B. Bluejacking

   C. CYOD

   D. Jailbreaking

6. What principle is most important in setting up network accounts?

    A. Least privileges

    B. Password expiration

    C. Password complexity

    D. Separation of duties

7. Tom is responsible for account management in his company. For user John Smith who is an administrator, which of the following would be the best name for him to choose?

    A. Admin001

    B. Admjsmith

    C. Ajsmith

    D. jsmith

8. Juanita is responsible for setting up network accounts for her company. She wants to establish an account for the SQL Server service. Which of the following would be the best type of account for her to use?

    A. A user/service account

    B. Domain admin account

    C. Guest account

    D. Shared account

9. Which of the following fully implements the 802.11i security standards?

    A. WEP

    B. WPA

    C. WPA2

    D. WAP

10. Which of the following would be best at preventing a thief from accessing the data on a stolen phone?

    A. Geotagging

    B. Remote wipe

    C. Geofencing

    D. Segmentation

11. Janet is a network administrator for a small company. Users have been reporting that personal data is being stolen when using the wireless network. They all insist that they only connect to the corporate wireless access point. Reviewing the logs for the WAP shows that these users have not connected to it. Which of the following could best explain this situation?

    A. Bluesnarfing

    B. Rouge access point

    C. Jamming

    D. Bluejacking

12. You find that users on your network are getting dropped from the wireless connection. When you check the logs for the wireless access point, you find that a deauthentication packet has been sent to the WAP from the users' IP addresses. What seems to be happening here?

   A. Bluesnarfing

   B. Bluejacking

   C. Session hijacking

   D. Disassociation attack

13. What is the primary weakness of infrared communications?

   A. Line of sight

   B. Low bandwidth

   C. Poor authentication

   D. Cannot be encrypted

14. Which wireless technology uses TKIP?

   A. WEP

   B. WPA

   C. WPA2

   D. WAP

15. Which acronym describes devices provided by the company?

   A. BYOD

   B. COPE

   C. CYOD

   D. CYOP

Chapter

12

Disaster Recovery and Incident Response

THE FOLLOWING COMPTIA SECURITY+ EXAM OBJECTIVES ARE COVERED IN THIS CHAPTER:

✓ **1.4 Explain penetration testing concepts.**

- Active reconnaissance
- Passive reconnaissance
- Pivot
- Initial exploitation
- Persistence
- Escalation of privilege
- Black box
- White box
- Gray box
- Pen testing vs. vulnerability testing

✓ **1.5 Explain vulnerability scanning concepts.**

- Passively test security controls
- Identify vulnerability
- Identify lack of security controls
- Identify common misconfigurations
- Intrusive vs. non-intrusive
- Credentialed vs. non-credentialed
- False positive

✓ **5.4 Given a scenario, follow incident response procedures.**

- Incident response plan: Documented incident types/category definitions; Roles and responsibilities; Reporting requirements/escalation; Cyber-incident response teams; Exercise

- Incident response process: Preparation; Identification; Containment; Eradication; Recovery; Lessons learned

✓ **5.5 Summarize basic concepts of forensics.**

- Order of volatility

- Chain of custody

- Legal hold

- Data acquisition: Capture system image; Network traffic and logs; Capture video; Record time offset; Take hashes; Screenshots; Witness interviews

- Preservation

- Recovery

- Strategic intelligence/counterintelligence gathering: Active logging

- Track man-hours

✓ **5.6 Explain disaster recovery and continuity of operation concepts.**

- Recovery sites: Hot site; Warm site; Cold site

- Order of restoration

- Backup concepts: Differential; Incremental; Snapshots; Full

- Geographic considerations: Off-site backups; Distance; Location selection; Legal implications; Data sovereignty

- Continuity of operation planning: Exercises/tabletop; After-action reports; Failover; Alternate processing sites; Alternate business practices

As a security professional, you must strive not only to prevent losses but also to make contingency plans for recovering from any losses that do occur. This chapter deals with the crucial aspects of business continuity and vendor support from an operations perspective. It also looks at incident response and the basic forensic procedures with which you should be familiar.

A solid grasp of these concepts will help you prepare for the exam because they appear in multiple objectives. It will also help you become a more proficient and professional security team member. The process of working with, helping to design, and maintaining security in your organization is a tough job. It requires dedication, vigilance, and a sense of duty to your organization.

Disaster and Incident Related Terminology

Rounding out this book, there are a number of terms associated with disaster recovery and incident response of which you need to be aware for the exam. The following terms (also found in the online glossary) are those CompTIA is fond of using and testing on in this category. They are provided in order to make it easier for you to know what each is intended to convey.

Security+ Terminology

cold site   A physical site that can be used if the main site is inaccessible (destroyed) but that lacks all of the resources necessary to enable an organization to use it immediately.

differential backup   A type of backup that includes only new files or files that have changed since the last full backup. Differential backups differ from incremental backups in that they don't clear the archive bit upon their completion.

disaster recovery   The act of recovering data following a disaster in which it has been destroyed.

disaster-recovery plan   A plan outlining the procedure by which data is recovered after a disaster.

failover The process of reconstructing a system or switching over to other systems when a failure is detected.

false positive A flagged event that isn't really a notable incident and has been falsely triggered.

forensics In terms of security, the act of looking at all the data at your disposal to try to figure out who gained unauthorized access and the extent of that access.

full backup A backup that copies all data to the archive medium.

hot site A location that can provide operations within hours of a failure.

incremental backup A type of backup that includes only new files or files that have changed since the last full backup and then clears the archive bit upon completion.

intrusion The act of entering a system without authorization to do so.

intrusion detection system (IDS) Any set of tools that can identify an attack using defined rules or logic. An IDS can be network-based or host-based.

intrusion prevention system (IPS) Any set of tools that identify and then actively respond to attacks based on defined rules. Like an IDS (which is the passive counterpart), an IPS can be network-based or host-based.

intrusive tests Penetration-type testing that involves trying to break into the network.

nonintrusive tests Penetration/vulnerability testing that takes a passive approach rather than actually trying to break into the network.

offsite storage Storing data off the premises, usually in a secure location.

onsite storage Storing backup data at the same site as the servers on which the original data resides.

snapshot Image of a virtual machine at a moment in time.

system image A snapshot of what exists.

tabletop exercise An exercise that involves individuals sitting around a table with a facilitator discussing situations that could arise and how best to respond to them.

vulnerability scanning Identifying specific vulnerabilities in your network.

warm site A site that provides some capabilities in the event of a disaster. The organization that wants to use a warm site will need to install, configure, and reestablish operations on systems that might already exist in the warm site.

working copy backup The copy of the data currently in use on a network.

Penetration Testing

It is becoming more common for companies to hire penetration testers to test their system's defenses. Essentially, a penetration tester will use the same techniques that a hacker would use to find any flaws in a system's security. These flaws may be discovered by means other than directly accessing the system, such as collecting information from public databases, talking to employees/partners, dumpster diving, and social engineering. This is known as *passive reconnaissance*. In contrast to this, *active reconnaissance* directly focuses on the system (port scans, traceroute information, network mapping, and so forth) to identify weaknesses that could be used to launch an attack.

When doing penetration testing, it is important to have a scope document outlining the extent of the testing that is to be done. It is equally important to have permission from an administrator who can authorize such testing—in writing—to be conducted.

Hacking and penetration testing are areas that seem quite exciting to many people. Unfortunately, this has led to a number of unqualified (or at least underqualified) people calling themselves penetration testers. It is imperative when hiring a penetration tester that you ensure that the person in question has the requisite skill set. Check their references, and verify their training and skills. It is also important to do a thorough background check on the person in question, because you are giving this person permission to try hacking techniques on your network. You will want to be certain that they conduct themselves in an ethical manner.

Often, the weakest link may not be on the system that you are ultimately wanting to access, but on another, trusted system. When it is possible to attack a system using another, compromised system, this is known as doing a *pivot*. With pivoting (also known as *island hopping*), a compromised system is used to attack another system on the same network following the *initial exploitation*. If the compromise is introduced at a different time than the attack, then it is said to involve *persistence*. An example of persistence would be an employee having his or her laptop infected at a hotel while traveling for business and the company's network not being compromised until the employee is back in the office a week later and connected to the company's network.

One weakness a good penetration test looks for is *escalation of privilege*—that is, a hole created when code is executed with higher privileges than those of the user running it. By breaking out of the executing code, users are left with higher privileges than they should have.

What Should You Test?

One of the first steps in penetration testing is deciding what needs to be tested. This is a question of verifying what actual threats exist to your network. For example, if you are the network administrator of a public school, it is unlikely that highly skilled cyber terrorists are trying to infiltrate your network. The most likely threat to your network is a low-to-moderately skilled student. The most likely threats are what should determine the exact nature of a penetration test.

Essentially, all tests will have a few similar steps, regardless of the threat. Those steps include some attempt to bypass security controls. The penetration tester will attempt to bypass whatever security controls have been implemented on your network. This is the best way to actively test security controls.

The three types of testing are described here:

Black Box   The tester has absolutely no knowledge of the system and is functioning in the same manner as an outside attacker.

White Box   The tester has significant knowledge of the system. This simulates an attack from an insider—a rogue employee.

Gray Box   This is a middle ground between the first two types of testing. In gray box testing, the tester has some limited knowledge of the target system.

In addition to classifying a penetration test based on the amount of information given to the tester, it is also possible to classify the test as intrusive versus nonintrusive. *Nonintrusive tests* involve passively testing of security controls—performing vulnerability scans and probing for weaknesses but not exploiting them. *Intrusive tests* involve actually trying to break into the network. In the strictest sense, passive tests are really just vulnerability scans and not penetration tests, whereas active tests provide more meaningful results. With active tests, it is possible that they may disrupt business operations in the same way as a real attack.

Vulnerability Scanning

Many security experts view vulnerability scanning as separate from penetration testing. However, it should be either part of the penetration test or done alongside it. *Vulnerability scanning* allows you to identify specific vulnerabilities in your network, and most penetration testers will start with this procedure so that they can identify likely targets to attack. A penetration test is essentially an attempt to exploit these vulnerabilities.

The key element of a vulnerability scan is always to identify vulnerabilities: identifying common misconfigurations and identifying a lack of security controls. Once you have identified the vulnerabilities, it is time to attempt to exploit them. Of course, the most egregious vulnerability is any aspect of your system where vulnerability scanning reveals a lack of security controls. Some of the more common vulnerabilities involve misconfiguration. In fact, popular vulnerability scanners, such as Nessus (www.tenable.com/products/nessus), will help identify common misconfigurations.

Credentialed vs. Noncredentialed

Vulnerability scanning can be done in either a credentialed or noncredentialed manner. The difference is that a credentialed vulnerability scan uses actual network credentials to connect to systems and scan for vulnerabilities. Tenable Security, the creators of the Nessus vulnerability scanner, have the following to say about the benefits of credentialed scanning:

> **Not Disrupting Operations or Consuming Too Many Resources**   Because the scan is performed with credentials, operations are executed on the host itself rather than across the network. Everything from operating system identification to port scanning is done by running commands on the host and then sending the results of those commands back to the Nessus server. This allows Nessus to consume far less system and network resources than performing a traditional network scan that probes ports and services remotely.

> **Definitive List of Missing Patches**   Rather than probe a service remotely and attempting to find a vulnerability, Nessus will query the local host to see if a patch for a given vulnerability has been applied. This type of query is far more accurate (and safer) than running a remote check.

> **Client-Side Software Vulnerabilities Are Uncovered**   By looking at the software installed and its version, Nessus will find client-side software vulnerabilities that are otherwise missed in a traditional network-based audit.

> **Several Other "Vulnerabilities"**   Nessus can read password policies, obtain a list of USB devices, check antivirus software configurations, and even enumerate Bluetooth devices attached to scanned hosts.

> *Source:* `https://www.tenable.com/blog/the-value-of-credentialed-vulnerability-scanning`

Whether you use credentialed or noncredentialed vulnerability scanning, be prepared for false positives. A *false positive* occurs when the scan mistakenly identifies something as a vulnerability when it is not. No software program is perfect, and this means that any vulnerability scanner will yield some occasional false positives.

Issues Associated with Business Continuity

One of the oldest phrases still in use today is "the show must go on." Nowhere is that truer than in the world of business, where downtime means the loss of significant revenue with each passing minute. *Business continuity* is primarily concerned with the processes, policies, and methods that an organization follows to minimize the impact of a system failure, network failure, or the failure of any key component needed for operation—that is, essentially whatever it takes to ensure that the business continues and that the show does indeed go on.

Business Continuity Planning (BCP)   Business continuity planning is the process of implementing policies, controls, and procedures to counteract the effects of losses, outages, or failures of critical business processes. BCP is primarily a management tool that ensures that critical business functions can be performed when normal business operations are disrupted and alternate business practices must be employed. For each critical business task, there should be a minimum of one alternative business process identified during the crafting of a continuity plan. Those alternate business practices should be documented in such a way that someone unfamiliar with them could perform them with minimal training.

Critical Business Functions (CBFs)   Critical business functions refer to those processes or systems that must be made operational immediately when an outage occurs. The business can't function without them, and many are information-intensive and require access to both technology and data.

Two of the key components of BCP are *business impact analysis (BIA)* and *risk assessment*. BIA is concerned with evaluating the processes, and risk assessment is concerned with evaluating the risk or likelihood of a loss. Evaluating all of the processes in an organization or enterprise is necessary in order for BCP to be effective.

You need only a passing knowledge of business continuity issues for the Security+ exam. If you plan on taking the Project+ exam, also from CompTIA, you will need a more thorough knowledge of these topics.

Types of Storage Mechanisms

You might need to restore information from backup copies for any number of reasons. Some of the more common reasons for doing so are as follows:

- Accidental deletion
- Application errors
- Natural disasters
- Physical attacks
- Server failure
- Virus infection
- Workstation failure

The information that you back up must be immediately available for use when needed. If a user loses a critical file, they won't want to wait several days while data files are sent from a remote storage facility. Several types of storage mechanisms are available for data storage. These include the following:

Working Copies   *Working copy backups*, sometimes referred to as *shadow copies*, are partial or full backups that are kept at the computer center for immediate recovery purposes. They are usually updated on a frequent basis and are generally the most recent backups that have been made.

Working copies aren't usually intended to serve as long-term copies. In a busy environment, they may be created every few hours.

Many filesystems used on servers include *journaling*. A *journaled file system (JFS)* includes a log file of all changes and transactions that have occurred within a set period of time (such as the last few hours). If a crash occurs, the operating system can check the log files to see which transactions have been committed and which ones have not.

This technology works well, and it allows unsaved data to be written after recovery. The system is usually successfully restored to its pre-crash condition.

Onsite Storage   *Onsite storage* usually refers to a location on the site of the computer center that is used to store information locally. Onsite storage containers are available that allow computer cartridges and tapes or backup media to be stored in a reasonably protected environment in the building.

> As time goes on, tape is losing its popularity as a medium for backups to other technologies. The Security+ exam, however, is a bit dated, and it still considers tape the ideal medium.

Onsite storage containers are designed and rated for fire, moisture, and pressure resistance. These containers aren't *fireproof* in most cases, but they are indeed *fire rated*. A fireproof container should be guaranteed to withstand damage regardless of the type of fire or temperature, whereas fire ratings specify that a container can protect its contents for a specific amount of time in a given situation.

If you choose to depend entirely on onsite storage, make sure that the containers you acquire can withstand the worst-case environmental catastrophes that could happen at your location. Make sure as well that they are in locations where you can easily find and access them after the disaster (for example, near exterior walls, on the ground floor, and so forth).

> General-purpose storage safes aren't usually suitable for storing electronic media. The fire ratings used for safes generally refer to paper contents. Because paper does not catch fire until 451° Fahrenheit, electronic media would typically be ruined well before paper documents are destroyed in a fire.

Offsite Storage   *Offsite storage* refers to a location away from the computer center where paper copies and backup media are kept. Offsite storage can involve something as simple as keeping a copy of backup media at a remote office, or it can be as complicated as a nuclear-hardened, high-security storage facility. The storage facility should be bonded, insured, and inspected on a regular basis to ensure that all storage procedures are being followed.

Determining which storage mechanism to use should be based on the needs of the organization, the availability of storage facilities, and the available budget. Most offsite storage facilities charge based on the amount of space required and the frequency of access needed to the stored information.

Although it is easy to see the need for security at any location where your files are stored, don't overlook the need for security during transportation as well.

Crafting a Disaster-Recovery Plan

A *disaster-recovery plan*, or scheme, helps an organization respond effectively when a disaster occurs. Disasters may include system failure, network failure, infrastructure failure, and natural disaster. The primary emphasis of such a plan is reestablishing services and minimizing losses.

In a smaller organization, a disaster-recovery plan may be relatively simple and straightforward. In a larger organization, it may involve multiple facilities, corporate strategic plans, and entire departments. In either case, the purpose is to develop the means and methods to restore services as quickly as possible and to protect the organization from unacceptable losses in the event of a disaster.

A major component of a disaster-recovery plan involves the access and storage of information. Your backup plan for data is an integral part of this process. The following sections address backup plan issues and backup types. They also discuss developing a backup plan, recovering a system, and using alternative sites. These are key components of a disaster-recovery plan: they form the heart of how an organization will respond when a critical failure or disaster occurs.

An order of restoration should always be followed after a disaster to ensure that dependent services are not restored before the ones they are dependent on. It is highly recommended that network maps or diagrams be used to illustrate dependencies. These maps can be invaluable in executing the order of restoration after the crisis.

Understanding Backup Plan Issues

When an organization develops a backup plan for information, it must be clear about the value of the information. A *backup plan* identifies which information is to be stored, how it will be stored, and for what duration it will be stored. You must look at the relative value of the information you retain. To some extent, the types of systems you use and the applications you support dictate the structure of your plan.

Let's look at those different systems and applications:

Database Systems   Most modern database systems provide the ability to back up data or certain sections of the database globally without difficulty. Larger-scale database systems also provide transaction auditing and data-recovery capabilities.

For example, you can configure your database to record in a separate file each addition, update, deletion, or change of information that occurs. These transaction or audit files can be stored directly on any type of archival media, such as magnetic tape cartridges, solid state drives, etc. In the event of a system outage or data loss, the audit file can be used to roll back the database and update it to the last transactions made.

Figure 12.1 illustrates the auditing process in further detail. In this situation, the audit file is directly written to a digital audio tape (DAT) that is used to store a record of changes. If an outage occurs, the audit or transaction files can be rolled forward to bring the database back to its most current state. This recovery process brings the database current to within the last few transactions. Although it doesn't ensure that all of the transactions that were in process will be recovered, it will reduce potential losses to the few that were in process when the system failed.

FIGURE 12.1   Database transaction auditing process

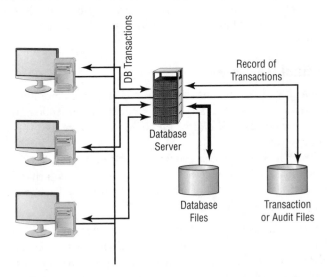

Most database systems contain large files that have only a relatively few records updated in relation to the number of records stored. A large customer database may store millions of records; however, only a few hundred may be undergoing modification at any given time.

User Files   Word processing documents, spreadsheets, and other user files are extremely valuable to an organization. Fortunately, although the number of files that people retain is usually large, the number of files that change after initial creation is relatively small. By doing a regular backup on user systems, you can protect these documents and ensure that they're recoverable in the event of a loss. In a large organization, backing up user files can be an enormous task. Fortunately, most operating systems date-stamp files when they're modified. If backups that store only the changed files are created, keeping user files safe becomes a relatively less painful process for an organization.

Many organizations have taken the position that backing up user files is the user's responsibility. Although this policy decision saves administrative time and media, it isn't a good idea. Most users don't back up their files on a regular basis—if at all. With the cost of media being relatively cheap, including the user files in a backup every so often is highly recommended.

Applications   Applications such as word processors, transaction systems, and other programs usually don't change on a frequent basis. When a change or upgrade to an application is made, it's usually accomplished across an entire organization. You wouldn't necessarily need to keep a copy of the word processing application for each user, but you should keep a single up-to-date version that is available for download and reinstallation.

Some commercial applications require that each copy of the software be registered with a centralized license server. This may present a problem if you attempt to use a centralized recovery procedure for applications. Each machine may require its own copy of the applications for a recovery to be successful.

Knowing the Backup Types

The frequency at which you do backups should be based on the amount of data that you are willing to lose. If you do backups only weekly (never recommended), then you could lose up to a week's worth of data. Similarly, if you do them every day, the most data you would lose is 24 hours' worth.

Regardless of the frequency at which you back up, three methods exist to back up information on most systems. The difference between them is in the data that they include, and this has an impact on the amount of time it takes to perform the backup and any restore operations that may later be required:

Full Backup   A *full backup* is a complete, comprehensive backup of all files on a disk or server. The full backup is current only at the time it's performed. Once a full backup is made, you have a complete archive of the system at that point in time. A system shouldn't be in use while it undergoes a full backup because some files may not get backed up. Once the system goes back into operation, the backup is no longer current. A full backup can be a time-consuming process on a large system.

During a full backup, every single file on the system is copied over, and the archive bit on each file is turned off. The archive bit is essentially a flag associated with every file that is turned on when the file is created or accessed.

Incremental Backup   An *incremental backup* is a partial backup that stores only the information that has been changed since the last full or the last incremental backup. If a full backup were performed on a Sunday night, an incremental backup done on Monday night would contain only the information that changed since Sunday night. Such a backup is typically considerably smaller than a full backup. Each incremental backup must be retained until a full backup can be performed. Incremental backups are usually the fastest backups to perform on most systems, and each incremental backup tape is relatively small. Keep in mind that though we may use the word "tape" even when a different storage medium is used, the concept is still the same.

An incremental backup backs up only files that have the archive bit turned on. That is how it can identify which files have changed or which ones have been created. At the conclusion of the backup, the archive bit is turned off for all the files that were included in the backup.

Differential Backup   A *differential backup* is similar in function to an incremental backup, but it backs up any files that have been altered since the last full backup; it makes duplicate copies of files that haven't changed since the last differential backup. If a full backup were performed on Sunday night, a differential backup performed on Monday night would capture the information that was changed on Monday. A differential backup completed on Tuesday night would record the changes in any files from Monday and any changes in files on Tuesday. As you can see, during the week each differential backup would become larger; by Friday or Saturday night, it might be nearly as large as a full backup. This means that the backups in the earliest part of the weekly cycle will be very fast, whereas each successive one will be slower.

HSM   *Hierarchical storage management (HSM)* is a newer backup type. HSM provides continuous online backup by using optical or tape jukeboxes. It appears as an infinite disk to the system, and it can be configured to provide the closest version of an available real-time backup. So rather than using one of the three traditional backup strategies, you ensure that data is being continuously backed up.

The acronym HSM is used for more than one security-related entity. Not only does it stand for hierarchical storage management, as discussed here, but it's commonly used for hardware security module as well—a method of transient cryptographic key exchange. If you see a test question on HSM, make sure to read it carefully in order to know with which meaning it is being associated before answering.

When these backup methods are used in conjunction with each other, the risk of loss can be greatly reduced, but you can never combine incremental and differential backups in the same set. One of the major factors in determining which combination of these three methods to use is time—in an ideal situation, a full backup would be performed every day. Several commercial backup programs support these three backup methods. You must evaluate your organizational needs when choosing which tools to use to accomplish backups.

Almost every stable operating system contains a utility for creating a copy of the configuration settings necessary to reach the present state after a disaster and for resetting to them. In Windows 10, for example, this is accomplished with *System Restore*. Make certain that you know how to do an equivalent operation for the operating system that you are running.

As an administrator, you must know how to do backups and be familiar with all the options available to you. In Exercise 12.1, we'll show you how to perform a backup in SUSE Linux.

EXERCISE 12.1

Creating a Backup in SUSE Linux

This exercise assumes the use of a SUSE Linux Enterprise Server. Although backups are available in all Linux distributions, SUSE simplifies this task (and most other administrative tasks as well) by including the YaST (Yet Another Setup Tool) interface.

1. Log in as root and start YaST.

2. Choose System and System Backup.

3. Click Profile Management and choose Add; then, enter a name for the new profile, such as **fullsystemback**.

4. Click OK.

5. Enter a backup name (using an absolute path such as /home/mybackup.tar), and make certain that the archive type is set to a tar variety. Then click Next.

6. At the File Selection window, leave the default options and click Next.

7. Leave the Search Constraints at the defaults and click OK.

8. At the main YaST System Backup dialog box, click Start Backup. After several minutes of reading packages, the backup will begin.

Developing a Backup Plan

Several common models are used in designing backup plans. Each has its own advantages and disadvantages. Numerous methods have been developed to deal with archival backup; most of them are evolutions of the three models discussed here:

Grandfather, Father, Son Method   The *Grandfather, Father, Son method* is based on the philosophy that a full backup should occur at regular intervals, such as monthly or weekly. This method assumes that the most recent backup after the full backup is the son. As newer backups are made, the son becomes the father, and the father, in turn, becomes the grandfather. At the end of each month, a full backup is performed on all systems. This backup is stored in an offsite facility for a period of one year. Each monthly backup replaces the monthly backup from the previous year. Weekly or daily incremental backups are performed and stored until the next full backup occurs. This full backup is then stored offsite, and the weekly or daily backup tapes are reused (the January 1 incremental backup is used on February 1, and so on).

This method ensures that in the event of a loss, the full backup from the end of the last month and the daily backups can be used to restore information to the last day. Figure 12.2 illustrates this concept. The annual backup is referred to as the grandfather, the monthly backup is the father, and the weekly backup is the son. The last backup of the month becomes the archived backup for that month. The last backup of the year becomes the annual backup for the year. Annual backups are usually archived; this allows an organization to have backups available for several years and minimizes the likelihood of data loss. It's a common practice for an organization to keep a minimum of seven years in archives.

FIGURE 12.2   Grandfather, Father, Son backup method

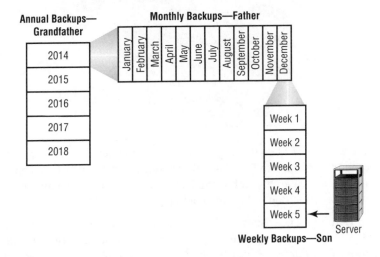

The last full backup of the year is permanently retained. This ensures that previous years' information can be recovered if necessary.

The major difficulty with this process is that a large number of tapes are constantly flowing between the storage facility and the computer center. In addition, cataloging daily and weekly backups can be complicated. It can become difficult to determine which files have been backed up and where they're stored.

Although the Grandfather, Father, Son method is the most common, and the one on which you will be tested, other obscure methods exist. One such method is called the Tower of Hanoi method. It is based on a mathematical word problem called the Tower of Hanoi. The details of this method are not important for the Security+ exam.

Full Archival Method   The *Full Archival method* works on the assumption that any information created on any system is stored forever. All backups are kept indefinitely using some form of backup media. In short, all full backups, all incremental backups, and any other backups are permanently kept somewhere.

This method effectively eliminates the potential for loss of data. Everything that is created on any computer is backed up forever. Figure 12.3 illustrates this method. As you can see, the number of copies of the backup media can quickly overwhelm your storage capabilities. Some organizations that have tried to do this have needed entire warehouses to contain their archival backups.

FIGURE 12.3 Full Archival backup method

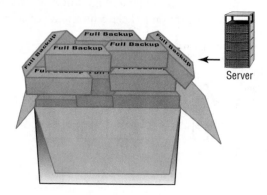

Think about the number of files your organization has: how much storage media would be required to accomplish full archiving? The other major problem involves keeping records of what information has been archived. For these reasons, many larger companies don't find this to be an acceptable method of keeping backups.

Backup Server Method The costs of disk storage and servers have fallen tremendously over the past few years. Lower prices have made it easier for organizations to use dedicated servers for backup. The *Backup Server method* establishes a server with large amounts of disk space whose sole purpose is to back up data. With the right software, a dedicated server can examine and copy all the files that have been altered every day.

Figure 12.4 illustrates the use of backup servers. In this instance, the files on the backup server contain copies of all the information and data on the APPS, ACCTG, and DB servers. The files on the three servers are copied to the backup server on a regular basis; over time, this server's storage requirements can become enormous. The advantage of this method is that all backed-up data is available online for immediate access.

FIGURE 12.4 A backup server archiving server files

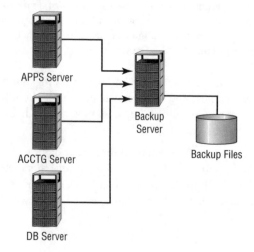

This server can be backed up on a regular basis, and the backups can be kept for a specified period. If a system or server malfunctions, the backup server can be accessed to restore information from the last backups performed on that system.

Backup servers don't need overly large processors; however, they must have large disk and other long-term storage media capabilities. Several software manufacturers take backup servers one additional step and create hierarchies of files. Over time, if a file isn't accessed, it's moved to slower media and may eventually be stored offline. This helps reduce the disk storage requirements, yet it still keeps the files that are most likely to be needed for recovery readily available.

Many organizations use two or more of these methods to back up systems. The issue becomes one of storage requirements and retention requirements. In establishing a backup plan, you must ask users and managers how much backup (in terms of frequency, size of files, and so forth) is really needed and how long it will be needed.

 Make sure that you obtain input from all who are dealing with governmental or regulatory agencies. Each agency may have different archival requirements, and compliance violations can be expensive. Both HIPAA and Sarbanes-Oxley are affecting—and driving—archival and disposal policies around the nation.

Recovering a System

When a system fails, you'll be unable to reestablish operation without regenerating all of the system's components. This process includes making sure that hardware is functioning, restoring or installing the operating systems, restoring or installing applications, and restoring data files. It can take several days on a large system. With a little forethought, you may be able to simplify the process and make it easily manageable.

When you install a new system, make a full backup of it before any data files are created. If stored onsite, this backup will be readily available for use. If you've standardized your systems, you may need just one copy of a base system that contains all the common applications that you use. The base system can usually be quickly restored, which allows for reconnection to the network for restoration of other software. Many newer operating systems now provide this capability, and system restores are very fast.

Figure 12.5 demonstrates this process further. Notice that installation DVDs are being used for the base OS and applications.

When the base system has been restored, data files and any other needed files can be restored from the last full backup and any incremental or differential backups that have been performed. The last full backup should contain most of the data on the system; the incremental backup or differential backups contain the data that has changed since the full backup.

Many newer operating systems allow you to create a model user system as a disk image on a server; the disk image is downloaded and installed when a failure occurs. This method makes it easier for administrators to restore a system than it would be to do it manually. It's all well and good to know how to make backups and the importance of doing so. There will come a time, however, when a recovery—the whole reason for disaster planning—will be necessary. As an administrator, you must be ready for this event and know how to handle it.

FIGURE 12.5 System regeneration process for a workstation or server

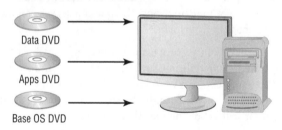

Data DVD

Apps DVD

Base OS DVD

An important recovery issue is to know the order in which to proceed. If a server is completely destroyed and must be re-created, ascertain which applications are the most important and should be restored before the others. Likewise, which services are most important to the users from a business standpoint and need to be available? At the same time, which services are nice but not necessary to keep the business running? The answers will differ for every organization, and you must know them for yours.

Backout vs. Backup

Although most attention deservedly is on backups, never overlook the need for a backout plan. A *backout* is a reversion from a change that had negative consequences. It could be, for example, that everything was working fine until you installed a service pack on a production machine, and then services that were normally available were no longer accessible. The backout, in this instance, would revert the system to the state it was in before the service pack was applied.

Backout plans can include uninstalling service packs, hotfixes, and patches, but they can also include reversing a migration and using previous iterations of firmware. A key component to creating such a plan is identifying what events will trigger your implementing the backout.

Planning for Recovery Sites

Another key aspect of a disaster-recovery plan is to provide for the restoration of business functions in the event of a large-scale loss of service. You can lease or purchase a facility that is available on short notice for the purpose of restoring network or systems operations. These are referred to as *recovery sites, alternate sites,* or *backup sites.*

Another term for *alternate site* is *alternative site;* the terms are often used interchangeably.

If the power in your local area were disrupted for several days, how would you reestablish service at an alternate site until primary services were restored? Several options exist to do this; we'll briefly present them here. These solutions are not ideal, but they are always considered to be significantly less costly—in terms of time—to implement than the estimated time of bringing your original site back up to speed. They are used to allow you to get your organization back on its feet until permanent service is available. An alternate site can be a hot site, a warm site, or a cold site:

Hot Site   A *hot site* is a location that can provide operations within hours of a failure. This type of site would have servers, networks, and telecommunications equipment in place to reestablish service in a short time. Hot sites provide network connectivity, systems, and preconfigured software to meet the needs of an organization. Databases can be kept up-to-date using network connections. These types of facilities are expensive, and they're primarily suitable for short-term situations. A hot site may also double as an offsite storage facility, providing immediate access to archives and backup media.

A hot site is also referred to as an *active backup model.*

Many hot sites also provide office facilities and other services so that a business can relocate a small number of employees to sustain operations.

Given the choice, every organization would choose to have a hot site. Doing so is often not practical, however, on a cost basis.

Warm Site   A *warm site* provides some of the capabilities of a hot site, but it requires the customer to do more work to become operational. Warm sites provide computer systems and compatible media capabilities. If a warm site is used, administrators and other staff will need to install and configure systems to resume operations. For most organizations, a warm site could be a remote office, a leased facility, or another organization with which yours has a reciprocal agreement.

Another term for a warm site/reciprocal site is *active/active model.*

Warm sites may be for your exclusive use, but they don't have to be. A warm site requires more advanced planning, testing, and access to media for system recovery. Warm sites represent a compromise between a hot site, which is very expensive, and a cold site, which isn't preconfigured.

An agreement between two companies to provide services in the event of an emergency is called a *reciprocal agreement.* Usually, these agreements are made on a best-effort basis; there is no guarantee that services will be available if the site is needed. Make sure that your agreement is with an organization that is outside of your geographic area. If both sites are affected by the same disaster, the agreement is worthless.

Cold Site   A *cold site* is a facility that isn't immediately ready to use. The organization using it must bring along its equipment and network. A cold site may provide network capability, but this isn't usually the case; the site provides a place for operations to resume, but it doesn't provide the infrastructure to support those operations. Cold sites work well when an extended outage is anticipated. The major challenge is that the customer must provide all the capabilities and do all the work to get back into operation. Cold sites are usually the least expensive to put into place, but they require the most advanced planning, testing, and resources to become operational—occasionally taking up to a month to make operational.

> Almost anywhere can be a cold site; if necessary, users could work out of your garage for a short time. Although this may be a practical solution, it also opens up risks that you must consider. For example, while you're operating from your garage, will the servers be secure should someone break in?

Herein lies the problem. The likelihood that you'll need any of these facilities is low—most organizations will never need to use these types of facilities. The costs are usually based on a subscription or other contracted relationships, and it's difficult for most organizations to justify the expense. In addition, planning, testing, and maintaining these facilities is difficult; it does little good to pay for any of these services if they don't work and aren't available when you need them.

> One of the most important aspects of using alternative sites is documentation. To create an effective site, you must have solid documentation of what you have, what you're using, and what you need in order to get by.

Management must view the disaster-recovery plan as an integral part of its *business continuity planning (BCP)*. Management must also provide the resources needed to implement and maintain an alternative site after the decision has been made to contract for the facilities. It is their responsibility to factor geographic distance into their selection criteria and include travel-related costs associated with the distance.

 Real World Scenario

Some Protection Is Better than None—Or Is It?

You've been tasked with the responsibility of developing a recovery plan for your company to have in place in a critical infrastructure failure. Your CEO is concerned about the budget and doesn't want to invest many resources in a full-blown hot site.

Several options are available to you in this situation. You need to evaluate the feasibility of a warm site, a cold site, or a reciprocal agreement with another company. The warm site and cold site options will cost less than a hot site, but they will require a great deal of work in the event of a failure. A reciprocal site may be a good alternative to both, if a suitable partner organization can be found. You may want to discuss this possibility with some of your larger vendors or other companies that may have excess computer capacity. No matter which direction you recommend, you should test and develop procedures to manage the transition from your primary site to an offsite facility.

Incident Response Procedures

An *incident response plan*, outlining action steps, or *incident response procedures* will define how an organization should respond to an incident. These policies may involve third parties, and they need to be comprehensive. The term *incident* is somewhat nebulous in scope. For our purposes, an incident is any attempt to violate a security policy, a successful penetration, a compromise of a system, or any unauthorized access to information. This includes system failures and disruption of services in the organization.

It's important that an incident response plan establish at least the following items:

- Guidelines for documenting the incident type and defining its category. This includes list(s) of information that should be collected about an incident and the procedures to gather and secure evidence.

- Resources used to deal with an incident.

- Defined roles and responsibilities for those who are involved in the investigation and response. This should identify members of the cyber-incident response team(s).

- Reporting requirements and escalation procedures including a list of outside agencies that should be contacted or notified and outside experts who can be used to address issues if needed.

According to CERT, a *Computer Security Incident Response Team (CSIRT)* can be a formalized or an ad hoc team. You can toss a team together to respond to an incident after it arises, but investing time in the development process can make an incident more manageable. Many decisions about dealing with an incident will have been considered in advance. Incidents are high-stress situations; therefore, it's better to simplify the process by considering important aspects in advance. If civil or criminal actions are part of the process, evidence must be gathered and safeguarded properly.

Let's say that you've just discovered a situation where a fraud has been perpetrated internally using a corporate computer. You're part of the investigation team. Your incident response policy lists the specialists that you need to contact for an investigation. Ideally, you've already met the investigator or investigating firm, you've developed an understanding of how to protect the scene, and you know how to deal properly with the media (if they become involved).

Your policies must also clearly outline who needs to be informed in the company, what they need to be told, and how to respond to the situation. Incidents should include not only intrusions but also attempts.

Just as fire drills are helpful for dealing with the real crisis when it comes, one of the best ways to be prepared to deal with an incident is to *exercise* responses to emergencies before they happen. Include the members of the team, and walk through mock incidences on a regular basis to identify weaknesses in your response and solutions for them.

The six steps of any incident response process should be as follows:

- Preparation
- Identification
- Containment
- Eradication
- Recovery
- Lessons learned

In the section that follows, we will walk through these steps in more detail to aid in understanding the incident response process.

Understanding Incident Response

Forensics refers to the process of identifying what has occurred on a system by examining the data trail. It involves an analysis of evidence found in computers and on digital storage media. *Incident response* encompasses forensics and refers to the process of identifying, investigating, repairing, documenting, and adjusting procedures to prevent another incident. An *incident* is the occurrence of any event that endangers a system or network. We need to discuss responses to two types of incidents: internal incidents and incidents involving law enforcement professionals.

It's a good idea to include the procedures that you'll generally follow in an *incident response plan (IRP)*. The IRP outlines what steps are needed and who is responsible for deciding how to handle a situation. The Computer Science department at Carnegie Mellon pioneered this process.

Law enforcement personnel are governed by the rules of evidence, and their response to an incident will be largely out of your control. You need to consider involving law enforcement carefully before you decide that you do not want to handle the situation without them. There is no such thing as dropping charges. Once they begin, law enforcement professionals are required to pursue an investigation.

The term *incident* has special meanings in different industries. In the banking and financial areas, it's very specific and involves something that includes the loss of money. You wouldn't want to call a hacker attempt an *incident* if you were involved in a bank network because this terminology would automatically trigger an entirely different type of investigation.

The next five sections deal with the phases of a typical incident response process. The steps are generic in this example. Each organization will have a specific set of procedures that will generally map to these steps.

However, before an incident occurs there needs to be substantial preparation. Preparing for incident response involves multiple factors. The first step is outlining how you intend to respond to specific incidents. Formulating an IRP is part of that preparation. You also will need to identify the personnel and resources required for your response. For example, if you intend to take a server offline in the event that it is breached, do you have a backup server available? In the event of a suspected computer crime, which of your personnel are qualified to perform the initial forensic processes? If no one is qualified, you need to identify a third party that you can contact.

An important concept to keep in mind when working with incidents is the *chain of custody*, which covers how evidence is secured, where it is stored, and who has access to it. When you begin to collect evidence, you must keep track of that evidence at all times and show who has it, who has seen it, and where it has been. The evidence must always be within your custody or you're open to dispute about possible evidence tampering. It is highly recommended that active logging be used during the strategic intelligence/counterintelligence gathering phase to document every access and visuals (pictures and video) recorded to show how the evidence is secured.

The process that is used during *data acquisition* for the preservation of all forms of relevant information when litigation is reasonably anticipated is known as *legal hold*.

Step 1: Identifying the Incident

Incident identification is the first step in determining what has occurred in your organization. An internal or external attack may have been part of a larger attack that has just surfaced, or it may be a random probe or scan of your network.

An event is often an IDS-triggered signal. Operations personnel will determine if an *event* becomes an *incident*. An easy way to think of the two is that an event is anything that happens, whereas an incident is any event that endangers a system or network.

Many IDSs trigger false positives when reporting incidents. *False positives* are events that aren't really incidents. Remember that an IDS is based on established rules of acceptance (deviations from which are known as *anomalies*) and attack signatures. If the rules aren't set up properly, normal traffic may set off the analyzer and generate an event. Be sure to double-check your results because you don't want to declare a false emergency.

One problem that can occur with manual network monitoring is overload. Over time, a slow attack may develop that increases in intensity. Manual processes typically will adapt, and they may not notice the attack until it's too late to stop it. Personnel tend to adapt to changing environments if the changes occur over a long period of time. An automated monitoring system, such as an IDS, will sound the alarm when a certain threshold or activity level occurs.

When a suspected incident pops up, *first responders* are those individuals who must ascertain whether it truly is an incident or a false alarm. Depending on your organization, the first responder may be the main security administrator, or it could consist of a team of network and system administrators.

The very first step, even with a suspected incident, is isolation. If you think, for example, that a given machine is infected with a virus, you must isolate that machine, even before you are sure that it is indeed infected. This involves quarantining the machine(s) that you suspect of being infected. Literally disconnect them from the network while you analyze the situation. In some cases, this is accomplished with simple device removal—just remove the device from the network by unplugging the network cable.

After you've determined that you indeed have an incident on your hands, you need to consider how to handle it. This process, called *escalation*, involves consulting policies, consulting appropriate management, and determining how best to conduct an investigation into the incident. Make sure that the methods you use to investigate the incident are consistent with corporate and legal requirements for your organization. Bring your Human Resources and Legal departments into the investigation early, and seek their guidance whenever questions involving their areas of expertise arise.

If you work for a multinational corporation, it is important to have a legal department that proactively offers advice on geographic matters such as *data sovereignty*. This is the concept that data is subject to the laws of where it is stored and legal implications of this should factor heavily into server location selection, backup facilities, and all other aspects of business operations.

A key aspect, often overlooked by system professionals, involves information control. When an incident occurs, who is responsible for managing the communications about the incident? Employees in the company may naturally be curious about a situation. A single spokesperson needs to be designated. Remember, what one person knows runs a risk of one hundred others also finding out.

Real World Scenario

The Email Incident

You're the administrator of a small network. This network has an old mail server that is used for internal and external email. You periodically investigate log and audit files to determine the status of your systems and servers. Recently, you noticed that your email log file has been reporting a large number of undeliverable or bounced emails. The addresses appear to be random. Upon examining the email system, you notice that the outbound mail folder seems to be sending mail every second. A large number of files are being sent. After inspecting the workstations in the business, you determine that several of them have out-of-date antivirus software. How should you handle this situation?

For starters, you may have one or more viruses or worms in your system. This type of virus sounds like a Simple Mail Transfer Protocol (SMTP) virus, and a virus can gain access to the address directory and propagate itself using SMTP.

You should investigate why the antivirus software is out-of-date, upgrade these systems as appropriate, and add server-based and mail-server virus-protection capabilities to your network.

Step 2: Investigating the Incident

The process of investigating an incident involves searching logs, files, and any other sources of data about the nature and scope of the incident. If possible, you should determine whether this is part of a larger attack, a random event, or a false positive. False positives are common in an IDS environment and may be the result of unusual traffic in the network. It may be that your network is being pinged by a class of computer security students to demonstrate the return times, or it may be that an automated tool is launching an attack.

> It is sad but true: One reason administrators don't put as much security on networks as they should is because they do not want to have to deal with the false positives. Although this is a poor excuse, administrators still often use it. As a security administrator, you must seek a balance between being overwhelmed with too much unneeded information and knowing when something out of the ordinary is occurring. It is an elusive balance that is easier to talk about than to find, but it's one for which you must strive.

You might find that the incident doesn't require a response if it can't be successful. Your investigation might conclude that a change in policies is required to deal with a new type of threat. These types of decisions should be documented and, if necessary, reconfigurations should be made to deal with the change.

What if the Intrusion Is Now?

Suppose a junior administrator rushes into your office and reports that an alert just notified him that the guest user account has logged in remotely. A suspected attack is occurring this very moment. What should you do?

You should respond to an attack that's occurring at this moment the same way that you would respond to one that happened before you knew about it. You need to determine what the account is doing and try to figure out the identity of the attacker and where they're coming from. As you collect any information, you should treat it as evidence and keep careful watch over it.

Although collecting as much information as possible is important, no one can be blamed for trying to protect their data. Damage and loss control are critical; you need to minimize the impact of the incident. Though it may be admirable to catch a crook deleting your data, if you can keep the data from being deleted, you will stand a much better chance of still being employed tomorrow. As soon as it becomes apparent that data is at risk, you should disconnect the user. Catching a bad guy is a noble task, but the security of the data should be considered paramount.

Step 3: Recovery/Repairing the Damage

One of your first considerations after an incident is to determine how to restore access to resources that have been compromised. Then, of course, you must reestablish control of the system. Most operating systems provide the ability to create a disaster-recovery process using distribution media or system state files.

After a problem has been identified, what steps will you take to restore service? In the case of a DoS attack, a system reboot may be all that is required. Your operating system manufacturer will typically provide detailed instructions or documentation on how to restore services in the event of an attack.

If a system has been severely compromised, as in the case of a worm, it might not be possible to repair it. It may need to be regenerated from scratch. Fortunately, antivirus software packages can repair most of the damage done by the viruses you encounter. But what if you come across something new? You might need to start over with a new system. In that case, we strongly advise you to do a complete disk drive format or repartition to ensure that nothing is lurking on the disk, waiting to infect your network again.

In some cases, it may not be possible to repair the problem completely. If data has been stolen, you cannot go back in time and prevent the loss of that data. In such cases, you must take mitigation steps. These are steps to lessen the damage. For example, if data has been stolen, you might do the following:

1. Immediately change all passwords.

2. Notify the relevant parties.

3. Make procedural changes so that the information stolen cannot be used to affect additional breaches.

 Real World Scenario

The Virus That Won't Stop

A virus recently hit a user in your organization through an email attachment. The user updated all of the programs in his computer and also updated his antivirus software; however, he's still reporting unusual behavior in his computer system. He's also receiving complaints from people in his email address book because he's sending them a virus. You've been asked to fix the problem.

The user has probably contracted a worm that has infected the system files in his computer. You should help him back up his user files to removable media. Then completely reformat his drives and reinstall the operating system and applications. After you've replaced these, you can install new antivirus software and scan the entire system. When the scan is complete, help the user reinstall data files and scan the system again for viruses. This process should eliminate all viruses from system, application, and data files.

 Just as every network, regardless of size, should have a firewall, it should also be protected by antivirus software that is enabled and current. ClamAV (www.clamav.net) is an open source solution once available only for Unix-based systems that is now offered for most operating systems.

Step 4: Documenting and Reporting the Response

During the entire process of responding to an incident, you should document the steps you take to identify, detect, and repair the system or network. This information is valuable; it needs to be captured in case an attack like this occurs again. The documentation should be accessible by the people most likely to deal with this type of problem. Many help-desk software systems provide detailed methods that you can use to record procedures and steps. These types of software products allow for fast access.

If appropriate, you should report/disclose the incident to legal authorities and CERT (www.cert.org) so that others can be aware of the type of attack and help to look for proactive measures to prevent it from happening again.

You might also want to inform the software or system manufacturer of the problem and how you corrected it. Doing so might help them inform or notify other customers of the threat and save time for someone else.

 **Real World Scenario**

How Incident Response Plans Work

Emergency management (EM) personnel routinely stage fake emergencies to verify that they know what to do in the event of an actual emergency. For example, if you live in a town with a train track that is routinely used by railcars carrying toxic chemicals, it isn't uncommon for EM personnel to stage a fake spill every few years. Those organizing the practice drill won't tell those responding what type of spill it is, or the severity of it, until they arrive at the scene. The organizers monitor and evaluate the responses to see that they're appropriate and where they can be improved.

Responding to security incidents requires the same type of focus and training. You should plan a fake incident at your site, inform all of those who will be involved that it's coming, and then evaluate their response. You should evaluate the following items:

1. Was the evidence gathered and the chain of custody maintained?

2. Did the escalation procedures follow the correct path?

3. Given the results of the investigation, would you be able to find and prosecute the culprit?

4. What was done that should not have been done?

5. What could have been done better?

Practice makes perfect, and there is no better time to practice your company's response to an emergency than before one really occurs.

Step 5: Adjusting Procedures

After an incident has been successfully managed, it's a worthwhile step to revisit the procedures and policies in place in your organization to determine what changes, if any, need to be made.

Answering simple questions can sometimes be helpful when you're resolving problems. The following questions might be included in a policy or procedure manual:

- How did the policies work or not work in this situation?

- What did you learn about the situation that was new?

- What should you do differently next time?

These simple questions can help you adjust the procedures. This process is called a *postmortem*, and it's the equivalent of an autopsy.

Forensics from the Security+ Perspective

The five steps outlined here will help in all incident response situations. For the exam, however, there are a number of procedures and topics about which CompTIA wants you to be aware that are relevant to a forensic investigation. We strongly recommend that you familiarize yourself with these topics as you prepare for the exam.

Act in Order of Volatility   When dealing with multiple issues, address them in order of volatility (OOV); always deal with the most volatile first. *Volatility* can be thought of as the amount of time that you have to collect certain data before a window of opportunity is gone. Naturally, in an investigation you want to collect everything, but some data will exist longer than others, and you cannot possibly collect all of it once. As an example, the OOV in an investigation may be RAM, hard drive data, CDs/DVDs, and printouts.

Capture System Image   A *system image* is a snapshot of what exists. Capturing an image of the operating system in its exploited state can be helpful in revisiting the issue after the fact to learn more about it. As an analogy, think of germ samples that are stored in labs after major outbreaks so that scientists can revisit them later and study them further.

Document Network Traffic and Logs   Look at network traffic and logs to see what information you can find there. This information can be useful in identifying trends associated with repeated attacks.

Capture Video   Capture any relevant video that you can. Video can later be analyzed manually in individual frames as well as run through a number of programs that can create indices of the contents.

Record Time Offset   It is quite common for workstation times to be off slightly from actual time, and that can happen with servers as well. Since a forensic investigation is usually dependent on a step-by-step account of what has happened, being able to follow events in the correct time sequence is critical. Because of this, it is imperative to record the time offset on each affected machine during the investigation. One method of assisting with this is to add an entry to a log file and note the time that this was done and the time associated with it on the system.

Take Hashes   It is important to collect as much data as possible to be able to illustrate the situation, and hashes must not be left out of the equation. NIST (the National Institute of Standards and Technology) maintains a *National Software Reference Library (NSRL)*. One of the purposes of the NSRL is to collect "known, traceable software applications" through their hash values and store them in a Reference Data Set (RDS). The RDS can then be used by law enforcement, government agencies, and businesses to determine which files are important as evidence in criminal investigations. More information on the RDS can be found at https://www.nsrl.nist.gov/.

Capture Screenshots   Just like video, capture all relevant screenshots for later analysis. One image can often parlay the same information that it would take hundreds of log entries to equal.

Talk to Witnesses   It is important to talk to as many witnesses as possible to learn exactly what happened and to do so as soon as possible after the incident. Over time, details and reflections can change, and you want to collect their thoughts before such changes occur. If at all possible, document as much of the interview as you can with video recorders, digital recorders, or whatever recording tools you can find.

Track Man-Hours and Expenses   Make no mistake about it; an investigation is expensive. Track total man-hours and expenses associated with the investigation, and be prepared to justify them if necessary to superiors, a court, or insurance agents.

After-Action Reports   Never, after recovery from any disaster/incident, fail to have the recovery team meet for an after-action review. This debriefing needs to include a sharing by team members of the steps taken, along with an open discussion of what worked and what should be changed in future crises. An evaluation of recovery objective performance, and any metrics used during or following the event should be reviewed.

Tabletop Exercises

A *tabletop exercise* is a simulation of a disaster. It is a way to check to see if your plans are ready to go. There are five levels of testing:

Document Review   A review of recovery, operations, resumption plans, and procedures.

Walkthrough   A group discussion of recovery, operations, resumption plans, and procedures.

Simulation   A walkthrough of recovery, operations, resumption plans, and procedures in a scripted "case study" or "scenario."

Parallel Test   With this test, you start up all backup systems but leave the main systems functioning.

Cutover Test   This test shuts down the main systems and has everything fail over to backup systems.

You should never do a cutover test if you have not already done a simulation and parallel test. If the cutover test fails, your entire system is offline; in essence, you have created a disaster. The larger the system, the more wide-ranging an impact the system being down can have. Because of this, doing a cutover test can be very difficult, but you should never simply ignore those systems in your disaster-recovery planning just because of the challenge they entail.

Summary

In this chapter, you learned about the many aspects involved in the operations of a secure environment. You studied business continuity and vendor support. Business continuity planning is the process of making decisions about how losses, outages, and failures are handled within an organization. Business impact analysis includes evaluating the critical functions of the organization. This information is used to make educated decisions about how to deal with outages should they occur.

The issue of reliable service from utility companies, such as electricity and water, should be evaluated as part of your disaster-recovery process. Addressing potential problems as part of your business decision making can prevent unanticipated downtime.

Disaster recovery is the process of helping your organization prepare for recovery in the event of an unplanned situation, and it's a part of your organization's business continuity plans.

The process of dealing with a security problem is called incident response. An incident response policy should clearly outline what resources, individuals, and procedures are to be involved in the event of an incident.

Exam Essentials

Understand the aspects of disaster recovery.   Disaster recovery is concerned with the recovery of critical systems in the event of a loss. One of the primary issues is the effectiveness of backup policies and procedures. Offsite storage is one of the most secure methods of protecting information from loss.

Know the types of backups that are typically performed in an organization.   The three backup methods are full, incremental, and differential. A full backup involves the total archiving of all information on a system. An incremental backup involves archiving only information that has changed since the last backup. Differential backups save all information that has changed since the last full backup.

Be able to discuss the process of recovering a system in the event of a failure.   A system recovery usually involves restoring the base operating systems, applications, and data files. The operating systems and applications are usually restored either from the original distribution media or from a server that contains images of the system. Data is typically recovered from backups or archives.

Be able to discuss the types of alternative sites available for disaster recovery.   The three types of sites available for disaster recovery are hot sites, warm sites, and cold sites. Hot sites typically provide high levels of capability, including networking. Warm sites may provide some capabilities, but they're generally less prepared than a hot site. A cold site requires the organization to replicate critical systems and all services to restore operations.

Be able to describe the needed components of an incident response policy.   The incident response policy explains how incidents will be handled, including notification, resources, and escalation. This policy drives the incident response process, and it provides advance planning to the incident response team.

Understand the basics of forensics.   Forensics is the process of identifying what has occurred on a system by examining the data trail. It involves an analysis of evidence found in computers and on digital storage media. When dealing with multiple issues, address them in order of volatility: capture system images as a snapshot of what exists, look at network traffic and logs, capture any relevant video/screenshots/hashes, record time offset on the systems, talk to witnesses, and track total man-hours and expenses associated with the investigation.

Review Questions

You can find the answers in the Appendix.

1. Which plan or policy helps an organization determine how to relocate to an emergency site?

   A. Disaster-recovery plan

   B. Backup site plan

   C. Privilege management policy

   D. Privacy plan

2. Although you're talking to her on the phone, the sound of the administrative assistant's screams of despair can be heard down the hallway. She has inadvertently deleted a file that the boss desperately needs. Which type of backup is used for the immediate recovery of a lost file?

   A. Onsite storage

   B. Working copies

   C. Incremental backup

   D. Differential backup

3. You're trying to rearrange your backup procedures to reduce the amount of time they take each evening. You want the backups to finish as quickly as possible during the week. Which backup system backs up only the files that have changed since the last backup?

   A. Full backup

   B. Incremental backup

   C. Differential backup

   D. Backup server

4. Which backup system backs up all the files that have changed since the last full backup?

   A. Full backup

   B. Incremental backup

   C. Differential backup

   D. Archival backup

5. You're a consultant brought in to advise MTS on its backup procedures. One of the first problems you notice is that the company doesn't use a good tape-rotation scheme. Which backup method uses a rotating schedule of backup media to ensure long-term information storage?

   A. Grandfather, Father, Son method

   B. Full Archival method

   C. Backup Server method

   D. Differential Backup method

6. Which site best provides limited capabilities for the restoration of services in a disaster?

   A. Hot site

   B. Warm site

   C. Cold site

   D. Backup site

7. You're the head of information technology for MTS and have a brother in a similar position for ABC. The companies are approximately the same size and are located several hundred miles apart. As a benefit to both companies, you want to implement an agreement that would allow either company to use resources at the other site should a disaster make a building unusable. What type of agreement between two organizations provides mutual use of their sites in the event of an emergency?

   A. Backup-site agreement

   B. Warm-site agreement

   C. Hot-site agreement

   D. Reciprocal agreement

8. The process of automatically switching from a malfunctioning system to another system is called what?

   A. Fail-safe

   B. Redundancy

   C. Failover

   D. Hot site

9. Which of the following types of penetration testing focuses on the system, using techniques such as port scans, traceroute information, and network mapping to find weaknesses?

   A. Active reconnaissance

   B. Passive reconnaissance

   C. Operational reconnaissance

   D. Constricted reconnaissance

10. Your company is about to invest heavily in a new server farm and have made an attractive offer for a parcel of land in another country. A consultant working on another project hears of this and suggests that you get the offer rescinded because the laws in that country are much more stringent than where you currently operate. Which of the following is the concept that data is subject to the laws of where it is stored?

   A. Data sovereignty

   B. Data subjugation

   C. Data dominion

   D. Data protectorate

11. Which of the following would normally *not* be part of an incident response policy?

    A. Outside agencies (that require status)

    B. Outside experts (to resolve the incident)

    C. Contingency plans

    D. Evidence collection procedures

12. Which of the following is the process used during data acquisition for the preservation of all forms of relevant information when litigation is reasonably anticipated?

    A. Chain of custody

    B. Order of volatility

    C. Legal hold

    D. Strategic intelligence gathering

13. Which of the following types of vulnerability scans uses actual network authentication to connect to systems and scan for vulnerabilities?

    A. Credentialed

    B. Validated

    C. Endorsed

    D. Confirmed

14. What is another name for working copies?

    A. Functional copies

    B. Running copies

    C. Operating copies

    D. Shadow copies

15. Which of the following is a reversion from a change that had negative consequences?

    A. Backup

    B. ERD

    C. Backout

    D. DIS

16. Karl is conducting penetration testing on the Pranks Anonymous servers and having difficulty finding a weakness. Suddenly, he discovers that security on a different company's server—a vendor to Pranks Anonymous—can be breached. Once he has compromised the completely different company's server, he can access the Pranks Anonymous servers and then launch an attack. What is this weakness/exploit known as?

    A. Fulcrum

    B. Pivot

    C. Swivel

    D. Twirl

17. According to CERT, which of the following would be a formalized or an ad hoc team you can call upon to respond to an incident after it arises?

   A. CSIRT

   B. CIRT

   C. IRT

   D. RT

18. Which of the following is a concept that works on the assumption that any information created on any system is stored forever?

   A. Cloud computing

   B. Warm site

   C. Big data

   D. Full archival

19. Which of the following is a newer backup type that provides continuous online backup by using optical or tape jukeboxes and can be configured to provide the closest version of an available real-time backup?

   A. TPM

   B. HSM

   C. SAN

   D. NAS

20. Which type of penetration-style testing involves actually trying to break into the network?

   A. Discreet

   B. Indiscreet

   C. Nonintrusive

   D. Intrusive

Appendix

Answers to Review Questions

Chapter 1: Managing Risk

1. C. Guidelines help clarify processes to maintain standards. Guidelines tend to be less formal than policies or standards.

2. A. It does not matter how frequent a loss is projected (only once every 60 years, in this case). What does matter is that each occurrence will be disastrous: SLE (single loss expectancy) is equal to asset value (AV) times exposure factor (EF). In this case, asset value is $2 million, and the exposure factor is 1.

3. D. ALE (annual loss expectancy) is equal to the SLE times the annualized rate of occurrence. In this case, the SLE is $2 million, and the ARO is 1/60.

4. A. ARO (annualized rate of occurrence) is the frequency (in number of years) that an event can be expected to happen. In this case, ARO is 1/60, or 0.0167.

5. B. Risk avoidance involves identifying a risk and making the decision no longer to engage in the actions associated with that risk.

6. B. The exception policy statement may include an escalation contact in the event that the person dealing with a situation needs to know whom to contact.

7. A. A separation of duties policy is designed to reduce the risk of fraud and to prevent other losses in an organization.

8. D. False positives are events that were mistakenly flagged and aren't truly events to be concerned about.

9. C. Change management is the structured approach that is followed to secure a company's assets.

10. E. Risk transference involves sharing some of the risk burden with someone else, such as an insurance company.

11. C. The risk-assessment component, in conjunction with the business impact analysis (BIA), provides an organization with an accurate picture of the situation it faces.

12. D. The accountability policy statement should address who is responsible for ensuring that the policy is enforced.

13. D. Risk mitigation is accomplished any time you take steps to reduce risk.

14. C. If you calculate the SLE to be $4,000 and that there will be 10 occurrences a year (ARO), then the ALE is $40,000 ($4,000 × 10).

15. B. The acceptable use policies describe how the employees in an organization can use company systems and resources, both software and hardware.

16. C. Collusion is an agreement between two or more parties established for the purpose of committing deception or fraud. Collusion, when part of a crime, is also a criminal act in and of itself.

17. C. The ISA (Interconnection Security Agreement) specifies the technical and security requirements of the interconnection.

18. A. If you calculate SLE to be $25,000 and that there will be one occurrence every four years (ARO), then the ALE is $6,250 ($25,000 × 0.25).

19. C. The principle of least privilege should be used when assigning permissions. Give users only the permissions that they need to do their work and no more.

20. A. Risk acceptance necessitates an identified risk that those involved understand the potential cost or damage and agree to accept it.

Chapter 2: Monitoring and Diagnosing Networks

1. C. A periodic update that corrects problems in one version of a product is called a service pack. Answer A is incorrect. A hot fix is an immediate and urgent fix for a specific problem. Answer B is incorrect; an Overhaul is not a term used in the industry. Answer D is incorrect. A patch is done to fix a specific problem.

2. B. An IDS monitors network traffic, but it does not take any specific action and is therefore considered passive. Answer A is incorrect because sniffers tend to be run for a specific period of time by a human operator. Answer C is incorrect; a firewall is for blocking traffic, not monitoring, and is thus not passive. Answer D is incorrect; a web browser is for viewing web pages.

3. A. A honeypot is a system specifically designed to be being broken into. Answers B, C, and D are not the terms used in the industry.

4. B. An administrator is the term for someone setting security policy in an IDS. Answers A, C and D are not the terms used in the industry.

5. C. Hardening is the term used for making a system as secure as it can be. Answers A, B, and D are not the terms used in the industry.

6. C. DMZs are meant to set public facing servers. The exterior firewall of the DMZ is more permissive than the interior, making the DMZ somewhat less secure. Answer A is incorrect. A honeynet is designed to catch attackers, and it should not be obviously less secure than the actual production network. Answer B is incorrect; a guest network is not meant to be accessible from the outside world. Answer D is incorrect. It would be completely insecure, not just somewhat less secure.

7. C. The other answers are other standards.

8. D. SED or Self Encrypting Drive is what is being described in this scenario. The other answers are related to cryptography but are not automatic. For example, FDE, or Full Disk Encryption, would fully encrypt the hard drive, but it would not be automatic.

9. C. This violated vendor diversity. He is using the same vendor for all of his anti-malware. If there is any flaw in that vendor or the algorithm used by that vendor misses a specific virus, then it will be missed everywhere.

10. A. An air-gapped backup is not exposed to the network and thus is far less likely to become infected. In fact, the only possibility for infection at the moment is that a backup is transferred to the air-gapped storage. If anti-virus is run just prior to this action, then the chances of malware in the backup become extremely small. The other answers have nothing to do with protecting backups.

Chapter 3: Understanding Devices and Infrastructure

1. C. Routers can be configured in many instances to act as packet-filtering firewalls. When configured properly, they can prevent unauthorized ports from being opened.

2. A. Packet filters prevent unauthorized packets from entering or leaving a network. Packet filters are a type of firewall that blocks specified port traffic.

3. D. Routers store information about network destinations in routing tables. Routing tables contain information about known hosts on both sides of the router.

4. B. Switches create virtual circuits between systems in a network. These virtual circuits are somewhat private and reduce network traffic when used.

5. A. IPsec provides network security for tunneling protocols. IPsec can be used with many different protocols besides TCP/IP, and it has two modes of security.

6. C. A load balancer can be implemented as a software or hardware solution and is usually associated with a device—a router, a firewall, NAT, and so on. As the name implies, it is used to shift a load from one device to another.

7. A. Switches are multiport devices that improve network efficiency. A switch typically has a small amount of information about systems in a network.

8. D. A heuristic system uses algorithms to analyze the traffic passing through the network.

9. A. Since encrypting data is very processor-intensive, SSL accelerators can be used to offload the public-key encryption to a separate plug-in card.

10. C. With WORM (write-once-read-many) protection, information, once written, cannot be modified thus assuring that the data cannot be tampered with once it is written to the device.

11. C. IPsec can work in either Tunneling or Transport mode. In Tunneling mode, the data or payload and message headers are encrypted. Transport mode encrypts only the payload.

12. A. With a full tunnel configuration, all requests are routed and encrypted through the VPN, while with a split tunnel, only some requests (usually all incoming) are routed and encrypted over the VPN.

13. B. With round-robin load balancing, the first client request is sent to the first group of servers, the second is sent to the second, and so on.

14. A. An active-active configuration means that more than one load balancing server is working at all times to handle the load/requests as they come in.

15. D. SSL decryptors work by decrypting encrypted traffic (SSL or TLS), inspecting it, and then re-encrypting it before sending it on to its destination.

16. B. TPM (Trusted Platform Module) is the name assigned to a chip that can store cryptographic keys, passwords, or certificates.

17. A. With MAC Filtering each host is identified by its MAC address and allowed (or denied) access based on that.

18. C. Bridges are used to divide larger networks into smaller sections by sitting between two physical network segments and managing the flow of data between the two.

19. D. Loops can occur when more than one bridge or switch is implemented on the network and the devices confuse each other by leading one another to believe that a host is located on a certain segment when it is not.

20. D. To combat the loop problem, technologies such as the Spanning Tree Protocol (STP) enable bridge/switch interfaces to be assigned a value that is then used to control the learning process and prevent loops.

Chapter 4: Identity and Access Management

1. B. Least privileges means to grant just enough privileges to do the job and no more. The other answers do not describe least privileges.

2. A. Discretionary access control allows users to define access. Answer B is incorrect, as this would be more restrictive. Answer C is role-based access control. Answer D is not an access control mechanism.

3. A. LDAP, or Lightweight Directory Access Control, is a directory access protocol. The other answers are simply not related to directory access.

4. A. Mandatory Access Control cannot be modified by users and is considered more secure. Answer B is incorrect—DAC provides the users flexibility and is less secure. Answer C is incorrect. RBAC is not based on pre-established access, but rather roles. Answer D is incorrect. Kerberos is an authentication protocol, not an access method.

5. C. Role-Based Access Control is based on the user's role, in this case the office administrator. Answers A and B are incorrect and are not based on user roles. Answer D is not related to access.

6. B. Kerberos uses a KDC or Key Distribution Center. The other answers do not.

7. A. Multifactor authentication uses more than one method. Answers B, C, and D are all one-factor methods.

8. A. Tokens are secure and can be one-time tokens. Answers B, C, and D can all be used more than once.

9. C. Two parties authenticating each other is mutual authentication. The other answers do not describe this.

10. D. This is a classic example of transitive access. Answer A is incorrect. LDAP is a directory access protocol. Answers B and C are not access descriptions.

11. D. The CAC is the smart card used by the U.S. Department of Defense.

12. D. CHAP periodically re-authenticates. Answers A, B, and C are all authentication methods but do not re-authenticate.

13. A. This is the output from arp -a. The other answers will not produce this output.

14. C. tracert (or traceroute in Linux) will show the complete path to the IP address. Answer A is incorrect—ping shows if a site is reachable, but not the path to it. Answer B is incorrect—arp shows address resolution protocol tables. Answer D is incorrect; nslookup is used with DNS.

15. A. Software is subject to copyright, and unauthorized software might be copyrighted software.

16. C. Kerberos was invented at MIT and uses tickets for authentication. Answers A and B are Challenge Handshake Authentication Protocol, which does not use tickets. Answer D also is an authentication protocol that does not use tickets.

17. C. You want a crossover error rate, also called equal error rate, and you want it to be low.

18. A. SAML is used with web page authorization. Answer B is incorrect—PIV is a type of smart card. Answer C is incorrect—CHAP is a type of authentication protocol. Answer D is incorrect—RBAC is an access control protocol.

19. D. Attribute Based Authentication looks at the entire environment. Answers A, B, and C are all access control methods but do not consider the entire environment.

20. A. Although three items are used, they are all Type I, something you know. Two-factor or strong, authentication requires two authentication methods from two different categories (Type I, II, or III).

Chapter 5: Wireless Network Threats

1. A. An IV attack is usually associated with the WEP wireless protocol.

2. B. The initialization vector (IV) that WEP uses for encryption is 24-bit.

3. A. TKIP places a 128-bit wrapper around the WEP encryption with a key that is based on things such as the MAC address of the host device and the serial number of the packet.

4. A. Near Field Communication (NFC) is used to send data between phones that are in close proximity.

5. D. WPS (Wi-Fi Protected Setup) is intended to simplify network setup for home and small offices.

6. B. RFID (Radio Frequency Identification) technology is used to identify and track tags attached to objects.

7. A. A replay attack captures portions of a session to play back later to convince a host that it is still talking to the original connection.

8. C. The 802.1x standard defines port-based security for wireless network access control.

9. D. Bluejacking is the sending of unsolicited messages over a Bluetooth connection.

10. C. With a disassociation attack, the intruder sends a frame to the AP with a spoofed address to make it look like it came from the victim and disconnects them from the network.

11. B. A rogue access point is any unauthorized wireless access point on a network.

12. C. An authentication process that requires the user to do something in order to complete the enrollment process is known as Wi-Fi Protected Setup (WPS).

13. A. Wired Equivalent Privacy (WEP) is a security protocol for 802.11b (wireless) networks that attempts to establish the same security for them as would be present in a wired network.

14. B. Jamming is purposely obstructing or interfering with a signal.

15. C. A disassociation attack is commonly referred to as a deauthentication attack.

16. C. While there is no hard-coded standard defining "near," the industry tends to use 4cm (1.6 inches) as the distance.

17. A. One of the simplest ways to secure Bluetooth devices is not to set their attribute to Discoverable.

18. B. Bluesnarfing is the gaining of unauthorized access through a Bluetooth connection.

19. D. Cloaking is a method of protecting the network that involves turning off the SSID broadcast. The access point is still there and accessible by those who know of its existence, but it prevents those who are just scanning from finding it.

20. B. In an evil twin attack, a rogue wireless access point poses as a legitimate wireless service provider to intercept information that users transmit.

Chapter 6: Securing the Cloud

1. C. In the Infrastructure as a Service (IaaS) model, the consumer can "provision" and is able to "deploy and run," but they still do not "manage or control" the underlying cloud infrastructure.

2. A. A private cloud delivery model is implemented by a single organization, and it can be implemented behind a firewall.

3. B. In the Platform as a Service (PaaS) model, the consumer has the ability to create applications and host them.

4. B. A public delivery model could be considered a pool of services and resources delivered across the Internet by a cloud provider.

5. A. In the Software as a Service (SaaS) model, the consumer has the ability to use applications provided by the cloud provider over the Internet.

6. C. A community delivery model has an infrastructure shared by several organizations with shared interests and common IT needs.

7. D. The hybrid delivery model can be considered an amalgamation of other types of delivery models.

8. A. Security as a Service (SECaaS) is a subscription-based business model intended to be more cost effective than smaller individuals/corporations could ever get on their own.

9. D. Cloud access security brokers are on-premise or cloud-based security policy enforcement points.

10. B. Elasticity is a feature of cloud computing that involves dynamically provisioning (or de-provisioning) resources as needed.

11. D. Sandboxing is the term used for restricting an application to a safe/restricted resource area.

12. A. Multitenancy implies hosting data from more than one consumer on the same equipment.

13. C. Ultimately, the organization is accountable for the choice of public cloud and the security and privacy of the outsourced service.

14. C. VM sprawl can be a result of creating virtual machines without the disciplines and controls of the physical world. This can result in over-provisioning (too much CPU, memory, or disk), or consuming resources after they are no longer required.

15. B. While a hybrid cloud could be any mixture of cloud delivery models, it is usually a combination of public and private.

16. A. Type I hypervisor implementations are known as "bare metal."

17. B. Type II hypervisor implementations are known as "hosted."

18. B. Cloud bursting means that when your servers become too busy, you can offload traffic to resources from a cloud provider.

19. B. QoS (Quality of Service) makes load balancing/prioritizing possible.

20. C. The machine on which virtualization software is running is known as a host, whereas the virtual machines are known as guests.

Chapter 7: Host, Data, and Application Security

1. A. Baselining is the term for establishing a standard for security.

2. B. Hardening is the process of improving security in a network operating system, or any operating system.

3. D. Fuzzing is testing by entering incorrect data to test the applications response.

4. A. Normalization is one of the most fundamental aspects of database configuration.

5. B. This is fuzzing or fuzz testing.

6. A. Open Web Application Security Project (OWASP).

7. C. A three-tiered architecture has an intermediary server.

8. A. A service pack is a bundle of patches and hot fixes.

9. C. Hotfixes usually can be installed without rebooting the machine.

10. B. Regression testing tests to see if the change caused any other problems.

11. B. Relational.

12. C. Patching.

13. B. Always apply least privileges, and in this case that is Delete.

14. B. An IPS will stop many attacks thus keeping the system online.

15. B. Input validation can stop most SQL injection attacks.

16. A. Encrypt all transmissions.

17. A. Always use change management.

18. A. Sandboxing the application would be the most secure.

19. C. Race conditions.

20. D. Waterfall is a good approach when the requirements are firm.

Chapter 8: Cryptography

1. A. long key sizes are not applicable to hashing algorithms.

2. A. The National Security Administration is responsible for cryptography in the U.S. government, even though those standards by then become NIST standards.

3. A. RSA is the most widely used asymmetric cipher today, though ECC is quickly becoming more widely used.

4. C. The Request for Comment is how you propose a new standard.

5. D. This is nonrepudiation.

6. A. TLS is the replacement for SSL.

7. C. This is a Message Authentication Code.

8. B. Key transmission is a concern.

9. C. For a hard drive, you want a symmetric cipher and AES is more secure than DES.

10. A. Environmental controls would be the least important issue.

11. A. This is a certificate authority.

12. C. A Certificate Revocation List should be used.

13. A. The Registration Authority identifies an individual for issuing a certificate by a Certificate Authority.

14. C. The key will have to be re-activated.

15. A. The certificate policy describes how a certificate can be used.

16. A. A key escrow should be used.

17. D. Online Certificate Status Protocol is done in real time.

18. D. A message authentication code will reveal any tampering, accidental or intentional.

19. A. Twofish.

20. D. PGP is an excellent choice for email security.

Chapter 9: Threats, Attacks, and Vulnerabilities

1. B. A DDoS attack uses multiple computer systems to attack a server or host in the network.

2. C. In a backdoor attack, a program or service is placed on a server to bypass normal security procedures.

3. A. A man-in-the-middle attack attempts to fool both ends of a communications session into believing that the system in the middle is the other end.

4. C. A replay attack attempts to replay the results of a previously successful session to gain access.

5. A. A DoS attack is intended to prevent access to network resources by overwhelming or flooding a service or network.

6. A. A logic bomb notifies an attacker when a certain set of circumstances has occurred. This may in turn trigger an attack on your system.

7. A. An armored virus is designed to hide the signature of the virus behind code that confuses the antivirus software or blocks it from detecting the virus.

8. B. A stealth virus reports false information to hide itself from antivirus software. Stealth viruses often attach themselves to the boot sector of an operating system.

9. D. SQL injection occurs when an attacker manipulates the database code to take advantage of a weakness in it.

10. C. Session hijacking occurs when the item used to validate a user's session, such as a cookie, is stolen and used by another to establish a session with a host that thinks it is still communicating with the first party.

11. D. XSRF involves unauthorized commands coming from a trusted user to the website. This is often done without the user's knowledge, and it employs some type of social networking to pull it off.

12. D. When a hole is found in a web browser or other software, and attackers begin exploiting it the very day it is discovered by the developer (bypassing the one-to-two-day response time that many software providers need to put out a patch once the hole has been found), it is known as a zero-day attack.

13. D. A shim is a small library that is created to intercept API calls transparently.

14. C. Refactoring involves testing to identify the design flow and then modifying, as needed, to clean up routines without changing the code's visible behavior.

15. A. Man-in-the-browser is a type of man-in-the-middle attack in which a Trojan horse manipulates calls between the browser and its security mechanisms yet still displaying back the user's intended transaction.

16. B. Pass-the-hash attacks take advantage of a weak encryption routine associated with NTLM and LanMan protocols.

17. B. The command monlist can be used with an NTP amplification attack to send details of the last 600 people who requested network time.

18. A. Clickjacking involves an attacker using multiple transparent or opaque layers to trick a user into clicking a button or link on another page when they were intending to click the top-level page.

19. C. With DNS poisoning, also known as DNS spoofing, the DNS server is given information about a name server that it thinks is legitimate when it isn't.

20. D. Typo squatting involves creating domains that are based on the misspelling of another.

Chapter 10: Social Engineering and Other Foes

1. A. Social engineering attacks take advantage of our inherent trust as human beings, as opposed to technology, to gain access to your environment.

2. C. Wetware is another name for social engineering.

3. A. Tailgating is best defined as following someone through a door they just unlocked.

4. D. Phishing is the form of social engineering in which you simply ask someone for a piece of information that you want by making it look as if it is a legitimate request.

5. D. Vishing involves combining phishing with Voice over IP.

6. C. Shoulder surfing is best defined as watching someone enter important information.

7. A. High-security installations use a type of intermediate access control mechanism called a mantrap. Mantraps require visual identification, as well as authentication, to gain access. A mantrap makes it difficult for a facility to be accessed by a large number of individuals at once because it allows only one or two people into a facility at a time.

8. C. Type C fire extinguishers are intended for use in electrical fires.

9. B. Electrical devices, such as motors, that generate magnetic fields cause EMI. Humidity control does not address EMI.

10. A. Perimeter security involves creating a perimeter or outer boundary for a physical space. Video surveillance systems wouldn't be considered a part of perimeter security, but they can be used to enhance physical security monitoring.

11. C. A security zone is an area that is a smaller component of the entire facility. Security zones allow intrusions to be detected in specific parts of the building.

12. A. Biometrics is a technology that uses personal characteristics, such as a retinal pattern or fingerprint, to establish identity.

13. A. Shielding keeps external electronic signals from disrupting operations.

14. D. TEMPEST is the certification given to electronic devices that emit minimal RF. The TEMPEST certification is difficult to acquire, and it significantly increases the cost of systems.

15. A. Gas-based systems work by displacing the air around a fire. This eliminates one of the three necessary components of a fire: oxygen.

16. B. Type K fire extinguishers are a subset of Type B fire extinguishers.

17. C, D. Proximity readers work with 13.56 MHz smart cards and 125 kHz proximity cards.

18. A. With hot and cold aisles, cold air is pumped in from below raised floor tiles.

19. B. If RF levels become too high, it can cause the receivers in wireless units to become deaf, and it is known as desensitizing. This occurs because of the volume of RF energy present.

20. C. RFI is the byproduct of electrical processes, similar to EMI. The major difference is that RFI is usually projected across a radio spectrum. Motors with defective brushes can generate RFI, as can a number of other devices.

Chapter 11: Security Administration

1. C. CYOD has employees select from a list of approved devices. COPE has the company buy the devices, and BYOD provides very little control. BBBA is not a term used in this context.

2. C. Company Owned and Provided Device describes company provided smartphones. The other acronyms/answers refer to alternative approaches to mobile devices.

3. D. Geofencing prevents a device from working outside a geographic area. WPA2 is a wireless security technology. Company-Owned and -Provided Equipment has the company buying mobile devices, and geotracking simply locates the device.

4. C. USB OTG is the use of portable devices as USB. Bring Your Own Device is simply a method for allowing employees to bring their own devices into the company network. Blue-jacking is a Bluetooth attack. Choose Your Own Device allows employees to select a device from a pre-approved list.

5. A. Bluesnarfing extracts data via Bluetooth. Bluejacking simply sends messages to the device. Choose Your Own Device allows employees to select a device from a pre-approved list. Jailbreaking refers to gaining root or admin access.

6. A. Least privileges is the most critical principle in account management. The other options are all important, but not as critical as least privileges.

7. D. This is the only name choice that does not give any hint as to the role of that user. The others all reveal, or suggest, the user's role.

8. A. All services should be assigned a service account. The other options are not secure.

9. C. WPA2 fully implements 802.11i, while WEP and WPA do not. WAP is Wireless Access Point, and it is not a security mechanism.

10. B. Remote wiping allows you to remove all data from a stolen phone. Geotagging would merely allow you to locate the phone. Geofencing would prevent the phone from working, but not prevent access of the data. Segmentation is used to separate user data from company data.

11. B. This is a classic example of a rogue access point. None of the other attacks would explain this scenario.

12. D. This is a disassociation attack. Bluesnarfing and bluejacking are Bluetooth attacks. The question does not describe session hijacking.

13. A. Line of sight is the primary weakness of infrared communications. All of the other answers are not true. Infrared connections can support each of these.

14. B. WPA uses Temporal Key Integrity Protocol (TKIP), while WEP and WPA2 do not. WAP is a wireless access point.

15. B. BYOD, or Bring Your Own Device, as well as CYOD, or Choose Your Own Device, are both employee-owned equipment. CYOP is not a real acronym for portable devices.

Chapter 12: Disaster Recovery and Incident Response

1. A. The disaster-recovery plan deals with site relocation in the event of an emergency, natural disaster, or service outage.

2. B. Working copies are backups that are usually kept in the computer room for immediate use in recovering a system or lost file.

3. B. An incremental backup backs up files that have changed since the last full or partial backup.

4. C. A differential backup backs up all of the files that have changed since the last full backup.

5. A. The Grandfather, Father, Son backup method is designed to provide a rotating schedule of backup processes. It allows for a minimum usage of backup media, and it still allows for long-term archiving.

6. B. Warm sites provide some capabilities in the event of a recovery. The organization that wants to use a warm site will need to install, configure, and reestablish operations on systems that may already exist at the warm site.

7. D. A reciprocal agreement is between two organizations and allows one to use the other's site in an emergency.

8. C. Failover occurs when a system that is developing a malfunction automatically switches processes to another system to continue operations.

9. A. Active reconnaissance is a type of penetration testing that focuses on the system, using techniques such as port scans, traceroute information, and network mapping to find weaknesses.

10. A. Data sovereignty is the concept that data is subject to the laws of where it is stored.

11. C. A contingency plan wouldn't normally be part of an incident response policy. It would be part of a disaster-recovery plan.

12. C. The process that is used during data acquisition for the preservation of all forms of relevant information when litigation is reasonably anticipated is known as legal hold.

13. A. A credentialed vulnerability scan uses actual network credentials to connect to systems and scan for vulnerabilities.

14. D. Working copies are also known as shadow copies.

15. C. A backout is a reversion from a change that had negative consequences.

16. B. In the realm of penetration testing, using a weakness in another—usually trusted—entity to launch an attack against a site/server is known as a pivot.

17. A. A CSIRT is a formalized or an ad hoc team that you can call upon to respond to an incident after it arises.

18. D. Full archival is a concept that works on the assumption that any information created on any system is stored forever.

19. B. HSM is a newer backup type that provides continuous online backup by using optical or tape jukeboxes. It appears as an infinite disk to the system, and it can be configured to provide the closest version of an available real-time backup.

20. D. Intrusive testing involves actually trying to break into the network. Non-intrusive testing takes more of a passive approach.

Index

Note to the Reader: Throughout this index **boldfaced** page numbers indicate primary discussions of a topic. *Italicized* page numbers indicate illustrations.

Numbers

2G networks, 364, 365
3DES (Triple-DES), 240
3G networks, 364, 365
4G networks, 364, 365
802.11a standard, 366
802.11ac standard, 366
802.11ad standard, 366
802.11af standard, 366
802.11ax standard, 366
802.11b standard, 366
802.11g standard, 366
802.11n standard, 366
802.11n-2009 standard, 366
802.1x standard, 271

A

acceptable use policies (AUPs), 24–25
access management
    ABAC (attribute-based access control), 161
    ACLs (access control lists), 161
    authentication. *See* authentication
    authorization. *See* authorization
    biometrics, 153–154
    DAC (discretionary access control), 160
    database servers, 163
    file servers, 163
    MAC (mandatory access control), **159**
    RBAC (role-based access control), 160
    RBAC (rule-based access control), 160–161
    review questions, 165–168
    review questions, answers, 423–425
    smartcards, **161–162**
    tokens, **162**
    transitive access, 154–155

access points, **108–111**, 170
    antennas, 109–111
    cloaking, 172
    controller-based, 110–111
    evil twin attacks, 174
    fat, 110–111
    MAC filtering, 109
    misconfigured, 145
    rogue, 171, 174, 177, 368
    stand-alone, 110–111
    thin, 110–111
account lockout, 375
account management, 374
    account types, **375–376**
    least privileges, 376
    offboarding, 377–378
    onboarding, 377
    privilege audits, 377
    time-of-day restrictions, 377
    usage audits, 377
accountability statements, 18
ACLs (access control lists), 161
active backup models, 401
active IDS, 97
active logging, 405
active reconnaissance, 387
active responses, **100–102**
active vulnerability scanners, 132
active-active load balancing
    configuration, 108
active/active model, 401
ad hoc networking, 374
ad hoc wireless, 59
Ad-Aware, 292
AD-IDS (anomaly-detection IDS), 82,
    95–96, *96*
Adams, Carlisle, 240
Adaptive Software Development, 216

X

Comprehensive Online Learning Environment

Register to gain one year of FREE access to the online interactive learning environment and test bank to help you study for your CompTIA Security+ certification exam—included with your purchase of this book!

The online test bank includes the following:

- **Assessment Test** to help you focus your study to specific objectives
- **Chapter Tests** to reinforce what you've learned
- **Practice Exams** to test your knowledge of the material
- **Digital Flashcards** to reinforce your learning and provide last-minute test prep before the exam
- **Searchable Glossary** to define the key terms you'll need to know for the exam
- **eBooks in Multiple Formats** for you to read on your favorite device

Register and Access the Online Test Bank

To register your book and get access to the online test bank, follow these steps:

1. Go to bit.ly/SybexTest.
2. Select your book from the list.
3. Complete the required registration information including answering the security verification proving book ownership. You will be emailed a pin code.
4. Go to http://www.wiley.com/go/sybextestprep and find your book on that page and click the "Register or Login" link under your book.
5. If you already have an account at testbanks.wiley.com, login and then click the "Redeem Access Code" button to add your new book with the pin code you received. If you don't have an account already, create a new account and use the PIN code you received.

A Wiley Brand